CHILD LABOR

ISSUES IN WORK AND HUMAN RESOURCES

Daniel J.B. Mitchell, Series Editor

CHILD LABOR

AN AMERICAN HISTORY

Hugh D. Hindman

M.E. Sharpe
Armonk, New York
London, England

Library of Congress Cataloging-in-Publication Data

Hindman, Hugh D.
  Child labor : an American history / Hugh D. Hindman.
    p. cm. —(Issues in work and human resources)
  Includes bibliographical references and index.
  ISBN 0-7656-0935-5 (alk. paper)
    1. Child labor—History—United States. 2. Child labor. I. Title. II. Series.

HD6250.U3 H53 2002
331.3′1′0973—dc 21

2002066517

Printed in the United States of America

The paper used in this publication meets the minimum requirements of
American National Standard for Information Sciences
Permanence of Paper for Printed Library Materials,
ANSI Z 39.48-1984.

BM (c) 10   9   8   7   6   5   4   3   2   1

TABLE OF CONTENTS

ILLUSTRATIONS

Figures

Tables

FOREWORD

Daniel J.B. Mitchell

To many Americans, "child labor" sounds like a topic of interest only to historians. At one time the United States had a child labor problem, but many believe that it was fixed some time ago— maybe back in the 1930s. Of course, while there is less child labor today than in the distant past, it remains an issue, even in a developed country such as the United States. Indeed, the twin phenomena of growth of wage inequality and large-scale immigration by relatively unskilled persons into the American workforce are likely to exacerbate the problem of child labor.

The fact that child labor remains a current issue does not mean that history has nothing to teach us about it, however. In this volume, Hugh D. Hindman draws on the history of social attitudes, economic development, and public policy in the United States to illuminate the subject. At what age is someone considered a "child"? What kinds of employment are harmful to children, however they are defined? What has been the impact of U.S. public policies designed to repress the use of child labor?

It is clear that economic development is associated with more schooling and less child labor over the long haul. But what of countries at an early stage of advancement? Should we expect that they will simply repeat the history of the United States with regard to child labor? One difference between modern developing countries and the United States of an earlier time is that unlike the United States, these countries typically base their development strategies on trade with countries whose labor standards are markedly more stringent than their own. For much of American history, in contrast, concepts such as "export-led growth" did not exist. And most other countries with which America traded were no more economically advanced than the United States. In the modern world, poor countries' labor practices are subject to scrutiny by their more developed trading partners.

The issue of child labor and other labor standards today is therefore bound up with world trade and investment. A current area of controversy is the degree to which such standards should be embodied in, or linked to, trade treaties. The degree to which international agencies such as the International Labor Organization and the World Trade Organization should intervene to encourage higher labor standards and reduce child labor has been much debated in recent years. Pressure has been placed on multinational firms, particularly those with retail brand images to protect, to avoid use of child labor in the countries in which they—or their manufacturing subcontractors—operate.

Also part of the modern debate is the notion of "deregulation" of markets. Perceived failures of economic planning in developing countries—along with the demise of the Soviet model of growth—have led to a revival of laissez-faire as an economic strategy. Of course, much of the impetus for deregulation and privatization is focused on product markets. But as such product-market deregulation occurs, the deregulation concept is inexorably extended to labor market protections of various sorts.

Issues of child labor are nowadays swept into the notion that government intervention in the marketplace is harmful to long-run growth. And to this argument is added the proposition that children in poor countries are better off working relative to the dismal alternatives available to them. Thus, despite the differences between the modern world and the era in which key child labor reforms were enacted in the United States, there is much that can be learned from Hindman's masterful review of child labor in the American context and its lessons for the current world debate.

Daniel J.B. Mitchell
Ho-Su Wu Professor
Anderson Graduate School of Management
and
School of Public Policy and Social Research
UCLA

ACKNOWLEDGMENTS

This book has been the single largest project of my career to date. As with all major projects, it was not accomplished alone. Too many are owed thanks to be acknowledged here, but certain intellectual debts must be recognized.

First, I would like to thank my colleagues in the Management Department of the Walker College of Business at Appalachian State University. Thanks for approving my research sabbatical (and for covering my classes while I was out), and thanks for the fertile intellectual climate. Appalachian's University Research Council provided two summer research grants that enabled collection of the primary source material. Numerous colleagues, mentors, and students, at Appalachian and elsewhere, provided assistance in many ways, often unknowingly. Two warrant special mention as sources of inspiration: Thanks to Professor Stephen M. Hills of Ohio State University and Professor Charles G. Smith of Otterbein College.

Invaluable research assistance was provided by Nicholas Graham, Brian Grigg, Cherie Hampton-Smith, and Julie Schmidt. Thanks also to the librarians at the Library of Congress, especially Bruce Kirby in the Manuscript Reading Room. Librarians of the Belk Library at Appalachian and the Wilson Library at the University of North Carolina–Chapel Hill also provided valuable assistance. Michael Siede was my principal advisor in illustrating the book. Catherine Fauver, Susan and Paul Jensen, and Daniel J.B. Mitchell reviewed early drafts and made wise, if often critical, suggestions. Each of them improved the final product.

Finally, my wife, Brenda C. Hindman, also provided critical assistance in collecting primary resource material (not to mention the infinite patience and support needed to carry this project to fruition). Thanks, Babe.

Part I

The Child Labor Problem

1. INTRODUCTION

Child Labor as a Social and Economic Problem

Out, Out!

The buzz-saw snarled and rattled in the yard
And made dust and dropped stove-length sticks of wood,
Sweet scented stuff when the breeze drew across it.
And from there those that lifted eyes could count
Five mountain ranges one behind the other
Under the sunset far into Vermont.
And the saw snarled and rattled, snarled and rattled,
As it ran light, or had to bear a load.
And nothing happened: Day was all but done,
Call it a day, I wish they might have said
To please the boy by giving him the hour
That a boy counts so much when saved from work.
His sister stood beside them in her apron
To tell them "Supper." At that word, the saw,
As if to prove saws could be hungry too,
Leaped out at the boy's hand, or seemed to leap—
He must have given the hand. However it was,
Neither refused the meeting. But the hand!
The boy's first outcry was a rueful laugh,
As he swung toward them holding up the hand
Half in appeal but half as if to keep
The life from spilling. Then the boy saw all,
Since he was old enough to know, big boy
Doing a man's work, though a child at heart.
He saw all spoiled. "Don't let him cut my hand off—
The doctor—when he comes. Don't let him, sister!"
So. But the hand was gone already.
The doctor put him in the dark of ether.
He lay and puffed his lips out with his breath,
And then—the watcher at his pulse took fright.
No one believed. They listened at his heart.
Little—less—nothing! and that ended it.
No more to build on there. And they, since they
Were not the one dead, turned to their affairs.

Robert Frost

From "Out, Out!" from *The Poetry of Robert Frost*, ed. Edward Connery
Lathem. Copyright 1916, 1944 by Robert Frost. Reprinted by permission of
Henry Holt & Co., LLC. Reprinted from *Poems of Child Labor*, NCLC
Publication 316, p. 43.

Figure 1.1 *Dangerous Work.* Beaumont, Tex. Nov. 1913. Dangerous work. Charlie McBride. Said twelve years old. This twelve year old boy has a steady job with Miller & Vidor Lumber Company. He takes slabs out of a chute, which has a moving endless chain to carry the wood up the chute. He passes the slabs on to the other boy who saws them on an unguarded circular saw. Charlie runs the saw himself whenever he gets the chance. He is exposed not only to the above danger, but to the weather—no roof even. Has been here for some months. "Get four bits a day." Fifty cents. Works ten hours. This is the only mill that I found around Beaumont that employed boys, likely because they are located some distance out of town.* *(Courtesy of the Library of Congress, Prints and Photographs Division, Lewis Wickes Hine National Child Labor Committee Collection, LC-USZ62–19574. Photographer Lewis W. Hine.)*

Global child labor is correctly perceived as a problem of economically underdeveloped nations. But we know of no major advanced nation that did not go through a stage of pervasive child labor on the path to advancement. If widespread child labor is viewed as predictable during certain stages of economic development, then the economic history of advanced nations may serve as a guide to its eradication in the developing nations of today and tomorrow. This book examines U.S. child labor history with the intention of identifying lessons learned that might be applicable to persistent problems of global child labor.

---

*All photo captions are reproduced verbatim from Hine's original caption cards.

Child labor is a problem of immense social and economic proportions in many developing regions of the world today. It came to be viewed in the same way when the United States was, industrially speaking, a developing nation. But child labor was not always seen as a problem. We came to recognize the problem only gradually, then to resolve it even more gradually and still incompletely. Though history can never quite repeat itself, a retrospective appraisal of the U.S. experience may inform the struggle against child labor in the world today. To the extent that we better understand the causes and effects of child labor in U.S. history, see why it matters socially and economically, understand how our nation came to grips with and made its accommodation to the child labor problem, understand the how and why of effective reform in our own history and the how and why of our failures to achieve effective reform, we may to able to contribute more effectively to solving the global child labor problem.

No nation has developed an advanced industrialized sector without going through this "dirty" phase of development. In early-twentieth-century America, young boys worked their fingers often literally to the bone in the coal breakers, young boys and girls continued to work sixty- and seventy-hour weeks in the cotton textile industry that they had helped build, and children were drawn into work in agriculture and food processing at such a young age that the term "infant labor" would not have been entirely inappropriate. Child labor stands as one of the more persistent social and economic problems in history and in the world today. This book sheds new light on child labor in U.S. history in a way calculated to shed light on the problem in the world today.

Child Labor in U.S. History

The American experience with child labor is, in many of its general contours, typical of that in other early industrializing nations. With industrialization, poor children and their families were drawn off the family farm, out of the home workshop, or out of the urban tenement into the mines, mills, and factories. The children, who had always worked alongside their parents in preindustrial times, naturally followed their parents into industrial employment. Several industries became dependent on child labor. Eventually, there developed a growing sense that there was something not quite right about this new industrial child labor, and a reform movement emerged. Over the next couple of generations, our society reached a general accommodation on the question, and most industrial child labor was eliminated.

While our history with child labor is not entirely unique, it is exceedingly rich in its unique details. In myriad industries in specific times and places, particular children, with their own names, identities, and histories, went to work. Their collective stories illustrate not only what they have in common with industrial child workers everywhere and always, but also point out much that is specific to the American experience. We developed our own cultural icons—especially in the breaker boys. American ingenuity probably generated more variations on the theme of the family wage than anywhere else in the world. Our reformers and antireformers were individuals—often characters—with their own ideas on aims and methods. We flirted with a constitutional amendment on child labor, but did not finally outlaw the practice until it had already been virtually eliminated. In these and many other ways, the history of child labor in America is richly original.

Children Have Always Worked

Children have always worked. This truth is evident in the history of childhood throughout the world. That simple declaration, "Children have always worked," appears, often verbatim, in many scholarly treatises on child labor. For example, Walter Trattner opens *Crusade for the Children* this way:

> Children have always worked. During early human history, the young of wandering tribes shared in hunting, fishing, and trapping animals. Later, when tribes and clans separated themselves into families, children continued to work with their elders in the woods and fields and in caring for crops and animals. They also helped in the handicrafts, as these developed.[1]

The generalization that children have always worked serves a number of useful purposes. First, it reminds us of the need to justify treatment of child labor as a "problem." Either explicitly or implicitly, most writers treat child labor as a social and economic problem. But if work has been central, integral, and essential to childhood throughout most of human history—if, in the main, even while acknowledging its abuses, child labor was a good thing—the burden remains on scholars to explain how it became a "problem." If child labor was good but is now a problem, how, when, and why did it go bad? What changed? What distinguishes "good" child labor from "bad" child labor? No one has seriously suggested that children should not do work. But where is the line to be drawn between work that children should do and work they should not do?

Today, however, the notion that children have always worked is a dangerous generalization. First, it has never been true that all children worked. Child labor, at least those forms considered to be a social and economic problem, has always been closely associated with poverty. With few exceptions, children of the well-to-do never had a serious child labor problem. Second, even if it once had been so, it is no longer true that children have always worked. In the world today, there are now several dozen nations where it is fair to say that, in the main, children no longer work. In some nations, there have been several consecutive generations of children who have never known child labor. For the most part, most economically advanced nations have largely solved their child labor problem. For them, child labor is a thing of the past.

This is not to suggest that any nation has solved the problem once and for all. In the United States, we have yet to overcome persistent problems in migrant agricultural labor; garment sweatshops have reemerged on domestic soil; and children remain vulnerable to exploitation in the street trades. But we do have child labor laws on the books that are generally respected and enforced. Nearly all the children are in school, even the children of the poor; and very young children no longer work. Indeed, we have gone so far in sheltering our children from work that our social and economic problem is no longer child labor but rather youth employment. That is, policy is now more oriented toward socializing people to the world of work as they approach adulthood than toward protecting them from working during their childhood.

It is no longer necessary to approach child labor as a problem, like poverty, that will always be with us, as some have contended. We know it is a problem that can be solved. Today it is possible to approach the topic from the perspective that—while it remains true in most of the world that children have always worked, and until recently in all parts of the world—child labor is not inevitable. It is now possible to embrace and express an optimism that is grounded in historical fact, not simply in utopian vision.

A Theoretical Framework for Approaching
the Child Labor Problem

Child labor has long been a topic of interest to a wide array of disciplines, from economics to history, from sociology to occupational health, from literature to poetry, and many others. Work in these various disciplines on the issue has often remained fragmented. Nevertheless, there is a considerable body of historical, sociological, and economic literature on which to draw. More complete discussion of a theory of child labor is reserved for chapter 10, where findings from this study are integrated with the previous literature, but it is useful to have a theoretically guided framework before proceeding with the inquiry. Thus, it is not necessary at this point to present a formal or exhaustive theory of child labor, or even a comprehensive literature review, but it is important to sketch the broad contours of a framework that can guide the inquiry that follows.

My main thesis, simply stated, is that industrialization is the cause of both the child labor problem and, later, its eradication. Before industrialization, children generally worked, but their labor was not seen as a problem. The ideal arrangement involved having children, from as early an age as possible, and within the confines of a kinship-based household, contributing to production for the group's own consumption. As production shifted to production for markets—that is, toward industrialization—children accompanied their elders into industrial employment. But industrial employment of children came to be seen as a social and economic problem—an evil, if you will. So society reacted to protect itself and its children. Restating the thesis: During early industrialization, forces conspired to create the child labor problem; during continuing or later industrialization, forces conspired to eradicate the problem. In the early phases of industrialization, factors such as habit, custom and tradition, uneven technological advancement, and lack of alternatives (especially schools), virtually ensured that children would be put to work. In later stages of industrialization, factors such as emergence of a reform movement, continued technological advancement, and growing availability of alternatives (especially schools) operated to curb child labor.

Previous literature makes clear certain fundamentals. Child workers were supplied to the labor market by the household. Supply can generally be understood within the framework of the household economy, for which there is a rich theoretical and empirical literature in both economics and sociology. In turn, emphasis on family economy encouraged attention to the availability of alternatives (especially schooling), family wage, and other, more subtle, issues such as parental altruism. Demand for child workers was provided by employers. If previous literature on the supply of child workers is fairly well understood, the literature tells us much less about the demand for child workers. We know that child labor is cheap labor, but we also know that it is low productivity labor. What is the interplay of these factors? What other factors might create a demand for children over adults? In examining demand, it will also be important to take into account the available technology. Finally, it is important to take into account the reform movement itself, since it seeks to reduce both supply and demand for child workers. What are the effects of law and regulation on the child labor problem?

Plan of the Book

The book is organized into three parts. Part I, comprising the first three chapters, presents "The Child Labor Problem." Part II, "Child Labor in America," comprising the middle six chapters, is the heart of the book. And Part III, "Child Labor's Legacy," offers a synthesis in two chapters to conclude the book.

Part I relies largely, but not entirely, on secondary sources to establish child labor as a persistent social and economic problem. Building on the theoretical framework sketched here, chapter 2, "Industrialization of Child Labor," traces the industrialization process in America and its intersection with child labor. It begins by establishing the centrality of child labor to family life in preindustrial America, where child labor is considered essential to the child's upbringing, then proceeds into industrialization—the transformation that changes everything—where child labor comes to be seen as morally repugnant. Chapter 3, "Child Labor Reform," chronicles American society's reaction against child labor, the efforts of reformers and counterreformers, and the evolution of state and federal law.

Part II, "Child Labor in America," presents the book's most important original contribution to the literature. It relies largely but not entirely on primary sources to portray child labor in six key industries in early-twentieth-century America. Chapter 4 examines child labor in the coal mines. Chapter 5 considers the light manufacturing sector by highlighting children in the glasshouses. Chapter 6 examines the textile industry, especially southern cotton textiles. In these three sectors—mines, factories, and mills—we achieved nearly complete eradication of the child labor problem. In the remaining three industry chapters, we remain vulnerable to child labor exploitation. Chapter 7 looks at sweatshops and industrial (tenement) homework. Chapter 8 considers the street trades, emphasizing two occupations in particular—the night messengers and the newsboys. And finally, chapter 9 examines agriculture, the first and last bastion of child labor in the United States.

At the core of my primary sources are the investigation reports of the National Child Labor Committee (NCLC). The Note on Sources at the end of the book provides details on primary and secondary sources. The NCLC, established in 1904, was at the center of child labor reform in America. In the early stages of its reform efforts, the NCLC had to first confront public ignorance of the problem. It did so by investing heavily in a program of investigation aimed at systematically documenting the nature and extent of child labor in the American economy. Field investigators were dispatched to document conditions in key industries in key regions. Their investigative reports proved to be of immense strategic value in educating and persuading both the public and public policymakers on the question of child labor. Today, these same investigative reports remain valuable as an exceptionally fertile, and as yet largely untapped, data source on child labor in American history.

Many of the NCLC investigators will be introduced in subsequent chapters. The NCLC attracted many distinguished individuals connected with the broader Progressive Era reform movement of the day. But most of its frontline field investigators remain largely unknown. A few names may be familiar, and one deserves mention here. Lewis Wickes Hine, who achieved widespread acclaim for his social photography,[2] was one of the NCLC's more active and meticulous investigators. It is my privilege to present a sampling of Hine's photographs—some of them famous, some of them never before published—to augment the text.

I try to allow the NCLC investigative reports to carry the story of child labor in America as much as possible. Where necessary, however, the reports are supplemented and complemented by a variety of other sources. Occasionally, other papers located in the NCLC collection provided useful information. Lewis Hine's photo-caption cards, on which he meticulously documented each of the over 7,000 photos in the collection, are a rich data source in themselves. The NCLC issued a large number of publications, many of which summarize information from investigative reports. The NCLC also published the *Child Labor Bulletin* (later renamed *American Child*), in which numerous articles provide information on committee investigations. NCLC sources are augmented by various government reports and documents (special mention should be made of the massive nineteen-volume report by the U.S. Bureau of Labor, *Report on Conditions of Woman and Child Wage-Earners in the United States*, published from 1910 to 1913) and a variety of secondary sources.

Part III of the book, the final two chapters, summarizes some of the key lessons learned and insights gained from the American experience; takes stock of our successes and failures; integrates the findings from this study into what is known about child labor from other sources; advances a theory of child labor; and projects the American experience into the realm of the global economy and the globalization of the child labor problem.

2. INDUSTRIALIZATION OF CHILD LABOR

Figure 2.1 The Only Animal Alive . . .

No fledgling feeds the father-bird!
No chicken feeds the hen!
No kitten mouses for the cat—
This glory is for men.

We are the Wisest, Strongest Race—
Loud may our praise be sung!—
The only animal alive
That lives upon its young!

Charlotte Perkins Gilman

Reprinted from NCLC, Poems of Child Labor, *NCLC Publication 316, p. 18.
The cartoon is from the* Detroit Times, *artist unknown.*

"The only animal alive that lives upon its young." How did America
come to this? Generally, animals suckle and nurture their young until
they are able to hunt, hide, fly or freely contract for their labor. How and
when did child labor become a commodity to be bought and sold on the
labor market for the household's succor? The short answer is industrialization. It is true, in the historical sense, that children have always worked.
Indeed, depending on how work is defined, all children continue to do
work today. But child labor is another matter. Child labor conjures up
images of something unwholesome, unhealthy, unholy. What is it that
distinguishes beneficial child labor—to the child, the household, and
society—from the child labor we condemn?

This chapter begins by examining the history of child work prior to
industrialization, before it came to be condemned as child labor, and then
follows the work of children into industrial pursuits. Industrialization—
the great transformation—also transformed child labor from what industrial society generally considered a social and economic good—a normal,
healthy, and educational aspect of a child's growing up—into not merely
a social and economic problem but a moral evil. The child labor problem
in America closely parallels the industrialization of America.

Child Labor in Preindustrial America

Child Labor in Rural America: The Yeoman Ideal

The image of the yeoman household wresting a living from the earth
represents the ideal of sturdy self-sufficiency. This is pure householding.
Within this framework, it is assumed that the children will work, often

very hard, and will do so from a very early age. And yet, we tend not to condemn this work as child labor. Even today, when the work of a child can be described as being within the household or on the family farm, evoking dim recollections of yeomanry, it is not subject to the same moral disapprobation as factory work. The yeomanry is the social and economic ideal against which industrial child labor came to be measured.

The extent to which rural and agricultural self-sufficiency was representative of early America may be debatable. The extent to which it was idealized is not. Family members were part of an economic unit organized to ensure self-sufficiency. Within that framework, the original division of labor was based on sex and age. As Thurnwald noted, "The division of labor is by no means the result of complicated economics, as rationalistic theory will have it. It is principally due to physiological differences of sex and age."[1] Tullos described the division of labor as it prevailed in the preindustrial South:

> On the farmsteads of the Carolina Piedmont, a general division of labor by sex and age prevailed. Men (and boys in their teens) cut trees and cleared land, built cabins and barns, erected snake fences that kept out free-grazing livestock, hunted and trapped and did most of the field labor. . . . Most women's work on Piedmont farmsteads consisted of tending children, preparing and preserving food, washing and cleaning, perhaps helping to plant, hoe, and harvest field crops, tending gardens, providing medical care, and making clothes, coverlets, and quilts. The oldest and youngest family members, male and female, were set to such tasks as spinning thread, making baskets, gathering herbs, milking cows, and feeding chickens.[2]

The children's work was integrated with their education. The pace of the work was oriented to circadian and seasonal rhythms that, while demanding, always permitted pauses for rest or instruction. In fact, the work of the children was valued as much for its preparation of the child for a productive adult life as for its immediate utility.

> The children received practically their entire education either in the home or in the adjoining fields. Certainly in those days the child received his best education under the supervision of this own parents. . . . The children were nearly always in the sight of their parents. Both parents worked, and the children worked also; but the parents could stop in their work at any time for the purpose of instructing the children. In a word, the home was the centre of the moral, educational, industrial, and social life.[3]

Figure 2.2 *Work That Educates.* Twelve-year-old boy tending bees under the direction of his father, John Spargo. Bennington, Vermont, Aug. 1914. *(Courtesy of the Library of Congress, Prints and Photographs Division, Lewis Wickes Hine National Child Labor Committee Collection, LC-H5–3996A.)*

Child labor reformers were guilty of romanticizing and idealizing the yeoman household in extolling "work that educates" over work in factories. An example is the Lewis Hine photograph (Figure 2.2) taken for the National Child Labor Committee, as part of a series showing a young boy engaged in educational tasks under the supervision of his father.[4]

The fact that early America was a frontier nation reinforced the appeal of the yeoman ideal. The steady westward march—from early colonial days up to the closing of the frontier in the 1890s—provided an outlet for independent-minded families dissatisfied with their current situation and sturdy enough to survive the rigors of frontier life.[5] Certainly the availability of the frontier limited the ability of employers to exploit workers during America's early industrialization, even while it also slowed the progress of labor organization by draining off discontented workers.

This opportunity offered to the artisan a free choice between wage service and farming, constantly depleted the ranks of mere laborers, operated to keep wages as high as the earnings of a "no-rent" homestead, and kept fresh and vigorous that feeling of independence which has been the distinguishing mark of the American workingman.[6]

The legacy of yeoman self-sufficiency has made it difficult to regulate child labor in certain industries and occupations historically aligned to that ideal, especially agriculture. Because it represents rural self-sufficiency, agriculture has remained, in spite of its obvious industrialization, relatively free of intrusive regulation. Also, industrial activity carried out within the home has been presumed to be beyond the scope of labor regulation. The yeoman ideal is predicated on viewing the household, as a collective unit, to be the locus of both production and consumption—that is, pure householding. Any intrusion into the rights of a household to utilize the labor of its children remains inherently suspect. (What? Will household chores be subject to government regulation?)

While it is easy to admire, respect, and romanticize the yeoman farmer and his family, we must continually remind ourselves that children shared not only in the bounty of the household but also in its privations and hardships. As a further antidote to overromanticism of preindustrial child labor, it is worth briefly considering that children fared much worse under two other institutions of preindustrial America—indentured servitude and slavery.

Child Labor in the Trades: The Role of Indentured Servanthood

Indentured servitude in the United States served both as an immigration policy and as a "market" for allocating child workers. It figured prominently in the early republic in the skilled trades, in agriculture, and in domestic work. Indentured servants "consisted of runaway apprentices, penniless debtors, kidnapped children, honest laborers, vagrants, and criminals of all kinds."[7] At its best, the system operated to the mutual benefit of both master and servant. But it was easily and often abused and would not be recognized as a legitimate form of employment under today's universal human rights canons.[8]

As immigration policy, it is estimated that between half and two-thirds of the colonists came to the New World under some form of indenture[9] and "took their place as wholly free citizens only after working out their terms of contract."[10] Likewise, the economist Richard Ely quotes, but does not cite, statements that "Nearly all the immigrants that came (to Virginia) between 1620 and 1650 were bondsmen," and cites a British estimate that 10,000 people "were kidnapped or spirited away to America every year."[11] The "spirit" was a familiar figure in seventeenth-century London folklore:

> He was a shadowy character who was either hired by merchants to gather a servant cargo or worked independently and sold individuals to shipmasters. Spirits won the dubious honor for leading thousands of English people to the New World through notorious recruitment methods. Roaming the streets of London in search of human cargo and armed with sweets and strong drink, the spirits coaxed unsuspecting children and adults onto ships bound for the colonies. The unwilling captives were then transported to the colonies and sold into servitude.[12]

A similar class of immigrants was the redemptioners. They included not only English, but especially German and Swiss families who booked passage to the New World on the promise to pay on arrival. They were given a period, usually fourteen days after arrival, to repay the ship's captain for their passage. If they could not, they were sold into servitude. Of course, to garner the cost of their transport and to secure a better deal than the ship's captain could on the open market, many families sold themselves into servitude.

As a market for child labor, indentured servitude proved an effective way to deal with the problem of orphans and children of poor and dependent parents in England and continental Europe. Domestically, it could also serve as an instrument of upward mobility, as when a relatively poor family indentured a son or daughter to apprentice in a skilled trade, though the degree to which this circumstance occurred is debatable.[13] Indenture could also be a solution for a household with too many mouths to feed.

The indenture was commonly for a four-to-seven-year period, but sometimes an age for liberation was set—typically either eighteen or twenty-one years of age. Masters were required, by both law and contract, to provide adequate food, shelter, and clothing. If the master was a skilled tradesperson, a good-faith apprenticeship was also required. At the end of the indenture, the freed servant was to be provided with some form of "freedom's dues," which included at least clothing, usually tools or livestock or both, often a sum of money, and rarely a grant of land. In return, the master received not only all rights to the labor of the servant, but effective ownership of the servant for the term of the contract. Runaway servants were hunted down and dragged back as aggressively as were runaway slaves. Foster Rhea Dulles and Melvyn Dubofsky report:

> [T]he servants were rigidly confined to the immediate vicinity of the place where they were employed, tavern keepers were not allowed to entertain them or sell them liquor, their terms of service might be extended for a long list of minor offenses, and they were subject to whippings and other corporal punishment by their master for disobedience or laziness. Servant girls could be held in longer bondage because of bastardy, and their masters were sometimes not above conspiring to this end. "Late experiments shew," read one report, "that some dissolute masters have gotten their maides with child, and yet claim the benefit of their services."[14]

By the 1820s, indentured servitude had receded to the margins, no longer comprising any substantial portion of the labor supply in America. Little is known about what happened to the former indentured servants after they earned their freedom. Some undoubtedly went West to help settle the frontier, while others remained in the East to help provide emerging industrialization with its requisite supply of free laborers. While indentured servants were sometimes subject to the most inhumane treatment, "because they had white skins, they soon melted into the free population and never created a race problem."[15] Not so with black slaves, soon to become former slaves, who were released from the bondage of slavery just as the American industrial revolution was about to take off.

Child Labor in the Slave Economy

In colonial America, slaveholding was common everywhere, North and South alike. In fact, when the number of indentured servants is added to the number of slaves, there was very little in the way of a free labor market in colonial America. Well before the industrial revolution, however, slavery was effectively abolished in the North. But the rise of large-scale commercial agriculture, coupled with the plantation system, led to the persistence of slavery in the South. It is generally recognized that the slave economy, commercial agriculture, and the plantation system all conspired to delay the industrialization of the South. In contrast, others argue that southern commercial agriculture, by virtue of the slave economy and the plantation system, was the first truly industrialized sector of the American economy. After all, the plantation was its own self-contained center of production of a key industrial commodity (whether cotton, sugar, tobacco, rice, or some combination). It had its own internal labor market, its own division of labor into specialized tasks, its own management hierarchy, and its own distinctive production processes. It lacked only a free labor market.

At any rate, on the eve of America's industrial revolution, the only substantial slavery that remained in America was the slavery in commercial agriculture in the plantation South. The role of children in the slave economy was, essentially, to restock the plantation's labor supply. From the master's perspective, that is why they were bred. From the time they were able to learn work, they learned work. From the time they were able to work, they worked.

Child labor in slavery was condemned not so much because of the labor but because of slavery itself. There is no doubt that slave children worked from a very young age, especially during peak periods such as the harvest. They were subject to the disciplinary regime of the plantation, however harsh or benevolent it happened to be. Still, even within the regime of the slave economy, there were a few factors that worked to limit the exploitation of the children's labor. First, it was not in the master's interest to overwork the children. If a child slave's value lay in restocking the labor supply, then a healthy child was worth far more to the master than a child broken by excessive or premature labor. Neither did the adult slaves want to overwork their own children. Certainly the adult slaves' interest in buffering their children from hard labor is more obvious than the master's. But even beyond the fundamental impulse of parental concern—the plantation produced a communal culture among the slaves in which all the adults shared a responsibility in raising all of the children—there was the simple fact that very young children were often more hindrance than help. The adults were responsible for getting the work done. Where a child could help, such help was valued. But the first work-related responsibility the children were required to learn was to stay out of the adults' way.

Slavery means, literally, a captive labor supply. Slaves composed a large share of the master's capital stock, a share second only to the value of the plantation itself. Thus, the slave's value was not simply the value of a day's labor or a season's labor. The value of the slave lay in the lifetime of labor the slave would yield. Under these conditions, and precisely because the role of the children was to restock the labor supply, masters were motivated to be judicious about overworking the children.

During certain peak periods, such as the harvest, all hands, including the children, were in the fields. At other times children might be seen wherever the adults were working. The youngest children and girls were likely to be found near the women who performed the domestic chores. Older boys were usually with the men. But the children were there principally to help and to learn. They could fetch water, carry things, and help to clean up, but the adults did the bulk of the real work. Gradually, as they grew older, they were expected to contribute more and more to the real work. As this happened, they also gradually came to be less under the effective control of the adult slaves and more under the control of overseers and the master.

To the extent that child slaves were under the direction and control of the adult slaves, the work of the children resembled traditional patterns where work combined helping and learning and could even be viewed as beneficial to the children. It was not the labor that was wrong, but the slavery. Of course, overseers and masters retained ultimate direction and control over the children, and they certainly had an interest in ensuring that the children developed sound work habits, but it was generally not in their interest to be overly intrusive of parental and adult authority.

Abolition of slavery can be properly considered the first major child labor reform in America. While the reform effort was directed at the institution of slavery, it had important consequences on the institution of child labor as well. The abolition of slavery released large numbers of working children from bondage and ensured that no future children would labor as chattel. Abolition of all forms of bondage (including the indenture system to which white children were subject) eliminated some of the most exploitative forms of child labor. But the indirect effects of the abolition of slavery may have been equally important. Abolition helped create the free labor market required for mass industrialization. Even though child labor persisted for several generations, it would ultimately prove unsustainable under conditions of a free market for labor.

In this sense, America's Civil War was truly a watershed event in the industrialization of America. It can be regarded as much as a war for industrial revolution as a civil insurrection. There is no doubt that the industrialization of America exploded after, and as a partial result of, the Civil War. Railroads expanded and the armaments industry strengthened core sectors, including textiles, iron, coal, and steel. Wartime profiteering created huge pools of capital, some controlled by men who would later come to be known as robber barons. But perhaps the most important contribution of the Civil War was that it set our economy unalterably on a course toward creation of a free labor market. Industrialization could begin on the basis of captive labor markets, but it could not be sustained on a massive scale without a free labor market. To be sure, many labor markets remained substantially unfree for many years—this is why child labor could persist—but the abolition of slavery was the single largest step in the creation of a free market for labor, just as the institution of slavery obviously retarded its development. Children were thrust into a free labor market in which they, ultimately, could not compete.

Industrialization: The Great Transformation

It is generally understood that the industrial revolution changed everything. Industrialization fundamentally altered social and economic relations. It turned the household economy inside out. Increasing wage dependence redefined the role of the household in production and consumption of goods and services. In doing so, it altered relations between and among parents and children. Industrialization also redefined relations between worker and work, worker and fellow workers, and masters and servants. That industrialization also altered the character of child labor is no surprise. Industrialization redefined the concept of childhood itself. That industrialization redefined child labor and transformed it from a social "good" into a social and economic "problem" seems generally understood. That industrialization not only created the child labor problem but also paved the way for its elimination is less well understood.

The turning point on the child labor question came with the shift in household economy from production for consumption to production for markets. At one extreme, in preindustrial society, the household is the locus of both production and consumption. The pattern is the closed group. The group, whether a narrow kinship group or an extended communal group, simultaneously ensures adequate production and sufficient consumption. Standards of output were culturally expected, standards of input were likewise reciprocated, all within the equity principles of the self-contained closed society. At the other extreme, in advanced industrial society, production is separated from consumption. The household remains the locus of consumption, but production is on the market. Ultimately, labor—more strictly, labor power—is treated as a commodity produced for sale, according to the dictates of supply and demand, on the market. People produce for markets, they are dependent on their wages for their standard of living, and, most decisively, they compete for available work (and, thus, comparative standard of living) in an open labor market. A perfectly free and open labor market assumes individual workers, not families or other groups, vying for the available opportunities. For the most part, child labor in America did not survive into the more advanced stages of industrialization.

Between the extremes of pure householding and pure market labor are a number of transitional stages. Each had important implications for our understanding of America's child labor problem. First, most yeoman households practiced one or more industrial occupations in which the children invariably participated. Most production was for the household's own use, but surpluses could be bartered for goods produced by friends and neighbors or for goods available from local merchants. Some families specialized in particular household industries and could attract "bespoke" work or custom work made to order. These cottage industries were the first step toward production for markets, but they fell short of creating industrial employment as it would come to be understood. First, "cottage industry" connotes only incidental and probably sporadic production for markets—most production, and the dominant orientation of life, continued to center on household use. Second, there was no clearly identifiable employer and so no employment relationship. As long as households and their friends and neighbors, local merchants, or even purchasers of custom work did not develop expectations about ongoing production for remuneration, none saw themselves in an employment relationship. But cottage industry did condition households to the possibility of outside income, whether in the form of bartered goods, cash, or credit. In rural areas, the fortunes of the yeoman still depended on a good piece of land, the right mix of crops and livestock (and prices for same), the labor of the entire household and, at peak times, neighbors as well, frugal household management, perhaps some cottage industry, and luck. Increasingly, however, yeomen's fortunes also came to depend on relationships with local merchants who could extend credit or lend machinery, who owned gins and gristmills, and who often marketed the farmer's crops and the product of the cottage industry.[16] Cottage industry provided a supplemental source of household subsistence and, if subsistence through traditional means was threatened, dependence on industry was likely to grow.

The next transitional stage was generally referred to as protoindustrialization and was characterized by the "putting-out" system. This stage was decisive for the child labor question because it was in this stage that the seeds of the child labor problem were sown. To the extent that children participated in the putting-out systems, it was clearly industrial employment of children. It was organized production for markets for the benefit of an identifiable employer.

The classic arrangement was for merchant capitalists to put orders for goods out to neighboring households; the merchant would supply the raw material and tend to the market, and the household would produce the goods. This arrangement differed from "bespoke" work in that goods were less likely to be custom-made to order and more likely to be commodity goods such as ready-made clothing, shoes and boots, yarn, cloth, and the like. It was also different from the occasional barter that occurred in the preindustrial period. The merchant capitalist and households developed a mutual dependence, and a true employment relationship emerged. The merchants did not directly employ children of the household, but neither did they directly employ the parents. What they employed was the collective labor of the household.

Considering the putting-out system a transitional stage of proto-industrialization can be misleading. First, it is important to recognize that most families came to their industrial employments straight from the farm or straight off the boat without themselves going through this intermediate stage. In many key industries and many key regions, America did not have an extensive putting-out system prior to industrialization. While most households may have had a spinning wheel or loom, they tended to produce only coarse goods for household or neighborhood consumption. There was no extensive putting-out system in the Piedmont South prior to the growth of cotton textiles. Even in New England where these systems were more widely established, they were never the dominant mode of economic activity. Second, the notion that putting out was a transitional stage may suggest that it ceased with full-blown industrialization, but that would be incorrect. Once industrialization was under way, putting out remained as an option for getting the work done. In its methods of employment, the "sweating system" found in urban tenement districts is a direct descendent of the putting-out system.[17]

In its early stages, the putting-out system retained important buffers that protected children.[18] The locus of work remained the home, and children worked directly under the supervision of parents. Pauses for rest, instruction, or household duties could be taken at will. Under the right conditions, intensity of child labor could be subdued and integrated into a regimen approximating that of the preindustrial household. Under more adverse conditions, however, any pressure for intensified industrial production that could be put on the parents could also be passed along to the children.

The next stages in industrial development involved progressively removing the locus of production from the home, perhaps first to a larger workshop operated by a neighbor, next to a "manufactory" where traditional hand methods were still used but workers were aggregated and organized under one roof, and finally to the modern factory with its modern machinery. With these moves, labor, and whatever child labor followed, came into direct contact with the market and increasingly fell under the market's sway. Subjecting labor to the laws of the market would ultimately separate labor from its traditional basis in the household. The integrated household group played a smaller and smaller role in the labor of its members, and the market, with its emphasis on the principle of freedom of contract, came to the fore. For a time, during the putting-out period, the household was buffered from direct contact with the market. Even after being thrown onto the market, households attempted for a while to maintain cohesion by hiring out as a single unit. The family wage, in its multitude of manifestations, was prevalent during early industrialization. Ultimately, however, the labor market won out, and household members were forced to adopt more individualistic and atomistic relationships with it. As industrialization progressed, households finally became disaggregated individual employees. Household members no longer worked together. In the realm of production, each household member had joined a new "family." Hugh Cunningham sums up some of the key changes occurring from protoindustrialization forward:

> First, in contrast to agricultural work, and to a lesser extent proto-industrial work, their work had a regular quality extending throughout the year; the trade cycle might bring with it periods of slump and lay-off, but in principle work achieved a regularity on a daily, weekly, and annual basis far removed from pre-industrial practice. Secondly, entry into the labour market was no longer phased; one day you were not a worker, and the next day you were. Thirdly, it was by no means certain that children would be working under the supervision of members of their own families, a point which was also true under proto-industrialization, but which had added impact in a work unit as large as a factory. Add to this the fact that

children often started work under the age of ten, and the industrial revolution period begins to regain the reputation it had until recent years as a
black moment in the history of childhood. The family as an institution
may have survived the industrial revolution, but many individual children did not.[19]

The Industrialization of America

As early as the Revolutionary War, there were all manner of mills, dis-
tilleries, paper and gunpowder factories, shipyards, and docks employing both skilled and unskilled labor up and down the Eastern seaboard.
In 1769, a Boston manufacturing house ran four spinning mills and, six
years later, a Philadelphia concern employed 400 women and girls producing cotton goods.[20] But these were relatively primitive "manufactories" which placed traditional hand-operated equipment in one location
and aggregated a group of workers. Production processes remained iden-
tical to those used in homework. In fact, most of the work continued to
be put out for homework.[21]

The Revolutionary War, and later the War of 1812, put the United
States on a path of independence from Great Britain, first politically,
then economically. The events of 1776 announced that we were, once
and for all, politically independent of England. There was the necessity
of war to gain that independence. But inevitably, during that war, America
was cut off from the product of British industry. Where import substitution could occur, we shifted to France, Spain, and other European nations with an interest in the New World. But, also inevitably, the war put
America on its own resources. It provided a powerful spur toward development of industry.

If 1776 announced our political independence, 1812 cemented our
economic independence. Again, wartime animosities choked off vital
elements of trade between Great Britain and the United States. Britain
remained, at least up until this period, not only our most important trading partner but also the economic fatherland to whom we looked for
guidance, advice, and innovation. The War of 1812 not only established
the principle of coequal sovereignty on the high seas and ensured that
Canada would forever remain beyond American reach,[22] but it also re-
deployed "large amounts of capital, which had previously been employed
in trade and shipping, into manufactures. The growth during this period
of isolation was extraordinary."[23]

Thus, early steps toward industrialization date to the colonial period. By the end of the War of 1812, the developmental pattern was clear— the North would emphasize industry and the South commercial agriculture. Industry continued to develop in the North through the period of the Civil War, but industrialization on a large scale did not occur in the South or the Midwest until after the Civil War, so the Northeast set the tone.

Samuel Slater, considered the father of American manufactures, was attracted to an America that, having recently won its political independence, appeared determined to secure its industrial independence as well. Slater had apprenticed to an English manufacturer of textile machinery, and was especially knowledgeable about Richard Arkwright's machines and processes (considered state of the art at the time). In 1789 in Pawtucket, Rhode Island, Slater established the first cotton factory in America that used modern factory methods and machinery.[24]

Other textile complexes soon appeared in Lowell and surrounding areas of Massachusetts, constituting the first truly large-scale factory operations in America. From their beginnings in the early 1800s, but especially from the 1820s through the 1850s, they sponsored an innovative labor policy that, in many ways, remains unique in American labor history. While the boardinghouse system implemented in the Lowell mills was relatively short-lived, it has been thoroughly studied.[25]

The Lowell mills were initially staffed by the "Lowell girls," single young women and girls recruited from the New England countryside— Yankee farm girls. Because labor was relatively scarce, and because the mills were recruiting young women of strict Protestant background, mill owners were compelled to avoid some of the more unwholesome labor practices that accompanied early stages of the industrial revolution in much of Europe. To house the women and girls, companies built large boardinghouses.

While it lasted, the boardinghouse system was remarkably effective in meeting the employers' problem of labor supply without being unduly harsh on the workers. Hours were long, and, certainly by today's standards, conditions did not measure up. But many of the Yankee farm girls who staffed the mills sought only to earn to a specific target amount and then return home, so maximizing hours was perceived as one way to achieve the target earnings quickly. Furthermore, they might have been willing to tolerate conditions they would not otherwise, since they saw themselves only as short-term employees. The boardinghouse system never produced conditions as harsh as those in the early British textile industry. One reason the boardinghouse system was effective was that it was consistent with tradition in the local culture.

> Since the labor of very young children was not a tradition in the New England sea towns where the mills first started, it was not adopted in the mills. Since there was a neighborly interest among the townsfolk in spite of differences in wealth and position, a friendly relationship pervaded the early mills. Since at the time no world markets were sought, and the difficulties of shipping gave a good margin of protection against the importing of goods of the coarser sort which New England made, the industry could set its own standards. Hence, although hours were long and conditions hard, the mills conformed so well in their demands and conditions to the standards of their time that in the early days of the industry young women of middle-class families did not hesitate to eke out the family income by working in the mills.[26]

The boardinghouse system offers equivocal proof that industrialization can occur without child labor. Most of the Yankee farm girls were from sixteen years of age into their early twenties. Very few children under sixteen were employed, and there is no evidence to suggest that these few made any meaningful or necessary contribution to production. At the other end of the age spectrum, very few middle-aged women, married women, or widows were employed and most of these ran the boardinghouses rather than working in the mill.[27] The boardinghouse system was very successful for its time, but it is only equivocal proof that industrialization can occur without child labor because, ultimately, the system could not be sustained.

For a while, the boardinghouse system seemed almost too good to be true. Charles Dickens, master critic of British industrialization, toured the Lowell mills in 1842. In contrast to "those great haunts of misery" of his own country, he found clean, well-ordered, well-lit, and ventilated factories, model boardinghouses well chaperoned and furnished with pianos and circulating libraries, and, most of all, he found happy, contented, and well-mannered young women and girls.[28]

But the boardinghouse system was too good to be true. Ultimately, the system, and the conditions that it implied, could not be sustained. First, the early Lowell girls were typically "spot" wage earners. That is, they worked to amass a dowry or to support their rural family, and when sufficient funds had been accumulated, they left the mill. Many frequently moved back and forth from farm to mill, but few entered with the intention of remaining. These girls were not the basis for a permanent industrial workforce, and the mills' owners continued to face chronic labor shortages in spite of their benevolent paternalism. Second, external competitive pressures in product markets were forcing mill owners to skimp on amenities in the boardinghouse and to impose stricter controls on hours and wages in the mills.

The owners needed a labor force that would work more regularly under harsher conditions, and they found it in immigrants. The Irish potato famine of the 1840s was driving many Irish families to America where, compelled by starvation, they were willing to take whatever work they could find at whatever wages and hours were offered. By 1855, Irish women constituted half the New England textile workforce.[29] The employers had not intentionally set out to replace the Yankee farm girls with Irish immigrants, it was simply that the Irish were showing up at the same time the Yankee girls were abandoning the mills because of falling wages and increased work pressure. The arrival of the Irish did not halt the fall in wages, but their response was different. When wages began falling with the depression of 1837, Yankee girls returned to the farm. When wages continued to fall in the 1850s, the Irish, having nowhere else to go, responded by sending their children into the mills.[30]

As the rural New England Lowell girls gave way to Irish immigrants, the Massachusetts "boardinghouse" model gave way to the "Rhode Island" model pioneered by Samuel Slater in his Pawtucket Mill.[31] Based on the family wage and the mill village, the Rhode Island system became the dominant mode for recruitment of children into industry in America. Slater's original workforce of 1790 consisted entirely of mothers and their children in family groups. By 1816, his workforce of sixty-eight included one family with eight members working, one family with seven members working, eleven more families with three to five members working, and eight single men and four single women. The two largest families alone made up nearly 25 percent of the total workforce.[32] Edith Abbott recounts a story, perhaps apocryphal but eerily prophetic, about Slater's efforts to recruit his original labor force:

> A man by the name of Arnold was living with his wife and ten or twelve children, a few miles away in the woods, in a den formed by two rocks and some rough slabs of wood. When the woman was asked by Mr. Slater if she would come and work with her children in his new mill she consented upon the express condition that she should be provided with as good a house as the one in which she then lived. The first time lists for the

mill, for the winter 1790–91, which have fortunately been preserved, contained the names, therefore, of Ann, Torpen, Charles, and Eunice Arnold.[33]

Industrial Expansion

Industry in the Northeast grew steadily from the early 1800s through the Civil War. But after the war the entire nation began a program of rapid industrialization. As the country grew westward, industry developed in the midwestern states of the former Northwest Territory. The lure of the frontier was much more than the yearning for independence and the chance to build a new life. It turned out that the frontier contained vast stores of raw materials valuable to industry. Industry dotted western Pennsylvania and moved westward through West Virginia, Ohio, and on to Indiana, Michigan, and Illinois following discoveries of coal, oil, and natural gas. Soon, industry spanned the continent, and was concentrated in hub cities like Chicago, St. Louis, New Orleans, and San Francisco and in the areas where valuable raw materials and minerals were abundant.

> This phenomenon of the contemporaneous existence of several industrial stages, side by side, under the same government, has laid upon this country some of the hardest problems which it has had to solve. The ever present but ever receding frontier has continually created a set of interests antagonistic to those of the settled industrial and commercial communities.[34]

Prior to the Civil War, the Piedmont was the back country of the South. Sparseness of the population and absence of the large cotton plantations throughout most of the Piedmont region during the antebellum period encouraged the proliferation of local handicrafts throughout the rural countryside. "Nearly every home had its cards, spinning wheel, and loom."[35] In addition, a wide variety of crafts emerged from potters to sawyers to tanners to millwrights, carpenters, coopers, and others. But though a few early mills had been constructed, there was little industrial employment.

The southern cotton textile industry did not really begin to flourish until the 1880s. One key development was the completion of the Air-Line Railroad in 1873. "At the end of the Civil War, the railroads of both North and South Carolina lay in sorry shape. . . . The rebuilding of the Carolina's railroads began slowly."[36] The Air-Line Railroad ran from

the iron, coal, and steel regions of Alabama through Atlanta and Charlotte and all the way to Richmond, Washington, D.C., and all points
east. Paralleling both the Blue Ridge escarpment to the west and the
coastal plains to the east, virtually all of the Piedmont region lay within
a hundred miles of the railroad trunk line. Connectors and spurs linked
the rest. Before this, some inland cities had been connected by rail lines
to port cities on the eastern seaboard. But now, the entire Piedmont was
connected to itself. The completion of the rail line enabled the Piedmont
to develop as an industrial region.

Southern advantages included ready access to raw material, undeveloped water power, the rise of an entrepreneurial capitalist class, and a
seemingly endless supply of "cheap and contented labor." Geographic
proximity to cotton meant the southern mill could purchase the raw
material more cheaply, forgoing both transportation costs and often the
fees of a commodity broker. Plentiful and undeveloped sources of water
power were important, in the first instance, for providing the power for
the first mills and enabling the industry to establish a foothold in the
region, and later, when mills converted to electrical power, for providing relatively inexpensive electricity. Next, after the ravages of the Civil
War followed by the ravages of Reconstruction, a new entrepreneurial
class emerged preaching the gospel of industry, and specifically the cotton textile industry as the salvation of a New South. The mill building
boom that was launched in the 1880s was accompanied by a chorus of
civic boosterism:

> A mill was sometimes a sort of community project, begun by an indi-
> vidual who hoped to benefit not only himself, but his neighbors as well.
> If employment was furnished to many poor people, the condition of the
> community was improved in a corresponding proportion. Sometimes this
> aspect of the question took on almost a religious fervor, so that the build-
> ing of a mill was in a way regarded as public philanthropy.[37]

But the decisive factor in the rise of the southern cotton textile industry was labor supply. Industry constructed mill villages to draw whole
households from the surrounding farming and mountain regions. In turn,
whole households went to work in the mills. Households came to the
mills in abundance:

> What was hardship to the farmer was a boon to the manufacturer, and the
> number of mills erected varied inversely with the price of raw material.

Table 2.1

Gainful Workers, Aged 10–14, in the United States: 1870–1930
(in thousands)

Year	Workers 10–14	% Nonfarm	Population 10–14	Total workers	Children as % of workforce	Activity rates of children (%)
1870	765	47.00	4,786	12,925	5.92	15.98
1880	1,118	50.64	5,715	17,392	6.43	19.56
1890	1,504	57.38	7,034	23,318	6.50	21.38
1900	1,750	62.47	8,080	29,073	6.02	21.66
1910	1,622	68.98	9,107	37,371	4.34	17.81
1920	1,417	73.02	10,641	42,434	3.34	13.32
1930	667	78.55	12,005	48,830	1.37	5.56

Source: Historical Statistics of the United States, Colonial Times to 1970 (U.S. Census Bureau, 1997), Series A119–134 and D75–84.

Added to theses advantages was an abundant supply of cheap labor, much of it drawn from the farms which were burdened with the production of a single unprofitable crop.[38]

The New Industrial Workforce

After the Civil War, over the course of a single lifetime, the American economy was transformed. Industrialization's impact on the household was wrenching. It fueled a mass migration of labor—off the farm and out of the mountains; from countless cities, villages, and regions throughout Europe; from China and Mexico; from east to west and south to north—families were uprooted from traditional patterns of life and drawn to the industrial centers, both urban and remote, springing up across the landscape. Families relocated geographically. And as a consequence, they were required to relocate themselves in society. Lifestyles in the industrial centers were very different from what they had known, and conditions of work were even more radically different. If the transformation was difficult enough for adults, it could be especially wrenching for children.

Table 2.1 presents a broad overview of child labor in America, according to the U.S. census from 1870, the first year the census counted gainful child workers, through 1930. The table presents gainful workers aged 10 to 14 (under 15, at least 10). In absolute numbers, child labor peaked in 1900 at 1.75 million children. The trend shows strong growth from 1870 through 1890, a sustained peak from 1890 through 1910, and a substantial decline thereafter.

Children constituted 5.92 percent of the total workforce in 1870. From 1870 through 1900, this figure remained fairly stable, hovering between 6 and 6.5 percent. After 1900, child workers as a proportion of the workforce declined steadily and substantially. Activity rates, or labor force participation rates, of children peaked around 1890 to 1900 at 21.38 and 21.66 percent, respectively. As early as 1870, however, 16 percent of children ten to fourteen years old were gainful workers, and the number remained persistently high through 1910, declining thereafter.

To provide at least some context for these numbers, Table 2.1 also provides the proportion of nonfarm workers in the economy (relative to total workers). While admittedly sparse context, this proportion is sometimes taken as a proxy for industrialization.[39] As the table shows, by the time we began counting child workers in 1870, the labor force was already equally divided into farm and nonfarm workers. From this threshold between 1870 and 1880, industrialization proceeded apace. It is generally understood that, prior to the Civil War, industry was concentrated in the Northeast and that, after the war, it exploded throughout the nation. Still, it is clear that industrialization had developed considerably before we started counting the working children. Unfortunately, the census did not count child workers during the earliest period of industrialization. Further, it can be seen that child labor did not begin to turn downward until a substantial majority of the workforce were in nonfarm occupations (62.47 and 68.98 percent in 1900 and 1910, respectively).

American industry encountered periodic labor shortages, especially of skilled labor, but for the most part, and at all the key stages in its development, industry was blessed with a more than ample labor supply. When the first large industrial complexes were built, the Yankee farm girls showed up. When they left, the Irish showed up. During the decade from 1846 to 1855, 3 million immigrants arrived in America. The pattern was repeated on an even more massive scale from 1881 to 1914. During the 1880s alone, over 5 million emigrated from Europe to the United States.[40] Europeans, escaping famine, political oppression, and economic depression, populated the urban centers and dispersed throughout the industrial Northeast and Midwest. Farther west, Chinese were imported to build the railroads, cut timber, and work the hard-rock mines. In the South, falling prices for cotton (and later, the boll weevil), under the economic system of the crop lien system, forced sharecroppers and tenant farmers off the land at precisely the time they were most needed in the mills.[41] Likewise, timber and mineral interests dispatched indigenous families from the southern Appalachian Mountains during the boom years of the Piedmont textile region.[42]

At the risk of only some exaggeration, it was almost as if we witnessed a reversal of Say's Law—that supply creates its own demand. During this period of rapid industrialization, demand for labor seemed always to create its own supply. A labor supply was obviously a necessary factor for industrialization. But for much of our industrial history, it appears that demand was the sufficient factor. Wherever employers demanded labor, the labor was there. Families desperate with poverty could always be found. Wherever the mine, mill, or factory was established, the workers showed up. And wherever the employer demanded the labor of children, workers could be found who offerred up their young.

Women and Children First

Supplying their labor, women and children fueled the industrialization of America. Perhaps even more than in Great Britain, America's first industrial workers were predominantly women and children. Why were women and children the first to be called? Why were they the first to go? In the preindustrial household economy, the division of labor was based almost entirely on sex and age. There was men's work, and there was women's work. Even during periods of peak activity, where men and women devoted their labor to a common goal, a division of labor deemed appropriate for men and women was generally recognized. Likewise, there was a differentiation between children and adults. But, unlike the male-female dichotomy (you are either one or the other), age is a graduated measure.

Even in the bustle of activity that characterized the yeoman household, there were slow periods. For the ambitious yeoman, usually the adult male head of the household, slow periods meant time to fix the roof while the sun was shining. They could mend fences, make and repair tools, put up a new shed, or explore exchange relationships with the surrounding community. Even when they took a holiday to hunt or fish (which would restock the larder), they were constantly engaged in productive economic activity. In contrast, activities of women and children tended to be more closely confined to the proximity of the home. After they had completed the routine chores in and around the house, which should not be minimized but which required only some finite amount of time, what were the women and children to do with the rest of their time? For the children the options were play, work (if it could be found), or learning. For the women, many turned to domestic industry, and since the women supervised the children, they brought the children along.

Claudia Goldin and Kenneth Sokoloff have studied the role of women and children in the industrialization of America as closely as anyone.[43] They show that the rapid development of industrialization in the American Northeast was associated with the relatively low productivity of women and children (as compared to men) in the Yankee household economy.[44] This circumstance created an excess supply of woman and child household labor that could be, in turn, made available to the external labor market. Industrial entrepreneurs and investors began their work in the Northeast, rather than elsewhere, at least in part because of the ready availability of a relatively cheap labor supply.

Goldin and Sokoloff studied the period from 1820 to 1850, which was, in fact, a period when the Northeast industrialized rapidly but the South and Midwest did not. There is evidence to suggest that the prevalence of women and children in industry predates this period. Women and children constituted the dominant share of the workforce in most of the primitive, transitional "manufactories" (and were an even larger share if the entire putting-out network is included). Men were owners, overseers, clerks, and, where needed, filled in certain key positions requiring strength or special skill. Women and children did the basic factory production.

Obviously, both supply and demand factors were related to the employment of women and children in the early factories. Did one set of factors dominate the other? If growth in supply of women and children was the dominant factor, one would expect their relative wages to fall as their proportion of the workforce increased, and rise as they withdrew from the workforce. But this is the reverse of the historical pattern observed in the United States. It is well established that relative wages of women and children increased over time while their share of the labor force was increasing.[45] Then, as their wages began to approximate those of adult males, employers began to substitute adult males for the women and children. The best available evidence suggests a demand-driven phenomenon.

Certainly manufacturers were aware of the opportunities presented by this excess supply of domestic labor. Early advocates for the devel-

opment of an American manufacturing sector encouraged the employment of women and children as necessary to the development of industry. Alexander Hamilton only echoed the view of many when he stated,
in his *Report on Manufactures*:

> Extensive manufactures can only be the offspring of a redundant . . .
> population. . . . [I]n general, women and children are rendered more use-
> ful, and the latter more early useful, by manufacturing establishments
> than they would otherwise be.[46]

The Family Wage

One distinctive feature of much of the child labor in the United States
was its close connection with family wage systems.[47] So much of American history of child labor is embedded within these systems, and we
invented such a great variety of them, that one wonders whether they
were a necessary adjunct to child labor in America. The most highly
developed—that is, the most highly rationalized and institutionalized—
family wage systems probably were those in the mill villages of the
southern cotton textile industry.[48] But the family wage was prevalent in
many other industries and occupations, sometimes in gender-specific
(father to son or mother to daughter) forms. The purest family wage
systems were found in agriculture and industrial homework, and it is no
mere coincidence that agriculture and homework are the two sectors
most closely connected to the preindustrial household economy.

In these family wage systems, the household hired itself out as a gang
of workers. All able-bodied family members might be part of the bargain. Whether family members all worked together or each worked independently, whether their wages were pooled into a literal family wage
or each worker was paid separately, whether the men and boys went one
way and the women and girls went another, the signal characteristic of
the family wage system is a group-hire for at least one adult and at least
one child. For the household, it meant that children could contribute to
adult earnings and, often no less important, that the children would have
someplace to go while parents were at work. For the employer, it meant,
at the very least, a reduction in the transaction costs associated with
employee recruitment. To the extent the employer was successful, it
might also mean a reduction in labor costs, a more docile and compliant
workforce, and a secure future labor supply (through early socialization
and on-the-job training).

The family wage system was usually also a community wage system. When augmented by such institutions as company towns, mill villages, tenement neighborhoods, and padrone systems, strong traditions reinforcing child labor were created. Most of one's friends and neighbors participated in the same system, further reinforcing the role of custom, habit, and tradition. Wages could be kept low, in part because of the variety of in-kind payments many received. In the mill village or company town, the company might provide housing, fuel, and other amenities from schools to churches, stores, and recreation facilities. The village itself was as integral a part of the company's capital investment as were factory and machinery. Consequently, the owner had a strong incentive to maximize the productive efficiency of its housing, schools, churches, and stores. Family members who were not currently working were either liabilities or investments. The aged and the infirm, including those whose infirmities were caused by work in the mill, were liabilities that the company was forced to carry by continuing to provide housing and subsistence even though they were not likely themselves to contribute to productive efficiency. Those too young to have begun productive work were investments. They could be carried in the company's program of housing and subsistence so long as a return on investment could be foreseen; that is, on the assumption that they would eventually turn to the mill.

But the critical factor was the current number of employees furnished by the family. Specific arrangements varied. Daniel Augustus Tompkins, a prominent mill owner who was best known as a builder of cotton textile mills and mill villages, recommended a ratio of one mill worker for each room of company housing provided. Others thought each family should provide a minimum of three workers to the mill. Possibly the most advanced forms were the famous "Pelzer Contracts" of the Pelzer "show mills" of South Carolina, owned and operated by Captain Ellison Smyth. All children under twelve were required to be in school; all children twelve and over were required to be in the mill; exceptions required written authorization from the mill superintendent; violations were subject to discharge and eviction (of the entire family).[49]

Tough Cases

Widows and Orphans

The "widders and orphans" problem has been a vexing social problem throughout history. As regards child labor, "widows and orphans" denotes a class including literal widows (and their children) and literal orphans, but includes children of disabled fathers as well. The commonality is a household where one or both of the adult breadwinners are disabled or absent. The common resulting tendency is a magnification of the pull of the labor market on the child. Whatever the prevailing trials and tribulations of both preindustrial and industrial life, widows and orphans bore a disproportionate share. Very few could remain independent. If they could join an extended family household, they would. When there were no relatives or willing neighbors to take them in, they often became dependent on public or private charity. Many were placed in asylums. Both public and private charity was scarce, and asylums were often harsh. Widows and orphans were objects of pity and public concern.

The orphan problem became particularly acute in New York City. By the mid-1880s, the city was overrun with orphans. The problem became so great, and the inadequacy of the asylums became so obvious, that new solutions were sought. Charles Loring Brace, founder of the New York Children's Aid Society, concluded "that the best of all Asylums for the outcast child, is the *farmer's home*" [emphasis in original].[50] Through the latter half of the nineteenth and the early twentieth century, as many as 350,000 orphans were shipped out of New York by the Children's Aid Society and other charitable organizations on the orphan trains "bound westward, and, to them, homeward."[51] Children from ages five to fifteen emigrated en masse to the rural Midwest. When the trains pulled into the station, dense crowds of eager farm families waited for the opportunity to choose the youngest, brightest, and healthiest of the group. Those not chosen rode the train further and further west until it was finally depleted of its orphan cargo. Some were signed over to tradesmen as virtual apprentices, but most were taken in by farm families.[52] Unfortunately, at least a few were gathered up by unscrupulous loafers looking to recruit a captive force of child workers. For many of the children, probably most, placement with Midwest farm families was the opportunity of a lifetime and, whatever the rigors, life was much better than what they faced in the asylums. But for many others, it was a Dickensian nightmare—nothing more than an interstate trafficking in child workers. Some were indentured into virtual slavery. Others were mistreated, abused, and neglected. Still others were shipped back to New York after the first harvest only to ride the orphan trains again the next season. Most of the charities provided replacement orphans on request.

Early industrialization exemplified by the textile industry promised a new form of asylum—a new and arguably better solution to the widows and orphans problem. The cotton mill village could provide shelter and the opportunity to earn food and clothing in exchange for the labor of the family. This was undoubtedly a better alternative than commitment to an asylum, but it was also, undoubtedly, a situation ripe for exploitation. Many of the earliest cotton mills, including Samuel Slater's mills in Rhode Island but also including the first textile mill villages in the South, provided work to indigent widows and orphans, sometimes without wages, as a "community service."[53] In the South, there were essentially two broad patterns of migration to the mill villages. First came the widows and orphans, second came the depressed subsistence and commercial farm families from the southern Appalachians and the cotton tenant farms. During the early phases of southern cotton textiles, widow-headed households were in the majority in many mill villages. Throughout the Piedmont textile region, widows headed from one-third to one-half of all households.[54]

As depressed farm families moved to the mills, widow-headed households eventually declined in proportion to the whole, but always constituted a significant minority of the total community. The image of the mill village as a benign asylum for widows and orphans was persistent, and until alternatives, such as widows' pensions, were provided, employers could claim a moral high ground in providing subsistence that could not be found elsewhere. The claim extended far beyond the mill village, however. It seemed that everywhere children worked, employers claimed that some substantial proportion worked to support indigent widowed mothers. Reformers argued it was wrong that orphans should be twice punished—first through loss of one or both parents, second by being condemned to a childhood of labor—but the argument was hollow as long as the child labor system enabled widow-headed households to survive and society offered no better alternatives.

Vagrants and Deserters

Ultimately, most fathers were devout breadwinners and remained steadfast throughout their lives in supporting their families. But everywhere and always, there have been a few who shirked. Nearly every industrial town or mill village had a few deadbeat dads, drunkards and loafers who lived off the labor of their children. Other fathers deserted the family altogether, leaving mothers and children to fend for themselves. The effect, at least in terms of child labor, was no different than if the mother

Figure 2.3 *The Dependent Widower.* Meridian, Miss. Apr. 1911. The Dependent Widower. WANTED;—A BACKBONE. *(Courtesy of the Library of Congress, Prints and Photographs Division, Lewis Wickes Hine National Child Labor Committee Collection, LC-2070.)*

had been widowed and the children orphaned. The women and children were placed in the same economic position. Whether the father was dead or simply a deadbeat, the children had to work.

To pity for the women and children, the public added scorn and disdain for the cowardly fathers. Reformers were especially biting in their disdain for such fathers. To illustrate this reaction, when Lewis Hine was investigating Mississippi cotton mills in 1911, he interviewed a father about the closing of a particular mill. His report contains the following mix of fact and commentary, but Hine's photo caption leaves no doubt about his opinion (Figure 2.3):

> His comment on the effect of the closing of the Meridian Cotton Mill is illuminating;—"They closed down about a year ago, and most of the men got work at other factories in town, while some moved away, — *but the greatest hardship was on the children. Now they have to go to school.*" His sanctimonious disquisition on his *"love for his family"* was nauseating. (See photos #2069 to #2071 showing his favorite occupation, and also one of the youngsters deprived of his right to toil.)[55]

It is easy to condemn the vagrants and deserters for their irresponsible lifestyle. The vagrants were parasites, the deserters cowards. Individual moral culpability attaches; thus, it is assumed, with a certain justification, that the cause is individual moral weakness. But that is only part of the explanation. Robert Hunter emphasized the important distinction between the poor and the paupers—dependence. Suggesting an analogy between sociological pauperism and biological parasitism, Hunter notes, "Paupers are not, as a rule, unhappy. They are not ashamed; they are not keen to become independent; they are not bitter or discontented. They have passed over the line which separates poverty from pauperism. . . . [T]hey live miserably, but they do not care."[56]

Otherwise upright fathers could fall to desperation by temporary disability, long-term illness, layoffs, reduced hours and short time, or any number of circumstances beyond their control. Any of these events could put the father in a position of temporary economic dependence on his children. For some proportion of fathers, this was so heavy a psychological blow that it pushed them over the line to become Hunter's happy vagrants in miserable lives. Some became dependent vagrants. Others escaped not poverty but pauperism by flight and became deserters. It was especially demoralizing for fathers willing and able to work to be put on layoff or reduced hours while their children continued regular work. A few mills openly preferred women and children and would hire fathers only when short of help, and then often placed them in menial positions. Ironically, many of the early child labor laws, by granting exceptions to age minimums in cases of widowhood or indigency, encouraged vagrancy and desertion. In any case, children of such fathers were an especially pathetic segment of the workforce—they might as well have been orphans.

Child's Play

If industrialization imposed a wrenching adjustment on adults, the children in the household were likewise caught up in it. The children were largely left to their own devices to adjust—they were rootless. Further, having no memory of any other kind of life and no grounding in the customs, habits, and traditions of preindustrial life, this new society thrust new rules upon the children, and, whatever society handed them, they were obliged to accept. But industrial society made no provision for the children:

These present day problems of the child . . . are all due to one underlying cause. There has been an entire revolution in industry during the last century, and nearly all the social problems of child life have grown up as a result of this revolution. The best thought of this entire period has been given to industrial development, — to economy, wealth, profits, and wages. That the needs of the child have been overlooked, if not entirely forgotten, in the readjustment of society to the new conditions, cannot be questioned.[57]

What were the children to do with their time? What were parents to do about their children? In contrast to previous generations, where children were rarely out of the sight of their parents, where "the home was the centre of the moral, educational, industrial, and social life," and where the child's activities were paced by the circadian and seasonal rhythms of the home, now both parents were out of the home for most of the waking day.[58] A mother with very young children might remain at home for a time, but as soon as the children were old enough to be left alone— and sometimes, under duress, even sooner—the mother returned to work. Where were the children to be left? In many industrial communities, from city tenement to mining camp, the house was no longer a home in the sense of centering the child's activities. What were parents to do with their children?

One option was to leave the children to their own devices. An older daughter could look after the younger children. Girls and very young children could remain in the home, now a center of domestic activity and little else. And boys could be boys and roam the neighborhood with their mates. It takes little thought to recognize the flaws in such a plan. Girls became trapped in an isolated domestic servitude. They were made prematurely responsible for the home, given little in the way of education to handle that responsibility, and were kept indoors, often in unsanitary or unhealthy environments, where opportunities for interaction with those in the world outside were limited. In contrast to the girls, who worked the home, the boys worked the neighborhood. Their energies were expended outside the home. In an earlier time they might have gathered firewood, tended livestock, run errands, and generally helped out. In industrial times, there was no one to direct their activity into such useful channels. Boys will be boys, and having an industrial neighborhood at their disposal—a neighborhood devoid of both parental supervision and constructive alternatives—they could readily become a class of loafers and budding criminals.

A second option was to send the children to school. In retrospect, we can readily assert that schooling was the best option for the children. Schooling would remove children from their industrial pursuits—at least for some portion of the day, week, or year—and whatever evils accompanied those industrial pursuits. Not only were they under adult supervision in an ostensibly more wholesome environment, but just maybe they would acquire some knowledge or skill that would be valuable in their future. Unfortunately, such clarity about the benefits of schooling often eluded parents of the time.

There were at least three reasons that schooling was not seen as the preferred alternative by many during this period. First, schooling was not yet widely available. Before industrialization, there were private schools for the wealthy and charity schools for the orphans and children of widowed, disabled, or otherwise dependent parents. Only with industrialization did the movement to educate the masses, implying universal and compulsory education, gain force. This meant, seemingly inevitably, that there was a lag between industrialization and creation of an equitable and effective system of public schools. For many working parents, schooling was simply not yet available for their children. For others, schooling came at such a cost, required traveling such a distance, or involved other difficulties, that when weighed against the opportunity costs of the child's lost wages, schooling could be more trouble than it was worth.

Second, even if available, schooling was not always highly valued by all. How were parents, especially those who had little or no formal education themselves, to fully understand the value of schooling for their children? Even for those parents who wanted only the best for their children, there was no adequate frame of reference for evaluating potential future value against opportunity costs. As for employers, they might understand, in the abstract, that a better-educated workforce could be a more productive workforce. But that did not address their concerns for production in the here and now.

Third, even if schooling was available and could ensure a better future for the children, it did not fully solve the fundamental problem confronting the parents—what to do with the children while the parents worked. Parents worked year round, when they could, and usually worked six days a week. But the typical school term of early public education was well short of even the 180-day term common today. Further, parents often worked ten and twelve hours a day, while the school day averaged around six hours. In short, if the parents' concern was what to do with the children while parents were at work, schooling could fill a portion of the time but still left children to fend for themselves for many hours and days.

A third option was to take the children along to work. Where schooling was a less than optimal choice and leaving the children to their own devices was an even poorer choice, taking the children to work was often the only practical alternative. Then what were the children to do at work but, well, work. It is important to recognize that for many parents during these early stages of industrialization, while schooling was just an emerging option, work was not the worst choice they could make for their children. At least there was adult supervision, often close to the parents, the children escaped idleness and contributed something to the family's economic well-being, and finally, just maybe, the children would acquire some knowledge or skill that would be valuable in their future.

Wherever they were—in the home, on the streets, in school, or at work—the children would be children. Having no frame of reference to support expectations that things ought to be otherwise, they would adapt to whatever environment they were placed in. But they would engage in the behavior and exhibit the behavioral characteristics of children. Above all, the children would play. Imbued with youthful exuberance and seemingly boundless energy, they would take their joy where they could find it. With a sense of curiosity that often bordered on recklessness, easily led by the passions of the peer group (magnified, especially among the boys, by a childish braggadocio), and with an ill-formed sense of morality that led them to take their cues as to right and wrong and acceptable and unacceptable behavior from their environment, the children would play. It is often said that child workers were deprived of their childhood, and this was certainly an apt assertion regarding many. But most children would have their childhood, whether in an environment well-suited to childhood or not.

3. CHILD LABOR REFORM

The Change After the Change

Declaration of Dependence by the Children of America in Mines and Factories and Workshops Assembled

Whereas, We, Children of America, are declared to have been born free and equal, and

Whereas, We are yet held in bondage in this land of the free; are forced to toil the long day or the long night, with no control over the conditions of labor, as to health or safety or hours or wages, and with no right to rewards of our service, therefore be it

Resolved, I—That childhood is endowed with certain inherent and inalienable rights, among which are freedom from toil for daily bread; the right to play and to dream; the right to the normal sleep of the night season; the right to an education, that we may have equality of opportunity for developing all that there is in us of mind and heart.

Resolved, II—That we declare ourselves to be helpless and dependent; that we are and of right ought to be dependent, and that we hereby present the appeal of our helplessness that we may be protected in the enjoyment of the rights of childhood.

Resolved, III—That we demand the restoration of our rights by the abolition of child labor in America.*

Alexander J. McKelway's "Declaration of Dependence" very nicely summarizes the nature of the appeal the child labor reform movement attempted to convey to the public. In many respects, the sentiments expressed speak for themselves. But two points are worth considering here.

First, this was not a declaration that could have been written by the children themselves. It was necessary that someone like McKelway write it on their behalf. Even assuming working children could acquire the

---

*Walter I. Trattner, Crusade for the Children, *attributes authorship of the "Declaration of Dependence" to Alexander J. McKelway and establishes the date as 1913. But a handwritten notation on one copy of the declaration suggests that it must have been written several years earlier. The copy, found in the NCLC papers housed in the Library of Congress, bears this notation, "June 29, 1910—John C. Winston Co—10,000—$167.50–Furnishing paper & tissues & printing."*

literacy skills to compose such elegant prose, they could not have written it. By virtue of their very helplessness and dependence, the children themselves were incapable of resorting effectively to self-help, either individually or collectively. If adults might be justifiably left to fend for themselves, individually and collectively, in a free labor market, no similar justification could be advanced on behalf of children.[1] While there are numerous instances of strikes by child workers in U.S. history, they tended to be spontaneous acts of rebellion over transitory issues, short-lived with gains limited to the moment. Children may have been assembled "in mines and factories and workshops," but they were incapable of exercising their right to full freedom of assembly to act for their own betterment. Someone had to speak for the children.

Second, McKelway's "Declaration of Dependence" was a twentieth-century assertion of the rights of children. While it expressed sentiments that had been gradually emerging and coalescing since the post–Civil War industrialization boom, it could not have been written at the time of the Civil War (at least not in the United States) and certainly could not have been written in the eighteenth century—it simply would have made no sense. The child labor problem was not understood, from our colonial period through the Civil War, in the same way that McKelway and early twentieth-century reformers understood it.

The First Child Labor Problem

It is important to recognize that the child labor problem of early-twentieth-century America, the one reformers came together to solve, was not the same as the child labor problem of eighteenth-century America. The later problem was defined and understood on different terms—nearly polar-opposite—than the earlier problem. From the preindustrial period through the protoindustrial period and well into the early stages of industrialization, the problem was not that children worked, it was that too many children were idle too much of the time. That is, it was a problem not of the employment of children but of the unemployment and underemployment of children.[2] It was not until much later that the work of children came to be seen as a social and economic problem calling for an abolitionist reform movement. By then, reform had to undo the work of the first reform movement, which, if the problem was unemployment and underemployment of children, then the solution was clear: Put the children to work.

Colonial poor laws, modeled after British laws, sought to prevent children from becoming a public charge or burden by putting them out to work, often under programs of bondage or indenture. The perceived need for these laws was reinforced by the British practice, applauded by the colonists, of shipping orphans and poor children to the American colonies. Underpinning the view that children ought to work for their subsistence were Puritan beliefs, dominant in the New England colonies, and Quaker beliefs, dominant in the middle colonies, in the virtue of industry and the sin of idleness.[3] All children were expected to be industriously employed, so much so that merely to "keep cattle" was not considered sufficiently industrious. "[M]asters of families should see that their children and servants should be industriously implied so as the mornings and evenings and other seasons may not bee lost as formerly they have bene." Thus, orders followed such as "all hands not necessarily imployed on other occasions, as woemen, girles, and boys, shall and hereby are enjoyned to spin according to their skill and abilitee."[4] In the Virginia colony, unencumbered by Puritan or Quaker morality, similar provisions encouraging and requiring the industrious employment of children were adopted based on more purely commercial interests. Eventually, these commercial interests came to dominate, even in the New England and middle colonies.

America had a continent to settle and a wilderness to tame. No hands could be spared; even more, none could be allowed to become a burden on society. As tensions with the mother country increased and the necessity of an independent manufacturing sector became evident, pressures for putting the women and children to work only increased. With independence, child labor was deemed to be in the national interest. Indeed, it helped to reconcile the schism between the Jeffersonian agrarian ideals and the Hamiltonian commercial ideals. Nowhere is this revealed more clearly than in the debates over early tariff policies. Hamiltonian interests ultimately won the day by showing how industrial work by women and children could redound to the comfort of adult male farmers without draining off necessary agricultural labor. Child labor was, in its day, a win-win situation. The children could be kept busy, escaping the sin of idleness. The household itself only stood to gain through any added contribution from the work of the women and children. Agrarian interests were protected by keeping the adult male yeoman farmer at the work of agriculture and by retaining the availability of women and children during peak (e.g., harvest) periods. Commercial interests, the most obvious and direct beneficiary of high tariffs, could claim to be advancing the national interest in an independent manufacturing sector without jeopardizing the agricultural sector and, equally important, providing useful employment for women and children who otherwise would be less than fully utilized.

A Growing Moral Repugnance: Society's Countermove

During the earliest stages of industrialization, the proportion of the industrial workforce comprising women and children was exceptionally high. But as long as industry itself was only a small portion of total economic activity and the absolute numbers of women and children remained small, little concern was expressed about working children. The turning point occurred around the time of the Civil War. Abolition of slavery set our economy unalterably on a path toward creation of a free labor market. And the postwar industrialization boom dramatically magnified the numbers of workers, including women and children, in industry. As unfettered industrialization proceeded apace, a growing moral repugnance set in. There seemed to be something not quite right about child labor in these new and newly emerging industrial settings. Society eventually reacted to protect itself. In the case of child labor, very young children were excluded from the labor market altogether, and youth were protected from exploitation and abuse through regulation of hours and conditions.

When labor became industrial labor, it not only engendered a fierce wage dependence, it also subjected labor to the conditions of the free, self-regulating market, that "stark utopia" that Karl Polanyi argues would have annihilated society. Naturally, society took protective measures. In a collective refusal to be treated as a commodity, society established limits. Child labor restrictions may be seen as a public expression defining who should be subject to the self-regulating commodity labor market and who should be exempt.[5] With the market's emphasis on freedom of contract, child labor was inherently suspect.[6]

William Morris, artist, poet, and founder of the British Socialist League, once wrote, "Ill would be the change were it not for the change beyond the change."[7] Eventually society would react to protect the children. The countermove involved the emergence of reform movements. But, as a reaction to the perceived evils of industrial child labor, the movement lagged industrialization. "All institutions for the common good undertaken by the community have developed more slowly than those institutions which have been initiated by individuals for the purpose of gaining profits."[8]

This inevitably meant that, by the time the anti–child labor movement gained substantial force, not only had the industrial child labor phenomenon existed for some time, but the parties to the process had developed habitual interests in the child labor system that they reflexively sought to protect. Industries had grown dependent on child labor and sought to defend their position. In turn, reformers labeled such industries as "parasitic."[9] Robert Hunter, with equal color, referred to the child labor system as "a kind of cannibalism" where "some of us live, and even win our pleasures and luxuries, by the ruin of others."[10] "Those industries which coin into profits the vitality of childhood—and leave to the world, for its mercy to support, wrecks of manhood—rob the country of something which they can never return."[11]

Reformers recognized that child labor was systemic and institutional. Wherever child labor was pervasive, there was a system of employment that had become institutionalized that led to its practice. While the motivation of individual employers and individual parents was always relevant, it was the systems that had to be destroyed if the institution of child labor was to be destroyed. Many individual employers were, at least on relative terms, motivated to treat their child workers well. Likewise, many individual parents sought the best for their children, given the range of available alternatives. Yet in spite of the enlightened motivations of some proportion of employers and parents, child labor persisted. If child labor was to be abolished, the institution of child labor would have to be attacked as an institution. As Edgar Gardner Murphy, one of the cofounders of the National Child Labor Committee, remarked:

> More than a generation ago it was argued, for the system of slavery, that there were good plantations upon which the slaves were well treated. That statement was true, but the argument was weak. The presence of the good plantation could not offset the perils and evils of the system in itself, any more than the "good factory" can justify the system of child labor. . . . There can be no "good" child labor and this system is monstrous, not only in principle, but in its results.[12]

The Reformers

The child labor reform movement reached the height of its prominence and influence during the Progressive Era of the early twentieth century.

During this period, the movement centered around and was best exemplified by the National Child Labor Committee. But well before the NCLC came into being, other organizations had initiated the reform movement. Through most of the nineteenth century the only organized opposition to child labor came from the trade unions. The first efforts of the trade unions were not aimed directly at reducing child labor, but rather were aimed at equalizing educational opportunities. At the time, the only schools available to those who could not afford private institutions were the "charity schools." Labor organizations, and especially their labor parties, argued that, as future voting citizens, equal education for all children was a democratic imperative. Dulles and Dubofsky cite the platform of the Workingmen's Party of New York, calling in 1829 for "A system that shall unite under the same roof the children of the poor man and the rich, the widow's charge and the orphan, where the road to distinction shall be superior industry, virtue and acquirement, without reference to descent."[13]

The national labor organizations that emerged in the second half of the nineteenth century all incorporated provisions calling for the abolition of child labor into their constitutions. When the Knights of Labor was founded in 1869, its constitution included such a position. The Knights were responsible for introduction of the very first labor legislation into the South in the 1880s. Likewise, when the Federation of Organized Trades and Labor Unions (FOTLU) was established in 1881, its constitution also called for the abolition of child labor. When FOTLU reorganized to become the American Federation of Labor in 1886, the child labor provisions were carried forward into the AFL constitution.[14] Thus, the AFL was on record as opposing child labor from its beginning, and the federation remained a consistent voice supporting the reform efforts, even if that voice was sometimes muted for strategic reasons.

Some of labor's motives were purely humanitarian, support for schooling being the primary example. This was, in no sense, labor protectionism. Certainly labor sought something that would benefit their own children, but it was to benefit all children. Certainly it would benefit children of trade unionists, but it would also benefit all comparably situated children, especially children of the poor. It was also to benefit society as a whole. Certainly it would benefit organized labor, but it would also benefit business by providing a better class of workers, and it would benefit government by providing a better class of citizens.

But organized labor had a mix of humanitarian and protectionist motives in seeking child labor legislation. It was recognized that children competed with adults for the available work, that child labor depressed adult wages, and that adults were less free to organize when children were scattered about the workplace. As other reform groups came on the scene, labor, because its self-interest was obvious, often remained strategically behind the scenes. This was especially so in the South where mill owners often believed that proposed child labor legislation was merely labor's "entering wedge" and that before long, labor would be pressing on for minimum wages, factory safety laws, and other restrictions on adult labor. Opponents were more effective when they could cast child labor proposals as labor legislation. Proponents found it more effective to cast them as child welfare legislation. So, while organized labor generally supported child labor reform, it often stayed in the background, allowing federations of women's clubs, church organizations, and, when they were established, state child labor committees to lead the movement.

The reform movement that emerged in the 1890s and flourished in the early twentieth century was by no means unitary. It consisted of an intricate web of organizations and agencies that cooperated on issues of child labor. While the National Child Labor Committee was the most prominent national organization, other national organizations were involved as well—most notably labor, which remained involved throughout, and the National Consumers League which, before the NCLC, had initiated the national movement. At the state and local level, not only was there an array of state and local child labor committee, labor federations, and consumers leagues, there was also an endless array of philanthropic and charitable organizations, religious groups, women's clubs, social service organizations, and settlement houses involved in the reform effort.

The National Child Labor Committee was formally organized on April 15, 1904, by Edgar Gardner Murphy and members of the New York Child Labor Committee.[15] Murphy had been the leader of the reform movement in the South and had organized the Alabama Child Labor Committee in 1901, the first state child labor committee in the nation. After a prolonged effort, significant reforms were attained in Alabama and the Carolinas in 1903. Murphy recognized the importance of a national approach to the problem and a national organization. He approached Felix Adler, a founding member of the New York Child Labor Committee (formed in 1903), with the idea for creating a national organization. Thus, Murphy, from among the most backward communities and recalcitrant states, hooked up with the New York committee, working in the very financial capital of industrial America, to form the NCLC and spearhead the national child labor movement. At the time of the founding of the National Child Labor Committee:

> Ten-year old boys were commonly found in the blinding dust of coal breakers, picking slate with torn and bleeding fingers; thousands of children sweltered all night for a pittance in the glare of the white-hot furnaces of the glasshouses. Young girls toiled in damp, dust-laden cotton mills for long hours, six days a week. Unsanitary factories and tenement sweatshops, canneries, and the street trades, including the night messenger service, all took their toll from the home, the schoolhouse, and the playground while most Americans looked on with approval or indifference. Child labor had few effective opponents.
>
> Motivated by pity, compassion, and a sense of patriotism, they argued that, for the child, labor was a delusion; for industry it was a fallacy; and for society, a menace. Child labor meant the spread of illiteracy and ignorance, the lowering of the wage scale and hence the standard of living, the perpetuation of poverty, an increase in adult unemployment and crime, the disintegration of the family, and, in the end, racial degeneracy.[16]

From the beginning, the NCLC comprised, and attracted support from, some of the most prominent philanthropists and social progressives in America. Its long-time chair was Felix Adler, founding head of the American Ethical Culture movement and a professor at Columbia University. Samuel McCune Lindsay, a sociology professor at the University of Pennsylvania, was named general secretary. Two ministers were chosen for the assistant secretary positions, Owen R. Lovejoy (who would later become general secretary) for the North and Alexander J. McKelway for the South. Other prominent members during the committee's early years included Jane Addams of Hull House fame; William H. Baldwin, president of the Long Island Railroad; Robert W. de Forest, president of the New York Charity Organization Society; Edward T. Devine, general secretary of that society; Florence Kelley, general secretary of the National Consumers League; James H. Kirkland, chancellor of Vanderbilt University; V. Everit Macy, director of the Title Guarantee and Trust Company; and investment bankers Paul M. Warburg and Isaac N. Seligman.

A first aim of the committee was to document the nature and extent of child labor in America in order to educate the public about the problem. To this end, it hired investigators and dispatched them strategically into the field. First, to the coal mines, and then to the glasshouses and cotton mills. Then they branched out more broadly studying street trades in cities all over the country, tenement homework especially in and around New York City, and fruit, vegetable, and seafood canneries along the East and Gulf Coasts (and later agriculture throughout the country). But the NCLC investigators did not compile and publish hundreds of investigation reports on child labor simply because they thought it was an interesting research topic. They, too, were reformers. The committee itself was a reform organization, and its investigation reports were intended from the first to serve as instruments of reform. Committee investigators shared the mission and operated from a context deeply embedded in the reform movement.

Investigators who spent many years in the field could easily become frustrated. The not-yet-famous social photographer Lewis W. Hine, a long-time investigator for the committee, recognized early on that he and his colleagues faced an uphill struggle. "[W]ith the parents, the employers, and the children against us, our task of liberation is not an easy one."[17] Public opinion had yet to be turned against child labor:

> Most of the children I have questioned say they would rather work than go to school. Recently I was laying some evidence of this nature before a superintendent of schools, a man who seemed fairly progressive, when he turned on me with the query: "Are they happy?" and I admitted that many of them seemed to be. "Are they healthy?" he continued; and I acknowledged that in spite of all the difficulties and irregularities in their lives, they seemed to be rather healthy. "Well," he commented, "what are you worrying about then?"[18]

As the reform movement became national in scope, northern progressives dominated the NCLC, and the southern textile industry became the seat of the opposition, with the result that North-South sectional prejudices and hatreds were rekindled. Though it had been founded by Edgar Gardner Murphy of Alabama, the NCLC had a decidedly northern cast. In fact, Murphy and many of the southern moderates did not stay with the NCLC for long. In 1906, Senator Albert Beveridge (Republican of Indiana) planned to introduce federal legislation that would ban the product of child labor from interstate commerce. Naturally, he sought the endorsement of the NCLC. But for Murphy and several others, especially those from the South, even discussion of support for federal legislation was out of bounds. When, after contentious debate, the NCLC board voted to endorse the Beveridge bill, Murphy was convinced that "the Board has departed from a compact which I regarded as inviolable," and he resigned. From this time forward, the board reflected a decidedly northern composition, and the larger committee itself was never successful in securing a substantial southern membership base.[19]

The departure of Murphy and the southern moderates, and the tentative embrace with the federal government, might not have irreconcilably soured relations with the South had it not been for the untimely appearance of some damaging publications. First came *The Woman That Toils* by the Van Vorst sisters, followed by a series in the *Saturday Evening Post*.[20] The Van Vorsts were well-to-do social workers who had interned at Hull House and took jobs in southern cotton textile mills. Their portrait of southern cotton textiles was decidedly unflattering. In 1906, John Spargo published *The Bitter Cry of the Children*.[21] Spargo was a socialist and a firebrand who pulled no punches in his descriptions of the abuses of child labor or his conclusions on who was to blame. Finally came Edwin Markham's "Children at the Loom," first published in *Cosmopolitan* in 1906.[22] This one was not simply unflattering, many found it insulting. The image of emaciated children chained to the looms insulted mill owner and mill worker alike. Markham apparently did not know his warp from his weave because anyone who knew textiles knew that very few children had ever worked on the looms—the children were spinners, doffers, and sweepers who worked in an entirely different department. While the NCLC had nothing to do with these publications or their authors, they reinforced the idea that the whole of the child labor movement was something that was coming out of the North and focusing inordinately on the South. Sensitivity to sectionalism was such that the NCLC came to be seen by many in the South as just another instrument of northern aggression.

The Counterreformers

Just as development of industrial child labor spawned a reform movement, development of the reform movement spawned a counterreform movement. Employers and their trade associations reacted to defend their interests. They sought to retain their laissez-faire right to manage as they saw fit, but they also sought to maintain any competitive advantages that child labor might yield and avoid competitive disadvantages that reform might impose. When reforms were proposed at state and local levels, affected state and local industries and employer associations acted to protect employer interests. As the reform movement became a national movement, the counterreform came to be centered in the southern cotton textile industry.

By the early twentieth century, southern mill interests were justifiably proud of the industry they had built since the Civil War, an industry hailed as the industrial salvation of an indigenously reconstructed New South. Earlier historians portrayed the owners and builders during the mill crusade as having been motivated principally by humanitarian motives.[23] They were public servants redeeming the South and its poor whites from poverty. If mills happened to make a profit, that was almost a secondary consideration. While later historians have largely discredited this view,[24] it is fair to say that the mill owners felt entitled by virtue of their achievements to deal with any problem—including child labor problems—without interference or intervention by outsiders.

Any number of mill owners might be cited as representative of the group. Here, let two prominent figures speak for the rest. Lewis W. Parker of South Carolina was owner of the Parker and Pacolet "show mills" of Greer and Greenville and held interest in several other mills. As an early leading spokesperson for the industry, he asserted that a full generation of child labor had been absolutely essential in building the industry, but that the problem was now solving itself. He explained the evolution of the child labor system thus:

> The unfortunate families back in the backwoods drifted to the cotton mills. When they drifted to the cotton mills what was to be done? It is not possible for a man who has been working on a farm, who is an adult—after the age of 21 years, for instance—to become a skilled employee in a cotton mill. His fingers are knotted and gnarled; he is slow in action, whereas activity is required in working in the cotton mills. Therefore, as a matter of necessity, the adult of the family had to come to the cotton mill as an unskilled employee, and it was the children of the family who became the skilled employees in the cotton mills. For that reason it was the children who had to support the families for the time being. I have seen instances in which a child of 12 years of age, working in the cotton mills, is earning one and one-half times as much as his father of 40 or 50 years of age. . . . [F]or this reason, the child-labor question is solving itself by reason of the fact that we are now getting into the second generation and as we get into the second generation of employees we get the skilled employees.[25]

Parker, like many mill men, stressed that he was not, in principle, opposed to regulation of child labor. First, however, compulsory schooling laws were needed. He recognized the future value of a better educated workforce, but also asserted that work in the mill was better than rampant idleness. But he also argued that local communities should be allowed to deal with these local problems in their own way. He did not want to yield one of the South's key competitive advantages in cheap labor prematurely.

Daniel Augustus Tompkins was better known as a mill builder than as a mill owner. While he was chief owner of three cotton mills and director of another eight, he claimed to have built over a hundred cotton factories, and retained a financial interest in many. "More than anyone before him, D.A. Tompkins conceived and articulated the modern image of the Carolina Piedmont as an industrial region, distinctive yet incorporated within the national economic order."[26] Tompkins was active in both the National Association of Manufacturers and the National Civic Federation (serving as treasurer of its child labor committee) and supported their position in opposition to federal child labor legislation. Expressing views similar to those of most manufacturers of the day, he argued that mill work was good for the child. "It's as easy to teach a boy to love work with the result of capability as it is to let him drift into habits of idleness with the result of incapability."[27] In a speech to the National Civic Federation, he stated, "As long as there are tenderhearted women, there will be sentiments that are liable to injure children, as the tender mother so often spoils the child. I believe there are just about as many children spoiled by indulgence as there are by overwork."[28] But Tompkins, like Lewis Parker, was also pragmatic, recognizing that, on the question of child labor, a balancing of interests would best benefit industry. "As long as men are greedy men there will be need ultimately of some law to set a limit to the overwork of children."[29]

If Lewis Parker and D.A. Tompkins were fundamentally pragmatists, the same could not be said for the decidedly zealous and dogmatic David Clark. No one represented the counterreform movement better than David Clark, publisher of the *Southern Textile Bulletin* for over four critical decades. With the leading textile publication in the South as his mouthpiece, he served as self-appointed representative of the interests of mill owners on a wide variety of matters from tariffs to technology to labor relations, but his role in the child labor movement was decisive. In turn, he was such a strident and effective opponent of federal child labor legislation that he bore more than a small measure of responsibility for the public perception that the battle for child labor law was between the nation and southern cotton textiles.

David Clark was the offspring of two prominent southern families. His father, Walter Clark, had been a Confederate colonel before serving twenty-six years on the North Carolina Supreme Court, sixteen years as chief justice. As a progressive, liberal "jurist of the Populist movement," the elder Clark claimed the friendship of men such as Theodore Roosevelt, William Jennings Bryan, Samuel Gompers, and Robert La Follette. He was considered by Woodrow Wilson for appointment to the U.S. Supreme Court, but was, by then, thought to be too old for the job. Clark's mother was a Graham and his grandfather, William A. Graham, had served as governor of North Carolina, United States senator, secretary of the Navy, Whig candidate for vice president, and a senator of the Confederacy.[30]

In contrast to the liberal leanings of his father, David Clark was an uncompromising conservative. Initially, he vigorously supported the child labor practices of the southern mills, recognizing that relatively cheap labor was the South's major competitive advantage over the well-established New England textile industry.[31] He saw the New England textile interests behind every effort to abolish or restrict child labor. He assailed the "long-haired men and short-haired women" and the "professional agitators and parasites" of the reform movement. In zealotry, he proved more than a match for the entire National Child Labor Committee and its reform coalition, and he was possibly the single most influential individual in bringing the Progressive Era reform movement to a close. His personal philosophy coalesced around two abiding principles in his fight against federal meddling on the child labor question. First, he was an ardent advocate of laissez-faire capitalism.[32] Second, he was an ardent advocate of state's rights.[33]

The counterreformers conducted few investigations of their own, but they were able to find a few investigators who were sympathetic to their cause. Two are especially worth mentioning. Thomas Dawley worked for the U.S. Bureau of Labor and participated in its massive study of the cotton textile industry published in 1910.[34] Dr. George W. Stiles headed the Rockefeller Hookworm Commission (more strictly—the Rockefeller Sanitary Commission for the Eradication of Hookworm).

Dawley was hired by the Bureau of Labor in 1907 to help investigate child labor conditions in the cotton textile industry. Twice Dawley traveled extensively through Georgia, Alabama, the Carolinas, and the

Appalachian mountain regions from which many of the mill families emigrated. He concluded that families were far better off in the mill villages where living conditions were at least decent, wages were regular, and children might have some opportunity for education in the mill school, than they were on the small, mountain, subsistence farms with no sanitation, few schools, backbreaking work, and abject poverty. But his conclusions did not sit well—in fact they caused something of a furor—with his superiors in the Bureau of Labor who, Dawley claimed, were eager to portray only the evils of the child labor system.[35] According to Dawley, officials suppressed his conclusions and threatened to fire him, so he resigned and published his results and conclusions independently in 1912 in a volume entitled *The Child That Toileth Not.*[36] Dawley's book was rapidly and widely disseminated throughout the Piedmont textile region and received considerable circulation in the rest of the nation. This was just the kind of carefully documented rebuttal the industry needed in response to the NCLC investigation reports and the coming onslaught of government reports.

Stiles had been studying hookworm in the sandy-soil regions of the South for years. He documented that hookworm was widespread, arguing that it accounted for the attribution that southerners were lazy.[37] In the mill villages he observed that hookworm was most common among those recently arrived from the farm. With a grant of $1 million from John D. Rockefeller, he established dispensaries in over two hundred counties and organized traveling exhibitions—health trains—to visit towns and mill villages curing southerners of their laziness. The diagnosis was easy, the cure was cheap, and the results were almost immediate. Stile's tours sometimes had "the rousing spirit of tent revival meetings" complete with the apparent miracle of faith healing.[38] Stiles, like Dawley, believed white southerners were better off in the mill villages than on the tenant farms from which they came. He made the curious suggestion that in order to more effectively eradicate hookworm from the South, the child labor laws should be suspended in order to encourage migration to the mills, thereby making it easier to get treatment to the people. Nevertheless, he was widely respected, and his opinion on the matter had great influence. Thus, both Dawley and Stiles influenced the debate by providing respectable rebuttal arguments, based on carefully collected data, that people were better off in the mill villages than where they came from—Dawley studied the southern Appalachian mountain regions and Stiles studied the sandy-soil cotton regions.

Evolution of State Law

Before the twentieth century there was no national reform movement, and there was no federal role on the question of child labor. Early reform efforts took place at the state level on a state-by-state basis. Well into the twentieth century, while the question whether there should be a federal role in child labor was debated, many of the most important advances continued to originate in the sovereign states. What emerged was a crazy quilt of legislation where state standards varied considerably, even between immediate neighbors. The situation could fairly be described as chaotic. It also permitted and engendered the worst sorts of sectionalism—of the "race to the bottom" sort where "the worse inevitably checks the progress of the better"[39]—as each state sought to preserve its competitive advantages, even at the expense of working children. But there was also real progress through this process of gradualism. It was not a patchwork merely in the sense that each state had its own unique standards, but also in the sense that patches were continually being stitched on top of patches. Within each state, the state's own patchwork of legislation evolved, and, generally, with this evolution came progress. States also tended to emulate similarly situated states so that a steady upward harmonization of standards occurred over time. More progressive states, usually but not always the more heavily industrialized states, led, and less progressive states tended to follow, lagging somewhat behind.[40]

From the beginning, laws directed at child labor and at child schooling have been inextricably interwoven. In the period of the first child labor reform—when unemployment and underemployment of children were the perceived problems—many of the early manufactories were called "spinning schools" and received their public support on account of their alleged educational value. The curriculum involved bringing girls in to learn the arts of industrial spinning and, when they had become proficient, putting them out to homework to spin. Later, as a reform movement emerged to remove children from the workplace and as schooling came to be seen as the preferred alternative to child labor, development of child labor legislation and schooling legislation were equally intertwined. "Although distinct from the movement for public education, it came hand in hand with it, and the success of one was accompanied or followed by that of the other."[41] In some areas, schooling legislation and child labor legislation came about simultaneously. In other areas, schooling legislation came first and child labor legislation followed, or vice versa.

In much of the North, concern for schooling provided the leading impetus. Tax-supported systems of free public education were established in most northern industrial states in the 1830s and 1840s. Schooling was not yet compulsory and in more remote areas was not widely available, but it was valued. The first regulatory concession sought by the working people was the opportunity to send their children to school. Children who worked too many hours could not properly attend to their studies, and so the first child labor laws provided restrictions on hours. It is important to note that these laws were not so much an attempt to reduce child labor as to redirect some portion of that labor to schooling.

By 1900, all the industrialized states of the North had statutes restricting child labor in mining and manufacturing. Though none measured up to the standards later espoused by the NCLC, and they were enforced or not enforced with varying degrees of vigor, at least there were laws on the books. Most common were restrictions on hours of working children. By 1900 most northern industrial states had adopted the ten-hour day and sixty-hour week as the legal maximum for women and children. Several states specified minimum ages, and most incorporated rudimentary compulsory schooling provisions.[42]

Resulting from a combination of early industrial leadership, greater relative wealth with a stronger middle class, and Puritan ethics, the New England states were the early leaders in progressive legislation. Massachusetts, influenced by its boardinghouse system of labor recruitment, was in the forefront, while Rhode Island, grounded in the family wage and mill village systems, lagged. After 1900, however, Massachusetts was no longer able to maintain its claim as the most progressive state on child labor matters. Tied so heavily to the textile industry, the tremendous growth of the industry in the South presented a competitive menace. Because part of the South's competitive advantage derived from pervasive child labor, Massachusetts found itself unable to continue advancing its child labor standards without harm to industrial interests. The mantle of most progressive shifted to states like New York and some of the midwestern states, especially Ohio and Illinois, that had been formed out of the old Northwest Territory with its strong commitment to education. It should be noted that a few nonindustrial western states also had relatively progressive laws, but they were less controversial as these states did not have a large child labor problem. It should also be noted that a few of the northern industrial states persistently lagged their neighbors. Pennsylvania, for example, proved to be a chronically difficult state in which to secure effective progressive legislation. While the reason is not entirely clear, it may have had something to do with the fact that Pennsylvania had a greater diversity of industries than did her neighbors. At any rate, Pennsylvania held the dubious distinction of having the largest number of child workers well into the twentieth century.

The South lagged the North considerably, both in development of industry and in enactment of progressive child labor legislation. The Piedmont South had been an industrial region for barely a generation. Before 1900, the only laws on the books in any of the southern states were of Knights of Labor vintage. Even some of these had been repealed or were no longer taken seriously.[43] But all this activity occurred prior to the most dramatic wave of industrialization. Earlier laws were passed with relatively little fanfare, attracting neither widespread advocacy nor strong opposition. After the turn of the century, debate over child labor legislation was inevitably more contentious. In 1900 none of the southern states had effective child labor legislation on the books.

Around the turn of the century, several southern states began considering legislative restrictions on child labor. In 1903 Alabama and both Carolinas passed laws prohibiting the work of children under twelve (with some exceptions for hardship). Alabama led the way. In 1901 church organizations, federations of women's clubs, and labor organizations urged enactment of both child labor restrictions and compulsory schooling legislation. While their efforts failed, they led to the formation of the Alabama Child Labor Committee. Edgar Gardner Murphy, then rector of St. John's Episcopal Church in Montgomery, who had been active in the campaign, recognized that ultimate success depended on building a sustained coalition. The Alabama Child Labor Committee was finally able to achieve success in 1903, passing what was then the most progressive child labor legislation in the South.

A few progressive southern governors attempted to push the envelope under the banner of educational reform. In North Carolina, Charles B. Aycock was elected governor in 1901 on a campaign pledge to establish a system of public education in the state. But he advocated child labor reform only insofar as it advanced his plans for a public school system. While North Carolina enacted legislation in 1903, its laws remained among the weakest in the South throughout the period of reform.[44] In South Carolina, proposals to limit child labor and require schooling were introduced in the legislature as early as 1900. Governor Miles B. McSweeney came out strongly in favor of the proposals. In his inaugural address he reviewed the laws of other states and nations and called it the duty of the state to enact similar laws. As a practical point, he urged that if South Carolina were to remain economically competitive, skilled and intelligent labor would be demanded. He pointed to the record from 1880 to 1900, when southern manufacturers had uninterrupted control, showing that child labor had increased in the South whereas in other areas it had been cut in half. South Carolina's first child labor and compulsory schooling law was enacted on February 11, 1903.[45]

In the South, as in the North, child labor legislation often went hand in hand with compulsory schooling legislation. But the movement toward universal and compulsory public schooling in the South had to overcome additional barriers, most notably "the Negro problem." The Democratic party—the party of white supremacy—was now firmly in power throughout the South. Democrats vehemently opposed compulsory schooling because it would mean educating black children as well as the white children of the mill workers.

Having only recently been emancipated from slavery, blacks did not participate in the great industrial development of the South.[46] They were generally barred from industrial employment and only began to secure industrial work following World War I after the commencement of the northern migration during the war. This was a decidedly mixed blessing for the black population. On the one hand, blacks were, on the whole, among the most desperately poor in the economy. Their children obviously worked, and obviously suffered, by virtue of their poverty. Ironically, however, discrimination against blacks operated to spare black children from the evils of child labor in the mines, mill, and factories. The one redeeming aspect of Jim Crow was that the child labor problem was not a problem for southern blacks.

Rigorous and arduous as it was, the labor of black children remained under the control and direction of the parents. Under such an arrangement, blacks were able to make considerable gains in educating their children. Even without significant public support and even in the face of a hostile white citizenry, black communities all over the South worked to establish at least rudimentary schools for their children. Larger numbers of black children were learning to read and write than at any time since blacks had arrived on the continent. While literacy rates remained substantially behind those of whites, they were gaining rapidly.

The NCLC and other reformers were able to use racial prejudice to great advantage. They pointed figuratively to the bright happy faces of black children eagerly learning to read and write and drew odious comparisons to the humorless, sunken-chested, and sallow-complexioned white children toiling away in the mills. Alexander J. McKelway, himself a man of the South and a white supremacist, invoked both patriotism and racial prejudice to battle child labor in the cotton mills. He cited the higher example of Jefferson Davis who, when it was proposed to lower the age limit for enlistment in the Confederate armies, replied, "We must not grind the seed corn." And he constructed a vision of the inevitable degeneration of the once proud white race coupled with the elevation and eventual supremacy of the blacks.[47]

Early in its history, the National Child Labor Committee recognized that legislative standards meant little without effective compliance and enforcement provisions. Many early laws contained loopholes that essentially nullified the intent of the law. For example, many of the ten-hour laws adopted by northern states in the 1850s contained exceptions for those working under "special contracts." Thus, employers could offer employment on condition that the hours provisions could be exceeded at will, and the employee's choice was to take it or leave it. Many of the first minimum-age laws contained "hardship exemptions," permitting younger children to work if helping to support a widowed mother, disabled father, or otherwise indigent families, thereby encouraging claims of indigency. Other laws required no proof of age but rather only a parent's oath, thereby encouraging perjury. Still others prohibited only "employment" of children, but not necessarily all productive work. So if children were kept off the payroll, they could still be required to help. Finally, many laws fixed employer liability only for "knowing" violations, thereby rewarding employer ignorance.

Furthermore, even good laws were often rendered ineffective through ineffectual inspection and enforcement regimes. While some employers voluntarily complied with the law, others had to be forced to comply. There had to be "compulsion incarnate" in the position of a factory inspector or school truant officer. Florence Kelley, a member of the NCLC and general secretary of the National Consumers League, who had previously been the chief factory inspector for Illinois, proposed three "objective tests" of the enforcement of child labor laws: (1) presence of children in school; (2) actual prosecutions of violators; and (3) public and published records of the enforcement agencies.[48]

While the reform movement concentrated most heavily on child labor legislation and compulsory schooling legislation, it also took an interest in a wide array of other issues, from widows' pensions to maintenance of birth records. Brief mention should be made of one important area that is often overlooked in other accounts of child labor reform; that is, the emergence of employer liability and workers' compensation laws, and the role of the courts and the insurance companies in their development. These had an important, if indeterminate, effect in reducing child labor in several sectors of the economy. Throughout the nineteenth century, employers were able to escape liability for disabling or fatal workplace accidents through a variety of legal defenses. One prominent defense was the contributory negligence theory that held the employer harmless when the employee's own negligence contributed to the accident. But early in the twentieth century, many courts began holding that the contributory negligence defense could not be applied in the case of children. Courts routinely held that where a child under the legal age was employed, employers could not plead contributory negligence. Some courts held that, even in the absence of a legal minimum age, the contributory negligence defense could not be used in cases involving children under a certain age.[49] As a result of these cases, employers faced increased risks in the employment of very young children. When most states adopted some form of worker compensation system between 1910 and 1920, the risks associated with hiring children were magnified.

In the latter half of the nineteenth century, the insurance companies exerted an important influence on plant design and operation in the interests of fire safety. They had urged elimination of pitched roofs (to prevent attic fires); required emergency exits, automatic sprinklers and fire hoses; and encouraged the use of "slow-burning" building materials.[50] In the early twentieth century, in conjunction with the emerging employer liability and workers' compensation laws, they also exerted some influence on the child labor problem. Since children posed higher risks of accident and injury (both to themselves and to others with whom they worked), employers that agreed not to hire children could sometimes qualify for lower insurance premiums. But the influence of insurance companies was also limited to those industries and sectors where insurance was most important. Insurance played no role in those aspects of agriculture involving child labor. Insurance concerns could be avoided by moving children out of the garment factories and into uninsured sweat-shops. And insurance companies were less influential in southern cotton textiles than they were in New England textile manufacturing.

Federal Benchmarks

As noted previously, before the National Child Labor Committee arrived on the scene, all regulation of child labor emanated from the states. Shortly after the NCLC was founded, however, it began to consider a federal role in the regulation of child labor. This turned out to be a long, difficult struggle, one in which the reform movement lost nearly all the major battles while steadily winning the war. But the move toward federal regulation also deeply split the NCLC itself, nearly leading to its premature destruction.

The Beveridge Child Labor Bill

In 1906, Senator Albert Beveridge planned to introduce a bill that would ban goods produced by child labor from interstate commerce. Naturally he sought the endorsement of the NCLC. While the committee was deeply divided over the question of federal regulation, after a rancorous debate, it voted to endorse the Beveridge bill. The endorsement resulted in the resignation of much of the committee's moderate southern element, and most notably cost the committee its founder, Edgar Gardner Murphy. These were progressives, but they were moderate progressives. Moreover, they were southerners. However much they abhorred the child labor system, they would pursue only legitimate aims to its abolition. And federal intervention was not deemed legitimate.

Constitutional principles aside, Murphy had observed how effectively appeals to states rights, noninterference, and northern intervention were used against the Alabama legislation finally achieved in 1903. Among those who spearheaded the defeat of the 1901 legislative proposal that led to the formation of the Alabama Child Labor Committee were representatives from the Dwight Manufacturing Company mills in Alabama City.[51] Dwight Manufacturing was northern Massachusetts capital. In spite of this, its representatives had been quite effective in portraying reform advocates—many of whom, including Murphy, were lifelong citizens of Alabama—as outside agitators bent on rekindling sectional hatred and trampling on sacred rights of mill owners and parents alike.

Murphy realized how vulnerable the reform movement was to charges of northern interference. As a southerner, he also understood that northern interference and federal intervention were one and the same.

For a while, Murphy's resignation disoriented the board. Even while the NCLC was on record endorsing the Beveridge bill, several members supported Murphy financially in his public campaign against the bill. With the reform movement itself fragmented, the Beveridge bill was going nowhere. President Theodore Roosevelt, while sympathetic to the aims of the bill, would not support it because of doubts over its constitutionality. In the face of a lost cause, the committee moved to salvage what they could. If Roosevelt would not support the Beveridge bill, might he support a study of the child labor problem conducted by the federal government? NCLC representatives pressed two ideas on Roosevelt, ideas that had been developed by a group of the Hull House social workers. One was for a large-scale federal study of the child labor problem. The other was for creation of a federal children's bureau. Roosevelt endorsed both.

Thus, even though the Beveridge bill was lost, the reform movement made important gains. With Roosevelt's backing, Congress approved the funds necessary for the federal study and assigned responsibility to the Bureau of Labor. With this much accomplished, in early 1907 the NCLC withdrew its endorsement of the Beveridge bill and agreed not to seek federal regulation until the study was completed. By 1910, the Bureau of Labor began releasing the results of its study. By the end of 1913, it completed its work, having released a total of nineteen volumes.[52] The idea for a children's bureau did not meet with immediate success in Congress. But after a six-year fight, the U.S. Children's Bureau was finally established in 1912 and charged to "investigate and report upon all matters pertaining to the welfare of children."[53] President William Howard Taft accepted the NCLC's recommendation and appointed Julia Lathrop as the first bureau chief.

The Keating-Owen Act

In 1914, soon after the final installment of the massive federal study of child labor was completed, the Palmer-Owen bill, designed to ban goods produced by child workers from interstate commerce, was introduced in the House of Representatives.[54] The bill adopted the age standards of the Beveridge bill, a minimum age of fourteen for factory work and an eight-hour day for workers fourteen to sixteen. Support for the bill was overwhelming, but what was even more surprising was the almost complete silence of the expected opposition. One of the few to testify against the bill was Lewis K. Parker, a prominent South Carolina mill owner famous for the welfare work engaged in his mill villages.[55] He disavowed any interest in perpetuating child labor and assured Congress that conditions were improving and the problem would soon solve itself. He was more concerned with the hours provisions that would apply to workers between fourteen and sixteen. Since the southern mills operated eleven- or twelve-hour shifts and since the work of children was fully integrated with the work of adults, it would be impossible for the mills to adjust to the law without discharging all mill hands under sixteen. The bill would effectively elevate the minimum age to sixteen.

The Palmer-Owen bill was reported favorably out of committee and passed the House on February 13, 1915, by a vote of 237 to 45. The pattern of voting was significant, and a similar pattern would accompany later votes in both the House and Senate on questions of child labor. The vote divided along sectional lines rather than party lines. Davidson notes:

> The vote was sectional, however, not in the sense of the whole South against the whole North, but rather of the manufacturing South against the rest of the country. Only from the Carolinas, Mississippi, and Georgia were a majority of votes cast against the measure. Alabama was divided, though a majority voted for the bill, and in the delegations from Kentucky, Tennessee, and Virginia the vote was as strong for the bill as any of the other delegations were against it.[56]

The Palmer-Owen bill did not make it through the Senate's crowded calendar that year, having been blocked by Senator Lee Overman of North Carolina. The child labor bill was reintroduced in 1916 as the Keating-Owen Act and received prompt and favorable consideration. The Keating-Owen Act, the "crowning achievement of progressivism,"[57] passed Congress and was signed into law by President Woodrow Wilson on September 1, 1916, to become effective exactly one year from that date. Support for the bill remained bipartisan, and opposition was still sectional.

But by now a new institutional actor had appeared on the scene to spearhead the opposition. In the spring of 1915, David Clark organized the Executive Committee of Southern Cotton Manufacturers for the explicit purpose of defeating the anticipated federal child labor laws. Along with Clark, the Executive Committee comprised eight militant mill owners, two from each of North Carolina, South Carolina, and Georgia, and one each from Alabama and Mississippi. The most prominent mill owner on the Executive Committee was Captain Ellison Smyth of South Carolina, who owned at least eight mills, including the famous Pelzer show mills that were home to the Pelzer Contract.[58] The Executive Committee hired former North Carolina governor W.W. Kitchen to lead the attack in Congress. Realizing that they were unlikely to defeat the child labor bill, their strategy was to delay its passage and "load" the *Congressional Record* with arguments that could be used later in litigation.[59] Aside from the testimony of southern cotton mill interests arranged by the Executive Committee, the only testimony in opposition to the Keating-Owen bill was offered by James Emery, general counsel of the National Association of Manufacturers (NAM). As it turned out, Emery was not representing any official position of the manufacturers association. He stressed that he personally endorsed the child labor standards embodied in Keating-Owen, but that he and a number of NAM's board of directors feared federal child labor legislation was merely an "entering wedge" for all manner of additional federal labor legislation that would inevitably follow.[60]

Even before the Keating-Owen Act had been signed into law, David Clark announced in the *Southern Textile Bulletin* that its constitutionality would be challenged.[61] Clark and the Executive Committee had a year to prepare. They raised funds from the mill owners, viewing support for their legal defense fund as more a matter of tithing than voluntary contributions. Clark had no qualms about haranguing those "Tight Wads and Slackers" among the mill owners who withheld their fair share of financial support.[62] The Executive Committee spared no expense in securing competent legal counsel. In fact, they retained the services of two prominent corporate law firms. Manly, Hendron, and Womble of Winston-Salem, North Carolina, handled matters on the ground. O'Brien, Boardman, Parker, and Fox of New York, one of the leading corporate law firms in the nation, was retained to formulate legal strategy and to carry the case to the Supreme Court. Next, the Executive Committee had to find a judge who would be sympathetic to their cause. The clear choice was Judge James Edmund Boyd of the U.S. Federal Court's Western District of North Carolina, known to be a conservative lawyer of the old school, and opposed to the progressive spirit of the times.

Finally, the Executive Committee had to choose the right case. They knew they had to wait until the law went into effect, but they wanted a case that could be carried to the Supreme Court at the earliest possible date.

One month before the law was to take effect, the Fidelity Manufacturing Company of Charlotte posted a notice of the law's requirements: that no one under fourteen could remain employed and that all under sixteen would be limited to an eight-hour day. On August 9, Roland H. Dagenhart, a Fidelity employee, filed a complaint in U.S. Court for the Western District of North Carolina on behalf of his two sons, Reuben and John. Reuben was then fifteen and had been working sixty hours per week. Under the law, his hours would be cut. John, who was under fourteen, would lose his job altogether. The father claimed the law violated his rights by depriving him of the earnings of his children to which he was entitled until they reached the age of twenty-one. Roland Dagenhart was a reluctant plaintiff at best. He was recruited by David Clark because the ages of his sons enabled a test of the key elements of the law. Clark had to coax Dagenhart into agreeing to serve as plaintiff, and all of his legal expenses were financed by the Executive Committee.[63]

Several years later, Reuben Dagenhart was highly critical of the constitutional rights the Executive Committee had secured for them. What had he and his younger brother gotten out of the lawsuit? "We got some automobile rides" and "They bought both of us a Coca-Cola. That's what we got out of it," he told an interviewer. At age twenty, after working twelve hours a day since the age of twelve, and now with a wife and child, he said, "Look at me! A hundred and five pounds, a grown man and no education. I may be mistaken, but I think the years I've put in the cotton mills have stunted my growth. They kept me from getting any schooling. I had to stop school after the third grade and now I need the education I didn't get." Even without an education, he seemed to understand his place in history: "It would have been a good thing for all the kids in this state if that law they passed had been kept."[64]

This was clearly a friendly lawsuit—one of those "collusive suits arranged to obtain quick and convenient adjudication of constitutional issues"[65] on behalf of a party that lost in Congress. The Executive Committee sat on both sides of the adversarial process. In fact, after the filing of the initial complaint and reply, neither the Dagenharts nor Fidelity Manufacturing participated any further in the case to which they were party. The obviously contrived nature of the case apparently did not bother Judge Boyd. The day before the law was to take effect, he issued an injunction against its provisions, finding them to be unconstitutional. The landmark *Dagenhart* case was set on a fast track for hearing before the Supreme Court.

The *Dagenhart* Court was divided between laissez-faire and progressive doctrines. By the 1890s, laissez-faire had triumphed in the Supreme Court, and its influence remained strong in 1917–18. But the Court had also acquired a strong progressive wing, decidedly less interventionist, and more inclined to permit the legislative branch to reflect the will of the people. Because the Court was so evenly divided ideologically, it was going to be a close case, but it looked like a Court that could have gone either way. The tension was between the Commerce Clause that authorized congressional regulation of interstate commerce and the Tenth Amendment clause that reserved all rights not specifically elucidated to the states. The Court had shown a reluctant tolerance for federal regulation of commerce in narrow instances where harmful or adulterated products were shipped across state lines. But the Keating-Owen Act called for regulation of otherwise harmless products because of the conditions under which they were produced. This had always been the province of the sovereign states. Ultimately, in a decision that marked the eclipse of progressivism, in a narrow 5 to 4 decision, the Supreme Court struck down the Keating-Owen Act on June 3, 1918.

An interesting footnote to this history involves Justice James Clark McReynolds, who voted with the majority to overturn Keating-Owen. President Wilson's appointment of Justice McReynolds to the bench was "one of the most perplexing in history. . . . It is doubtful that any President has nominated a justice whose views proved so foreign to his own."[66] This was the very same seat to which Wilson had considered appointing Walter Clark, David Clark's father. At the time, however, Walter Clark was sixty-seven years old and Wilson sought a younger appointee. Had Walter Clark received the appointment rather than McReynolds, it is likely that the vote would have been 5 to 4 to uphold the constitutionality of the federal child labor law, thereby scuttling his son David's efforts.

It is difficult to gauge the effects of the Keating-Owen Act and impossible to do so with any quantitative precision. The law was in effect for only ten months (except in the Western District of North Carolina), and vigorous enforcement machinery had not been implemented. In several of the northern industrial states, the Keating-Owen standard was already incorporated in state law, so no adjustment was necessary. Elsewhere, many employers brought their operations into compliance with the law, and some maintained those standards after the law was invalidated. But it is also clear that many other employers ignored the law, and some that had complied returned to lesser standards after it was invalidated.

By the time the Keating-Owen Act was overturned, the United States was into World War I, and the resulting domestic labor shortages created pressure to relax state child labor laws, as many European nations had done. But Felix Frankfurter, then chair of the War Labor Policies Board, had a clause inserted in all federal contracts requiring adherence to the Keating-Owen standards. Perhaps the strongest effect of Keating-Owen was indirect—the influence it had on state laws. The Keating-Owen Act contained the same age standards as the earlier Beveridge bill. Between the Beveridge bill in 1906 and Keating-Owen in 1916, a handful of states had adopted their age standards in state law, sometimes explicitly for the purpose of discouraging imposition of federal regulation. Finally, after Keating-Owen was declared unconstitutional, a number of the lagging states brought their statutes into line again, to discourage further attempts at federal meddling. If the Beveridge bill announced the basic contours of what would become the American standard on child labor, Keating-Owen hastened adoption of that standard.[67]

The Child Labor Tax Act

Shortly after the Keating-Owen Act was invalidated, another child labor bill was introduced in Congress. The bill retained the same child labor standards as the Keating-Owen Act. This time, however, since the Commerce Clause alone had failed to provide a constitutional basis for regulating child labor, Congress' taxing authority was invoked. The bill would impose a 10 percent excise tax on goods made by children (or where children performed work ancillary to production). The Pomerene Amendment to the Revenue Bill of 1919—also known as the Child Labor Tax Act—passed Congress in February 1919 and was to take effect that April.[68]

Once again, David Clark announced that the constitutionality of the act would be challenged. Eugene T. Johnston, an employee at the Atherton Mills, a D.A. Tompkins mill, complained on behalf of his son, John W. Johnston, who was then fifteen and would see his hours reduced. Once again, Judge Boyd issued an injunction against implementing the act on the basis that it was unconstitutional. Once again, the U.S. Supreme Court struck down the constitutionality of the Child Labor Tax Act.

This time, however, a number of peculiar things happened on the way to the Supreme Court. First, the injunction issued by Judge Boyd was extremely narrow. It applied only to John W. Johnston. Even Atherton Mills' other underage employees were not covered. Because the injunction was so narrowly tailored, the U.S. district attorney chose not to appeal. After all, the law remained in force, with only one exception. So to get the case to the Supreme Court, it was necessary to call the Atherton Mills back in to file the appeal, ostensibly insisting on their right to fire John W. Johnston (or to reduce his hours). In turn, these events made clear that this was another obviously contrived and collusive "friendly" lawsuit with David Clark and the Executive Committee sitting with both private parties.

Nevertheless, the case moved rapidly to the Supreme Court, where it was heard on December 10, 1919. By this time, young Johnston had already turned sixteen, so, in addition to whatever other concerns there might have been about the legitimacy of the case, "the purported controversy had become inescapably moot."[69] After the December hearing, another curious thing happened—nothing—and it happened for an unusually long time. David Clark had hoped for a decision before April, because mills would be required to file tax returns "admitting or denying liability for the 10 per cent tax."[70] But April came and went with no decision. In fact, two more Aprils came and went before a decision was finally issued in May 1922.

Reasons for the inordinate delay are not entirely clear, but Stephen Wood places Chief Justice Edward White and Justice Louis Brandeis at the center of speculation. White's problems were complex. For him, the case straddled a doctrinal fence, and it was difficult for him to come down on one side or the other. Delay may have enabled him to postpone a difficult decision. He was aging, and his infirmities were becoming more apparent. At the same time, "White was determined not to surrender the Chief Justiceship while the dangerous progressive, Wilson, could name his successor. . . . He died only a few weeks after Harding took office."[71] Brandeis, on the other hand, was deeply concerned about the jurisdictional defects of the case—both the lack of a legitimate controversy and its obvious mootness—and was urging the Court to dismiss without addressing the constitutional issues. Sometimes, as he later would remark to Felix Frankfurter, "The most important thing we do is not doing."[72]

When Warren Harding appointed William Howard Taft as chief justice, the case was scheduled for rehearing, and many observers recognized that the Child Labor Tax Act was doomed. For one thing, Harding's new solicitor general, James M. Beck, had published articles questioning the constitutionality of federal child labor legislation, he had heartily approved of the *Dagenhart* decision, and only three weeks before oral arguments, he publicly questioned the constitutionality of the Child Labor Tax Act.[73] Needless to say, his defense of the act before the Court was considered somewhat less than enthusiastic or persuasive.

But it was more than Taft's or the Harding administration's new philosophy that doomed the Child Labor Tax Act. From the beginning, it was understood that Congress had intended to regulate child labor. Since direct regulation had been foreclosed under the Commerce Clause in *Dagenhart*, Congress sought shelter in its taxing powers. But the use of taxing power was always a thin veil. Congress sought regulation under the guise of taxation. This was not intended as a revenue bill. That much had become clear over the period that the Child Labor Tax Act remained in force. Over its short life, the act had raised about $41,000 in revenue, but had cost over $310,000 to administer.[74] In an earlier era, the Court would not have second-guessed Congress. Even in the laissez-faire 1890s, it was considered improper for the Court to inquire into the motives of Congress. If this was exercise of a valid taxing power, so be it. It was no concern of the Court why Congress wanted this law. But in recent years, the Court had shown greater interest in the reasons for exercise of congressional authority. Once the reasons became relevant to the Court, and it was obvious that this was regulation in the guise of taxation, the Child Labor Tax Act had to fall if the holding in *Dagenhart* remained law.

Before *Johnston v. Atherton Mills* was heard for the second time, it was joined by two other cases—*Vivian Mills v. J. W. Bailey* and *Drexel Furniture v. J. W. Bailey*. These were both cases arranged by David Clark and the Executive Committee and brought to the Supreme Court by way of Judge Boyd's chambers in the Western District of North Carolina. Clark had become concerned about the jurisdictional weaknesses of the Johnston case and was well aware that it had been moot for some time. He wanted to have his bases covered. Ultimately, the Court dismissed the *Vivian Mills* case for jurisdictional defects. It was in the *Drexel* case that the Court ruled the Child Labor Tax Act unconstitutional. In this case Drexel had protested assessed taxes. It is interesting to note that David Clark had to go outside textiles to the furniture industry to find the right test case. Taxes had been assessed against numerous textile mills, including mills in the Western District of North Carolina, but apparently none had protested.

As for *Johnston v. Atherton Mills*, it was declared moot.

As with the Keating-Owen Act, it is difficult to assess fully the effects of the Child Labor Tax Act. Once again, it is clear that not all employers complied with the act and that some returned to lesser standards when the act was invalidated. But the law remained in effect for three full years—from May 1919 to May 1922—and many industrial employers had fully adjusted to operating without children and never turned back. To be sure, the law covered only industry (essentially, mining and manufacturing), and there was growing concern with child labor in other sectors (such as agriculture and the street trades), but within the covered sectors, child labor declined substantially. It was not simply that employers had three full years' experience under the act (though that was critical—new habits of industry can become well ingrained in three years' time), these three years happened to be very important in the history of several industries. In the textile industry, for example, these three years when child labor was subject to heavy taxation traversed the period from the boom years of World War I into a bust period of the postwar years.[75] Efficiency innovations along the lines of scientific management developed during the boom were carried over into the bust and became the notorious "stretch out"— that is, workers were required to operate more and more looms or spinning frames for the same pay. Worker productivity now mattered more than ever and, to preserve the available work, adults were put on work-sharing arrangements. To top it all off, the American Federation of Labor had launched a postwar organizing drive into southern cotton textiles. In sum, textile employers had enough to worry about. Many had learned to live without child labor, and now putting the children back to work was the last thing on their minds.

Another development in child labor reform from around this period is worth noting even though it had little immediate impact in the United States. As World War I came to a close, President Wilson's ill-fated support of the League of Nations gained prominence on the world stage. Wilson dispatched Samuel Gompers, long-time president of the American Federation of Labor, to Geneva as an emissary on labor affairs. Gompers was extremely influential in the creation of the International Labour Organization. Ironically, however, since the United States never joined the League of Nations, it did not join the International Labour

Organization at that time either. Gompers carried with him a resolution from the 1917 Convention of the American Federation of Labor that the Treaty of Peace should include a provision that "no article or commodity shall be shipped or delivered in international commerce in the production of which children under the age of 16 have been employed or permitted to work."[76] While Gompers was not successful in obtaining this particular provision, Convention 5, adopted at the first session of the International Labour Organization in 1919, called for a minimum age of fourteen in industry (mining and manufacturing). The International Labour Organization is, today, the only agency of the League of Nations to survive to become an agency of the United Nations.

The Proposed Constitutional Amendment

Following the judicial defeat of the second federal child labor law, the NCLC Board of Trustees voted on June 19, 1922, to support an amendment to the Constitution. The committee had discussed the advisability of pursuing such an amendment as early as 1906 when concerns were raised that the Beveridge bill might be found unconstitutional, but the decision was made to pursue federal legislation first. But after two successive federal child labor laws were invalidated, there seemed to be no other course of action if federal legislation was to be sustained.

Congress remained generally sympathetic to the cause of child labor reform. While there was spirited debate, both houses recommended the proposed amendment by the necessary two-thirds majority. On April 26, 1924, the House of Representatives passed the amendment by a vote of 297 to 69. Shortly thereafter, on June 2, 1924, it passed the Senate by a vote of 61 to 23. Thus, the proposed Child Labor Amendment to the Constitution was recommended to the states for ratification.

Provisions of the proposed constitutional amendment were elegant in their simplicity and parsimony. In two brief sections, it declared:

> Section 1. The Congress shall have power to limit, regulate, and prohibit the labor of persons under eighteen years of age.

> Section 2. The power of the several States is unimpaired by this article except that the operation of State laws shall be suspended to the extent necessary to give effect to legislation enacted by Congress.

Arguments for and against the proposed Child Labor Amendment were grounded in their time, but the general contours of the argument were familiar.[77] Proponents of the amendment argued that, in spite of progress, the child labor problem remained serious. The census of 1920 had reported 1,060,858 children between the ages of ten and fifteen at work, or 8.5 percent of the total children of that age in the country. Further, the enumeration did not take account of children under ten, nor the total number of children in agriculture (the census being taken in January), nor children doing seasonal work, industrial homework, or vacation work. Since the census was taken, child labor increased as a result of the withdrawal of the last federal child labor law—all industrial statistics show an increase.

Central to the reform argument were the harmful effects of premature or excessive work. It interferes with physical, mental, and moral development, and subjects the child to overstrain, fatigue, retarded growth, accident and injury, industrial poisons, night work, and conditions of moral danger. Most of the illiteracy of the country was attributed to early work. Children were deprived of the moral and spiritual balance that comes with natural childhood, play, and the opportunity for happiness. Moreover, child labor was an economic and social waste to the country. It reduced wages and increased unemployment among adults; it impaired future productivity; it constituted a political and social danger by lowering the quality of citizenship; and it led to increased poverty and crime.

Proponents claimed federal jurisdiction over the child labor problem was desirable because of the lack of uniformity and inadequate enforcement at the state level. In 1920, twelve states with about 30 percent of the children between ten and fifteen had nearly 60 percent of the nation's child workers. Finally, the constitutional amendment was seen as necessary, essentially as the only way federal jurisdiction could be asserted (the two prior federal laws having been found unconstitutional).

Opponents of the Child Labor Amendment argued there was no need for a federal law. Using the same official census numbers cited by the NCLC, opponents attempted to show that the problem was nowhere near as large as it might seem. Starting with the official figure of 1,060,858 and successively subtracting out various groups, they claimed, for example, that there were only 622 underage cotton mill workers nationwide, only 404 in the Piedmont South.[78] Besides, opponents continued, an absolute prohibition of child labor was uncalled for. Many young people were quite capable of earning a living, and many were called upon by necessity to do so. Gainful employment remained the best alternative open to some children who might not benefit from continued schooling and might otherwise be idle and on the street. Under proper conditions—on the farm, in the home, during vacation— no one should object to their working. Early work had, after all, been a factor in the lives of many successful men. Finally, parents were the best judge of necessity and the desirability of their children's entering gainful occupations.

Opponents contended that regulation of child labor should be left to the states. All states now had child labor laws on the books, and while they varied in their stringency and strictness of enforcement, steady progress in state regulation was observable.

James A. Emory, general counsel of the National Association of Manufacturers, stated the obvious most eloquently when he objected that "Everything back of this proposal speaks of 'compelling backward communities,' 'coercing recalcitrant states.' It is immediate reform by force rather than the patient but permanent method of persuasion. It urges 'dragooning' the community 'body' rather than 'replenishing' the community 'soul.'"[79] Furthermore, the problem was not one to be solved by legislation alone. As social conditions were improving, child labor was steadily disappearing by itself. As to the wisdom of a constitutional amendment, opponents urged it to be eminently undesirable. Aside from the general notion that we should not tamper with the Constitution lightly, the amendment conveyed powers that were simply too broad. By permitting Congress to prohibit and regulate the labor of all persons under eighteen, its implied powers were even greater, opening the way to a progressively expanded program of federal regulation extended to education and schools and all manner of wages, hours, and working conditions. Congress could be expected, over time, to exercise its power to the extreme limit. Even more troubling, it would give Congress the power to invade the sanctity of the home, subjecting parents to inquisition, domination, and tyranny of agents from Washington.

By the 1920s, other circumstances had changed throughout America and had brought into play factors that, in their combined force and effect, doomed the Child Labor Amendment. Underlying factors included a pulling back of trust in big government and government intervention that followed the conclusion of World War I. Another factor was the residue of the "Red Scare." Concern over subversives in our "foreign" population may have abated somewhat since the war, but concern over "foreign" ideals remained high. Reflecting the temper of the times, a

new objection was raised to the proposed constitutional amendment—
one that had not played a prominent role in opposition to earlier federal
efforts—that it was socialistic, bolshevistic, and communistic, and would
ultimately lead to federal control over the nation's children. Suggesting
that the federalization of the American child was a movement directed
from Moscow, Senator William H. King of Utah asserted:

> Every extreme Communist and Socialist in the United States is back of the
> measure. The Bolsheviks of Russia were familiar with the scheme that was
> about to be launched to amend our Constitution. . . . In conversation with
> one of the leading Bolsheviks in the city of Moscow, one of the educators,
> when I was there last September and October, I was remonstrating with
> him about the scheme of the Bolsheviks to have the state take charge of
> the children: "Why," he said, "you are coming to that." . . . "A number of
> Socialists in the United States," and he mentioned a number of names but
> I shall not mention them here, "are back of the movement to amend your
> Constitution of the United States, and it will be amended, and you will
> transfer to the Federal Government the power which the Bolshevik is
> asserting now over the young people of the state."[80]

The NCLC and the reform coalition had a number of problems convincing the nation of the merits of a constitutional amendment. First
and foremost, by the 1920s it was clear that industrial child labor, as it
had traditionally been conceived, was well on its way out. Child labor in
the mines, mills, and factories had, in fact, been reduced dramatically.
By the 1920s, the child labor problem in these industrial settings was
not the problem of earlier decades, that is, it no longer involved very
young children. Compared to the standards of 1900, by 1920 very young
children no longer worked, hours of child workers had been reduced,
and children had been removed from most of the most objectionable
occupations. The NCLC and the Children's Bureau could and did point
to numerous instances where state laws did not conform to national standards, where employers violated state laws, or where employers reem-
ployed younger children after federal laws were found unconstitutional.
But they could not convince the American public that the problem of
child labor in the mines, mills, and factories remained sufficiently grave
or pervasive to warrant constitutional amendment. Where child labor
persisted, it was concentrated among backward employers in recalcitrant states, and it was only a matter of time before these, too, would
abandon their child labor practices. The character of the child labor problem had changed.

So, what was the character of the child labor problem in the 1920s? In 1921, Felix Adler, long-time chair of the NCLC, retired and was replaced by David F. Houston, who had been President Wilson's secretary of agriculture from 1913 to 1920. Both his appointment and the program he pursued signaled the NCLC's perception of the current child labor problem. From this time forward, the committee expended very few resources investigating child labor in the factories, mines, and mills. From this time forward, the vast majority of its investigatory resources were expended in agriculture—and especially commercial agriculture. Several investigations were conducted in the street trades, especially of the newsboys, and an important investigation would be conducted in tenement homework.

Thus, with child labor in the mines, mills, and factories largely defeated, the reform movement shifted its attention to agriculture (and to a lesser extent, to the newsboys and tenement homework) at the same time the public was asked to consider the proposed Child Labor Amendment. This was, in important respects, new terrain. Social consensus had come to agreement with the movement to abolish child labor in mines, mills, and factories. But agriculture remained exempt from most state child labor laws. Likewise, newsboys were often covered under special provisions that reduced minimum ages on condition of licensing requirements. Similarly, industrial tenements were licensed, and compulsory schooling laws could be enforced, but work within tenements could not be regulated. When the reform movement turned on agricultural child labor, it attacked the preindustrial ideals of the "yeoman" farm family, an ideal that remained strong throughout rural America. When the reform movement attacked the newsboys, it not only attacked the "little merchant" ideal of Horatio Alger fame, it also attacked the powerful print media. Finally, when the reform movement renewed its attack on tenement homework, it was clear that what they proposed was government freedom to invade the sanctity of the home.

The NCLC and the reform coalition were in a public relations bind. On one hand, if the debate was framed around traditional forms of child labor (in mines, mills, and factories), it could generate public sympathy on the question of child labor, but little public support for a proposed remedy that might no longer be needed. On the other hand, if it attacked agriculture, the street trades, and homework, it could generate a public backlash that would, likewise, diminish public support for the amendment. The reform movement had gotten out ahead of public sentiment on the question of child labor and was unprepared for the organized opposition to the Child Labor Amendment.

Once again, the NCLC and the reform movement would lose a major battle. Once again, the leader of the opposition was none other than David Clark, editor of the *Southern Textile Bulletin*. Certainly no one individual defeated the Child Labor Amendment. But just as certainly, no one individual did more to defeat it than David Clark. By now his reputation had been cemented among southern manufacturers. They could be counted on to oppose the amendment. Over the years, Clark and southern cotton textiles had gained substantial influence within the National Association of Manufacturers, especially through NAM's general counsel, James Emory. Both NAM and other scattered manufacturing interests worked to oppose the amendment. Clark had also earned a solid reputation as an ardent defender of states' rights. The proposed constitutional amendment tapped a deep vein of sentiment, and it required no great prodding to enlist the support of various like-minded organizations committed to states' rights.

But the real genius of Clark's campaign to defeat the Child Labor Amendment was to reach beyond his natural allies and gain support of America's farmers against the amendment. Clark organized the Farmers' States Rights League and operated it out of the office of the *Southern Textile Bulletin*. Using a carefully cultivated network of contacts, the Farmers' States Rights League followed debate over ratification from state to state. Whenever the question of ratification was to be taken up, the Farmers' States Rights League was there to blanket the rural districts with literature. Using Clark's carefully cultivated rhetorical skills—honed over a decade of battle—the message persuaded many. When agricultural interests turned against the Child Labor Amendment, in combination with opposition from selected manufacturing interests, growing ambivalence in the media, and weakening resolve of the public, it was clear that the Child Labor Amendment was defeated. The reform movement had been totally unprepared for, and was totally outflanked by, Clark's capacity to crystallize sentiment in agriculture. By the time the reformers responded, the battle was over and all they could do was cry "foul."

Too late to have a bearing on the outcome, that cry gained credence from an American Federation of Labor investigation of the Farmers' States Rights League and the publication of a revealing expose.[81] The AFL's reporter first sought out the incorporators of the league. He found that Ben T. Wade, president, was not a farmer at all, but a clerk in a cotton mill bank in Troy, North Carolina (near Charlotte—Wade insisted "I own farms"). Even as its president, Wade knew little about the league:

> "What is the membership of your organization?" he was asked.
> "It is large," was the response.
> "But how many?—ten, twenty, fifty thousand, or what?"
> "I do not know."
> . . .
> "What dues do you charge?" he was asked.
> "No one has been asked for money," he replied.
> "How is your very extensive campaign of advertising supported?" was the next question.
> "By volunteer subscriptions."
> "In that case someone must be putting up some very handsome sums of money. Who are these people?"
> "I have no information to give out," was his response to this and all further questions.

A second incorporator, N.H. Williams, was storekeeper at one of the bank's client mills. Two of the incorporators, however, were honest-to-goodness farmers. The reporter found L.H. Hilton on his farm baling hay with his three sons. Asked about the Farmers' States Rights League, Hilton replied, "There are no farmers' organizations of any consequence around here." He recalled, however, that he had signed a petition opposing the Child Labor Amendment last summer when he was in town for jury duty. "I was told that it would forbid my own children to do work around the place." Had he paid any dues? "No. . . . All that was wanted was just our names." Did he know who the officers were? "I do not know." Did he know where the office was? "I do not know." The other farmer incorporator was G.H. Greene. He, too, remembered signing a petition, something about a child labor law, but he was not sure whether it was a state or federal law. He, too, had paid no dues and had no knowledge of the officers or offices of the league.

The reporter finally hit pay dirt when he contacted Jeff Palmer, who was listed as agent for the league. Palmer's office was located across the hall from David Clark's at the *Southern Textile Bulletin*. He was enthusiastic about the aims and purposes of the league ("To fight for states rights and against the child-labor amendment") and boasted openly about their extensive advertising campaign. Palmer clammed up only when the reporter began asking questions about sources of the league's financial support. At that point, Clark interrupted the conversation, "Tell him nothing. It's none of his business. He has nerve to come here and ask these questions."

In response to the AFL's expose, Clark was characteristically unapologetic. In an editorial titled "Bad Losers Howl,"[82] he boasted, "We set out to beat the Federal Child Labor Amendment and we have beaten it. If in the midst of their wailing and gnashing of teeth the pap-suckers and parasites vent some of their spleen upon us we are receiving that which we expected." He acknowledged organizing the Farmers' States Rights League "on exactly the same plan as the National Child Labor Committee." He insisted that Jeff Palmer was not on his payroll, and that the league was more than a mere alter ego of the *Southern Textile Bulletin*. At the same time he admitted that the *Bulletin* had "secured from the Farmers' States Rights League permission to distribute literature in their name." He remained defiant to the point of arrogance. "If our methods do not please those who lost, it makes no difference to us. . . . Let 'em rave." Once again, David Clark had won.

The defeat of the Child Labor Amendment is open to multiple interpretations. In the end, the reform movement might have lost another major battle but it appeared to be steadily winning the war. Child labor in mines, mills, and factories continued to decline. Lagging states continued to improve their laws. And the general public had become engaged in a national discussion of the issue, a discussion that included attention to new and nagging child labor problems in agriculture, the street trades, and tenement homework. But a federal role in regulating child labor appeared to be precluded—that is, until the Great Depression.

The NRA Codes

The next major federal intervention in child labor came with the National Recovery Administration (NRA) Codes adopted in response to the Great Depression of the 1930s. The National Industrial Recovery Act was President Franklin D. Roosevelt's "middle road" in dealing with the depression. It had become clear, even to the business community, that laissez-faire principles were contributing to cutthroat competition, chronic overproduction, and a downward spiral of prices, wages, and profits. Yet centralized economic planning was anathema to most Americans. Roosevelt's middle road envisioned a classic tripartite power-

sharing arrangement between government, industry, and labor. Government would establish and monitor the basic principles. Industry representatives would be given authority to set prices and allocate production.
And labor was to be given a voice at the table. In essence, each industry
would be permitted to plan its own growth out of the depression. Since
this entailed a substantial relaxation of antitrust law and a corresponding increased opportunity for predatory collusion, the government and
labor would monitor the process. The NRA Blue Eagle was the industrial symbol of patriotism. Most reputable employers wanted to post the
Blue Eagle to show they were doing their part to end the depression.
But, to qualify, employers were required to commit to a code of industrial conduct. The code was to be the product of tripartite negotiation
between industry, labor, and government, with government serving as
final arbiter. Labor provisions of the codes required recognition of rights
to organize and bargain collectively as well as provisions covering minimum wages, maximum hours, and working conditions.

Significantly, the Cotton Textile Code was the first of the industry
codes to be adopted. Manufacturers, especially southern manufacturers, were wary of the code's provisions regarding unions. They had
recently had their fill of unions, with two substantial regional organizing campaigns, one in the early 1920s and one in the late 1920s. They
were now relatively union free and intended to stay that way. Still,
given Roosevelt's political debts to labor, it was clear that some provision for unions would be included, and the proposed code provisions
were ambiguous enough, so employers reluctantly agreed. Employers
also agreed to a normal workweek of forty hours. On first impression,
this may seem like an astonishing concession from the industry, one it
did not have to make. It was, in fact, a dramatic departure from recent
past practice, and the industry would have fought it vigorously only a
few years earlier. But, in recent years, in response to the persistent
depression, most employers had adopted some form of a limited work
week in order to spread the available work around. Under current conditions, it cost employers little. Furthermore, though it was a long way
off, in planning for a return to full production, it made sense to consider the eight-hour day. To operate round the clock, shifts of either
eight or twelve hours are most efficient. Anything between leaves a
gap where machinery must be left idle. By this time, ten- and eleven-
hour days had become the norm in southern textiles, and a return to
twelve was unlikely. Besides, employers were willing to make a major

concession on hours, where it would cost little, because they planned to take a hard line on the question of minimum wages. For northern textile interests, a minimum wage might increase hourly labor costs modestly. But in the South, the effect would be substantial. Southern interests endeavored to maintain a North-South differential and keep the minimum wage at the lowest level possible.[83]

Child labor provisions of the Cotton Textile Code came about, seemingly, almost as an afterthought. But they, too, were a part of the industry's bargaining strategy. A series of hearings was held by the government. On the first day, the industry made an extended presentation of its basic proposal emphasizing its magnanimous gesture on hours but expressing strong reservations on the minimum wage and provisions for unions. Labor's presentation was scheduled for the second day, and they were expected to press hard for a high minimum wage. Before the day's hearing began, however, the industry announced that, in a dramatic emergency meeting the night before, it had decided to recommend an amendment to the code that would abolish child labor throughout the industry. It then offered a startling proposal for a firm sixteen-year minimum age, a proposal well above the prevailing minimum age at the time. The industry ploy effectively stole the thunder from labor's presentation, for the presentation could only begin after the mill owners had received a round of lavish praise for their obviously humanitarian motives.

But, once again, the industry had actually conceded little. Most of the children had already been driven from the mills by the depression. Mills could count on a more than plentiful supply of adult workers at whatever minimum wage was established. Finally, they recognized that pressures for enhanced productivity created by both the minimum wage and the limitation on hours made continued employment of children unprofitable.

Scholars disagree over the immediate effect of the child labor provisions of the Cotton Textile Code. James Hodges maintained that the provisions had little effect since nearly all the children had already been driven from the mills. He insists, "Child labor was not a problem that New Deal labor policy had to attack."[84] On the other hand, Liston Pope notes that implementation of the codes "revealed that between six hundred and one thousand workers under sixteen years of age had been retained until then in Gaston County."[85] At that time, Gaston County, North Carolina, was home to the highest concentration of textile mills in America. It is likely that a large portion of the young workers dismissed were fourteen and fifteen years old, of legal age under North Carolina law, but now illegal under the code.

While there is disagreement over the immediate effects of the NRA codes, there is general consensus that they were the final nail in the coffin of child labor in many sectors of American industry. Another scholar, Elizabeth Davidson, observed:

> With the establishment of the NRA codes in 1933, most of the employment of children under sixteen was stopped. After the codes were invalidated, some manufacturers re-employed workers under sixteen, but the indicators seem to be that many of them retained the code age standards even when state laws did not require it.[86]

Writing to Courtenay Dinwiddie, then general secretary of the NCLC, President Franklin Roosevelt offered mutual congratulations: "With the adoption of the Textile Code last July, I think we all realized that the end of child labor in America was at hand."[87] Even Herbert Hoover, who was certainly no fan of either the New Deal or the NRA Codes, acknowledged as early as 1934 that "The codes have served admirably to reduce child labor by about 25 per cent, and they have eliminated sweating in certain trades."[88]

While many credit the NRA codes with the final abolition of child labor from America's factories, it is often overlooked that they also elevated the national standard on child labor almost overnight. Prior to adoption of the codes, only four states had established a sixteen-year minimum age for factory work, when fourteen was the generally accepted standard. With the codes, the accepted standard minimum age was elevated to sixteen, and eighteen became the minimum for hazardous work, and hours were restricted for all workers. This rapidly became the new national standard for factory work, a standard that remains in place today. Ironically, a large share of the credit for this elevation in standards belongs to the textile mill owners who once fought the advancing standards so vigorously and passionately.

The Fair Labor Standards Act

After the National Industrial Recovery Act was invalidated by the Supreme Court in 1935 and after the 1936 elections provided a mandate to President Roosevelt and the Democratic Congress, work began on the

Fair Labor Standards Act. This act was intended to restore those provisions of the NRA codes that dealt with minimum wages, maximum hours, and child labor.[89] When the constitutionality of the Fair Labor Standards Act was upheld in 1941,[90] the United States had finally established its first enduring federal child labor law. But this was anticlimactic. At least as far as the mines, mills, and factories were concerned, the law was redundant. Child labor had already been effectively abolished. Still, there were other sectors where continued child labor reform efforts were called for. The Fair Labor Standards Act originally exempted agriculture altogether. Numerous exemptions and exceptions enabled child labor to continue to flourish in many of the street trades and permitted child labor to creep back into the sweating sectors of the economy.

Part II

Child Labor in America

4. CHILDREN IN
THE COAL MINES

Figure 4.1 *Chauncy Breaker, Outside View.* Jan. 1911. Breaker of the Chauncy (Pa.) Colliery, where a 15 year old breaker-boy was smothered to death and another badly burned, Jan. 7, 1911. (Photo of newspaper clipping #1946.) The Coroner told me that the McKee boy was but a few days past his 15th birthday when he was killed, and that the evidence seemed to show that he was at work in another breaker before his 14th birthday. (He will report to us on that point, further.) *(Courtesy of the Library of Congress, Prints and Photographs Division, Lewis Wickes Hine National Child Labor Committee Collection, LC-H5–1932.)*

Breaker Boy: American Cultural Icon

The anthracite coal region of eastern Pennsylvania was the first industry investigated by the NCLC. The great anthracite coal strike of 1902, which had brought to light the fact that thousands of young boys were working in and around the mines, was still fresh in the public mind. NCLC northern secretary Owen Lovejoy had investigated conditions in the region during the strike and, three months after joining the NCLC, returned to the region to conduct the committee's first field investigation. Lovejoy's published report set the rhetorical tone:

> The coal-breaker dominates the anthracite region. The most important object on the landscape, the largest building, with the most mysterious machinery—the coal-breaker paints the first deep picture on the mind of the miner's son. From the dawn of his intelligence he recognizes its power, and in it his destiny. He *may* go to school; he *will* go to the breaker. . . . Yonder is the miner's "patch"—thirty or forty black, squatty huts, with alleys of mud and coal-dirt winding among them—birthplaces of a hundred boys. Here stands the great building with a hundred narrow boards laid across the coal-chutes—seats for a hundred boys. The plan is complete. A boy is born; let him hasten through his babyhood! Can he not see the breaker needs his labor and the hut his wages?[1]

During the early years of the NCLC, child labor in anthracite coal mining received a disproportionate share of its attention. This was in part due to the role of anthracite coal in the committee's own institutional history. The anthracite coal strike of 1902 was the major labor event in recent memory—it was arguably the most important strike in American history up to its time. Facts revealed in hearings before the Anthracite Coal Strike Commission indicated that child labor was prevalent in the anthracite coal fields. The NCLC thought an investigation "would serve not only to illustrate prominent evils of premature child labor in other sections of our country, but also that, once known, would arouse public opinion."[2] Publicity of child labor conditions in the industry resonated with the public. Further, the anthracite region was geographically close to the major urban centers of New York and Philadelphia. Child labor in the anthracite mines demonstrated the national character of the problem, but did so in a way that brought the story close to home.

Finally, in anthracite coal the NCLC found a cultural icon—the breaker boy. The breaker boys, who endured some of the most grueling conditions among child workers anywhere, came to symbolize all that was wrong with child labor. If the chimney sweep is the symbol of British child labor, it was the breaker boy in America. Lewis Hine, who investigated the anthracite region in 1911, observed:

> I have found an almost universal sentiment,—expressed individually by various school principals, truant officers, coroners, and others,—that the

physical danger to health is much greater in the breaker than it is inside the mine. The Coroner's Docket showed more deaths to breaker-boys than to those inside.[3]

The basic job of the breaker boy was to pick slate and other impurities from the coal before it was shipped. There was a variety of methods for doing this, but, most commonly, coal was run by a conveyor from the bottom of the breaker diagonally to the top. Boys were positioned on wooden benches above the conveyor and manually picked slate from the coal as it rushed by. Hine described their work, calling attention to the dangers associated with it:

> The boys working in the breaker are bent double, with little chance to relax; the air at times is dense with coal-dust, which penetrates so far into the passages of the lungs that for long periods after the boy leaves the breaker, he continues to cough up the black coal dust. Fingers are calloused and cut by the coal and slate, the noise and monotony are deadening; and, worse still grave danger from the machinery to those boys who persist in playing about the breaker, and even for those at their regular work. While I was in the region, two breaker boys of 15 years, while at work assigned to them, fell or were carried by the coal down into the car below. One was badly burned and the other was smothered to death. This was at the Lee Breaker at Chauncy, Pennsylvania, January 6th, 1911, the boy who was killed was Dennis McKee. The Coroner told me that this boy had reached his 15th birthday only a few days before his death and the evidence seems to prove that he was working in another breaker before he was 14 years old.[4]

While reformers and progressives in New York, Philadelphia, and other parts of the country were provoked to righteous indignation over the plight of the breaker boys, no such reaction was observed in the anthracite region itself. "The little devils like it," one breaker boss remarked to Lovejoy. The use of youngsters was so deeply ingrained in the fabric of the anthracite communities that Lovejoy was moved to caution his readers:

> The welfare of the breaker boy is of very minor concern in the coal region, and readers of this paper must not suppose that "child labor" is a vital topic here. No subject is less frequently discussed. The churches are almost wholly silent. Nobody seems disposed to "dodge the issue." No issue is recognized.[5]

Figure 4.2 *Pennsylvania Breaker, Inside View*. South Pittston, Pa Jan. 1911. A View of the Pennsylvania Breaker. The dust was so dense at times as to obscure the view. This dust penetrates the utmost recesses of the boy's lungs. *(Courtesy of the Library of Congress, Prints and Photographs Division, Lewis Wickes Hine National Child Labor Committee Collection, LC-USZ62–23751.)*

But here, in the breaker boy, was the raw material that constituted the social, economic, and political future of the nation. If given the opportunity to flourish, the future of the nation would benefit from the moral character and sturdy stock produced by the mining regions. But if the future was sacrificed for present output, all that the nation would yield would be a bunch of men, too dissipated by their early work to contribute to the nation's future (Figure 4.2). Owen Lovejoy made the following appeal on behalf of the breaker boys:

> The typical breaker-boy is proud of his breaker and boasts of its daily output. He is proud of the independence which personal economic value gives him in the home. Every mine-center affords many examples of strong young lives, full of energy, rich in possibilities that, if wisely directed, might help to inspire men to that social awakening which is the sole hope of our democracy. But they will not be wisely directed. They will be dwarfed by a daily round of monotonous slate-picking.[6]

The NCLC and the Anthracite Coal Industry

It was the anthracite strike of 1902, coupled with Owen Lovejoy's familiarity with the anthracite region, that prompted the NCLC to give its first attention to the industry. Then, having gained an early understanding of the industry and region, the NCLC facilitated follow-up investigations. Lovejoy himself conducted investigations in 1905 and 1907. Lewis Hine investigated in 1911, followed by Edward Brown in 1912 and Florence Taylor in 1916. Because of these repeat visits, and because the industry was concentrated in a compact geographic region in eastern Pennsylvania, the industry and the NCLC came to know each other quite well.

The great anthracite coal strike ran from May through October of 1902. Then, with winter coming on and no coal coming out of the region, President Theodore Roosevelt appointed the Anthracite Coal Strike Commission to arbitrate. For four months the commission held hearings at which over five hundred witnesses testified. The hearings were followed closely by the media and their reading public. Child labor was not an issue in the strike, but it came to play a prominent role in the hearings. At the time in Pennsylvania, fourteen was the minimum age for work in mining above ground; sixteen was the minimum age for work below ground. But no proof of age was required. Miners insisted their wages "are so low that their children are prematurely forced into the breakers,"[7] which, in turn, kept adult wages low. Employers insisted they did not knowingly employ underage boys.

In the aftermath of the great strike, the anthracite industry was understandably sensitive about its public image. During the strike, the difficult conditions under which the miners and their families worked and lived had received widespread attention, and the industry's use of child labor had become an embarrassment. So when the NCLC came poking around looking for more evidence of child labor, it was bound to stir controversy. When Owen Lovejoy investigated in 1905, Pennsylvania law had been amended to require an affidavit attesting to the child's age. But Lovejoy's published report concluded that there were no fewer than 9,000 and up to 12,800 boys under fourteen illegally in the mines and breakers of the region.[8]

The chief of the Pennsylvania Department of Mines, a Mr. Roderick, took umbrage at the report. He replied that this "man by the name of Lovejoy [who] made a tour of the anthracite counties inquiring into the ages of boys employed at the mines" had made "a very extravagant statement" that was published "in blazing headlines" in the daily papers. A department official estimated that "there were not more than 2,000 boys who were below the employment age, and even they had certificates from their parents or guardians to show that they were over fourteen."[9] Later, when the department investigated more fully, it concluded there were no more than 760 boys under fourteen employed.

As a consequence of this public squabble over the numbers, the National Civic Federation intervened. The federation was a tripartite organization of prominent representatives of business, labor, and the public that, during these years, was committed to promoting industrial peace. During the anthracite strike, and before President Roosevelt's arbitration commission brokered a settlement, United Mine Workers President John Mitchell had proposed that the issues in dispute be submitted to a panel appointed by the National Civic Federation.[10] The federation felt entitled to challenge Lovejoy to justify his numbers:

> It is claimed on the one side that there are 12,000 boys under fourteen years of age in the anthracite coal breakers, whereas officials of the State of Pennsylvania, after investigating the matter, claim that there are not over 8,100 all told under sixteen, and that with only 760 of them is there any doubt about their being over fourteen—the age beyond which no attempt is made to prevent employment.[11]

Lovejoy eagerly accepted the challenge. What was it, 9,000 to 12,800 boys or 760? He felt his estimate was constructed fairly conservatively; he knew the state's estimate was preposterous. He explained his methodology in detail. Through intensive study in a single borough, then extrapolating to the entire anthracite region, he arrived at his estimate of 12,800. In his follow-up investigation, he applied the same methodology to two additional boroughs and arrived at estimates as high as 18,000. He then surveyed school superintendents from seven boroughs on causes of absences and nonenrollments, and arrived at a pooled estimate of 14,760. Finally, using occupational data of the Department of Mines and totaling jobs known to be reserved for boys, he showed that a reasonable estimate could run as high as 27,393. Whatever the true number, Lovejoy concluded, it was large, and his own original estimate had clearly been on the conservative side. He then simultaneously exposed the fallacy in the state's estimate and the flaw in its enforcement scheme, by pointing out that the state's number of 760 referred only to boys who had not presented the required certificates of age.[12]

Lovejoy's reply to the National Civic Federation's challenge enhanced the NCLC's reputation for fair reporting, at the same time demonstrating the untrustworthiness of many official sources. This would not be the last time the committee's numbers were challenged, but they were generally thereafter accorded presumptive credibility. The reply also enhanced the NCLC's commitment to ongoing study of the anthracite region. Over the next twelve years, the committee came to know the region well. In turn, the region also came to know the committee. Subsequent to Lovejoy's early investigations, three systematic investigations were conducted in the region. Lewis Hine visited with his camera in 1911; Edward Brown investigated in 1912; and Florence Taylor followed in 1916. Their reports suggest how mine operators became increasingly wary of the NCLC investigators. When Hine visited the Ewen Breaker at Port Griffeth, South Pittston, in 1911, he reported:

> January 10th, I took a number of photos of the Breaker-boys at work in the Ewen Breaker, and outside at the noon hour. The boys I found Sunday were all in evidence, and many more. One of them complained that they were not allowed to play around the Breaker any more because some one had injured the machinery and the boys had been blamed for it.[13]

When investigator Brown visited the same breaker one year later, he noted:

> At first I was warned not to take any pictures. The reason given was that some time ago a photographer took pictures of the place which were subsequently used in an action for $25,000 damages for the death of Ely Ross, a breaker boy who it was alleged was about 12 years old at the time of his death.[14]

Finally, when investigator Taylor visited the same breaker in 1916, she was refused entry altogether.[15]

The NCLC and the Bituminous Coal Industry

In contrast to the attention paid to use of child labor in anthracite mining, the NCLC conducted only two systematic field investigations into bituminous coal mining. The first of these investigations was conducted by Owen Lovejoy in 1906 and covered western Pennsylvania, Maryland, and northern West Virginia.[16] The second was conducted in 1908 in West Virginia by Edward N. Clopper, accompanied by Lewis Hine.[17] While reports from state child labor committees to the national association, especially from Ohio, Indiana, Illinois, Kentucky, and Alabama, along with Pennsylvania and West Virginia, frequently mentioned the bituminous mining industry, these reports were generally not the product of field investigations.

There are a number of important contrasts between the anthracite, or hard coal, and the bituminous, or soft coal, industries. Anthracite was the fuel preferred by the railroads to stoke their steam locomotives (railroad interests owned or controlled 95 percent of anthracite coal production at the time). Likewise, anthracite was the preferred commercial and residential heating fuel. It was considerably more expensive per ton than bituminous coal, but it was also considerably more dense. Because it was more dense, it was more compact, requiring less storage space, and it burned hotter and longer per ton. Softer bituminous coal was preferred by the emerging steel industry (for its coking properties) and by the electrical power plants that were newly and rapidly gaining prominence on the industrial landscape.

The NCLC never developed a close, almost personal, relationship with the bituminous industry as it had with anthracite. The bituminous coal region was far more widespread than the compact anthracite region of eastern Pennsylvania. The bituminous fields stretched from western Pennsylvania into Ohio and West Virginia, extending southward through Kentucky, Virginia, and eastern Tennessee and picking up again around Birmingham, Alabama, and extending westward through Ohio, Kentucky, Indiana, and Illinois. It was a vast region, and even where the NCLC investigated, it did not conduct repeat investigations as it did in the anthracite region. Still, an adequate portrait of child labor in soft-coal mining emerges from the scattered investigations that were conducted.

Another important contrast: There was no slate picking in soft coal and consequently no breaker for the young boys. Most child labor in bituminous mining was underground. Boys worked as runners, drivers, door boys, and couplers, but the largest percentage worked with their fathers at the coal face as loaders. It should be noted that, by the early twentieth century, children had been removed from the coal face in anthracite mining "thanks to an awakened humanity and improved machinery,"[18] but in bituminous mining child loaders remained common underground. Under Pennsylvania law in the early 1900s, while a boy had to be sixteen to work underground in anthracite, he only had to be twelve to work underground in bituminous mining, so long as he accompanied his own father.

Miners were paid per ton of coal delivered to the tipple on the surface where the coal was loaded into railroad cars. The mine provided mules (and later electric haulage), cars, drivers, runners, couplers, and door boys to get the coal from the face to the tipple, but the miner was responsible for the coal face. He was responsible for cutting and blasting the coal, loading it into the car (while sorting dirt, shale, and rock), and, in these early days, building his own bracing to protect himself from roof falls. Time spent away from cutting coal was money out of the miner's paycheck. So, fathers took their sons in as loaders.

In West Virginia in 1908, miners generally received $.40 per ton and could earn from $5 to $9 per day. The helpers or loaders were usually not paid, which explains why the miner took his own sons in, and also helps explain why loaders were often some of the very youngest children. When a boy could get on as a trapper, earning his own money at $.75 to $1.25 per day, he generally did. Furthermore, at many locations, the miner was awarded an extra "half turn" if he brought in his own loaders. This meant he was given 50 percent more cars to fill. Since many mines faced a chronic shortage of cars, this was another way for the miner to increase pay, whether the boys did much actual work or not. A school superintendent in western Pennsylvania told Lovejoy, "Men take boys in the mine actually so small they can hardly carry their dinner bucket without dragging it, in order to claim an extra half turn."[19]

Brief mention should be made regarding the role of company housing and especially the company stores. These institutions played a more prominent role in the bituminous coal-mining communities than they did in anthracite, the anthracite fields being located closer to the urban industrial centers of eastern Pennsylvania.[20] Company housing and company stores were essential in recruiting a labor force to areas where houses and stores did not otherwise exist. But they also enabled the coal companies to recapture nearly all the wages they paid out. Of course, the company incurred the additional outlay in the cost of housing and the goods sold at the company store, but it proved an extremely valuable device in reducing the circulating capital, or cash flow, requirements of the business. It was a common practice that, where miners were in debt to the company store, they were paid not in cash wages but in "scrip" redeemable only at the company store. Furthermore, to the extent that the company store (more than company housing) became a profit center in its own right, it could buffer the coal company's bottom line against the rise and fall of coal prices. The upshot of all this was that it created incentives toward labor-intensive operation and away from capital-intensive operation. That is, coal companies had an incentive to hire more workers who would spend their wages at the company store and employ less machinery that had no money to spend. A school superintendent remarked to Lovejoy, "[T]here are too many workers in the mine so as to have more tenants for the company houses and more customers for the company stores. All are expected to trade at the company store."[21] In turn, this created incentives to employ more child labor. A policeman in western Pennsylvania told Lovejoy, "I take my boy to the superintendent and tell him a hard luck story, and especially if I have a big family and trade at the company store, he will take him in. They do not ask for certificates of age in the mines here."[22]

Boys' Work

Lovejoy and the NCLC recognized that coal mining in America began on a "higher plane" than in England of a hundred years earlier where a large proportion of the underground workforce were women and young girls.[23] In America, he noted, we started with "little boys."[24]

There was a more or less definite career ladder for the boys to follow in both anthracite and bituminous mining. In anthracite, youngest boys started in the breakers. In bituminous mining, youngest boys started as loaders working for their fathers. From these entry-level positions, there was a great variety of jobs in the career progression. Most common next steps, in both anthracite and bituminous, were the jobs of door boy and then driver. After this career stage, boys made the transition from boys' work to men's work.

Door boys, or "nippers," tended doors within the mines, opening them when a car, or "trip," came through and closing them behind. Between trips the nipper simply waited in darkness and isolation. The doors were part of the mine's ventilation system, helping to keep methane and other gases out of the chambers where they did not belong and helping to route fresh air into the chambers where it was needed most. Thus, nippers were important to the safety of all who worked below ground. It was not until after electric haulage systems became prevalent in the mines that operation of the doors was automated. Hine described the work of the "nippers," or door boys:

> The chief drawback to their work is the deadening monotony of it and the mental stagnation that must inevitably follow in its trail. Sitting by himself for nine or ten hours a day, in absolute darkness, save for his little oil lamp and the lamps of the passers-by; breathing air that is far from fresh air, fouled by smoking oil-lamps and loaded with moisture; his chief work being to open the door when called to, and to close it after the cars have passed through;—small wonder is it that he sometimes falls asleep and fails to respond to the summons to open the door, thereby increasing the dangers of collision between cars in opposite directions, or that he wanders off, leaving the door open, increasing the dangers of explosion. If his monotony is broken, as it too often is, by calls to come and help the driver of a "trip," it means increased physical danger.[25]

Next in the career progression came the drivers. They were responsible for hauling the loaded coal from the coal face to the surface and then returning with the empty car. In anthracite mining and much of bituminous mining, the cars were large and were pulled by mules, so the driver's task was to drive the mules. In some bituminous mines where the coal vein was thinner, shafts were narrower, so smaller cars were used. In some of these mines, boys themselves pushed the cars to the surface. Hine described the work of the drivers:

> These drivers, or leaders, are not as a class so young as the nippers, but many of them are under 16 years of age. Their work is to guide and urge the mules down with loaded cars and back with the empties. Some entries are dangerous. In some, footing is uncertain. There is always the danger of getting in the way of moving cars, or of being jammed between them or by them, especially as all present are called upon to help when difficulties arise. Then, there is ever the menace of bad-tempered mules that are not any too well treated. One day, a boy showed me where a mule had just kicked him when he wasn't looking. Another driver, that day, had neglected to tie a "bad mule," (as he had been directed to do,) and it ran away, crashing into a moving trip and endangering all those near by.[26]

The career ladder in coal mining might more aptly be called a career circle, because miners who survived a career underground often ended up back where they started. In anthracite, the career progressed from breaker to nipper to driver to runner to laborer to miner—and back to the breaker. As one older miner told a government investigator in 1919,

"You begin at the breaker, and you end at the breaker, broken yourself."[27]

> If rheumatism, asthma, or old age chance to reach him before the casualties of falling rock, run-away car, broken rope, powder blast, or fire-damp befall him, he comes from the mine prematurely old and enfeebled, and finds his place again in the breaker, there to end his career where he began.[28]

Putting older, perhaps enfeebled, men to do boys' work became a more common alternative as law and enforcement made it more difficult to employ young boys. In some bituminous mines, where breakers were not available:

> [O]ld crippled men, instead of boys, are employed to tend the trap-doors, and this arrangement is certainly an improvement over the employment of children, inasmuch as it affords the means of earning a livelihood to men incapacitated for other work and does not deprive boys of the opportunity to acquire some education.[29]

Coal mining was dangerous work, and whatever their specific job, boys in mining were exposed to various dangers. NCLC investigation reports were filled with anecdotes and evidence of accidents and injuries. In this and other industries, the NCLC frequently used the figure "300 percent" to indicate that the injury and accident rate to children (under sixteen) was three times higher than for workers sixteen and over. While their data were inadequate to prove the estimate, and it does not seem reasonable for all industries, it appears a reasonable estimate in mining. Thus, in an already dangerous industry, boys were approximately three times more likely than men to incur accident or injury. Hine made these cryptic comments during his 1911 investigation:

> On January 2, 1911, the Superintendent of the Pennsylvania Coal Co., at South Pittston issued a letter of congratulation and rejoicing to the foreman of the mines in that district, marveling that these mines had gone two months without a fatal accident. (Within a few days a serious and fatal explosion occurred at the Hoyt Shaft, ending this wonderful record.) The foregoing, alone, should be sufficient to warrant putting the minimum age limit of 16 years, but, if one doubts the grave dangers attending mine work, let him spend a few days actually going through the interior of a busy mine, and let him bear in mind continually that what are dangers

for any adult are manifolded in the case of careless boys, bubbling over with the untrained animal spirits of youth.[30]

Underground, the greatest dangers were the roof falls that occurred most commonly at the coal face. In bituminous mining, children who worked as loaders and the men were at equally great risk. In anthracite mines, where young men did the loading, boys were at less risk of roof falls. Then there was the danger of explosion that threatened whoever happened to be underground: "These explosions occur often in the most unforeseen places and without known cause. A door left open by a careless door-boy, may cause an accumulation of gas that results in explosion when one enters with a lighted lamp."[31]

Drivers and nippers, in addition to the risk of explosion, risked being jammed by or between cars. In the case of runaway cars, they risked being run over. And boys in the breakers faced risks all their own. Lewis Hine made notes from the county coroner's docket during his 1911 investigation:

> Notes from the Coroner's Docket for Luzerne County for 1910. The ages are not given in the Coroner's records except for young boys, so I am not sure I found all under 16 who were killed in 1910. This record is for the county, only, and does not show those injured, but not killed.
>
> 1. Charles Nojenski
>   "About 15 years of age. Caught in breakery machinery while throwing coal at other boys, and killed. The Company is exonerated from all blame in the matter." Auchincloss Colliery, D.L.&W. Nov. 15, 1910.
> 2. Joseph Martonik
>   "About 15 years of age. Caught in the machinery and horribly mangled. Aug. 31, 1910 at Cranberry Colliery. If he had obeyed instructions, or if the machinery had been properly protected, the accident might not have happened."
> 3. Thomas Caffrey
>   "Fourteen years old. A door-tender at #9 Colliery. Sugar Notch, Pa. Was assisting in hauling a trip and was jammed and killed, January 4th, 1910."[32]

In 1912, investigator Brown visited the Susquehanna Coal Company (No. 7) breaker in Nanticoke. His notes included the following about two boys on the list of breaker boys: "Raymond Kozofosky. Working here 9 months, Refused to give age. Looks about 12. Brother to Assistant

Foreman." And "Charles Safinsky, 19 W. Church Street. Started to work July 13, 1910. Claims 14. Looks 13." Then Brown related this story:

> A few months ago, Chas. Safinsky and Raymond Kozofosky, slate pickers, fell in the coal pockets and were buried under 30 tons of coal. Charles' cap fell in the pocket and he went after it. Feeling himself go down he grabbed Raymond's leg in an attempt to arrest his fall. This precipitated Raymond too, and both went down. They were rescued after much misgiving. They received no pay for the time they could not work owing to this accident.[33]

The threat of disabling accidents and premature death was real enough. But the effect of premature work and excessively arduous work took their own toll. A single incident makes the case: During the great anthracite strike of 1902, the U.S. Navy sent a Lieutenant J.P. Ryan to recruit sailors from among the idled miners. After a short stay in the region, he was ordered to leave for the following reason:

> One curious outcome of the recruiting was that very few of the strikers who applied for enlistment could pass the physical requirements. Lieutenant Ryan found that nearly all of those who were willing to go into the navy are under size, weak-chested and round-shouldered, and physically undesirable in nearly every way. This is attributed to going to work at an early age, lack of nourishment, and hard labor in unsanitary surroundings.[34]

What was it like to break into coal mining as a child in early twentieth-century America? How did the boys themselves see their work and its relation to their lives? First, we know that miners' sons went to the mines. That is, nearly all of the child workers in mining were children of parents who were involved in mining. Few from outside the mining community entered; few from within the mining community escaped. Thus, entering the mines became a rite of passage from boyhood to manhood. In the anthracite communities, the coal breaker served also as a figurative "breaker"—a socializing institution designed to introduce the boys to work in mining, to break them in. In bituminous mining, boys were broken in by their fathers.

Today, we are inclined to say they were boys doing men's work. But in their own day, the boys understood they had to do boys' work before they could earn the privilege of doing men's work. Yet they were boys who would be boys, "careless boys, bubbling over with the untrained animal spirits of youth."[35] They would have their childhood and they would have their play. It was probably a good thing that the boys were started aboveground in the breakers or belowground with their fathers. Regarding the breaker boys:

> It was not that the coal operators put the boys in the breakers in the more dangerous places, for slate picking is possibly attended with less danger than any other operation around a coal mine. The difference was due wholly to the fact that the men were men and the boys were boys. . . .
> When a man sits for nine hours a day picking slate, if anything happens in the coal mine to stop the operation for five minutes, he sits up and stretches his back and rests. . . . When a 14 or 13 or 12-year-old boy sees the coal chute running empty for five minutes, does he straighten his back and rest? No, he strikes the next boy on the back and there is a game of tag on in a minute; and these little boys, 40 or 50, perhaps a hundred of them, are scurrying around like rats over this darkened building with coal dust so dense at times that one cannot see at six feet distant, and the first thing you know one stumbles and falls headlong into the great grinding machinery with its steel jaws that crush and kill, and is ground to pulp before he can be rescued.[36]

Lunchtime in the breaker was a scheduled daily pause in the work routine. As a recess from work, boys looked forward to the opportunity to play. In many ways the breaker served the boys as a great industrial clubhouse. It was where they gathered to play. Investigator Edward Brown visited the Stanton number 7 colliery of the Wilkes-Barre and Lehigh Company at lunchtime. He counted thirty-four boys inside, of whom he estimated sixteen were under the age of fourteen and three were no older than twelve. He described the scene:

> They were all running about the breaker playing. Some climbed to a dangerous height on the beams. Others were sliding down the coal passage. The boys on top threw the fine coal dust which had settled on the beams down on the boys below. It would go into the boy's eyes which resulted in the flinging of coal at one another. A single misstep might have hurled the top boys down, while those below were in danger of falling in the coal pockets and being smothered. I was ordered out by the breaker boss as soon as he discovered me. It was against the rules to allow anyone in the breaker.[37]

If the breaker served as clubhouse where the boys gathered to play, it also served to socialize the boys into the world of mining. It was where they gathered to collectively contemplate and act out their journey to manhood. To be a miner was to be tough, and lessons in toughness were part of the curriculum from the first day on the job. Owen Lovejoy described breaking in as a breaker boy:

> During the first weeks of labor his hands are cut and torn, his nails are broken off, and the pain of handling the sharp stones and slate is intense. But he does not complain. Does a twelve-year-old boy ever complain of what other boys endure? He looks back afterward with haughty contempt on the days when he had bleeding finger-tips, and much of the suffering of the new boy in the breaker is from the ridicule of his "red tops."[38]

The Hine photo provides another glimpse into the psyche of the boys in the coal mines. As the caption indicates, the photo was taken in West Virginia, so it was a bituminous mine that did not have a breaker. Here, young boys typically broke in underground loading coal for their fathers at the coal face. There is another photo, a close-up of this same young lad in the picture, striking a similar posture, that has become one of Hine's most famous child labor photos. The lad's posture—a cocky, self-assured swagger, if nothing else—is instructive. But where does the swagger come from? The photo of the entire crew suggests an answer. Here is a boy among men. He has progressed up the career ladder to the point where he no longer does boys' work. He is expected to pull his own weight on the crew, to carry his share of the load. According to all the cultural trappings of his world, he can now claim to be a man. Yet he is not a man, he is still a young lad. That swagger, and the frame of mind underlying it, undoubtedly helped the lad to get where he was at such a young age. And it also helps him project his manhood in spite of his slight frame. Where the men stand erect and proud, the boy swaggers, equally proud (Figure 4.3).

Frustrating Attempts at Regulation

Establishing effective regulation of child labor in the anthracite region proved extremely frustrating. In many respects Pennsylvania was a very progressive state. In others it was extremely recalcitrant. Pennsylvania's public school system was more advanced than those of its coal-mining neighbors Maryland, West Virginia, and Ohio. Its compulsory schooling laws were as progressive as any in the nation.[39] Even before the NCLC arrived on the scene, night schools had been established

Figure 4.3 *Tipple Crew.* Tipple Crew, Turkey Knob Mine, MacDonald, W. Va. Oct. 1908. Witness E.N. Clopper. *(Courtesy of the Library of Congress, Prints and Photographs Division, Lewis Wickes Hine National Child Labor Committee Collection, LC-USZ62–23739.)*

throughout the anthracite region to accommodate the work schedules of the boys. But availability of schools and compulsory schooling laws did not necessarily translate into enrollment and attendance. Peter Roberts, who interviewed a number of school officials, noted that it was comparatively easy to enforce the compulsory schooling laws when the breakers were idle. Indeed, during the recent strike activity, several school districts moved to open new schools to handle the influx of students. But when the strikes ended and the breakers were running, school populations were depleted.[40]

If public schooling in Pennsylvania was relatively advanced, child labor laws lagged. It was difficult to secure adequate legislation and even more difficult to secure adequate enforcement. It was estimated that the powerful railroad interests owned or controlled as much as 96 percent of the anthracite deposits.[41] And as has been previously noted, Mr. Roderick, the state's chief mining inspector, viewed it as among his duties to defend the industry from outside attacks. Even with a corps of sympathetic inspectors, the mines took precautions to avoid being pinched for any child labor violations. One underage lad described to

Lovejoy the drill used to foil the inspectors, a drill that also reveals the career ladder for the boys in the mines. "De boss put drivers nippin' an' de runners drivin' an' de laborers runnin' an' hid us away on de gob. Dat was a cinch to get pay for sleepin' all day on de gob."[42]

Owen Lovejoy asserted there was another reason for the difficulty in securing adequate regulation in the anthracite region—ethnic prejudice. By 1900, the English, Welsh, German, and Polish miners had given way to the Slavs of southern and eastern Europe, who now dominated the labor force. Efforts to restrict child labor were opposed or resisted, Lovejoy insisted, because these were not the "American child" but were rather the children of ignorant Slavs. The truth was, he pointed out, they were American children of foreign-born parents. Most were, indeed, descended from southern and eastern European immigrants. But only 3 percent of the children themselves were foreign born, and roughly half the parents were American born. In truth, they were American children—first- and second-generation American children. Nevertheless, ethnic prejudice suggested that education would be wasted on these children, that they were suited to nothing more than a life of brute labor.[43]

Pennsylvania law had established a minimum age of fourteen for work in the breakers and sixteen for work underground in anthracite, but until 1905 no documentation of age was required. In 1905 the law was amended to require such documentation. County squires (or ordinaries—known today as notary publics) were authorized to issue affidavits on oath of a parent or guardian. The new law took effect on May 1, 1905, shortly before Owen Lovejoy's first visit to the region on behalf of the NCLC. A breaker boss remarked to Lovejoy, "It's queer how all these little fellows who have come to us this spring are just fourteen and were all born on the first of May."[44] According to Lovejoy, the employers knew they were employing underage boys but did not care:

> While these men are certain that they are employing boys younger than the prescribed age, they are not guilty of violation of the law, since every boy has come with an official document, issued by authority of this great state, declaring him to be of the legal age for employment.[45]

During his first investigation in 1905, Lovejoy's field notes include the following roster from one breaker:

> Here, twenty-two boys were interviewed at the noon interval, all of whom admitted they were under fourteen except one Scotch boy (whose age, by the school record was found to be ten) and one Irish boy of fifteen, who

has been out of school and at work for more than six years. Of the others, one was nine (eight by the school record), three were ten, two were eleven, six were twelve, and three were thirteen (although the school record showed one of the thirteen-year-old boys to be eleven).[46]

On his return to the same breaker in 1907, despite the storm of public controversy caused by his first report, he found that of the original twenty-two boys, sixteen were still at work, three had returned to school, one had moved away, and three could not be located.[47]

During Lewis Hine's 1911 investigation, he spoke with a Dr. Dodson, coroner in Nanticoke (Luzerne County). Dr. Dodson shared information about a breaker boy who was killed three years earlier in 1908:

> He went on to tell how the parents swear falsely about the ages of the boys. He gave me the record of a ten-year-old breaker boy, killed January 4, 1908, by falling from the breaker at Wanamie, Pennsylvania. His age certificate said he was 14 years old, but his baptismal record showed he was only ten. Name, Stanley Letuvinak (American name recorded as Thomas Long). On the Coroner's Docket I found the Jury reported, "We find the said Company not responsible for the accident, as they hold affidavit from the father that he was 14 years old," and the boy was away from his working place at the time of the accident.[48]

On reflection it can be seen how the system of requiring affidavits on parental oath could lead to widespread petty corruption. So long as the mines had the proper paperwork on file, they were immune to prosecution or liability. County squires and parents were more than willing to cooperate in supplying child workers, circumventing the intent of the Pennsylvania law through "the perjury of the parent and the pathetic greed of the notary public."[49] The practice throughout the region was that squires issued "work permits" on application of parents for 25 cents apiece. In one publication Lovejoy heaped scorn upon the parents for their complicity in the exploitation of their children:

> [I]t left it to the imagination of the parent and the credulity of the official to determine the age of the child who applied for a permit to work. Sometimes parents found that the years of taking care of the little child had dragged on so heavily that a child of eight years seemed to them to be 14 or 16 years of age. They felt that they had had the little darling in their arms so long now, it must become an adult and add its efforts to those of the natural wage-earners of the family in order to eke out an existence.[50]

In another publication, Lovejoy was more sympathetic to the plight of the parents. He noted that most of the anthracite parents were not literate in written English, and many did not even understand spoken English. Many thought they were simply applying for a work permit for their children. They raised their right hand, swore a solemn oath, and made their mark that they had duly applied for a work permit for their child. They were simply unaware of their perjury—that they had just sworn under oath and signed that their child was of legal age for work in mining.[51]

By the time Lewis Hine and Edward Brown investigated in 1911 and 1912, respectively, Pennsylvania law had been amended (and by the time Florence Taylor investigated in 1916 it had been further amended). In 1910, the law had been amended in an effort to address the abuses of the notorious affidavit system operated by the county squires. Age standards remained the same—fourteen for work in the breakers, sixteen for underground work—but the responsibility for certification was shifted to school officials. Furthermore, the law required documentary proof of age and not just the parent's oath. It also required school officials to certify that the child had met the compulsory school attendance requirements and required the child to pass a basic literacy exam. While the new law was a considerable improvement over the old, it still left the coal companies off the hook as long as they kept their paperwork in order. They could knowingly hire underage boys as long as the boy brought work papers. In 1912, investigator Brown visited the Baltimore number 5 colliery of the Delaware and Hudson Company. He asked the outside foreman, John Moore, for permission to tour the facility. The foreman replied:

> I cannot permit entrance to breakers or shaft. No young boys are employed here as formerly. When the new child labor law went into effect the Company sent me notice that I would be held personally responsible for any fine imposed for violation of this law. Children must produce work papers.[52]

But Moore's assistant foreman admitted to Brown, "Some of the kids in the breaker is no more than 12 years old, but they all got papers. That lets us out." The assistant foreman continued, "No boy of mine will ever go in that hell. About 20 boys in breaker, and I bet that you could shovel 50 pounds of coal dust out of their systems."[53] As a result of the new law, investigators Hine and Brown spent a good deal of time interviewing public school officials about its effectiveness. Brown summarized

the ways in which the authority of school superintendents and principals was circumvented in the issuance of work certificates:

> There are three ways in which under aged child get permits.
>
> 1. If they are refused here, they go to the Justice of the Peace and swear
>   they are 16. The law does not cover these at all. If over 16, Superin-
>   tendent has no jurisdiction. No educational qualification is required.
>   This is not done very often.
> 2. Where child 14 years of age are unable to pass examination and are
>   refused, they send substitutes to take examination.
> 3. By buying fake work paper. There appeared a number of privately
>   printed certificates. It has not been discovered who is responsible for
>   these fake papers. They bring from $5 to $75.[54]

Among school officials, Hine and Brown found substantial differences the ways they approached their responsibilities in administering
the new law. Some were extremely diligent and conscientious, winning
the admiration of the NCLC investigators. Others, however, saw themselves essentially as working for the coal companies and tried to administer the law in such a fashion that the breakers would retain their labor
supply. Still others simply saw the law as a nuisance, adding more bureaucratic red tape to their responsibilities without compensating them
for the extra work.

A.P. Diffendaefer, superintendent, Nanticoke, was one of the company men who might as well have been employed by the coal companies. He had good relations with the companies. He trusted them to do
what was right and saw it as his job, at least in part, to ensure that their
developing labor supply was not "detained" in school too long. He told
Hine, in 1911, "He thought conditions are not bad in the mines around
Nanticoke, as the Coal Companies try to do what is right."[55] In 1912, he
assured Brown:

> The child labor law is very well enforced here, owing to the care of the
> operators and to the activity of the truant officer. Very few children
> employed—none under fourteen. When new law first went into effect
> there was an increase of nearly 150 in the school enrollment. This was due
> to the return of some children to school and owing to the increased number
> who were detained in school. I established what was known as the "Breaker
> Boy's School" in which were enrolled the boys who were under age and
> had already been employed, but were unqualified educationally to meet

new child labor law. I did not attempt to teach them the general branches, but just brushed them up to the standard of reading and writing and got them out again to work.[56]

In contrast, there was Charles A. Judge, superintendent, Pittston. He was very diligent in attempting to administer and enforce the law, but he faced great difficulties. For his efforts, he earned the respect and admiration of investigators Hine and Brown. Both of their reports include detailed accounts of their discussions with Superintendent Judge. In 1911, he told Hine:

> The law is being persistently violated, not only around here, but I am convinced it is so all over the state. I try to do my duty in the matter, and if a child, between 14 and 16 applies for a certificate, and cannot read or write satisfactorily, I refuse the certificate. Then the company sends him to the Squire where a parent swears that the child is sixteen (although it may not be over 14) and the company accepts the child. The coal companies are largely to blame for the child labor here. Some months ago the companies were badly in need of boys. Knowing that I was the strictest of the principals around here, the Pennsylvania Coal Co., sent a representative to me asking me to "ease-up" in my requirements. This man said, "You stick by them and they'll stick by you as they did in the case of that other principal who was pinched for careless certification." When they found they couldn't work me, they proceeded to go over my head by having Squires issue certificates on parents' oath, and sometimes without their oath. Then they thought they had the laugh on me. The total number of certificates I issued in 1910 is only 117. I know I have turned down several hundred, but they have probably gotten a Squire's certificate and been at work all the time. In some ways conditions are worse now than they were before the 1910 law went into effect. The law should *force Squires to demand proof of birth*. The Chief Mine inspector, Roderick, has tried all the year to get evidence on us principals. He succeeded in having three principals pinched last summer, and that will be their main fight this year, contending that the school principals are no better qualified to issue certificates than the Squires. As long as my duties are as plain as they are, I shall continue to keep myself up to them, regardless of what others may do.[57]

Hine toured the Pittston area with Superintendent Judge's truant officer. His investigation report includes the following notes:

> Spent part of the day looking up the homes of the boys whose names I have been collecting in Pittston. In company with the Truant Officer, Mr.

Kearney, and an interpreter, I obtained some interesting and damaging evidence. In the first place, all the boys between the ages of 14 and 16 years, should have certificates from Principal Judge, but none of these boys had obtained certificates from the school. The only alternative, if the Company requires certificates as they should, is for the boys to obtain a certificate of 16 years from a Squire, which we found they have done,—some of them being not only 14 but 13 years old. Following are some cases;—

1. Willie Bryden (see photo 1920) a door-tender, inside the mine at Shaft #6. We found Willie at home ill. He had been complaining that the dampness was affecting him, when I saw him in the mine. His mother admitted Willie to be only 13 years old. Said the boss told his father, who works in the mine, to bring Willie to work, four months ago;— and that they had gone to Squire Barrett, who had issued him a certificate (three years ahead of time). He will be 14 next July. The older brother also works in the mine, and the home is that of a frugal, German family, showing no need for Willie's work.

2. Philip Kurato, 177 S. Main Street, (See Photo #1930). We found his stepmother at home. She said he is 13 years old, and that is the age he gave Principal Judge the other day, (but he told me 12). She said he has been working two years in the breaker, and that Squire Barrett made out his working papers for him. Also that his birth certificate shows he is 13 now. This woman owns a house near by that is worth about $1,500. Not paid for yet. The truant officer says he has, in his possession, a baptismal record on which the data is altered to make the boy look old enough to work. The parent said Squire Barrett altered the date, and the parents do not seem intelligent enough to do it themselves.

3. The mother of Jo Pume, 163 Pine Street, (See photos #1915 & 1923), showed passport which shows Jo to be 14 years old. He has no school certificate although working underground.

4. Found mother of Philip Barth (real name seems to be Balda) 67 So. Main Street. They said he is 15 years old, but he has no school certificate.[58]

The following year, Superintendent Judge was equally critical in his remarks to investigator Brown. While he still saw the coal companies as ultimately responsible for the child labor problem, he was now more openly critical of the corruption among squires and mining inspectors:

The child labor law is very unsatisfactory. It is not much harder to swear children are 16 and go to squire for a certificate than it was to swear to 14 and get one. To every 25 certificates squires issue, I issue one. They go to squire, swear to 16 and pay 25 cents and get certificate. No proof of age or educational qualification required. I venture to say there are several hundred children from 9 to 13 years working in breakers. Foremen of mines advise children to go to squire and avoid me. Three supervising principals recently issued certificates to children under age, without educational examination and for a fee. All were arrested and fined. *This is a campaign on the part of companies to show that issuance of certificates by school authorities is a failure and a hint to restore power again to squire.*[59]

Then there was Louis P. Bierly, principal in West Pittston, who seemed to regard the new child labor law as just so much more bureaucratic red tape imposed from above—another unfunded mandate from Harrisburg. It seemed he would really rather not be bothered at all. According to Hine, Bierly thought "the largest problem in the whole matter to him was the question of how the Principals are to get compensation for extra time spent issuing certificates. There has been some trouble and considerable discussion, and it is still unsettled."[60] Apparently Mr. Bierly took the matter into his own hands. On investigator Brown's return visit the next year, he noted, "Last year Mr. Bierly was arrested for charging a fee for issuing certificates."[61]

When investigator Taylor visited in 1916, she was able to report a dramatic reduction in the employment of boys in the mines and especially in the breakers. Two factors had brought this about: (1) a tough new compulsory schooling law; and (2) installation of mechanical slate pickers in the breakers. The new law extended the age of compulsory schooling to sixteen. The child labor law had not changed, so boys could still work in the breakers at fourteen, but now they were also required to attend school. The law resulted in the creation of a system of what were called "continuation schools"—later to be called junior high schools, then middle schools—to accommodate the influx of students fourteen to sixteen years of age.

The new law put school officials in a stronger position than they had been under the former law. By the time Florence Taylor visited Pittston in 1916, a Mr. McGuigan had replaced Superintendent Judge. McGuigan was equally diligent and zealous and, with the weight of the new law behind him, seems to have been much more effective than Judge. He had reported a fellow superintendent to the state superintendent for selling certificates. He sued the Pennsylvania Coal Company when it refused to provide certificates for two boys he alleged were under fourteen (before trial the boys were back in school). And he provided evidence that other coal companies were generally in compliance with the law.

Still, there were difficulties. McGuigan reported to Taylor that a "Catholic priest in town says he is losing his congregation because he will not issue false birth certificates."[62]

Coal companies adapted to the continuation school law in various ways. Some could not be bothered with it and discharged all boys under sixteen, preferring to install mechanical pickers. Others established alternating school and work arrangements. Taylor describes one such:

> Susquehanna Coal Co. No. 7. Mr. Yonk, foreman. Employs 150; 30 boys, 24 under 16. Employs them in three shifts, some going to school Monday and Tuesday, some Wednesday and Thursday, etc. Has not taken on any boys under 16 since law went into effect but kept boys he had.[63]

The overall effect of the continuation school law was to dramatically reduce child labor in the breakers. But in some cases, it actually appeared that a larger number of boys were employed after the law, but that each boy worked fewer hours because of the continuation school requirement. For example, she noted, "Greenwood Breaker, Delaware and Hudson Co. Assistant foreman said they employ 45 boys, 38 under 16. Had to employ 12 extra when the law went into effect."[64]

Where some mines complied with the new law by discharging all boys under sixteen, other mines took advantage of their competitor's mode of compliance. Investigator Taylor was told by Mr. Coyne, superintendent of schools in Old Forge, that "The Jermyn breaker has dismissed boys under 16 since law went into effect but they have been taken on at the Pennsylvania Coal Co.'s colliery."[65]

On the Role of Technology and Mechanization

If technology is taken to mean machinery, it is clear that technologies in use can be important determinants of child labor. On one hand, the coal breaker, itself one large complex machine, enabled the employment of large numbers of children in picking slate. On the other hand, installation of mechanical slate pickers within the breakers enabled the elimination of child labor. If, however, technology is taken in a broader sense to mean modes of production, then additional factors become relevant.

In Owen Lovejoy's published report of his 1907 investigation in the bituminous coal regions of Maryland and western Pennsylvania, he entertained a couple of working hypotheses on why child labor was higher in some mines than others. One hypothesis was that it was the "attitude of management" that mattered most. He described two mines in central Pennsylvania, both on the same hillside where the thickness of the veins were about equal and the conditions of mining were similar. At one mine, owned by railroad interests, 10 to 15 percent of all employees were boys under 16. The superintendent himself had gone to work at eight, thought it was the best thing that had ever happened to him, and opined that children should have all the education they need by twelve. At the other mine, an independent mine, no boys under sixteen were employed. This mine superintendent was a former superintendent of schools who happened to cherish education.[66]

A second hypothesis was that what Lovejoy called "conditions of labor" determined the amount of child labor employed. Again, he described two mines in Maryland located on opposite sides of the same mountain. One, owned by railroad interests, employed no boys under sixteen. In this mine, the vein was 8½ to 9 feet thick, the work was very heavy, and extra large cars were used. In the other mine, an independent, 40 percent of the employees were under sixteen. Here, the vein was only 3½ to 4 feet thick. The boys could work some of the tight spaces better than men. This was "because the company does not care to excavate more earth than is necessary to get the coal out from the headings."[67]

Lovejoy's field notes from his investigation provide more detail on the comparison and contrast between these two mines. The mine with the thick vein that employed few children was owned by the Consolidated Coal Company. But it was not that the company, in its "attitude of management," was averse to hiring children. Lovejoy visited another Consolidated Coal Company mine where as many as half the workers were under sixteen:

> A young man working at No. 9, Consolidated, says 25 are employed there—small mine—and half of these are boys under 16. Some are only 11 or 12. George Hoover who works with him is a little fellow who looks 12, but says he's 17. "All the boys are supposed to have certificates that they are 16 years old!" he says.[68]

The mine with the thin vein that employed a large number of boys was the Washington number 2 mine owned by the Piedmont and George Creek Coal Company:

> About 100 are employed at this small mine and nearly all were seen going in. Several pictures were taken. Of those seen, not more than 40 were

boys of 16 and under, about 20 were apparently under 14 and 5 or 6 were evidently from 9 to 12 years old. Mr. William Hines, inside foreman, whose father is one of the principal owners of the mines, explained the large number of boys saying that the veins are very low—3½ to 4 ft., and the boys can work in many places to better advantage than the men. If a miner takes in three boys he can keep them loading and he can "cut coal all the time." Wages are apparently good $2½ to $4 a day. There are twenty mule drivers whose wages are $1.20 a day. Mr. Hines says all the mines employ many boys but believes they may have more up here on account of the nature of the work. They are preparing to install electric haulage which will do away with some of the mule drivers.[69]

But now, back to the anthracite region and the question of hard technology—that is, machinery. Owen Lovejoy had long argued that "From the standpoint of industrial cost, it does not pay to try to run a kindergarten in a coal breaker."[70] By 1916, when Florence Taylor investigated, the coal companies were finally starting to agree. As noted previously, Taylor observed a dramatic reduction in the number of young boys employed, especially in the breakers. The new continuation school law had made it much more difficult to hire underage boys, and mines had difficulty recruiting sufficient boy labor. Even more decisively, most mines had begun installing mechanical slate pickers to replace the breaker boys.

Taylor identified three different types of pickers in use in the region: (1) emery pickers, which were good only for dry coal and required some use of boys on the "tailings" as the picker leaves about 15 percent of slate and it must be reduced to 2 or 4 percent; (2) spiral pickers, which were not considered satisfactory at all; and (3) jigs, which were very satisfactory, at least for wet coal, and required no boys at all. On the effects of the mechanical pickers in eliminating child labor, her report contains the following notes from interviews with mine officials:

Raub Colliery, Raub Coal Co. Mr. Rovett, foreman. Said he employed no boys under 16 because he could not bother with continuation school law. . . . About 10 boys employed and mechanical pickers in use. Foreman said one jig replaces 10 boys.

Susquehanna Coal Co. No. 7. Mr. Yonk, foreman. . . . "Give us enough jigs and we wouldn't have any boys—jigs do work much better." 4 jigs replace 35 boys and cost $500 a piece. Hard to get boys for company's new breaker. 16-year-old boys won't work for breaker boy's wages. Nothing else for boys under 18 to do around breaker because of dangerous occupations clause.

Babylon Breaker, Temple Coal and Iron Co. Foreman said he used to employ 110 boys but now only 23, none of whom are under 16. He is using jigs mainly and expects to eliminate all boys.

Greenwood Breaker, Delaware and Hudson Co. Breaker has both jigs and Emery pickers but company is going to put in all jigs this summer. Will need about 12 boys then—used to employ 120. "Got to have some boys 14 to 16 for odd jobs—hard to get them over 16 as they go into the mines then."

Marvin Breaker, Delaware and Hudson Co. Mr. Nichol, superintendent. Thinks the law is a good thing and says that jigs will eliminate boys—employs 38 now.

Archbold Breaker, Archbold Coal Co. Mr. More, superintendent. . . . Employs 7 boys and is putting in jigs as fast as possible to get rid of them. Thinks the law is a good thing.

Price-Pancoast Breaker. McArthur, foreman. . . . Has 20 boys now—used to have 50 but discharged all under 16 when new law went into effect. Using Emery pickers and finds them satisfactory—is going to put in more and get rid of more boys.[71]

Effects of mechanization were echoed by others interviewed by investigator Taylor. From Mr. Robinson, a superintendent of schools, Taylor noted that "most of the breaker boys in his continuation school come from the Lackawanna Co.'s old breaker. Not many under 16 are employed in the more modern one." Finally, S.J. Phillips, a local mine inspector, affirmed that "the installation of mechanical pickers has supplanted a good deal of youthful labor."[72]

There was no clear cause-and-effect relationship between the newer tougher schooling law and the installation of mechanical pickers in the breakers. Still, both clearly had an effect in reducing the employment of boys. To the extent that the continuation school law made it more difficult to recruit young breaker boys, it created incentive to install the mechanical pickers. To the extent that older boys would not work for breaker boy wages, this incentive was strengthened. Ultimately, the mechanical pickers accounted for the demise of child labor in the breakers. If a jig cost $500 and could replace roughly ten boys, clearly even at the meager wages of the breaker boys, a jig would pay for itself within a year. Further, once purchased, a jig was likely to be installed. Once installed, there was no further need for young boys. Once the young boys were gone, they would not return.

The NCLC paid scant attention in their investigation work to other segments of mining and extraction. It was understood that in some sectors, such as iron ore or oil and gas, relatively few children were working. In other sectors, however, such as timber and some of the Western hard-rock mining camps, it was known that substantial numbers of children worked. But, investigations were rarely commissioned. In one investigation outside of coal mining, investigator Harry Bremer visited iron and zinc mines in New Jersey in 1913 and found very little evidence of child labor. Regarding the iron mines, Bremer reported:

> No child labor was found in any of these mines. Only four children were found to be employed, and these were water boys for men engaged in outside work or in one of the shops. Eighteen years is the very youngest age permitted below the surface, and usually none under twenty-one are sent into the mines.[73]

He visited the zinc mines at Franklin Furnace, "claimed to be the richest zinc deposit in the world, extending over a diameter of three miles and to a greater depth than 1,700 feet. . . . The superintendent at this mine, Mr. Catlin, said children never went into the mine. The youngest miners are all over twenty-one years of age. The youngest workers on their books are two boys of fifteen and one half and sixteen years, and these work in one of the buildings above the surface."[74]

Continuing Legacy: The Missouri Tiff Mines, 1937

After 1916, the NCLC conducted no further investigations in coal mining and, with one exception conducted no more investigations in any sector of the mining industry, leaving the field to the U.S. Children's Bureau, which followed up with several investigations of its own.[75]

After 1916, the only special investigation conducted by the NCLC in mining came in 1937, investigating the Missouri "tiff" mines. What triggered the investigation was a new Missouri child labor law establishing a minimum age of sixteen in manufacturing and eighteen in mining. During debate on the bill, a significant exemption was added to protect Missouri's "tiff" miners. The NCLC had been watching events in the Missouri statehouse and became curious. What was "tiff," and who was mining it, and under what conditions?

"Tiff"—or barite—is a mineral that was then used in the production of paint, enamel, lacquer, floor coverings, textiles, rubber goods, paper, glass products, and so forth. In 1937 it was mined in five other states, but only Missouri, the leading state with 57 percent of national production, was still mining barite by hand. NCLC Director of Investigations Charles E. Gibbons found the "tiff" miners in a corner of Washington County on the edge of the Ozark Plateau. There some eighty families comprising five hundred individuals, including three hundred children, lived in abject poverty mining "tiff."[76] Here was a scene like none that had been observed in the annals of NCLC investigation. Child labor was already virtually eliminated, and had been for some time in mining and extraction. This scene was more prescient of some of the conditions observed in primitive mining operations in developing nations today than it was reminiscent of anything seen before in U.S. history.

The barite industry began in Washington County around 1900, about when the timber industry was giving out. Here is how it worked:

> The first step in becoming a tiff miner is to find a place to live. There are practically no houses available in the tiff area except those possessed by tiff owners. In return for a house, which he secures rent free, the miner agrees to dig tiff on the land of the company or individual who owns the house.[77]

This was an arrangement carried over from the timber boom. Indeed, it appears that many of the earlier timber interests had retained mineral rights and were now mining barite. Furthermore, it appears that most of the families had been on the land through the timber boom and, indeed, were descended from the original stock of Scotch-Irish settlers.

Mining barite was a straightforward economic proposition and a pure illustration of the family wage. The family was given a house, most typically a two-room "shack" with neither electricity nor running water, in exchange for agreeing to dig tiff. On the positive side, they were not put on any schedule, nobody supervised their work, and they were free to adopt whatever rhythms of work most suited their needs. On the negative side, they were paid a strict piece rate—according to the amount of tiff delivered to the mill—but were provided none of the tools that might have raised their output to levels that would have provided a comfortable subsistence. Equipment such as front-end loaders, bulldozers, and various mechanical shovels were common by this time. Yet the Missouri tiff miners were equipped only with their own picks and shovels.

Hand-digging tiff involved sinking a shaft into the ground, typically and roughly five by five feet square. Dirt was thrown to one side. Tiff was most commonly located anywhere from five feet to as deep as thirty or forty feet below the surface. Tiff was thrown to the other side of the hole. When the shaft became too deep, a crude windlass was erected to remove the dirt and tiff (not to mention the miner).

Under these circumstances, the entire family was pressed into the mining operation. Men and older boys most typically worked down in the hole. Women, girls, and younger boys most typically worked above (the women and girls also having responsibility for the domestic labor). Even infants were taken daily to the pits—where else would they stay? Any contribution any family member could make to the growing tiff pile enhanced the family's subsistence. Tiff had to be "scraped" to remove the residual dirt and debris. This was a good job for the women and younger children. It enabled the men and older boys to stay in the hole throwing tiff. If the family was large enough, dirt and debris could be "scrapped"—or scoured for pieces of tiff that were discarded. This was the job of the youngest children.

In 1937, the family was paid $7 for each ton of tiff delivered to the local mill. From this, $.60 to $1.75 per ton was deducted for hauling, depending on the distance from the mill, and another $.75 to $1.00 per ton might be deducted for royalties on land use, leaving the family with anywhere from $4.50 to $6.40 per ton. The NCLC estimated that this yielded the equivalent of $.075 per hour for the children, this at a time when a federal minimum wage of $.25 per hour was about to be established.

What was once a highly literate and self-sufficient region had been effectively debased. First, the settlers were dispossessed of their land by the timber interests. Then, they were thrown into abject poverty by the barite interests. The result was predictable. Few adult tiff miners were literate. Illiteracy in Washington County, at 16.1 percent, was the highest in Missouri and far exceeded the national rate of 4.3 percent. Furthermore, illiteracy had actually increased from 1920 to 1930, while it had decreased nearly everywhere else. Relatively few of the children of tiff miners attended school.[78]

Conclusion

The NCLC's investigations of child labor in mining were among the first conducted and they were concentrated in the early years of the committee. The last study in anthracite was conducted in 1916, and the committee would not commission another investigation in mining and extraction until 1937, when it stumbled across the Missouri "tiff" miners. The elimination of child labor in mining was an important early win for the NCLC. While every industry stubbornly resisted giving up its child workers, mining and extraction yielded relatively early. It was just such a horrendous occupation for children that, in most states, mining came under more stringent regulation than other employment. In turn, this enabled the NCLC to strategically shift some of its investigation resources to other problem industries it felt needed attention.

5. LIGHT MANUFACTURING

Children in the Glasshouses

Figure 5.1 *Glass Blower and Mold Boy.* Morgantown, West Virginia. Oct. 1908. A Blower and Mold Boy, Seneca Glass Works.*(Courtesy of the Library of Congress, Prints and Photographs Division, Lewis Wickes Hine National Child Labor Committee Collection, LC-USZ62–20500.)*

By the early twentieth century, America had become a maturing industrial nation. Heavy industries, especially railroads, steel, and soon autos, were emerging. But heavy industries were less likely to employ young children. The work was either simply too heavy or required greater attention to productive efficiency. Where children were employed, they tended to work away from the core production processes, working as errand boys or water boys in service to the core workers.

There had been a few heavy industries that had employed large numbers of children. Meatpacking was one example. But, for a variety of reasons, child labor was already well on the way out of the meatpacking industry by the time the National Child Labor Committee came into being. One reason had to do with the competitive nature of the industry. By 1900, the modern meatpacking plant was a heavily capitalized major industrial complex. To provide a return on investment, the complex had to maintain consistent output at a high level. Work processes were rationalized earlier than in many industries, and this pushed children off the disassembly lines and into secondary errand boy, water boy, and service worker roles. Second, because of concern over consumer food-product safety, meatpacking was among the first industries to come under government regulation. This regulation opened the production processes to public scrutiny. When the light shined in and caught glimpses of child labor, the children scurried (or were shuttled) to the recesses of the production process and were eventually phased out. Finally, since the center of the meatpacking industry was Chicago, its proximity to the Florence Kelley, Jane Addams, and Hull House social workers helped accelerate the effect of public pressure. Insights into child labor in the meatpacking industry are provided in several sources of fiction and nonfiction.[1] But the NCLC never investigated meatpacking.

While the large industrial complexes in auto, steel, and meatpacking dominated the industrial landscape, industrial America was dotted with many thousands more smaller factories, plants, and workshops supplying the major factories and producing all manner of consumer goods. Child workers were common in match factories, potteries, furniture factories, machine shops, broom factories, print shops, and many other sectors of light manufacturing. Many of the smaller manufacturing establishments operated along traditional lines. That is, one of the owners, proprietors, or partners was an entrepreneur and possibly a tinkerer-inventor. This person was usually considered a skilled craftsperson in the trade and fulfilled the role of the master. In the next tier, there were often several adult, skilled workers, many of whom had been brought up in the trade. These filled the role of journeymen. Finally, there were the apprentices, whose job was to enable the skilled workers to do their job. Ostensibly, they were learning the trade and would, if they stayed with it, one day assume the role of journeyman. Many of these were children.

The National Child Labor Committee and its agents visited numerous small manufacturing facilities and documented their child labor conditions. But, for a variety of reasons, they focused their attention on the glass industry. The glasshouses were caught between the traditions of the small manufacturing workshop and the major industrial complex. That is, plants of massive size were in operation, but they operated largely under traditional methods. The plant was more a series of semi-independent workshops than it was an integrated manufacturing facility. Each workshop was operated under the direction of skilled glassblowers, and each shop had its array of "dog boys" as helpers. But important traditions were beginning to break down. In an earlier era, the dog boys would have been at the bottom rung of a clearly defined career ladder that progressed from helper to apprentice to skilled glassblower. By the early 1900s, conditions had changed in the industry, and it was unlikely that most helpers would ever rise above the status of dog boy.

Owen Lovejoy called the glass industry the "oldest and youngest" of American industries.[2] In his investigation report, Charles L. Chute provides this background on the industry:

> Glass making is one of the most ancient of industries. The use of glass began among the earliest civilizations and its importance has continually increased until today it is indispensable, entering in myriad forms into the daily life of every civilized man. Glass making is therefore one of the greatest of present day industries. Brought from Europe it did not assume importance in this country until the great deposits of coal and natural gas were discovered, first in Pennsylvania and then in the States lying directly west. A cheap and adaptable fuel being furnished by the seemingly inexhaustible supplies of natural gas for feeding the ravenous furnaces of the glass factory, the industry grew by leaps and bounds until it became as it is today one of America's foremost industries.[3]

While the first glasshouse in America dates to 1609 in Jamestown, Virginia, and the first manufactured exports from the colony were glass, the industry did not take off until much later. It was not until 1865 that a

Boston house produced flint glass of the quality used in European glassware. The dramatic expansion of the industry came after 1888 when the first continuous tank was introduced in Jeannette, Pennsylvania. The continuous tank, as the name implies, enabled the continuous production of molten glass rather than production in batches. This, in turn, enabled production at much higher volumes and also enabled, or rather required, production around the clock.

By the early 1900s, the glass industry stretched from New Jersey to Missouri, and the NCLC investigated glasshouses across the entire region. But the first investigations, conducted by Harriet Van der Vaart in 1904 and 1905, focused on the new center of the industry around East St. Louis. The East St. Louis region received follow-up investigations by Anna Herdina in 1910, who brought along Lewis Hine to take photographs, and Charles L. Chute in 1911. East St. Louis became the center of the struggle over child labor in the glass industry.[4]

East St. Louis: Industrial Slum

The East St. Louis region was a sprawling industrial slum. It had become the center of the glass industry by following the discovery of natural gas westward until it met the Mississippi River. Each westward step increased shipping costs to the industry, but at the Mississippi, shipping costs were reduced substantially. With an abundant fuel supply nearby, population centers to the east, and natural resources coming in from the west, it was an ideal location for the industry. The Illinois Glass works in Alton was the largest complex of glass factories in the world, comprising in 1910 eight factories with two more under construction and two others contemplated—employing 4,500 at capacity. Another large complex was the Obear-Nester works in East St. Louis, managed by Joseph Nester, president, and spokesperson for the industry association.

Officials of the Illinois Glass works and the Obear-Nester works were of the old school. They had grown up in the industry and, in turn, had helped the industry grow. Their plants were more closely tied to the craft traditions even as their industry achieved massive scale. But there were also major new players in the industry. Massive breweries were built across the river by August Busch, and the Anheuser-Busch Brewing Company required a massive and reliable supply of glass bottles. Busch interests controlled as many as four large glass factories, three in Streator and one in Belleville. For the Busch interests, brewing was their craft—bottles were a mere necessity. They were less wedded to the traditions of the glass industry even while they had become major players in it because of their dependence on it. They were more willing to depart from the old craft traditions of the industry, including the use of boys. They were less stubborn in their resistance to the aims of the NCLC and its investigators.

With such a concentration of glassworks, the demand for boy help readily outstripped the local supply. Later, these chronic shortages of boy labor would facilitate the reduction of child labor in the industry. But early on, the industry continued to recruit heavily for boys. Factories hired "boy getters," agents who recruited throughout the Midwest to bring boys, with or without the rest of their family, to the factories. There were also persistent, but not well documented, reports of a population of boat people living on ramshackle boats and rafts along the east bank of the Mississippi. Many of these people purchased, or otherwise obtained, orphan boys to work in the factories.[5] The optimum arrangement was to obtain two boys for each available sleeping space and put them out to work on opposite shifts, one on days and one on nights. This enabled many adults to live, however meagerly, on the wages of their orphan boys. Boys could be obtained from orphanages scattered about the Midwest, or from New York City on the orphan trains sponsored by Charles Loring Brace's Children's Aid Society. This was a far cry from the idyllic Midwest farm life Brace had envisioned for the boys. They merely exchanged the urban slum for the industrial slum. While their presence is amply documented, it is not clear just how prevalent the use of orphans was by the time the NCLC began its investigations.

Florence Kelley's Unfinished Business

While the investigations reported here were conducted under the auspices of the National Child Labor Committee, they could just as appropriately be credited to Hull House, or the National Consumers League, or to Florence Kelley herself. As general secretary of the National Consumers League, Kelley played an instrumental role in the founding of the National Child Labor Committee. But before this, she had served from 1893 to 1897 as the first state factory inspector in Illinois. While she spent much of her time in and around the Chicago area, the glass industry had become her major downstate concern, and she had become well acquainted with some of its principal representatives, especially

Joseph Nester of the Obear-Nester works. She had inspected some of the East St. Louis factories and found them rife with child labor. She had even documented numerous violations of the law. But, by the time she left Illinois for New York City, she really had not made substantial headway on the child labor problem in the glass industry.

In this sense, the early NCLC investigations can be seen as a continuation of her work. Like Kelley, both Harriet Van der Vaart, who investigated in 1904 and 1905, and Anna Herdina, who investigated in 1910, were associates of Hull House and the National Consumers League (Van der Vaart was general secretary of the Illinois branch of the Consumers League). While Owen Lovejoy was initiating the first investigations in the anthracite coal industry, and before the NCLC could organize for investigations in other industries, the Hull House/National Consumers League group moved on the glass industry.

Part of the impetus for investigation was a new Illinois law, which can also be credited largely to the efforts of the Hull House/National Consumers League group. Enacted in 1903, it set standards among the highest in the nation for factory work. Children under fourteen were prohibited from working in the factories. Children under sixteen were limited to eight work hours per day and were prohibited from night work, and factories were required to keep work permits on file. In 1904, Harriet Van der Vaart was dispatched to East St. Louis to see how the new law was working.

First she toured the Illinois Glass works complex in Alton, the largest glass factory in the world. She was accompanied by one of Illinois' deputy factory inspectors, a Mr. Reiger. According to factory records, in 1904 there were only thirty-four children between the ages of fourteen and sixteen, down from 316 in 1900. She and Reiger toured the facilities, both day and night. They took down names and checked certificates for all thirty-four children under sixteen. Everything checked out. This appeared to be a model factory. It all seemed too good to be true, and Van der Vaart had her doubts. After Reiger left for Chicago, she took the list of names, stopped by the school superintendent's office and obtained more names of boys not attending school, and began visiting the homes of the boys. At one home, the mother said, "My boy came home last night and said the factory inspectors were coming." At another house a "little" boy said, "We were all sent home last night because you were coming."

> Over and over I obtained evidence that the factory had been prepared for our visit. I then went back to the office of the Illinois Glass works and

told Mr. Smith, the President, and Mr. Levis, one of the Proprietors, what I had discovered. Mr. Smith said:—

"But Madam, what would you do if you were a proprietor and the enemy was out, wouldn't you take every precaution?" and he rather challenged me to find out how he obtained his information. Mr. Levis said:—

"Of course, you do not enter one factory without some one, possibly a glass blower will step to the phone and inform the next factory."

As I came out of the office, it was just the time for the night force to go in. I noticed a short distance to the right of the door a man standing, and about a half block behind him were a number of rather small boys. My driver said that he had overheard this man tell the boys they "must stay back until that rig goes away." He also heard one boy say to another: "Go and stay in the grocery story until that lady goes away."[6]

Van der Vaart was scheduled to present her findings at the Third Annual Meeting of the NCLC in 1907.[7] Since it had been two and three years since her initial investigations, she felt it would only be fair if she revisited the key sites. She revisited the Alton works, still the world's largest glass facilities, and the Obear-Nester works, managed by Joseph Nester, who had led the fight for the glassmakers against child labor legislation in Illinois.

At Alton, Charles Levis flatly refused to let her go through the plant. State factory inspectors had just been through and levied what would become $620 in fines. As far as he was concerned, "they had been painted quite as black as they could be," and he did not see what a tour by Van der Vaart might accomplish on their behalf. So, she stood at the factory gate, where she saw a number of "very young ones" going in, and visited some homes where she found several boys under sixteen sleeping in preparation for the night shift.

On her visit to the Obear-Nester works in East St. Louis, Van der Vaart tells of her encounter with two office girls:

On my way to the office I was overtaken by two girls, who told me that anyone could walk in, and one of them said, "I will take you where the children work; we girls hide the kids when the factory inspectors come in." I said: "Why do you do it?" "O, well, I would like to be hid if I was their age."[8]

On the basis of her previous research, and the return visits to these two key facilities, Van der Vaart concluded that employers were knowingly and deliberately engaged in widespread disobedience of the law. But she did not stop at criticism of the employers. Her reports and her presentation at the NCLC Annual Meeting in 1907 also included a substantial dose of criticism for the factory inspectors:

> I do not like to take the attitude of constantly criticising our inspectors, and, of course the enforcement of the law *is* one of the factors that is reducing the number, but I cannot help but be impressed with the *unreliability* of the figures in their reports. For instance, in one of the factories which in the factory inspector's report is given as employing eight between the ages of fourteen and sixteen, when I visited the factory I was told by the manager they employed one hundred and fifty, and in showing me the pay roll there were several pages of names.[9]

As it happened, Edgar T. Davies, the current chief factory inspector of Illinois, was also scheduled to speak at the annual meeting. He was not shy about returning verbal fire in the direction of Van der Vaart. At the time Illinois was the number three manufacturing state in the nation, but had the lowest level of child labor. Davies felt his office should get some credit for that and resented reformers like Mrs. Van der Vaart casting aspersions on his work. He especially took umbrage at her "broad statement that the child labor law is not being enforced against the glass companies in Illinois."[10]

Davies noted the presence of Florence Kelley in the audience and pointed out that she was his predecessor as chief factory inspector. In her capacity, "she had full authority to prosecute and convict" and, in her book, she states that she found eight hundred children employed at the Alton works, but "upon taking office I found no record of a conviction of a glass company in the state." In contrast, Davies declares, "During my administration, as chief inspector, I have secured the conviction of every glass company in the state. . . . There is not a glass company in the State of Illinois, not one of them, that I have not convicted." Indeed, he had just obtained another conviction (with a $620 fine imposed) of the Illinois Glass Company in Alton the day before Van der Vaart's most recent visit, "and this conviction, if you please, in the face of the fact that the Alton Glass Company is not only evasive, but constantly on the lookout."

Davies' presentation was aptly entitled, "The Difficulties of a Factory Inspector,"[11] and the exchange that took place at the annual meeting nicely illustrates how inspectors were often caught between the interests of the employers and the interests of reformers. Illinois not only had one of the more progressive child labor laws in the nation, it also had arguably the best system of inspection and enforcement. While there were certainly inspectors who were corrupt, ineffectual, or simply weak, Davies was not among them, and he asserted, "Officials who are charged with the enforcement of laws, and have tried to do their full duty, are naturally very jealous of their official reputation."[12]

Boys' Work

For all the attention the NCLC devoted to the East St. Louis region, working conditions for boys in East St. Louis were probably no worse, and, owing to the chronic shortages, may have been somewhat better, than working conditions found elsewhere in the industry. While conditions certainly varied somewhat from factory to factory, the essential job structure was very similar. Based on her early investigations of East St. Louis, Harriet Van der Vaart provided this description:

> Every glass blower has to have two or three boys to assist him in the work. The glass blower pours the molten glass into the molds; a boy sits and closes the molds; another one picks the bottles out of the molds and puts them on a long stick or handle, and puts them in front of a small furnace, which is called "the glory hole," where the top or the neck of the bottle is finished. Then they are placed on a long tray, and the boys carry them into the annealing furnaces, where they are gradually cooled.[13]

Based on his later investigations (1912 and 1913), Herschel H. Jones provided a very similar description of glasshouses in a different part of the country (western Pennsylvania). On boys' work, he observed:

> The different "jobs" done by boys in the glass factories each have a distinctive name. In the blown-ware factories at the side of the blowers and gatherer stands the little "cracker-off" boy who breaks the cooling, wax-like glass from the end of the blowpipe after the chimney or bottle has been left in the mold; sitting at the feet of the blower is the "holding-mold" boy, who opens and shuts the molds; then the "sticker-up" or "warming-in" boy, who takes the ware from the mold and holds it to the "glory-hole," reheating the mouth that it may be shaped by the gaffer, or finisher; from the finisher the "carry-in" boy takes the ware to the lehr, where it is properly tempered and made ready for packing.[14] [Figure 5.2]

Figure 5.2 *Boys at the Lehr.* Morgantown, West Virginia. Oct. 1908. Boys at the lehr, Economy Glass works. *(Courtesy of the Library of Congress, Prints and Photographs Division, Lewis Wickes Hine National Child Labor Committee Collection, LC-USZ62–29116.)*

The combination of common production methods in use and strong craft traditions that permeated the industry produced clear job hierarchies. There was boys' work and there was men's work, and all understood the difference. Each workshop in the glass factory was led by the glassblower, almost invariably the most highly skilled and most senior member of the team. Each team had two or three men. In addition to the blower, there was the gatherer, who measured out the proper amount of molten glass for the blower, and the gaffer, who finished the top. One of these may have been an apprentice. Then there were the boys. Holding molds, cracking off (or pulling off), snapping up (or sticking up), carrying in, and warming in were all boys' work. Over half the team did boys' work. It should be noted that, in most factories, a number of older boys, and even a few fully grown adult men, did boys' work.

One of the first features of the work environment that impressed investigators was the speed at which the boys worked. The blowers all worked on piece rates, while the boys were paid a flat hourly or daily rate. So, everyone on the team worked at the blower's pace, and the blower operated at the fastest pace that could be maintained steadily:

[T]he blowers all work on a piece-work basis and strain every nerve to make the out-put as great as possible. Recently, one of the trade journals has been complaining of the speeding which the men inflict upon themselves and their helpers in many factories. A blower who is slow or aged soon falls behind and his place is taken by a faster man, the trade being overcrowded with journeymen. The men frequently make as high as $12 a day, $8 to $10 being the average pay for a skilled blower. The boys are paid by the day and average about $1. The faster the men work the harder all the boys work with no increase in their wages.[15]

In contrast to the orderly layout of the textile mill, the glass shop was often chaotic and cluttered. Always taking their cues from the skilled blowers, the boys learned to perform their tasks as a tightly coordinated unit. It could almost be described as a repetitive dance, choreographed around the central figure of the blower, who remained stationary:

[T]he shop boys get into a regular swing or "gait" . . . and when these semi-automatic movements are once acquired the boys can pass each other to and fro in an extremely small space, and even regularly jostle their bodies against each other without much danger of striking one another with hot tools or hot glass. The constant changing of "small help," however, is continuously thrusting green boys into the shop, in which case there is real danger until all engaged in the "team" work get into a harmonious swing.[16]

The snapping-up boys were required to work very rapidly. They carried hot bottles held in a "snap" from the blower to the glory hole. New boys had difficulty keeping up. Carrying-in boys had greater variety in their work but, depending on the ware produced, it could be heavy work, and many plants had gone to older boys and men for this. For these jobs especially, there was much walking at a rapid pace. Many boys worked at a light trot, a "dogtrot," if you will—hence the term "dog boys." On a night shift at Federal Glass Company in Columbus, Ohio, Charles L. Chute observed:

At least a dozen of the carrying-in boys were probably under 16. Boys were working fast and too busy to talk with. These little boys did not look healthy, many of them, not fit to do their all-night work in the intense heat and hurry. They are on the walk all the time for ten hours and must travel many miles. Timed one boy and paced the distance; at his rate he walked a little over *20 miles per night*.[17]

Because they worked as a team, boys often developed an intense camaraderie. There were regular reports of boys singing loudly as they worked, or shouting boasts, put-downs, and stories (often bawdy) back and forth to one another. And, of course, they had their games. Herschel Jones described one:

> A very dangerous custom that the boys have is that of spitting into a defective bottle or glass while it is hot, sealing it, then throwing something at it to make it break with a loud report. A boy of fourteen at Rochester, was struck in the eye by a piece of flying glass while doing this and when visited by the investigator two months after the accident his eye was still bandaged and there was little probability that he would ever be able to see with it.[18]

The camaraderie could also produce a budding sense of solidarity among the boys. While they may have lacked a complete consciousness of their work situation, at least they could recognize when one of their own had been slighted in some way. Brief, spontaneous job actions and "spring fever" strikes were not uncommon.[19] Usually the boys gained very little from these bursts of militance, but the boy who did not stand with his fellows was quickly ostracized.

Another objectionable condition noted prominently by investigators was the heat. The environment around the furnaces was consistently well in excess of 100 degrees. Mold-boys and snapper-up boys were constantly subject to it, others intermittently. Boys lost copious amounts of body fluids during a work shift that had to be replaced. Water was the most common replacement fluid, but reports note that in many workshops, beer was the replacement fluid of choice. A related problem was the extreme temperature changes the boys experienced, especially in winter. Carrying-in boys experienced this many times per shift as their work took them back and forth from extreme heat to extreme cold. Others experienced the extreme temperature change when coming and going from the factory. On the basis of discussions with physicians, Charles L. Chute suggests that the rate of tuberculosis was twice as high among glass workers as among other workers.[20]

Another problem frequently mentioned was strain. This derived in part from the pace of the work and affected all the boys. But some were affected in other ways. Depending on the nature of the glassware produced, loads could be quite heavy for the carrying-in boys. But the boy most frequently mentioned in connection with strain was the mold boy. The holding-mold boys sat in one position at the foot of the blower manipulating mold handles. They worked bent over, in "a stooping attitude," for hours on end with only occasional opportunities to stretch. According to investigator Chute, "At one factory in Indiana, the foreman called the investigator's attention to the fact that nearly all the blowers were more or less 'round-shouldered' or bent, and said significantly 'they got that when they were mold-boys.'"[21]

Finally, there were concerns about working with glass. Mishandled or flying hot glass caused burns. Broken glass caused cuts (boys often worked in bare feet). A significant problem was "blow-over," fine floating glass dust. "[T]he small particles of glass float through the air and lodge in the eyes and nostrils of the men and boys, causing great pain."[22] Blow-over was a more pronounced problem in the older factories.

Night Work

Whatever objectionable conditions the boys may have endured on the day shift, they were magnified at night. Night work was the scourge of the glasshouses. Owen Lovejoy called it the "crowning offense" of the industry.[23] Obtaining legislative bans on night work was a high priority for the NCLC, so investigators documented its practice and its effects carefully.

Introduction of the continuous tank in the 1880s caused widespread adoption of the night shift. The molten glass had to be kept at a constant temperature round the clock so fuel and maintenance costs were spread throughout the day. A few plants did not operate night shifts, but most did.[24] Compounding the problem, most of the glasshouses adopted a system of alternating day and night shifts. That is, workers were on days one week and nights the next in perpetual rotation. Alternating shifts were apparently preferred by the blowers, and the others, as part of an intact work team, had to follow suit. Herschel Jones described the glasshouse at night:

> There is something very weird and uncanny about a glass house at night. To get the full effect of this one must visit it at twelve or one o'clock or later when streets are deserted and every one else is in bed. The yelling of the boys as they run back and forth to the lehrs; the popping of glass bubbles as the blower draws his pipe up from the mould; the swish of the wind and the clank of moulds; all these sounds break upon the stillness of

the night before you reach the factory. The glass men often tell how the boys in their factories are so happy that they sing while they work. But it isn't singing, it is a monotonous yelling that the boys keep up, not exactly to keep them awake as a resident of a glass house town outside of Pittsburgh seemed to think, but to counteract the dullness of their work. The boy must always be alert to keep up with the blower or presser.[25]

Everyone, from top to bottom, acknowledged the difficulties of night work. Chute recorded the opinion of the workers: "The general opinion among the workmen questioned seemed to be that night work was hard, physically and otherwise, that it was unnatural and undesirable. Also many said, 'It is harder for young boys than for men.' "[26] A foreman agreed:

It is a shame to employ young boys at night. I've been through it. I started myself at ten. While one boy can stand it, the most of them cannot. After a few years of night work, and what is worse, the changing of night and day shifts, they often show the effects badly.[27]

Even general managers were aware of the problem: "Night work is hard, unnatural and bad for boys. I've seen boys hurt and dwarfed by night work. I've worked nights myself and I know. It is always harder working at night and day sleep doesn't rest one like night sleep."[28]
But some managers expressed little concern:

Mr. W.J. Stuckert, Manager of Higbee Glass Company, Bridgeville, says that he likes the little boys at night because they are afraid to run away. He does not deny that he could get older boys for higher wages, but he says he prefers the smaller boys because he can handle them easier.[29]

Investigation reports also included numerous statements from physicians and school officials, both on the evils of child labor in the glasshouses and on the particular evil of night work. Illustrative comments include, first from a physician: "No one can sleep as well in day time as at night no matter how quiet the surroundings and the majority of these children are not in environments conducive to sleep. Many bright little boys who have worked at night have made very stupid men."[30] Another physician: "The boys frequently eat breakfast, loaf around the rest of the day before going to work and don't get more than four or five hours sleep in the daytime. Many of them have only two rooms and the noise from the other children in the family makes it impossible for the boy to sleep well. Anyhow, sleep in the daytime never does them as much good as sleep at night. I see them going off to work in the morning and they look like old men, not running and jumping like school boys."[31] A school official concurs: "Each year adds to the evidence that such night work saps the life from their tender bodies, giving the little fellows the appearance of dwarf-like old men."[32] Finally, a physician sums up the long-term effects: "Long working hours for children are a tax upon their vital resources, that must be paid for later on in life. The energy expended in childhood in overwork, on account of long hours, must be taken from the capital that should be expended in the physical development of the body."[33] According to investigator Jones: "The most frequent expression used by the physicians, school authorities, and workers themselves, when asked about the effect of night work upon the boys was, 'It makes them look like old men.' "[34]

Destruction of Craft: Apprenticeship and the Career Ladder

In the glass industry of the early 1900s, one observes the transformation in the mode of production from methods based on craft traditions to industrial modes of production. Most schools of thought, from neo-Marxist to institutionalist to neoclassical, tend to emphasize the role of technological advance in spurring such change. For examples, Harry Braverman emphasized the de-skilling of work brought about by machinery coupled with rationalization of management practices that captured the knowledge of the skilled craftsmen;[35] Frank Tannenbaum and Karl Polanyi emphasize the social reaction as workers attempt to right themselves in a sea of change;[36] neoclassicists gloss over the entire affair and focus only on the efficiency and productivity gains from advanced technology.[37] The role of technology cannot be dismissed in the destruction of the craft traditions of the glass industry. Emerging pressed glass technologies, as opposed to blown glass, diminished the skill and social standing of the glass blowers. Entrance into the industry of firms like Anheuser-Busch, who just wanted bottles and lots of them (and cheap ones) and did not particularly care how they were made, spurred management reforms that emphasized productive efficiency. Technology clearly pressed upon the craft traditions. But the causes of the destruction of the craft were more subtle and simple than mere technology.

Stated most simply, the beginning of the end of the craft tradition in glass occurred when fathers no longer saw the trade as viable for their sons. When fathers no longer brought their own sons into the glasshouses, the traditional craft career ladder was broken. Factories were forced to recruit boys on the open market, and such an arrangement was, in the end, unsustainable. Boys who did enter the industry had nowhere to go. Few, if any, would become apprentices on the road to journeyman. Boys' work became dead-end work and lost any of its remaining redeeming characteristics. More than the coming of technology and more than the pressure for productive efficiency, though both played an instrumental role, the destruction of the career ladder led to the destruction of the craft. And it also led to the elimination of child labor in the industry. Children as future apprentices might be tolerated; children as dog boys would not.

Traditionally, boys were required to work three to five years as helpers before they were admitted to the apprenticeship to learn the trade. "The average service in the bottle factory before the boy can begin his apprenticeship is approximately 5 years, in the tableware and chimney factory, 3 or 4 years." The apprenticeship itself lasted five years at 50 percent of the journeyman's wages. "Thus a boy entering the factory at 14 usually has 10 years of work ahead of him before he can hope to be classed as a journeyman."[38]

Opportunities to learn the trade were eagerly sought, but were hard to come by. This was attributable to two main factors. First, during the period of rapid expansion of the industry following the 1880s, large numbers were admitted to the apprenticeship, probably more than was wise. These were now working as journeymen, and most had many years remaining in their careers. So, opportunities created by attrition in the ranks of journeymen were rare. Second, mechanization and the concomitant productivity increases meant that, especially as growth in the industry slowed, there were fewer openings for journeymen. Anna Herdina obtained a description of the state of affairs at the Illinois Glass Company in 1910:

> The superintendent of the large machine and mold shop of the plant, a fine mechanic, gave some interesting facts. They are under the machinists union and are allowed 1 apprentice for the shop and 1 more for every 4 journeymen. Said the demand for a chance was great, for some time he had had about 25 boys on the waiting list. All Americans. Never had had to advertise or go far to get apprentices. Said they had no use for a boy at all until 16. Rather start a boy at 17 and 18. The more education the boy had the better. "Most of the boys starting hadn't had enough."[39]

Charles L. Chute reports that in 1909 no boys at all were admitted to the apprenticeship. By 1910, the American Flint Glass Workers were admitting two apprentices for every ten pots or one apprentice for every fifteen journeymen at continuous tanks. The Glass Bottle Blowers Association was allowing one apprentice for every twenty journeymen. "The bright, quick boy or more often the boy with a "pull" is picked out, the ordinary or slow boy has little or no chance."[40] By 1913 in western Pennsylvania, Herschel Jones estimated:

> [F]or every 100 boys under the age of sixteen that we permit to do this night work in the glass factories, not more than four stand any chance of becoming skilled tradesmen, and this chance comes only after working until they are eighteen or nineteen years old. At present, there is no prospect whatever for the boy learning the glass trade.[41]

Investigation reports contained numerous accounts of boys who hoped for the opportunity to enter the trade, but were unlikely to get it. Two illustrative accounts are these:

> Charles Barker, 17, was found employed as a boy by the Fostoria Glass Company, Moundsville, W. Va. . . . Boy first began work at 9 years old in this glass plant, working regularly there since he was 10,—7 years. He never got more than $1.20 a day. He is large, strong and able and has tried in every way to get a chance to learn the trade, but has been put off with promises so far.

> Thomas McCormick, 19, employed by J.T. & A. Hamilton (bottle factory) Pittsburgh, Pa., began at 10 years of age here. Worked 9 years straight,—boy's work all the time. No chances were given to learn the trade, although he expected and worked for it. His mother said the factory had treated the boy badly. He got discouraged and quit the job this year for a time. On trying to get back the company refused him.[42]

A traditional argument favoring the use of child labor in the glass industry, an argument grounded in the craft traditions of the industry, was losing its force. "The glass man points with pride to a blower or presser who draws a big pay, and spends proportionately, and informs you that there is a man who started as a little boy 'carrying-in.'"[43] Of course, the claim was true. Virtually all the journeymen working at the time had started as young boys. But the opportunity to learn the trade, to apprentice and to become a journeyman, was proving more and more elusive. No one recognized this sooner or more readily than the men who had come up through the trade themselves. In the past, their own sons would have had sufficient "pull" to virtually assure them a place in the trade. Now, there was no such assurance. Thus, NCLC investigators provided numerous reports from glass men on their views of the glass trade as a viable option for their own sons:

> A glass-worker at Uniontown in conversation with the investigator pointed to a boy who looked little more than sixteen and said, "That boy is nineteen years old and he don't know how to do anything else but that job of 'sticking up' that he has been doing for four years. There is no chance for a boy in this trade now. If I thought it was such a good trade, I would put my own boy in the factory, but I'm keeping him in school. He would never learn anything working in a glass house."[44]

> James Moore, factory manager and runner-in of boys talked freely. . . . said he wouldn't have his own boys in the glass factory. "They were going to stay in school." Said there was only one of the men in the factory who had his boys in.[45]

> Overseer told me that no boy of his will ever go into a glass factory. "If you want to spoil a boy, put him in a glass works."[46]

And finally, the most pointed statement of all: "I would rather send my boys straight to hell than send them by way of the glass-house."[47]

Substitutes for Child Workers

Scarcity of Boys

As the skilled adult men stopped placing their own sons into the trade, the industry was forced to recruit boys on the open market. The craft lost its traditional career progression, the employers lost an important reservoir of labor from which to recruit, and the child labor system lost the intergenerational basis that largely drove the system. Throughout the industry, but especially in areas such as western Pennsylvania and East St. Louis, where large concentrations of factories were found, there were chronic shortages of boy labor.[48]

The first response of many firms to the shortage of boy labor was to try harder to recruit boy labor.[49] Many factories hired boy-getters; that is, agents who scoured neighboring states recruiting boys. Anna Herdina's investigation report includes these entries:

Olney Bottle Co., Olney, Illinois
Mr. W.H. Modes, VP
James Moore, factory manager and runner-in of boys
Sent out the factory manager, a good boy getter, to bring in boys, mostly from Indiana. He said those brought in all 16 or over. Mr. Modes said he'd rather have them at that age "if he could get them." Blamed the laws some as making boys scarce and cost more.

Wilcox Glass Company, Robinson, Illinois (went from Findlay, Oh to Indiana to Illinois in 1905 for gas)
Mr. H.G. Wilcox
He said he had just been down to Tenn. and brought up 40 to 50 boys (all over 16). Got them in small towns and country, anywhere and paid their car fare up, guaranteeing them jobs. Said most of these boys couldn't read or write their own names.[50]

As the scarcity of boy labor persisted, the next response was to attract or retain older boys and men to do boys' work. Many firms attempted this strategy, but it too had its flaws. First, and as noted previously, older boys would not stay on unless they saw some opportunity to become tenured in the trade through the formal apprenticeship process. Second, if they were to stay, they would have to be paid a substantially higher wage. The problem with this was not only cost, but the fact that it violated custom and tradition in compensation practices. Men's work had its established rate of pay, and boys' work, whether performed by boys or men, had its established rate. Both the unions and the employers shared an interest in maintaining the traditional wage differentials, in relative terms, between men's work and boys' work. This kept boys' wages low and helped fuel the boy shortage.[51]

Negroes and Foreigners

As the chronic boy labor shortage persisted, and as older boys and grown men refused to do boys' work at the traditional rates of pay, employers were forced to turn to their other reliable sources of cheap labor—blacks and immigrants. Boy-getters became generalized labor recruiters. As early as 1904, Harriet Van der Vaart noted, "The Factories offer the unskilled labor, which *attracts* the Foreigners, and in large glass factories in Illinois the manufacturers send out agents to induce foreigners and ignorant people to come in; but it is because they cannot get the boys."[52]

Likewise, in 1910, officials of the Illinois Glass Company told Anna Herdina:

> As to scarcity of boys, said always some difficulty to get enough but have been getting along all right by using men. No difficulty experienced in getting men (Mostly foreigners and negroes) to work at boys pay ($1.25) at boys work except in the warm weather. Mr. Hurr figured that there were, entire plant, 350 men doing boys work. Said 4 years ago (when he came) there were easily 100 more boys used.[53]

In contrast to the Illinois Glass Company that recruited immigrants, Joseph Nester of the Obear-Nester works in East St. Louis recruited black girls to do boys' work. Anna Herdina observed:

> From 10 to 12 negro girls working right among the boys and men. Foreman said they took them only from 16 yrs old up. All get $1. day, here all work at "warming-in." . . . "Negro girls were good workers, better than boys." "Trouble getting the girls? Well, I should say not. All we have to do is to put an ad in the paper and the next morning the yard will be black with them."[54]

The substitution of blacks and immigrants for the boys was, as it was always, accompanied by controversy. Even those who generally supported progressive views, worker rights, and abolition of child labor were made uneasy by the changing composition of the workforce. Unions were clearly ambivalent. To illustrate, the Anheuser-Busch bottle plants were among the first to eliminate child labor. But, as Harriet Van der Vaart reported, this was not due to the endorsement of the local union:

> I went to the president of the glass blowers union. He advocated making the age limit *twelve* rather than fourteen, and thought it would be better to do away with all restrictions, rather than allow the cheap labor to come in that was taking the place of the boys. . . . I was told citizens generally in Streator regretted the large class of foreigners who were constantly being brought in to take the place of children in the factories, and it made many of them question the Child Labor Laws.[55]

When it came to the mixing of the races, even some of the NCLC investigators expressed concern. Anna Herdina noted, "Combination looks bad to me. Foreman said had trouble sometimes but watched things close. . . . Moral effect of this mixing must be bad."[56]

On the Role of Mechanization

Machinery, technological advance, and mechanization clearly played a profound role in the elimination of child labor from the glass industry. But it is important to distinguish the causes of technological advance from its effects. It often appears that the motivation to implement advanced technology often lay outside the technology itself in areas associated with child labor. That is, as in mining, the technology that would eliminate child labor was widely available well before it was widely implemented. But once advanced technology was introduced, it had its own profound effects in the further reduction of child labor.

In the early stages of industrialization in the glass industry, technological advance was associated with increased use of boy labor. The development of the continuous tank simultaneously enabled dramatic growth of the industry and drew thousands of children into its employment. In contrast, continued technological advance as the industry matured tended to reduce child labor. The next major development following the continuous tank was the semiautomatic machine that produced pressed glass. Relative to blown glass, this resulted in a substantial reduction in all labor, both boys and men. Production of fruit jars was the first to move away from blown glass and into pressed glass. In 1904, Harriet Van der Vaart was greatly impressed by her visit to the new Ball Jar factory, both for its magnificent modern machinery and production methods and for the fact that it employed very little child labor:

> By far the most interesting factory I visited was the Ball Brothers Glass works in Muncie. Interesting because it showed the progress that is coming in the glass industry through machinery. . . . They were just putting in $60,000.00 worth of new machinery. Mr. Ball said the advisability of putting in machinery and turning men out was a question the firm were discussing. The specialty of this house is making fruit jars, and all the blowing is done by machinery. Each machine requires two men and two boys. This does away with the employing of *one* boy. The gatherer, a man, takes the melted glass from the furnace and drops it into the mould. The presser, a man also, cuts off the required amount, turns the press and applies the machinery that blows the bottle. A boy sits on the other side and takes the bottle from the mould and another boy carries it to the

furnace. They had machinery at one time that carried the bottles but it was not a success, as it required two men to work the machine. It was taken out, but Mr. Ball said it would only be a short time until they had the right kind of machinery to carry the bottles. . . . In the room where the glass tops to the jars were made it only required one man to each machine. This man took the melted glass from the furnace and dropped it into the mould, the machine cut off the required amount, pressed it and turned it out onto a little plate, which dropped it into a groove where it ran down and dropped into a box. Several boys were stationed by the grooves to see that nothing impeded or interfered with each top finding its right destination. When this factory is running full force they employ about fourteen hundred people and four hundred between the ages of fourteen and sixteen.[57]

Others operating with the automatic machines also tended to rely less on child labor. At a new plant of the Thatcher Manufacturing Company in Streator, Illinois, Anna Herdina observed:

Plant here 1½ years old, running 2 Owens automatic machines making milk bottles only. Now building addition for two more machines. Mr. Niver, Supt. said not used no boys under 16 and never had here. Youngest 17 or 18. The law hadn't affected them at all. The automatic machine running continuously, he said, requires steady reliable help hence boys not used.[58]

Automated conveyor systems would, one day, perform much of the boy work in moving the product from one stage to the next in the production process. A number of employers experimented with different automated systems, but none had been found fully satisfactory. Automated conveyor systems would not come along until well after the boys had been removed from the glasshouses. But some methods of conveyance were resulting in the replacement of boys by men. Herschel Jones described a device coming into use in the glass factories of western Pennsylvania by 1912:

Several of the factories visited by the writer were using the "peanut roasters" or warming ovens into which the ware is put on trays as it is taken from the moulds. When a tray is filled it is taken from the oven and carried to the lehrs. In carrying these trays one man can do the work of two or more boys. In the Keystone Bottle Company factory at Uniontown two men were carrying for eight "shops" with no difficulty, while at least four boys would have been required without the use of the ovens.[59]

Eventually technology would displace most boys' work. In that sense, it is clear that technology caused much of the reduction in child labor. But what caused technology? Ironically, the child labor problem was often a direct or indirect cause for the introduction of technology. Where boys were scarce or expensive, machines could substitute. Lewis Hine received a letter from an official of the Travis Glass Company of Clarksburg, West Virginia, who understood the relationship of reciprocal causality between the child labor problem and technology. On one hand, he acknowledged that machines were eliminating boys. On the other hand, he credited the agitation over the boy labor problem for the introduction of those machines:

> In regard to the boy labor employed in glass houses operating by machine methods, would say that while the machine has reduced the number of boys required, it has not dispensed with them altogether, although it has made necessary the use of a larger and older class of boys than was formerly employed.

> The two things that have brought about the introduction of machinery into the glass trade have been first the arbitrary and extravagant demands of labor organizations, and second, the persistent agitation of the boy labor problem. While the old-time manufacturer is faced with new problems by the introduction of machinery, yet the business as a manufacturing business is not suffering thereby, in fact it is increasing and expanding in proper proportion to the expansion of the country, and were it not for this introduction of machinery the glass trade today would give employment to many thousands of people at a very much higher rate of wages than they are now able to earn. Whether or not the introduction of machinery and the removal of men and boys from glass houses has been or will be a good thing for them and the country in general, is, in our opinion, a debatable question that we are neither able nor disposed to pass upon.[60]

Similarly, officials of the Illinois Glass Company in Alton, Illinois, credited the 1903 Illinois law with providing the impetus for advanced technology:

> Charles Levis, Secy., very kind and willing to give information. Said, "When the law (night and 8 h.) was passed we thought it was going to put us out of business, but like everything else we found a way out." Said their way out had been to use men very largely when they couldn't

get older boys and to bring in the automatic machine. Claimed the laws had largely caused the invention and introduction of the automatic at this time.[61]

On the Role of the Law and Its Enforcement

In 1911, Charles L. Chute conducted an extensive study of the glass industry in Illinois, Indiana, Ohio, Pennsylvania, and West Virginia. Its main purpose was to compare the effects of law on child labor in the more progressive states of Ohio and Illinois with the more backward states of Pennsylvania, Indiana, and West Virginia. Ohio and Illinois both had a minimum age of fourteen, prohibited night work for those under sixteen and limited their hours to eight per day, and had what was considered an effective system of factory inspection. Reformers were gearing up for legislative campaigns in each of the other states. Pennsylvania and Indiana had the fourteen-year minimum age and limited the hours of those under sixteen to ten per day. West Virginia still had a twelve-years minimum age and no limitation on hours.

Particularly galling to reformers was the situation in Pennsylvania with the "infamous glass exception." In 1909, when the Pennsylvania child labor law was revised, reformers had sought, and obtained, a prohibition on night work for those under sixteen. But the prohibition contained an exception for "continuous industries"; that is, for the glasshouses. "The exception was obtained through the power of the glass manufacturers and is for their benefit expressly."[62]

Chute visited ninety-nine factories, representing 58 percent of all the plants in the five states and 39 percent of all the plants in the country.[63] Table 5.1 summarizes in the aggregate some of his key findings.

Chute acknowledged that his counts of boys under 16 were undercounts, but asserts that use of the numbers was suitable for comparative purposes.[64] Nevertheless, he found 2,045 of 32,308 employees (or 6.3 percent) to be under sixteen. Extrapolating this figure to the entire glass industry, he estimated 5,240 under sixteen nationwide.[65]

In Ohio and Illinois 685, 4.4 percent, of the workers were under sixteen, whereas in Pennsylvania, Indiana, and West Virginia 1,360, or 8.1 percent were under sixteen, a substantial difference.[66] It is important to remember that, while Chute counted the number under sixteen, the minimum age in all states except West Virginia was fourteen, so employing children fourteen to sixteen in all these states was legal.

Table 5.1

Children Under Sixteen in Ninety-nine Midwest Glasshouses, 1911

	Plants	Total employees	Under 16	% of Workforce
Illinois	11	5,520	209	3.8
Ohio	28	10,065	476	4.7
Indiana	31	10,280	692	6.7
West Virginia	14	4,245	382	9.0
Pennsylvania	15	2,198	286	13.0
Total	99	32,308	2,045	6.3

Source: Excerpted from table in Chute, NCLC Investigation Report 314, p. 20.

The lower levels of child labor in Ohio and Illinois were attributed to two other features in their laws: (1) the prohibition on night work; and (2) the eight-hour-per-day limit.

The prohibition on night work not only reduced use of boys under sixteen at night, but also reduced the use of boys under sixteen overall. In some Ohio and Illinois plants it was possible to obtain data from the time before night work was prohibited to compare with the 1911 data. Chute concluded, "In the sixteen plants where it was possible to secure actual figures of the number of children employed before the law was enforced it was found that less than one fifth as many were used now as were being used when law was passed."[67]

As a consequence of the law, many plants were using older boys and men, especially on the night shift. While they demanded somewhat higher wages, most employers acknowledged "there was no increased cost because of the greater efficiency of older boys and men."[68] The hours laws also made a difference in Ohio and Illinois. Illinois had adopted the eight-hour law for children under sixteen in 1903, Ohio in 1908. Indiana and Pennsylvania had ten-hour laws and West Virginia had no limit. The Glass Bottle Blowers Union had established 8½ hours as the normal shift, day or night.[69] Since the normal shift in unionized glass houses was 8½ hours, the hours laws presented problems only in Ohio and Illinois. Nearly all managers complained of the inconvenience this imposed. Most plants adjusted by dismissing the boys one half-hour early and either replaced them with older boys from the oncoming shift (who subsequently worked nine hours) or by suspending a portion of the plant's operations for this half-hour. Joseph Nester of the Obear-Nester Glass Company in East St. Louis complained, "I have to let off from 16 to 20 boys under 16 at 4:30 and close down 4 shops; 12 blowers have to quit then too." Chute was surprised to find that, "No cases were found of plants which have reduced the working hours of all their employees to 8 in order to employ children more conveniently, although the result has been predicted."[70]

It also appears that Ohio and Illinois had better records in regard to violations of the minimum-age provisions. While his search was by no means exhaustive, Chute was able to prove only three under fourteen in Ohio and one in Illinois. In Indiana, thirty-five violations were proven involving twelve- and thirteen-year-old boys. Fifteen of the thirty-one factories violated the law. In Pennsylvania two of fifteen plants violated the age limit. In West Virginia, the only state of the five without a four-teen-year age limit, eight of the fourteen plants employed at least forty-two boys under fourteen.[71] One problem with the Indiana law was that it still required only a notarized affidavit from a parent as proof of the child's age. Chute found that in a majority of the Indiana factories he visited, "some one of its officers or an employee who had taken out a Notary Public's license and was issuing affidavits from the office of the company."[72] This was a problem that had earlier caught the attention of Harriet Van der Vaart.[73] In an earlier period, when glass blowers still brought their own sons into the trade, this arrangement enabled them to put their boys to work at whatever age they saw fit. Later, as boys became scarce, and especially boys of legal age, the system created incentives to encourage parents to falsely state the age of their child. Chute noted:

> Abuses of this kind were found. In Dunkirk, Ind. at the Marling, Hart Bottle Co., Mr. Mat. Hart is owner, manager and his own notary and swears out all affidavits for himself in his own office. Many extremely young looking boys were seen in the plant who were to all appearances much under fourteen but all had affidavits.[74]

One of the most common arguments against any improvement in child labor laws was that it would put children out of work, and, as a result, both the child and the child's family would be made worse off by the loss of the child's wages. Chute was asked to address this question of the relation between child labor laws and poverty as part of his overall investigation. He chose Alton, Illinois, as "an ideal field for the study of 'the poverty question.'" While this aspect of his study was not as rigor-ous or systematic as others, he did spend three days in Alton making home visits and "interviewing city officials, school authorities, men and women engaged in relief work and others." His observations include:

> Until recently the glass industry was practically the only one in Alton employing boys. From 200 to 400 boys under sixteen, most of them working partly by night, were employed there at the time the present Illinois Child Labor laws began to be enforced. . . . At the time that the first raids were made upon this plant which led up to the strict law enforcement of to-day, the town of Alton was full of poor families many of whom existed, it would seem, through the labor of their young boys in the glass plant. Many of these boys were thrown out. There was little other work. What was the result? For a time suffering among some of the poorer families. That fact was well established by the testimony of those who at that time visited among the poor and dispensed relief. It did not last however. An adjustment took place. Public and private relief, ineffective before, was organized. Some of the boys went back to school. To-day there is less poverty by far than before the law was enforced.[75]

The organized private relief to which investigator Chute referred included a scholarship program developed by the Illinois Consumers League. Families of boys who were put out of work could apply for an income replacement subsidy on condition that the boy return to school. It was found that many families needed and benefited from this subsidy, but many families did not need it. Furthermore, of those who did, most did not need the subsidy for a long period of time.

Employer Response to the Law

Employers varied in their views of, and their responses to, the child labor laws. Some of the larger firms had bitterly opposed the laws and resisted compliance for a time, but were grudgingly moving toward acceptance and compliance. Typical of these was Joseph Nester of the Obear-Nester Glass Company in East St. Louis. Nester was not only manager of the factory, but he was also the chief spokesman for the industry in the Illinois legislature. Anna Herdina had a "long talk" with him in 1910:

> Objected to laws as tending to make boys scarce. Said they were getting along all right now (by depending on negro girls) but had had trouble

getting boys and getting them to stay. . . . Mr. Nester seemed to attack the Compulsory education laws more than law of 1903. We had a long and hot (but friendly) discussion of this. He said, "The American boys are not learning trades any more." Blamed this to schools and laws. "There is no possible chance of a boy who stays in school till 15 (just a possibility at 14) going to work and learning a trade." . . . Said they had been prosecuted a No. of times for using boys illegally. Were prosecuted by Davies and paid fines about five years ago. Said there was one time when they thought they couldn't obey the law without shutting down the plant so they took chances. Since had got adjusted and were living up to law strictly. Inspectors had tried hard to catch them but hadn't been able to lately. Last year about 8 inspectors surrounded the plant at 11 P.M. and stormed it, but found nothing wrong, he said. Found it best policy to obey law whether believing in it or not.[76]

Similarly, Charles Levis, secretary of the Illinois Glass Company in Alton, told Herdina:

"When the law (night and 8 h.) was passed we thought it was going to put us out of business, but like everything else we found a way out." . . . Said the law (of '03) was enforced on them gradually. They violated it a great deal, he intimated, and were prosecuted a number of times until 2 to 3 years ago they decided to live up to it absolutely and had since.[77] (See, for example, Figure 5.3)

In contrast, some employers were quite supportive of the child labor laws. Herdina also interviewed a Mr. Niver, superintendent of a relatively new factory in Streator, Illinois: "Mr. Niver said, as far as they were concerned 'the law could be made 21 and they would adjust to it O.K.' He believed that the law should require boys to stay in school till they were 16. Would rather have educated boys for his work or for any work."[78]

Another interesting company that never had much use for boy labor was the Standard Co-operative Glass Company of Marion, Indiana. The company was owned by the glassblowers themselves and was operated as a producer cooperative.[79] While it was apparently a profitable operation, it engaged in a number of unusual practices. For example, they did not operate a night shift. But most significantly, for purposes here, they did not use young boys.[80] They would have been happy to see a prohibition on night work and elevation of the minimum age in Indiana.

Figure 5.3. *Illinois Glass Company.* Alton, Illinois. May, 1910. Group of glass workers Shops 6 & 7, Illinois Glass Co. 12:45 P.M. Even the tiny chap on left end of photo was working. He is a Polish boy who cannot understand English. I saw him at work just before 1 P.M. *(Courtesy of the Library of Congress, Prints and Photographs Division, Lewis Wickes Hine National Child Labor Committee Collection, LC-1481.)*

Posture of the Unions on the Child Labor Question

As employer viewpoints varied, so too did the viewpoints expressed by union officials. A few adamantly opposed the child labor laws because they would result in bringing in blacks and immigrants to replace American boys. To keep out the "cheap labor" that was coming in to replace the boys, the local union president at one of the Anheuser-Busch bottle factories in Streator advocated reducing the minimum age to twelve and eliminating all restrictions of hours.[81]

More often, at least when pressed on the issue, union officials were generally supportive of the trend toward greater restrictions. In contrast to his colleague at the Anheuser-Busch factory, Mr. Hurley, president of the Glass Blowers Union at the Illinois Glass Company in Alton, assured Harriet Van der Vaart "that all associations stood for prohibition of children working under fourteen, but had never put themselves on record for sixteen." Even in Indiana, as early as 1905, a Mr. Robertson, president of the Glass Blowers Union of Terre Haute, said he was in favor of prohibiting night work for children under sixteen and he thought the association generally would stand for it.[82] Likewise, Herschel Jones reported that, by 1912, T.W. Rowe, president of the American Flint Glass Workers Union for western Pennsylvania, had "come out publicly" against children under sixteen on night work, saying that other states had adapted fine and it was neither necessary nor desirable.[83]

Clearly the unions had an important influence on the child labor question. As laws were enacted, the union had to accommodate its effects. For example, when laws prohibiting night work for boys under sixteen were adopted, some firms stopped the practice of rotating shifts—alternating day and night shifts—for the boys. Boys under sixteen were put on day shifts, and the night shift was staffed by older boys or blacks and immigrants. This mode of accommodation, however, required the consent of the skilled union workers, who remained subject to rotating shifts. Generally, the unions made the necessary accommodations. Mr. Hurley, the president of the Glass Blowers Union at the Illinois Glass Company in Alton, said glassblowers did not object to two sets of boys, or workmen, and that some preferred night work.[84]

In sum, there were union officials and union men who stood against child labor, and others who stood for it, and probably more of the former than the latter. But there was no consensus union position. More significantly, it did not occupy a high position on the union's bargaining agenda. The trade was already hard-pressed by encroaching mechanization, an oversupply of journeyman blowers, and the destruction or erosion of the craft traditions of the industry. The unions had other more pressing problems to worry about than the age of the helpers who staffed their furnaces. Furthermore, in contrast to some other industries, journeymen did not compete directly with boys for either wages or work. Because of the strength and influence of the unions, wages of adult men (who had come through the union apprenticeship program) were fixed at one scale; and wages of the boy labor (whether performed by boys, older boys, black girls, or immigrants) were paid on an entirely separate, nonunion scale. So long as the union could maintain the differential between men's work and boys' work, it cared little who performed the boys' work.

Ultimately, most local unions were indifferent to the child labor question. If they had to confront it, they would. But if they did not have to think about it, there were plenty of other things on their mind. As told to

Harriet Van der Vaart, the president of the Glass Blowers Union of Marion, Indiana, may have summed it up best when he said they did "not have definite ideas on the child labor question" and was "not sure where the men would stand."[85]

Conclusion

In the end, child labor was eliminated from the glass industry through the complex interaction of several key factors, including emerging law, the reform efforts themselves, increasing mechanization, the chronic scarcity of boys coupled with the growing availability of cheap substitutes, and the erosion of the industry's traditional career hierarchy.

Reformers emphasized getting good laws in place and then establishing effective inspection and enforcement programs. Law undoubtedly had important direct effects on the reduction of child labor, but it is easy to overemphasize these effects. Even Harriet Van der Vaart acknowledged that the law was not the most important factor. After touring Illinois in 1904, with its model law for the time, she toured Indiana, a state with a much more backward law, in 1905 and observed that the number of children in Indiana glasshouses was decreasing also. Reluctantly she concluded, "I am afraid that the 'Child Labor Law' is one of the smaller factors in causing the reduced number."[86]

But if it is easy to overstate the direct effects of law, it is also easy to overlook important indirect effects. The agitation of reformers to secure improved laws generated publicity that, of itself, had some effect in reducing child labor. Furthermore, the law hastened mechanization and exacerbated the boy scarcity that exerted further pressure to reduce the use of child labor. Mechanization, in turn, had powerful direct effects on reduction of child labor. But it, too, was, in part, an effect of developing law and the chronic scarcity of boys. Mechanization also had important indirect effects in the erosion of the craft traditions of the industry that made the employment of blacks and immigrants a more palatable alternative to boys. The availability of blacks and immigrants as substitutes for boys was important, but this would not have been considered an appropriate alternative were it not for the chronic boy shortages and the erosion of craft traditions when fathers stopped sending their sons into the trade.

In sum, just as a confluence of factors had created the child labor problem in the glass industry, a confluence of causally interrelated factors almost seemed to conspire to eliminate the child labor problem.

6. COTTON TEXTILES
Herod of Industries

Figure 6.1   The Golf Links

The Golf Links

The golf links lie so near the mill
That almost every day
The laboring children can look out
And see the men at play.

Sarah N. Cleghorn
New York Call, *November 11, 1917. Artist, Boardman Robinson.*

In many ways and for many reasons, cotton textiles (and especially southern cotton textiles) became the major battleground on which the social, political, and economic war over child labor was fought. Of all industries, it received the most attention from the National Child Labor Committee, and most of the focus was on the South.[1]

In 1870, when New England dominated cotton textiles, 13,767 or 14.5 percent of its workforce was children under sixteen. As a proportion of the workforce, southern mills employed a larger proportion of children—23 percent—but the number of working children was small—2,343. By 1905, the proportion of the New England cotton textile workforce under sixteen had fallen to 6 percent (9,385 children). In the South, the workforce continued at 23 percent children. But now the numbers were no longer trivial. By the most conservative estimate, from the Census of Manufactures, there were 27,538 under sixteen in southern mills.[2] According to the household census in 1900, the number was 60,000. Alexander McKelway, using data from the 1904–5 Industry "Blue Book," estimated that in the Carolinas, Georgia, and Alabama alone, there were 62,000 under fourteen; 75 percent of the spinners were under fourteen and only 30 percent of the entire workforce was over twenty-one.[3] Estimates varied widely, but even the most conservative estimates suggested a large problem that could no longer be ignored.

Child labor in southern cotton textiles was at its peak when Edgar Gardner Murphy of Alabama approached Florence Kelley and Felix Adler with his proposal for a National Child Labor Committee. In turn, abolition of child labor from the southern mills became one of the principal aims of the committee.

A Theory of Child Labor

Industry attempted to dismiss the child labor problem by arguing that reformers exaggerated greatly.[4] As the NCLC began providing irrefutable proof and denials became less effective, the industry and its apologists developed the theory that child labor in southern cotton textiles was inevitable, benign, and self-correcting. It was inevitable owing to certain factors unique to the southern industry. It was benign because it provided children with a better life than they would otherwise have had. And it was self-correcting within a few generations (and so there was no need for meddling by reformers or intervention by government).

Mrs. J. Borden Harriman, chair of the Welfare Committee of the National Civic Federation, articulated her version of this widely held theory of child labor in southern cotton textiles in her address to the NCLC annual meeting in 1910.[5] It seems that "poor whites" who had generally been "illiterate, immoral and indifferent" before the Civil War, found themselves even more desperate after the war: "[F]inding that they could not hold their own unless they moved away from the populous sections, isolated themselves in the mountain districts of North and South Carolina, Georgia, Alabama and Tennessee." Once living in the isolation of the mountains, their morals became "increasingly lax" so that "the tendency was for a lower social condition each year, and with each generation, until this class of people seemed nearly hopeless." Fortunately for the hapless mountain folk, the emerging textile industry offered, in addition to work for the whole family, "good, new houses," "kindergartens, schools, churches, and frequently clubhouses," and some provided welfare workers and even the occasional nurse. As to child labor, the only reason it existed was because "The first generation of operatives coming from conditions above described brought fingers so stiffened, hands so hardened by toil as to be totally unfit for handling the soft, unspun cotton; it followed that the children, with still supple fingers, were pressed into service as spinners." But Mrs. Harriman was able to reassure the audience in attendance at the NCLC meeting that this would soon pass. She pointed out "the significant fact that the second generation is awakening to the importance of sending its children to school and keeping them out of the mills during their tender years" and concluded, "[C]hild labor is one phase in the evolution of the Southern cotton industry. And it is surely passing."[6]

Always the gentleman, but always a southern patriot, Alexander McKelway replied to Mrs. Harriman's ruminations. As to her "theory of the settlement of the mountain regions" he ventured, "I was under the impression that the mountain regions had been settled before the Civil War, even before the Revolutionary War. I have a dim recollection that it was the mountain folk of the Watauga that won the battle at King's

Mountain and saved the Revolutionary cause when it was at its lowest ebb." As to Mrs. Harriman's characterization of the South's "poor whites" and their illiteracy, immorality, and indifference, McKelway countered, "This was a serious indictment of practically a whole people. . . . So far as my own memory and experience recall, we were all 'poor whites' after the war. Those who were not were under suspicion of having sacrificed too little for the Southern cause." McKelway asked why, if the cotton mills were the saviors of poor whites, illiteracy rates remained so high and health conditions so poor in the mill villages. Finally, on her theory of child labor, he charged that it "[I]gnores the whole history of the cotton-mill industry,—two hundred years of it in England and one hundred years of it in America. It was not an accident that the children were employed." Child labor had been a prominent feature in this "Herod of industries" wherever it had operated. It was hardly unique to the South.[7]

Mill Village and Family Wage

Borrowing from northern experience, but adding substantially to it, the southern cotton textile industry worked out the most highly evolved forms of the Rhode Island system of mill villages and family wages. The mill villages invariably provided housing for many or all of their employees. Most villages also provided a store, a church, and a school. Many mills went well beyond these minimums to provide: (1) an extensive array of social welfare programs, from medical care to gardens and libraries; (2) economic institutions, from banks to funeral parlors; and (3) all the services expected of a municipal government, from law enforcement to fire protection to streets and sewage.

The mill village, and whatever amenities it provided, undoubtedly represented a gain in material standard of living for those families who migrated in from the mountains and surrounding farms. What was hardship to the farmer was a boon to the mill owner. As prices for raw cotton fell, the farmer's loss was proportionate to the mill owner's gain. But the mill owner benefited doubly. As some proportion of farmers were forced from the land each year, they had few alternatives but to go to the mill. Low cotton prices first reduced the owner's cost of raw materials and second generated an ample labor supply by triggering the migration to the mills. Since those who were forced from their farms tended to be among the most hard-pressed, the mill villages provided valuable relief.[8]

Conditions in the mill villages were indeed better than the conditions that immediately preceded migration. But once in the mill village, there was often no going back. Few families were ever able to return to the mountains or farms when conditions there improved. Many families sold their rural property in the process of moving to the mills. Many others carried substantial debt as a result of their move. Once the move was made, the mill controlled everything, including the villagers: "Everything belongs to it—most of the men and all the kids."[9] An NCLC investigator described how the mill villages engendered a fierce dependency that could be almost impossible to escape:

> [O]ne of the unfortunate possibilities of the company store; these people from the country are lent the money for transportation, and are given house rent for a month. They arrive with no money, make very small wages while under a "learner," and usually even less for a time when finally started independently. During this time, unaccustomed to handling much money, and therefore, greatly overestimating the purchasing power of what they are getting, and expecting to get, they run heavily into debt to the store, very soon they learn that always the rent comes out at the two-weeks payday first, then transportation debts begin to come out, and finally clear of these two they give up hope of ever getting square with the store. This may partly account for a certain unpopularity of the company store, which at first I found difficult to account for, and for the pronounced preference for the "other store" to which I find many of them going when it is much farther from the house.[10]

The Family Wage and Child Labor

If the mill village imposed a fierce dependency of the family on the mill, it also, in turn, imposed a fierce dependency of the mill on the labor of children. Mill villages were a necessary expense, but they were still very expensive. Where only housing was provided, this still entailed a considerable capital investment. Further, it was a nonproductive capital investment. Little or no work for the mill was conducted in the homes. Mill owners had a strong incentive to spread the cost of the mill village over as many workers as possible. Where schools, churches, and other public amenities were provided, the incentive to employ as much of the village as possible was magnified. Where workers fell into debt to company stores, banks, hospitals, funeral parlors, and other potential profit centers, debt encouraged the workers themselves to offer up their children. In any given family, those too old, disabled, or cantankerous to work could be carried as a cost at the whim of the household or the mill. Those too young to work could be carried as an investment. But those who could work, and thereby pay returns to corporate investment and household debt, were most highly prized. Households and mill owners alike had strong incentives to get as many of the children as possible to work as early as possible. Similarly, large families with more available or potential hands had stronger incentives to go to the mills, and mills had strong incentives to recruit large families.

If initial recruitment efforts involved inducing families to migrate from the mountains and farms to the mill villages, once families were in the mill villages, their young children constituted a captive group of recruits to replenish the workforce. Specific arrangements varied from village to village; the so-called Pelzer contract associated with South Carolina's Pelzer "show mills" provided the model. Under the Pelzer contract, the mill contracted with the head of the household for the labor of the entire family. The contract provided that children over five were required to attend the company school every day it was in session and that children over twelve were required to work in the mill unless released from work by the superintendent. In this way, a new cohort of workers would be introduced to the mills each year.

Obviously, children had little choice about these arrangements. Grover Hardin, who entered the mill at age ten, recalled that children had to endure whatever conditions existed. So long as their parents were there, the children could not quit. Noting that the mills preferred large families, he recalled, "They're glad to get them big families. Then they can scatter them out, over the mill, and most of that time the children would have to stay, you know, till they got up big enough to set out on their own. Whether they liked the mill or not, why they'd have to stay. . . . They couldn't say, 'Well, I'll quit. I'll go somewheres else.'"[11]

The presence of children in the workplace also restricted the mobility of the parents. The superintendent of a small mill in Munford, Alabama, told an NCLC investigator that "he always makes a special effort to get workers in families because then he has a greater hold on them as they can't move about from place to place too readily."[12] Further, it was not just the mill owners who insisted that the children be put to work at an early age. Parents, too, would insist that their children be hired and would provide false statements of age if necessary. "They argued that if they raised the children to the age of ten or twelve they should begin to get money back on their investment. If the children went to school they would probably marry before going to work and the parent would lose all he had spent."[13]

The Helper System

By the time the children came of age for regular work in the mill—whatever the regular age was at the time and place, and in accordance with the child's status—they were already well socialized into the regimen of the mill and well trained in many of the work processes. The character of the training and socialization of very young children was conditioned on the presence or absence of a mill school.

Where there was no mill school, many families had few alternatives but to bring the children to work. Under this informal arrangement, youngest children played more than they worked. Their only real reason for being there was to keep them under parental supervision. As the children gained familiarity with the mill, they were expected to contribute to production in simple ways. At a small Mississippi mill, an investigator observed, "One little girl whose mother said she was seven years old, was industriously taking the waste off the roller covers of the spinning frames all the time I was there. Her mother said: 'I am jest keeping her out of mischief.' Another girl apparently nine years old was helping her mother at the spooling machine."[14]

The "helper system" enabled the mill to gain production from very young children and to train the workforce of the future while disavowing a direct employment relationship. The system was also beneficial to the parents. As children grew older and made a greater contribution to the work process, there were certainly economic gains. But where the youngest children were concerned, the greater advantage of the helper system was that it provided reassurance to parents. Investigator Herschel H. Jones described the "most shocking sight" of little Sally Daniel, age six, "busily working shifting bobbins at the same frame with her mother." The parents claimed she did not work regularly, but "only helped her mother" here today because she was "too sick to go to school so they brought her here where it was warm."[15]

Eventually, as the children were able to work more regularly, they would begin to receive their own wage. At this point the children began paying a return on the investment of both the mill and the parents. Investigator Harvey P. Vaughn described a family in a small mill in Athens, Georgia:

This Mill employs only about thirty hands. The whole family comes to the mill does just about as it pleases. Some very small children were playing in the mill. Sam Bowles, 11 years old, was working here. He was getting 40 cents a day. He stood near a woman, one of the weavers, as I talked to him she said she made about $1.00 a day. She said she was a widow and had secured an ordinary's certificate for Sam. She said another one of her children 13 years old worked there and made 75 cents a day, another one 15, made $1.00. Her husband had been dead six years. . . . I told her that with all that help she would be getting married if she didn't look out. She laughed, said she had been married four years already that her husband worked in a lumber yard right near.[16]

An account from another small Georgia mill describes Mattie E. Brown, "a poor widow." Between her own children and her younger brothers and sisters left to her care after her father's death, she had seven children working in the mill, ages ten, eleven, twelve, thirteen, two fourteen, and fifteen. "All seven have steady jobs. . . . She said she was lucky because all of the seven children from her family were healthy and looked older than they really are."[17]

Where a mill school was present, the socialization and training program of the helper system could be coordinated and integrated with the educational program of the mill. One famous practice was that of "dinner-toting" (Figure 6.2). NCLC investigators received numerous reports from schoolteachers and principals about the interruptions in the middle of the school day when children left school to carry dinners to their parents and older siblings in the mill.[18] While their elders ate, the children helped out by sweeping, cleaning, or tending their parent's machine. Many schools observed that, as children approached the age for regular work in the mill, they never returned from their dinner-toting mission for the afternoon session of school.

Children not only were available to help out and to train for their role in replenishing the labor supply, but also they could be a reserve labor supply, helping the mill accommodate to fluctuations in production schedules and product demand. Many schoolteachers commented on how enrollment and attendance plummeted when there was a "call to the mill." In 1907, investigator Alfred E. Seddon interviewed Miss O'Leary, teacher of the primary class at the Meridian Cotton Mill School in Mississippi. While she had ninety-three children on her class roll, only forty-five were present. "She accounted for the difference by saying that a number had left to work in the factory—that they wanted in the factory

Figure 6.2 *Dinner Toters.* Columbus, Ga., Eagle & Phenix Mill April, 1913. "Dinner-Toters" waiting for the gate to open. This is carried on more in Columbus than in any other other city I know, and by smaller children. Many of them are paid by the week for doing it, and carry, sometimes, ten or more a day. They go around in the mill, often help tend to the machines, which often run at noon, and so learn the work. A teacher told me the mothers expect the children to learn this way, long before they are of proper age. (See also Vaughn's Georgia Report, April, 1913) *(Courtesy of the Library of Congress, Prints and Photographs Division, Lewis Wickes Hine National Child Labor Committee Collection, LC-USZ62–47525.)*

all the children they could get."[19] Four years later, Lewis Hine interviewed this same Miss O'Leary, now principal of the Meridian School. The cotton mill had been closed for a year now and half of the mill houses were vacant. Still, school attendance was much better than when all the houses were occupied and the mill was running.[20] It should be noted that whatever schooling children may have received in the lower grades, most had gone to the mill by the time they would have reached the upper grades. In most mill schools, the upper grades were reserved for the sons and daughters of management.[21]

Spinners and Doffers: Girls at Work and Boys at Play

While children could be found in all work areas performing nearly the full range of work in the mills, they tended to be concentrated in certain occupations and rare in others. For example, few young children worked as weavers and virtually none worked as loom fixers. Of course, none worked as foremen, overseers, or other managers, though some of the older children in child crews may have assumed some informal supervisory roles. The industry claimed that "no child ever stood at a loom," but the NCLC was able to document a few cases in mills here and there.[22] Usually, the only children working in the weave room of the mill were sweepers. Weavers were adult men and women. The work required higher skill and was more physically strenuous than most work performed by children. Weavers were also better paid. For the men, weaving was often the first rung on a career ladder leading to higher-skill loom-fixing and maintenance work or into management.

Children were concentrated in the spinning rooms of the mills to the extent that, in some mills, the spinning room was referred to as the "Children's Department." Bertha Awford Black, who entered the mill at age eleven after moving from the farm with her family, recalled it as "Just nothing but children."[23] The children most commonly worked as spinners, doffers, and sweepers. Boys generally started as doffers and sweepers, but many progressed to spinning after gaining experience. Girls were more likely to start out as spinners.

Doffing involved replacing full bobbins, filled by the spinners, with empty ones. It was intermittent work involving relatively short bursts of high activity with extended rest (or play) pauses in between. At the required moments, the doffers invaded the mill and changed over every bobbin on every spindle as quickly as possible so that spinning could commence again. In mills with more modern machinery, which usually stood taller than earlier designs, boys often had to climb onto the spinning frames to replace the bobbins. Lewis Hine describes his visit to the Bibb Manufacturing Company, no. 1 and no. 2, Macon: "[F]ound the President of the Bibb Mfg Co. (an eccentric individual) in good humor and gained access to two of their mills. In the Bibb Mill No. 1, there were dozens of youngsters, some so small they could reach their work, at times, only by climbing up onto the spinning frames."[24] (Figure 6.3)

In some mills, doffers doubled as sweepers, sweeping up cotton lint in between the doffing runs. In larger mills, doffing and sweeping were more likely to be distinct occupations. After the doffing was completed, doffers could often leave the mill for hours at a time, remaining close enough to be called when needed. In a typical report, a mill superintendent said, "[T]he doffer boys played base ball, went swimming, and at

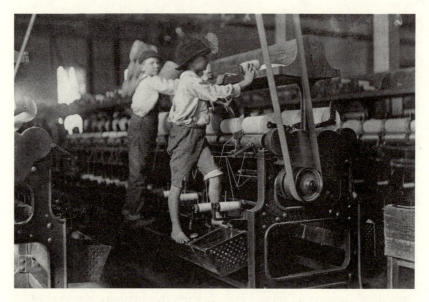

Figure 6.3   *Doffer Boys.* Macon, Georgia. January, 1909. Bibb Mill No. 1. Many young-sters here. Some boys were so small they had to climb up on to the spinning frame to mend the broken threads and to put back the empty bobbins. *(Courtesy of the Library of Congress, Prints and Photographs Division, Lewis Wickes Hine National Child Labor Committee Collection, LC-USZ62–23944.)*

least once, for a considerable period of time, played cards. Their actual working hours were about four hours each day."[25] Doffers were often able to play, on company time, more hours than they worked.

In contrast to doffing, spinning was real, continuous work. Spinning cotton into yarn involved tending spinning frames. Each frame contained multiple spindles, each with its own bobbin to be filled. Spinners tended as many frames as their skill and competence enabled them to tend. They were usually paid on a piece rate based on the number or weight of the bobbins they filled. Much of the work involved "piecing up," or tying together broken pieces of yarn. It was considered light work in that it did not require great physical strength. But it did require endur-ance, constant attention, nearly continuous movement, fine motor dex-terity, and if not high skill, at least a knack for accommodating to the pace of the work process—a knack that could be acquired only through experience. When performed for ten, eleven, or twelve hours per day, work as a spinner was quite physically and mentally demanding.

Spinners did get the opportunity to take breaks from time to time during the workday. When they got caught up on their work—when they were all "pieced up"—they could rest momentarily, though being caught up too much of the time only indicated a readiness to tend a greater number of frames. More significantly, when the boys were called in to doff the bobbins, the spinners could enjoy a break from their work even long enough to leave the mill for a while. As Bertha Awford Black recalled, "Well, we'd go out there behind the mill at the warehouse and us girls we'd build us a little playhouse until they'd whistle for us."[26]

One positive aspect of the mill village and family wage system as it evolved in southern cotton textiles is that it retained parental control over child discipline. Alexander McKelway cited several examples from New England of whipping recalcitrant child workers and pouring cold water on them to keep them awake.[27] But the southern mill village and family wage system assured that responsibility for disciplining junior employees remained with the parent, that parents never gave authority for child discipline over to the mill. A former child laborer described the system of discipline he experienced as a child in the mills in the Carolinas:

> Back years ago kids used to be brought into the mill to go to work. They'd make about ten cents a day. They'd get in there and start playing. You know how kids will do. And someone would go tell their daddy and the daddy would whip them. That's one thing about these people back then— they'd didn't let nobody else whip their children. If they did, somebody'd get their head cracked. You don't go around whipping other people's children. You go and tell their daddy, if they done something wrong.[28]

Overseers, foremen, and superintendents were authorized taskmasters, but they were not, generally, authorized disciplinarians. Overseers were expected to be taskmasters, and some were quite stern, but they were also friends and neighbors in the mill village. As respectful neighbors, they were reluctant to intrude, without invitation, into the parent-child relationships of other families. Their actual authority was limited. They could send a child out of the mill (suspension) or dock a child's pay, as they could dock the pay of or suspend any employee, but further discipline was left to the parents. Under the mill village system, a child's conduct was a reflection on the parents. As a tightly enclosed unit, everyone knew who did what. Everyone knew whose children got in trouble at the mill on any given day. As in all societies, parents were expected to discipline their children into conformity with cultural norms. A child who disrupted the mill brought embarrassment to the family. Under the family wage system, cultural norms were reinforced by economic incentive. The child who was less amenable to the factory regimen was of less value than the child who appeared to have a promising future in textiles. Under the family wage system, when a child was less valuable to the mill, the family was less valuable. In sum, parents, as heads of families, had strong incentives to enforce the disciplinary code of the mill. Discipline may still have been harsh. But at least it was discipline administered by the parents (and other adult relatives) under parental standards of the time and place.

NCLC vs. the Industry

The main aim of NCLC investigations in southern cotton textiles was simply to document and expose child labor conditions. Numerous broad-scale investigations were conducted. Over the years, there were very few mills, and even fewer mill villages, that did not receive at least one visit from an NCLC investigator. Before Lewis Hine joined the NCLC investigative staff, Alfred E. Seddon had toured mills in Mississippi and Georgia.[29] After Hine joined in 1908, he and other investigators, most notably Seddon, Harvey P. Vaughn, and Herschel H. Jones, blanketed the South.

Hine's first foray into the South was a tour of North and South Carolina mills late in 1908. In North Carolina he visited nineteen mill villages and investigated seventeen mills in the general vicinity of Charlotte (he was refused entry into the High Shoals and Atherton mills, both of which are D.A. Tompkins mills). At the time, according to North Carolina law thirteen was the minimum age in factories (twelve for apprentices), there was no night work under fourteen, and there was a sixty-six-hour-per-week limit under eighteen, but Hine had no difficulty finding violations everywhere he went. In a moment of candor, the president of the Ivey Mill in Hickory told Hine he could not afford to observe the law because no one else did. "Not over ten per cent of the mills observe it. . . . I now have a family of four girls nearly grown, all number one hands, and they are going to another mill because I will not employ a ten-year-old child."[30]

In South Carolina, where the minimum age was twelve (with exceptions for orphans and children of dependent parents) and there was a sixty-hour maximum workweek, it was worse:

> In general, I found these [mills] were considerably worse than in North Carolina, both as to age and number of small children employed, though

several of the mill towns in North Carolina approached the worst ones in South Carolina. . . . In Chester, South Carolina, an overseer told me frankly that manufacturers all over the South evaded the child labor law by letting youngsters who are under age help older brothers and sisters. The names of the younger ones do not appear on the company books and the pay goes to the older child who is above twelve.[31]

The following year, when Hine visited two large cities (Augusta and Macon) and two small towns (Tifton and Valdosta) in Georgia, he found conditions even worse. He observed that, while he found a larger number of children in the Carolinas, "there is a larger percentage of very young children in the cotton mills of Georgia than in either North or South Carolina."[32] In the larger cities, mill owners had enough sense to hide their child workers when dignitaries came touring. At the King Mill in Augusta, Hine got a tour along with an entourage that included the mill management team and several distinguished citizens of the city. He commented:

> It was an interesting fact that during our whole trip, no one saw any children (except those of us who were "wise" enough to keep an eye on unnoticed places such as elevator shafts and windows high up). I waited around after the party left and spent the noon hour in the mill yard. Photos #500 to 509 ought to convince any one that a good many little ones are working in that mill and the fact that we missed them all when we went through was something more than a mere coincidence.[33]

In the smaller towns no effort was made to conceal the extent of child labor: "at Tifton, Georgia, there is a cotton mill employing 125 hands. I obtained several photos of the entire force at noon (#486, 513, 514). This is the largest proportion of youngsters I have ever seen in a cotton mill. Every one in the photo (except the boy with the foot ball, who is the Supt's. son) works or helps regularly in the mill."[34] (Figure 6.4)

The NCLC received sharp criticism from the industry for its sensationalist reports depicting only the worst conditions in the worst mills. In response, the committee dispatched investigator Alfred E. Seddon to visit some of South Carolina's famous "show mills." Among others, he visited Lewis W. Parker's Monaghan Mills in Greenville and the Victor Mills in Greer, and Captain Ellyson A. Smyth's Pelzer, Belton, and Ninety-Six Mills. At the Monoghan Mills, of 250 hands in the spinning room, 85 were under 16; two said 10 and two said 9. At the Victor Mills,

Figure 6.4   *Tifton, Georgia.* January, 1909. Workers in the Tifton (Ga.) Cotton Mills. All these children were working or helping. 125 workers in all. Some of the smaller boys and girls have been there one year or more. *(Courtesy of the Library of Congress, Prints and Photographs Division, Lewis Wickes Hine National Child Labor Committee Collection, LC-USZ6–1221.)*

one said 10 and another said 8. At Ninety-Six, of 75 hands in the spinning room, 50 were children; two were 10 and three were 9. The minimum age in South Carolina was twelve. In addition to checking ages, Seddon administered a literacy test to as many of the children under fourteen as he could. In six mills he tested 142 children, finding ninety-two, or 65 percent, to be illiterate.[35]

As they gained experience, NCLC investigators learned to target their resources for maximum impact. Their purposive sampling methodology was especially effective in spotlighting the mills of the rich and famous among the mill owners. Alongside their broader investigative work, they almost seemed to enjoy targeting three strategic groups: (1) mill owners who also happened to be politicians or lobbyists, especially those who were vocal opponents of child labor legislation; (2) mills operated by northern interests, and especially those operated southern mills in order to avoid the stricter child labor laws up north; and (3)

Mississippi mills that were newly emerging at the far western edge of the southern cotton textile region.

Vocal Politicians and Lobbyists

F.B. Gordon was president of the Columbus Manufacturing Company, Columbus, Georgia, and was also president of the Georgia Cotton Manufacturers Association. Investigator Harvey P. Vaughn visited his mill in 1913, commenting, "From my own observation and the testimony of the teachers in the neighborhood I believe there is a larger proportion of children in this mill than in any other one I have visited." Gordon showed Vaughn an article in which he "paid his respects" to the NCLC calling them "an association of foreigners." Vaughn pointed out that "Mr. Gordon is himself a Bostonian and the capital invested in his mill is from the East."[36]

Gordon claimed to Vaughn that he had been responsible for the defeat of the child labor bill considered the previous year in the Georgia legislature. As president of the Georgia Cotton Manufacturers Association, he had also been an active lobbyist in Washington and sought continued protective tariffs on cotton textile goods. The juxtaposition of these lobbying roles prompted Alexander McKelway to remark, "Mr. Gordon has lately been as conspicuous in Washington lobbying for the protection of his infant industry as he has been in Atlanta for the continued exploitation of industrious infants."[37]

Another political figure spotlighted by the NCLC was Governor B.B. Comer of Alabama, who was also head of the Avondale Mills in Birmingham. Comer was elected governor in 1906 on a pledge to resist further factory legislation. He was once described by Edgar Gardner Murphy as "the most bitter opponent of child labor legislation I have ever known."[38] So Governor Comer's mills were an obvious target during Hine's 1910 investigation tour. And Hine obviously enjoyed this kind of investigative work. It did not take him long to find the evidence he sought. His own account of his investigation of the Avondale Mills is worth quoting at length:

> As Governor Comer's Mills at Avondale (Birmingham, Ala.) have been brought to the attention of the public by the newspapers, I expected to encounter difficulties, so to feel their pulse I first went to the Superintendent, Mr. Shinn, asking for permission to make some postal card photos

of the people during noon hour. He said he had no objection, personally, "But you better see Mr. Comer, the Secretary, who is the one to give you permission. A while ago a fellow got permission to go through the mill and then he went off and wrote it up for the newspapers and it kicked up a Hell of a Row. Then I got the Devil for letting him through." Instead of seeing Mr. Comer, I went off on a little tour of my own, that noon, and found a rear gate through which most of the workers go at noon and around which they hang out a good deal. Spent part of two days around that gate and got a number of striking photographs and interesting data to go with them. In every case, the youngsters told me their age as 12 years, even to the little Hop-o'-My-Thumb, whom the others dubbed "our baby doffer." They would hesitate when I asked them, but always succeeded in remembering that they were twelve. Entering by the back gate, I got up into the spinning rooms early one noon and spent the hour inside. Saw many of the youngsters whose photos I have, actually at work, some at noon and some when the mill started up. Saw a couple of very young girls helping in the weave-rooms. Saw Child Labor Laws conspicuously posted. Got some few photos of children at their machines. Then I sat down outside by the back gate and photographed and chatted with the doffer-boys who had an hour off after noon-hour, and who gave me some interesting data. (See photos and labels.) Then, in the afternoon, I went to see Mr. J. M. Comer, the Governor's Son, and Manager of the mills, as I had been directed.

This time I told him I wanted to get photos for postal cards and magazine use to see if I could get him started talking about things. He is, personally, a fine fellow and I think really wanted to help me out. At the same time it was evident that he did *not* want his people photographed. He hesitated a long time, as though unwilling to commit himself. Then he tried to discourage me by saying the photos would not be "pretty" and that the workers would object, etc. Then as I answered all of his objections, he came out with his real answer;—"There are persons who come around getting material for an Anti-Cotton-Mill crusade. Now, we have no objections to views being taken of the mill, inside or out, if Superintendent Shinn goes around with you, but I would *much* rather you didn't take groups of the people. They're all dirty, etc., etc." On the way out, I managed to get in a farewell tour of the entire mill while in operation all alone and counted seven very young girls working in the spinning rooms and helping in the weave-rooms. I have photos of some of them going home at noon. November 23rd, 1910.[39] (Figure 6.5)

NCLC investigators and publicists became a real thorn in the side of prominent mill owners. Not only was the NCLC wreaking havoc with

Figure 6.5 *Baby Doffer.* Birmingham, Alabama. November, 1910. "OUR BABY DOFFER" they called him. This is one of the machines he has been working at for some months at the Avondale Mills. Said, after hesitation, "I'm 12," and another small boy added, "He can't work unless he's twelve." Child labor regulations conspicuously posted in the mill. *(Courtesy of the Library of Congress, Prints and Photographs Division, Lewis Wickes Hine National Child Labor Committee Collection, LC-USZ6Z–18131.)*

their property and their industry, the NCLC reports were impugning the reputations of reputable men. Considering this, it is perhaps surprising that NCLC investigators apparently never encountered violence or overt physical hostility. Not that they were welcomed into the mill villages. There was plenty of hostile verbal sparring. One prominent Mississippi mill owner, for example, called an NCLC report in which he was featured "a pack of G__D__ black lies," labeled Alexander McKelway "a rotten, lying scoundrel,"[40] and later "paid his compliments very vehemently to the last Child Labor man 'who sneaked around here and took pictures of little tads that never went inside of our factory.'"[41] But, perhaps because the mill men had reputations to protect, expressions of hostility were rarely more than verbal.

Alfred E. Seddon described one time when he received a less than enthusiastic welcome at the Porterdale Mill (Bibb Manufacturing Company) outside Covington, Georgia. He became concerned for his safety, but he was never harmed. On his arrival, he checked in with the mill's gatekeeper and received a gruff dismissal. So he went to check into his hotel. But the proprietor, "with evident embarrassment informed me that the Mill Superintendent, Mr. Towers, had intimated to him that I was not to be accommodated at the hotel. He, however, informed me that Mr. Bowden would take me and indicated the house."[42] As it turned out, Mr. Bowden was the mill's gatekeeper, the very first person of whom Mr. Seddon had inquired on arrival at the mill. According to Seddon, Bowden was:

> a big, heavily built, ill-looking man, the front of his shirt copiously stained with tobacco juice. He was not, in appearance at least, the kind of man I would like to have for my host, and it was not therefore a great disappointment when he growled, "I don't keep no boarding house." A little later on I had occasion to view his refusal to take me in with great satisfaction when I learned that someone who, under similar circumstances had been sent to be that man's guest, had been badly beaten during the night.[43]

So, Seddon had to trudge the rain-soaked mud road back to Covington. The following morning, he set out once again for Porterdale. Along the road, who should happen to pass but the senior Mr. Porter. "[He] wanted to know what authority I had to visit the mill. I told him I was authorized to do so by the National Child Labor Committee. His vigorous reply was, 'That authority is not worth a damn, and you know it.'" Porter and his sons took Seddon to the train station, sent to the hotel for his valise, and waited with him four hours until he was put on the first train out of town.[44]

Northern Capital and Sectional Prejudice

As the southern textile industry grew, numerous northern firms attempted to protect their market position by locating manufacturing facilities in the South. In the Carolinas, many mills had significant northern financial backing, but most mills were under the financial and operational control of indigenous southerners. In Georgia and Alabama, however, several large mills were financed, built, and operated completely under the control of prominent northern textile firms. Once located in the South, these northern interests did not want to give up the advantages they enjoyed in cheap labor, and so were often involved in opposition to progressive child labor legislation. To the reformers, and particularly those with roots in the South, this was triply galling. First, northern interests were seen as attempting to escape northern progressive child labor legislation—that is, they were perceived as coming South explicitly to exploit southern children because they were no longer permitted to exploit their own at home. Second, when northern capital sought to influence southern legislation, it was perceived as meddling of the sort likely to rekindle sectional prejudice. Third, and perhaps most galling, these northern firms often tried to portray the reform effort as outside interference, agitation, and northern meddling. This last was especially galling to reformers like Edgar Gardner Murphy, who remembered how the Dwight Manufacturing Company, of Alabama City and Massachusetts, had defeated Alabama's 1901 child labor bill by portraying Murphy and other reformers as outsiders, labor agitators, and misguided philanthropists in service to northern interests.[45] It was also especially galling to Alexander J. McKelway, long-time NCLC secretary for the southern states and a true man of the South, and other southerners active with the NCLC. As a consequence, northern firms operating in the South, and especially those that had publicly opposed child labor legislation, became prime targets for NCLC investigations.

Among the largest mills in Georgia and Alabama were the Merrimack Mill in Huntsville, Alabama, and the Massachusetts Mill in Lindale, Georgia. Both the Merrimack and the Massachusetts Manufacturing Company were of Lowell, Massachusetts, fame, and both were under the control of the Lyman family of Lowell. The NCLC got to know these mills as well as any other two mills. Beginning in 1909, both mills were investigated heavily through 1915. Lewis W. Hine made multiple investigations of both mills, and also made multiple investigations of their northern counterparts for comparison purposes.

What apparently caught Alexander McKelway's attention and ensured that both Merrimack and Massachusetts Manufacturing would receive regular visits went back to before the NCLC even began to conduct investigations. On May 5, 1905, when the Georgia child labor law that would be approved in 1906 was under consideration, H.P. Meikleham, a member of the executive committee of the Georgia Industrial Association, published a letter opposing the agitation for a better child labor law in Georgia, in which he asserted:

> We wish to again call the attention of the public to the fact that behind these efforts is the energy of our competitors in the north and east. These northern competitors are feeling the weight of our superior advantage of climate, of our location beside the cotton fields, of our low cost of living,

of our cheap lands, and of all the advantages we enjoy—and they will leave nothing undone to secure the passage of labor laws, the regulation of freight rates, and the general adjustment of all economic conditions so as to deprive us of these advantages, and so as to compensate them as our competitors.

It was not so bad that a member of the Georgia Industrial Association would oppose child labor legislation, or even question reformers' sectional patriotism—that was to be expected. What really got McKelway steamed—"it does rather rile a southern gentleman"—was that Mr. Meikleham was superintendent of the Massachusetts Manufacturing Company in Lindale.[46]

The NCLC had investigated the two mills from 1908 through 1910 and had widely publicized the results, along with comparisons to the more favorable conditions of the mills in Lowell, Massachusetts. So when crack investigators Lewis W. Hine, Herschel H. Jones, and Harvey P. Vaughn returned in 1913, they expected find the situation considerably improved. When they found that conditions remained far short of ideal, their scorn occasionally turned to sarcasm. Hine described his return to the Massachusetts Mill in Lindale, at the time the largest mill in Georgia:

> First impressions are often lasting. Mine, as I entered the village, were distinctly favorable. Here was the group of well built mills, surrounded by well kept grounds,—homes that were, externally, at least, well-planned and cared for,—a school building and a church that pleased the eye,— *Everything well provided for,*—apparently. This was deepened as I went through the mill,—weave-rooms and card-rooms up-to-date,—no use to look for children here, I thought. Upon entering the spinning-room, however, I met a real set-back,—youngsters by the dozens, tiny little chaps, sweeping, doffing, spinning,—there were twenty-five of them that I judged to be under 12 years of age in the three spinning rooms alone, (and I found some more in the weave room, helping.) These little ones were all well-trained,—answering to the age of 12 or 14, no matter how youthful their appearance. Surely, I thought,—*Not a Thing Neglected,—Except the Children.*
>
> In order that I might be more sure on my age estimates, I made some visits to the homes of the people, where some of them showed me their family records, Life insurance papers, etc.,—From these sources and from conversations with the parents and children themselves, I proved nearly a dozen children to be working now, or during the past year at 10 and 11

years of age,—some of them having begun before they were 10. I found that many children who say they are twelve are really "going on" 12 and too often, *have a long way to go* before reaching 12. Others, who are 12 now, had been working one, two or three years, beginning at ten or before.

Now, this Massachusetts mill in Georgia has a sister mill in Lowell, Mass., run by the same Corporation. Let us compare with the foregoing what I found at the Lowell mill a while ago. Using the same effort and precautions in Lowell, to find whether many violation existed, I obtained a few photos of the *youngest workers there*, (see photos 2587 to 2590) and found that not one of them was under 14 years of age, and in the whole mill there were only a few under 16. The Agent, there, said he was opposed to having them in the mill under 16. They are not permitted to work more than ten hours a day, and we expect this to be reduced to eight hours before long.[47]

Similarly, when Hine returned to the Merrimack Mill in Huntsville, he had no difficulty proving that very young children still worked for very long hours:

At closing hours I counted about thirty-five children coming out of the mill who were apparently under fourteen years of age; one half of these were apparently under twelve years of age. By the end of the week I had proved (1) twenty of them to be under fourteen (and a large number that I did not question would admit that much) (2) thirteen of these I proved to be under twelve when they started to work here (some of them have recently reached twelve, but have been working so long they started at nine, ten, and eleven) (3) five of these proved to be eight and ten years old now, all with steady jobs.[48]

Hine called it "another example of Double Standards. The Merrimack Mill at Lowell, Mass. several times as large as the Huntsville Mill, maintains a very high standard in child labor matters." With about a thousand hands, the Huntsville mill ran eleven hours a day for five days, and five hours on Saturday, and employed children as young as eight and ten. Hine asked, "What is the reason?"[49]

Mississippi

Mississippi was not among the leading textile states of the South and, indeed, was outside the Piedmont region most closely associated with southern cotton textiles. Yet the NCLC devoted considerable attention to the mills of the state. Mississippi mills were among the first investigated in 1907 and were then investigated in each year from 1911 through 1914, inclusive. A number of factors combined to make Mississippi a fruitful field for investigation. First, the relatively small number of mills made it possible to conduct a more comprehensive investigation of conditions throughout the state. Repeated investigations over a number of years began to yield longitudinal data that more clearly revealed trends in the employment of children. Second, located at the far western edge of the southern textile region, the industry was newer and younger than that of the core Piedmont region. If the advance of child labor could be stopped here, at the industry's frontier, perhaps it could be stopped in other areas the industry would later develop. Finally, as one of the more "recalcitrant regions and backward states," Mississippi highlighted certain aspects of the child labor problem perhaps more clearly than other states. For example, NCLC investigators argued, though without a great deal of dispositive evidence, that Mississippi's failure to adopt child labor legislation after other southern states had done so was leading to an influx of "that unnatural class of parents who had become accustomed to subsist by their children's labor."[50] Alfred E. Seddon spoke with W.W. Robertson, editor of the Wesson Enterprise (Wesson was home to the largest mill in the state at the time), who was strongly opposed to a child labor law. His argument was that Mississippi's vagrancy law was adequate to deal with the problem. In an editorial, he pointed out, "Here is what section 5055 of the new code says, 'All persons who are able to work and do not work; but hire out their minor children, or allow them to be hired out and live upon their wages, shall be punished as vagrants.'" He described the case of a father who beat his children out of bed in the morning and set them crying to the mill without breakfast. All that was necessary to deal with such "lazy daddies," he concluded, was to enforce the vagrancy laws. Seddon wondered why, if Mr. Robertson was so concerned about these children, and if the vagrancy law was so effective, he did not simply report this father to the authorities.[51]

NCLC investigators developed almost personal relationships with a number of mill owners. In spite of his child labor practices, investigators seemed especially fond of J.H. Ledyard, president of the Tupelo Cotton Mills—from Alfred E. Seddon's first visit in 1907, where Ledyard "gave carte blanche to go wherever I pleased inside or outside of the Mill," to Lewis Hine's visit in 1911, to Herschel Jones in 1914, whose report notes, "Mr. Ledyard, the owner of the cotton mill is a *nice* man and he wouldn't do nothing in violation of the law."[52] On Seddon's first visit, Mr. Ledyard was surprisingly candid.

> He frankly told me that I might find some things that I could not approve of. He himself deplored some things that were in the system and would welcome legislation that would alter conditions. He did not approve of child labor. From a business point of view it was unprofitable, from a moral and social standpoint it was deplorable.[53]

Sure enough, Seddon did find some things of which he could not approve, most notably twenty-eight very young children (of a total workforce of 208) working in the spinning room. Likewise, when Hine returned in 1911, he gave Ledyard some credit where he felt credit was due, but also criticized his laxity, noting, "I found very few of the tiny little helpers that flourish in the mills of other states. On the whole, there is not a very large percentage of children under twelve years, but I do want to emphasize the fact that there are too many children who are obviously not yet twelve but who are posing at 'just past twelve.' "[54]

When Herschel Jones returned in 1914, Mississippi had just adopted a new law raising the minimum age to twelve for boys and fourteen for girls, and establishing an eight-hour day for boys under sixteen and girls under eighteen. Unlike Seddon, Jones was not given free access to Ledyard's Tupelo Cotton Mills. Still, he described how, "By enquiring for the supt. whenever there seemed to be any suspicion as to my presence, I was able to get thru the entire mill unmolested." Jones had no difficulty locating numerous specific violations of the new law:

> In the large spinning room on the first floor were at least five boys under 14, and three or four under 16. One boy of 13 who was cleaning spools said he began at 7 A.M. and worked till about 6 P.M. He said a boy of nine who was working with him was "just helping" him. Another boy of nine and a boy of 7 whose mother worked in the mill were also cleaning spools.[55]

In contrast to Ledyard, whom NCLC investigators liked personally in spite of his inability to come to grips with his child labor problem, there was T.L. Wainwright, president of the Stonewall Mills, the Yazoo Yarn Mills, and the Kosciusko Mill. Wainwright was the original mill man in Mississippi and was longtime president of the Mississippi Mill Owners Association. Wainwright was a strident, sometimes bitter, adversary. He is the mill owner who referred to the NCLC report as "a pack of G__D__ black lies," called Alexander McKelway "a rotten, lying scoundrel," and "paid his compliments very vehemently" to Hine.[56]

After Wainwright complained publicly about the NCLC report, investigator Alexander Fleisher was sent to Stonewall to interview him and to investigate the Stonewall Mills. Apparently Fleisher was less than successful in getting a good look in the mill, but he got his interview. "Mr. Wainwright states that the conditions in his mill are exceptional; that there are no idle fathers because the Deputy Sheriff would see that they immediately got to work or would be put in prison." Perhaps because he had little else to investigate, Fleisher's report contains some unusual notations, including the following, regarding the company-owned drug store: "The drug store uses about 10 oz. of morphine every three weeks and one lb. of cocaine. This is on the statement of the drummer of the Mobile Drug Company who supplies the drug store."[57]

When Herschel Jones returned to Mississippi in 1914 after the child labor law had been upgraded, he made sure to pay his respects to "Old Man Wainwright." Wainwright had been a "powerful political force" in opposition to the new law—he "claimed it was the most drastic in the country." In addition to upgrading minimum age and hours standards, the new law vested enforcement authority in the local public health official and the county sheriff. But Wainwright was not about to give in to the new law. "The Sheriff had never inspected the mill." Instead, he "appointed a Deputy at Stonewall who worked in the mill" and "left all these matters to him."[58] As an ironic consequence of his vocal opposition, however, when the new Mississippi child labor law was finally adopted, it was especially important that his mill conform to its basic provisions. Wainwright was apparently very careful about strict adherence to the law: he had affidavits on file for all boys under sixteen and girls under eighteen; he had adjusted work schedules to conform to the new hours requirements (doffer boys were sent out for two hours a day and young spinners were provided with relief crews). Nevertheless, on investigation, Jones found six underage girls and at least one hours violation.[59]

Some mills made an easier adjustment to the new Mississippi law than either Ledyard's Tupelo Mills or Wainwright's Stonewall (and other) Mills. One example was the Laurel Cotton Mill that was owned by a large lumber company. When Alfred E. Seddon first visited in 1907, he found it a real mess:

> This mill employs 376 hands of which about 100 are children. Cornett Foard ("a bad case") very little fellow, on the pay roll. Did not know his age, referred me to his father. Father said the boy is 7. Father has 3 daugh-

ters working in mill ages 10, 12 and 14 respectively. Father earning $1.50 per day. Says he cannot afford to do without the little fellow's earnings. I spoke severely to father told him the boy ought to go to school. Said he would probably be compelled to send him to school when the legislature meets. The man was a poor thriftless looking man with chin stained with tobacco juice. Said he had a sick wife and infant baby at home.[60]

But when Herschel Jones returned in 1914, after the new law was in force, "No boys were found under 12, nor any girls under 14." Jones credited the manager, J.S. Pleasant, noting:

This mill has adjusted itself admirably to the 8 hr. provisions in its arrangement for the spinners in groups that are relieved by a "relief crew" composed of 5, and sometimes 6 of the most expert older spinners. When the law was passed in 1912, Mr. Pleasant had copies of it printed at once and circulated among all the mill families, with the announcement that they would as promptly as possible readjust all their employees to conform to it. They promised to show preference to those children whose earnings were necessary for support of mothers and other children. The first step was to cut all girls under 18 out of the weaving room, and to concentrate all affected by the hour provision in one room, the spinning department. These were then divided into groups, each of which was relieved for two hours per day by the "relief crew." One experienced spinner of this crew can do the work of two beginners, and so most of the time the five, or six, are supplying for from 45 to 50 daily.

Mr. Pleasant figures that it costs them $3500 a year to conform to the law. He does not object to it applying to all under 16, but thinks that nothing is gained and much hardship is worked by applying the 8 hour restriction to girls between 16 and 18. He says he thinks the South has reached the place where it should fall in line with the states of the North in labor legislation.[61]

Whether the NCLC's strategy of targeting Mississippi mills deserves credit for preventing the westward spread of child labor in southern cotton textiles is not entirely clear. Nevertheless, it does appear that the spread was stopped at roughly the Mississippi River. In 1913, Lewis Hine was invited by the faculty of the University of Texas to conduct a wall-to-wall investigation of child labor in all industries in the state. In conjunction with this investigation, Hine visited ten cotton mills in the newly emerging Texas cotton textile industry and found very few children under fifteen. While he found serious child labor problems in numerous other industries—including agriculture, the street trades, and other manufacturing—cotton textiles had apparently emerged as a clean industry in Texas.[62]

On Compulsory Schooling

Like everywhere else, issues of schooling were inextricably intertwined with issues of child labor. Children, while in school, were not at work, and children at work were not in school. But the situation in southern cotton textiles was further complicated by additional factors. Unlike the North and most of the Midwest, where compulsory schooling laws long predated the NCLC, few southern laws provided for either public or compulsory schooling. In the North and Midwest, the more pressing concerns were extending the availability of schooling throughout the rural communities and, in urban areas, into secondary schooling, and in enforcement of the existing compulsory schooling laws. In the South, at the time the NCLC began investigating the southern cotton mills, there were few compulsory schooling laws on the books to enforce. Each state had begun to provide at least some public support for schooling, but none had yet required schooling for all children or provided for anything approximating universal availability. Whereas in the North the movement for compulsory and universal schooling preceded the period of greatest agitation for child labor reform, in the South the movements for compulsory schooling and child labor reform coincided.

Reformers understood from the beginning that compulsory schooling laws were among the best child labor laws. Many of the more progressive mill owners seemed to be in agreement on this point. For example, when Lewis W. Parker, one of the leading mill men in South Carolina, addressed the annual meeting of the NCLC in 1908, he asserted that the manufacturers had been "agitating" for a compulsory schooling law since 1900, stating that "compulsory education law is in itself the best child labor law." But there was an important difference between his position and that of the reformers. While he asserted that the mills were not opposed to child labor legislation, he was adamant that such legislation should be preceded by compulsory schooling law.[63] Otherwise, mill interests were concerned that if children neither worked nor attended school, but instead remained idle, that it would breed "a dangerous class of loafers and budding criminals."[64]

Mill owners claimed, with some justification, that the mill schools provided the only opportunity for schooling that many children would have. That is, schooling in the mill villages, in terms of both availability and quality, was far superior to that in the farming or mountain regions from where the families came. Even if the relationship between the mill and the mill school often disrupted children's education, many would have received no education at all had it not been for the mill school. Thomas R. Dawley's book, *The Child that Toileth Not*, published in 1912, appeared to confirm the superior educational opportunities for children in the mill villages as compared to the farms and mountain communities from which the mill families had come.

Wiley H. Swift, then field secretary for the North Carolina Child Labor Committee, decided to challenge Dawley by comparing school enrollments in Watauga County, a remote mountain county, with those in Gaston County, the leading textile county in the state. Gaston County, located in the very center of the Piedmont textile region, boasted the largest concentration of mills and spindles anywhere.[65] Liston Pope estimated that, in 1900, 30 percent of the workforce in Gaston County mills were boys and girls under fourteen.[66] Wiley Swift gathered school enrollment data for the two counties for two years. During the 1908–9 school year, he found only 65 percent of Gaston County's school-age population were actually enrolled in school, compared to Watauga County's more favorable enrollment of 74 percent. The following year, Watauga County's school enrollment grew to 77 percent, while Gaston County enrollment slipped to 62 percent. Swift argued that these numbers forcefully negated the claim of superior opportunities for schooling in the mill villages.[67] But Swift failed to disclose in his study that Watauga County was home to the Watauga Academy, a teachers college founded in 1899 and now known as Appalachian State University. The comparatively high school enrollments were almost certainly unrepresentative of other remote mountain counties.

If it was generally true, as mill owners claimed, that mill schools provided opportunities that many children otherwise would not have had, it was not true that mill owners were the steadfast advocates of universal and compulsory schooling they sometimes claimed to be. Their argument that compulsory schooling laws must precede child labor legislation was motivated as much by a desire to forestall the latter as to promote the former. Whatever their concern about "loafers and budding criminals" throughout the broader southern society, they clearly already had the capacity, without any legislation, to ensure that children in their own mill villages were not idle. Many mills explicitly required that children be either in school or in the mill. And there is no doubt that the mills had the means to enforce such a requirement. Thus, the mill owners already had the wherewithal to provide universal and compulsory schooling, at least in their own villages. Children in the mills belied the owners' sincerity as advocates for compulsory schooling.

Consistently high illiteracy rates among the mill workers also belied the owners' interest in educating their workers. In 1905, when the South Carolina legislature was considering a ten-hour law shortly after their first child labor law in 1903, a petition against the bill was submitted with 3,000 signatures from mill hands in Anderson, Spartanburg, Pelzer, Piedmont, and Greenville, proclaiming, "We are not overworked, and are satisfied, and only ask to be let alone." Of the mills represented on the petition, the Pelzer mills were considered the "show mills," famous for the Pelzer contract and what was considered a relatively progressive posture among mill management toward the education of the mill children and families. Thus, when 154 of the Pelzer operatives could not sign the petition, but rather made their "mark," it provided strong commentary on the need for stronger compulsory schooling laws.[68]

NCLC investigators made sure to highlight issues of literacy and illiteracy in their reports. In Alfred E. Seddon's first 1907 investigation in Mississippi, he carefully tested the literacy of 130 children under fourteen found working in five separate mills. He found that 89, or 68.5 percent, were illiterate.[69] Thereafter, most investigation reports made reference to illiterate children working in the mills, whether anecdotally or more systematically.

Compulsory schooling laws in the southern textiles states evolved over a series of steps. The first step was to require a minimum amount of schooling for employed children. In its 1906 child labor law, Georgia required employed children under fourteen to attend school for at least twelve weeks per year. The next step was to make schooling compulsory by local option. North Carolina's 1907 law permitted counties to make education compulsory for children eight to fourteen for up to sixteen weeks per year. The first true compulsory schooling law was enacted by North Carolina in 1913. It required four months of schooling per year for children eight to twelve years of age. South Carolina followed with a compulsory schooling law in 1915, Georgia in 1916, and Alabama in 1917.[70]

On "the Negro Problem"

Blacks did not work inside the cotton mills.[71] One popular explanation for the exclusion of blacks from the mills was that the hum of the machinery put them to sleep.[72] At some mills, outside jobs were performed by blacks. There might be a small crew of black men working the dock unloading cotton, but their work stopped at the bale-breaker, where cotton entered the mill. At the other end of the process, another relatively small crew of black men might handle the warehousing and loading of finished goods. Most of the blacks who worked the warehouses and docks were adult men, or at least older boys. But blacks did not enter the mill itself. At nearly all mills, the inside jobs were reserved for whites. In all their investigations in the South, the NCLC encountered only two mills where blacks worked inside: Savannah's only cotton mill had an integrated workforce, and a silk mill in Virginia employed blacks exclusively.[73] Notably, neither of these mills employed children.

Even during periods of chronic labor shortages, mill owners gave no more thought to hiring blacks than they gave to not hiring the children of their white mill workers. During one short period, a few owners recruited European immigrants, following the lead of their northern counterparts. But that effort was aborted after the first groups of immigrants migrated out of the textile region as soon after their arrival as they were able. There was no black or immigrant child labor problem in southern cotton textiles. Child labor was the exclusive province of indigenous whites.

The "Negro problem" was one reason for slow emergence of compulsory education laws in the South. Laws were opposed because they would also require compulsory education for blacks. While, on average, educational opportunities for blacks clearly lagged those of whites, in many areas of the South, blacks established schools that were far ahead of anything available to the mill children. Since black children were barred from industrial work, and demand for their labor on the tenant farm was intermittent and sporadic, what else was there for them to do but go to school? NCLC investigators did not hesitate to appeal to racial prejudice by contrasting model schools for black children with the sham programs provided the white mill children. As Hine commented while investigating Alabama Governor Comer's Avondale Mills, "the comparisons are odious."[74] He submitted photographs comparing the mill school and the school for black children. The mill school stood "in the very shadow of the mill." The mill gate was within fifty feet of the front door of the school, "And the workers passing back and forth in front of the school do not tend to lessen the Call of the Mill." According to Hine, "I have it on good authority that the children go here for the eight weeks of the year merely to comply with the requirements of the law." In contrast, "Within a stone's-throw of this school is located a school for negro children where the parents find the entire school year none too long for their children."[75]

Southern reformers allied with the NCLC developed a theory of the degeneracy of the white race that many southerners, even some of the enlightened mill men, found compelling.[76] As Jean Gordon, NCLC ally and Louisiana factory inspector, noted regarding the blacks, "They are at school, well nourished, playing out in our glorious Southern sunlight, waxing strong and fat; it is only your white-faced, sunken-chested, curved-backed little Christians who are in the mills and department stores."[77] Alfred E. Seddon, one of the NCLC's important southern investigators, made the following observations, reflecting on one of his early investigations in Mississippi:

> It seems as tho some people would allow the white children to degenerate thro ignorance rather than afford a chance to the negro to get an education. I am learning right along, and one thing that I think I have learned is this: that the present conditions are paving the way for the elevation of the colored man and the degradation of the white man in the South. The colored children are not admitted to the mills. As a consequence they are at liberty to go to school, and they do. I have been surprised at the number of well dressed and well behaved colored children I have seen both at Columbus and at West Point, going to and coming from school. These children are rising in the social scale, as surely as the little white slaves in the factories are sinking. Whatever our prejudices or wishes, we cannot reverse the law of nature that says the fittest shall survive. The ultimate victory will be to strong physique and cultivated intelligence regardless to skin-color. The Southerner, ardent upholder as he rightly is of perpetual white domination in the South, should be the most urgent in his demands that white children in the South should have at least an equal chance with the black children in developing the best that is in them.[78]

During and after World War II, more mills began admitting blacks inside. But blacks doing inside work did not become widespread until after the Civil Rights Act of 1964. While child labor had long been eliminated by that time, it seems likely that child labor would have been eliminated sooner than it was if blacks had been allowed to compete for inside work.

Elimination of Child Labor from the Cotton Mills

The NCLC conducted no further significant investigations in southern cotton textiles after 1915. It was not that they had succeeded in eradicating child labor from the mills. Indeed, child labor remained persistently and naggingly high. But they had succeeded in mobilizing significant public sentiment against the child labor system, and mill owners were on notice that their practices would come under scrutiny. Furthermore, southern states were well on the way to putting in place the broad contours of a regulatory framework. By 1916, all southern states but one had established fourteen as the minimum age for work in the mill (North Carolina's minimum age was thirteen) and had placed further restrictions on hours and night work even if enforcement of these laws remained uneven. All states required some minimum level of education for working children, a few states had enacted compulsory schooling laws, and the rest would do so within a few years. Finally, with the enactment of the Keating-Owen Act in 1916, the NCLC felt that the federal government would assume investigative responsibilities, and so the NCLC could focus its resources elsewhere. Even if child labor had not yet been eradicated, clearly the tide had turned.

Southern cotton textiles enjoyed an extended building boom from the early 1900s up to and through World War I. Throughout this period, production capacity swelled. When orders were reduced on the conclusion of hostilities, the industry found that it had dramatically overbuilt. Now in a state of significant overcapacity, the industry fell into depression, a depression from which it never fully recovered until after the Great Depression of the 1930s. This industry depression helped bring about a further dramatic reduction in child labor. As Liston Pope suggests, it took the depression to align economic interests with developing sentiment. "Elimination of children in the mills was effected only when economic advantage reinforced considerations of moral and social welfare to decree their dismissal."[79]

The Child Labor Tax Act remained in force as the industry entered this period. When the law was invalidated in May 1922, the industry was already well into its depression. Mill owners cut wages, laid off some workers, and put others on short time. At the same time, they installed new machinery and introduced rationalized work routines along the lines of scientific management, aimed at enhancing productivity and efficiency. When workers were required to run more looms or spinning frames for the same pay, they called it a "stretch-out" and resisted. A number of mills were eventually closed, but this was generally not the owner's first response to the heightened competitive pressure of the postwar environment.

From the employer's perspective, children were no longer such a bargain. Lower adult wages favored hiring adults. Not only were they now relatively cheaper, they were also more plentiful. The substantial tax on child labor, even if its enforcement was uncertain, created further incentives to shift away from children. Perhaps more important, children were utterly unsuited for management's newfound interest in efficiency. Child labor, as the epitome of low productivity labor, was an early casualty of the stretch-out. It was simply wasteful to have doffer boys spending up to half their shifts playing ball or horsing around on the river bank or railroad tracks. Young girls simply could not tend as many spinning frames as women could. Even if they had the speed, dexterity, attention span, and endurance, much of the new machinery was just too complex to be mastered by young girls. Added to these considerations was the fact that most Southern textile states had adopted worker compensation laws in the 1920s, rendering employment of children more economically hazardous. Whatever economic incentives the child labor system previously held for the mill owners had vanished, and most mills reduced or eliminated their reliance on children.

Worker economic interests likewise tilted against employment of children. While many workers wished for a better life for their children, we have seen that many others were either passively indifferent or actively favored mill work for their children. Nothing, however, seemed to clarify the economic competition between adult and child labor as layoffs and short time did. When mothers and fathers could not find work, or were only working short time, it became very clear that there would be more work for adults if the children were not in the mill. When, as sometimes happened in some mills during earlier temporary downturns, adults were put on short time while the children continued on their regular schedules, worker objections were increased. As Alfred E. Seddon commented, "Under ideal conditions the period of slack work would be the opportunity to fill the school house. The child's labor is always the cheapest and at times when the employer has the choice of the man or the child, it is the man who has to walk the streets, and the child who goes into the mill."[80] Herschel H. Jones observed just such a situation and its effect on worker sentiment:

> Employees of the cotton mills say that no one gets regular work but children. The men are allowed to work about half or two thirds of the time, they say, but the children are always kept busy. E.M. Adams, Doc Gravett, Barry Smith, Ed Hall and half a dozen others have lost their jobs during the past ten days, and children are doing the work they used to do. The men and grown women can make about $1. a day, and the children average from $2.00 to $2.60 a week. The men employees say they want a child labor law passed that will keep the children out of the mill. This statement is general in the mill settlement.[81]

The economic pressure on workers from wage cuts and job insecurity were exacerbated by workplace pressure associated with the stretch-out. As pressure cumulated, labor–management tension and conflict escalated. The American Federation of Labor launched a postwar organizing drive in southern cotton textiles. There were sporadic strikes in the early 1920s, and tensions remained high throughout the decade, culminating in the strike wave of 1929 and the General Textile Strike of 1934. Owners had demonstrated a willingness and ability to crush worker resistance. In this climate, it became increasingly clear to many parents that the mills were no place for their children at the same time that employers were realizing that they had more important things to worry about than keeping the children employed.

The final nail in the coffin of the child labor system was provided by the Cotton Textile Codes, adopted in 1933 under the National Recovery Administration. Not only did the codes prohibit child labor under standards much higher than those that existed in most states (children under sixteen were barred, no night or hazardous work for workers under eighteen), but provisions regarding minimum wages and maximum hours, by themselves, created incentives favoring the employment of adults. After the National Industrial Recovery Act was found unconstitutional, few mills returned to the earlier standards on child labor, and these were generally the most backward mills.

McKelway points out that the South, certainly when compared to England, but also when compared to the North, had actually responded fairly promptly to the child labor problem. He notes that it was not until

1902 that England raised the minimum age for work in the cotton mills to twelve; in 1903 Alabama, North Carolina, and South Carolina all did.[82] The consensus of history, that the South was slow to act compared with the North, is not quite correct.[83] It is certainly true that they were later to act than most northern industrial states, but given their later industrial development, the latency period between emergence and abolition of the child labor problem was certainly no longer, and arguably substantially shorter, in the South compared with the North.

7. TENEMENT HOMEWORK
Birthplace of the Sweatshop

Figure 7.1 *Artificial Flowers*. New York City. January, 1912. Julia, a six-year-old child, making pansies for her neighbors on top floor (Gatto) 106 Thompson Street, N.Y. They said she does this every day, "but not all day." A growler and dirty beer glasses in the window, unwashed dishes on the stove, clothes everywhere,—and flowers likewise. *(Courtesy of the Library of Congress, Prints and Photographs Division, Lewis Wickes Hine National Child Labor Commiitee Collection, LC-USZ62–38229.)*

"I like school better than home. I don't like home. There's too many flowers."

Such were the sentiments of little Angelina, a seven-year-old girl who spoke with NCLC and National Consumers League activist Mary Van

Kleeck. Angelina worked in her home until ten or eleven o'clock each night making artificial flowers to help her mother earn her sixty cents per day. She was a bright little girl who not only liked school, but wanted to do well there. But how was she to handle her schoolwork when all her after-school hours until late at night were taken up with flowers? Simple enough, she got up early each morning to do her schoolwork. "This morning, first I did the writing, then I did the two times, and then the three times, so I won't have so much to do tomorrow."[1]

Industrial homework—that is, manufacturing carried on in private dwellings—occupies a particularly troublesome niche in the struggle for the abolition of industrial child labor. While industrial establishments —mines, mills, and factories—did not surrender their child workers easily, they eventually did yield. But the home is the first and last refuge of child labor. Abolition of child labor from industrial homework was never fully achieved. Progress was always halting and difficult to sustain; regress was not uncommon.

Industrial Homework and the Sweating System

In its benign, even beneficial, preindustrial state, the home was where children learned values and responsibility, where they learned to perform chores and otherwise help out, where they developed primitive industrial skills and acquired primitive industrial habits. But the home was also the birthplace of the sweatshop.[2] Industrial homework represents a transitional form of productive activity, linking industrial production to preindustrial production methods. It is production of manufactured goods for markets, but the production itself remains within the confines of the preindustrial household economy. Industrial homework is the proto-industrial putting-out system (i.e., industrial goods are placed into private homes for manufacture) projected into a maturing industrial economy. The sweating system is a putting-out system carried to its logical (under laissez-faire assumptions) conclusion.

Children and child labor were often brought into industry through the putting-out system. In textiles, many of the Yankee farm girls who populated the Waltham System boardinghouses got their basic skills training back on the farm in the cottage industries. The child labor system in many industries (such as glass, textiles, other light manufacturing) was often imported directly from the home workshops into the factories. In turn, as the factories began to turn away from child labor, not all child labor was eradicated. The system began putting out children as well as industrial production. Some of the child labor was merely displaced back into the homework sectors of the industry. This was especially true in the further contracting sectors of the garment industry and the needle trades. As reform came to the mines, mills, and factories, child labor and other conditions connoted by the term "sweatshop" retreated to the backwaters of the industry—back toward the home.

America had never developed the extensive putting-out system that prevailed in Britain and throughout most of northern and western Europe. To be sure, we had our proto-industrial exemplars in glass, textiles, shoes, and other mercantile goods often produced by skilled craftspeople. But these moved off to the factory as soon as technology or economies of scale called for them. As a result, a sweating system did not really develop in the United States until the 1880s or 1890s. In those industries where widespread patterns of homework emerged, it was not because of strong preindustrial traditions, it was more because economic incentives enabled and encouraged the movement of work from the factory to the home. During the 1880s this movement "spread like a fungus" so that by the 1890s "it was a universal blight."[3] In America, industrial homework came to be concentrated most clearly in that group of industries loosely identified as the garment and needle trades.[4] Because industrial homework was so closely associated with the garment industry and needle trades, it was also closely associated with urban tenement environments. While the garment industry operated homework networks in many urban centers such as Chicago, Cincinnati, Milwaukee, and Rochester, the focal point was New York City, the center of the garment industry. The tenements of New York City epitomized urban congestion. Factory workers, earning bare subsistence wages in seasonal work, preferred to save the nickel carfare and live close to the factory. Homeworkers, who made less and had the added burden of picking up materials and delivering finished goods, were also advantaged by living close. In one Manhattan block alone, there were seventy-seven factories employing 40,000 workers.[5] Ringed around the factories and contract sweatshops were the tenements—the home workshops. In New York City's tenement sweatshops, a variety of goods were produced, including paper bags, shelled and packaged nuts, and stripped tobacco and cigars and cigarettes. Nearly all the artificial flowers consumed in America, whether sold as ornamentation on hats, purses, or clothing, or sold separately, were made in New York tenements.[6] By far, however, most industrial homework was connected to the garment industry and the needle trades. Most custom clothing and upper-end men's wear and women's fashion were produced in factories as inside work. Finishing work—for example, hand-sewing the lining to the garment—might be outsourced to the tenements, but the skilled work remained under strict management scrutiny. In lower-end ready-to-wear clothing, more of the work could be profitably performed outside, as it was subject to less rigorous quality standards. At the same time, there were some homework tasks that required fine skill and high quality, such as glove stitching, embroidery, and crocheted Irish lace (produced mostly by Jews and Italians).

Wherever it existed in America, industrial homework was inextricably linked to the sweating system. According to John R. Commons, "The term 'sweating,' or 'sweating system,' originally denoted a system of subcontract, wherein the work is let out to contractors to be done in small shops or homes." Thus, "the system to be contrasted with the sweating system is the 'factory system.' " A typical arrangement in many of the garment trades was for the manufacturer to operate one or more "inside shops" along with a network of "outside shops." The inside shop was the factory where the manufacturer hired employees to work under the supervision of management on the manufacturer's own premises. In the factory, the cloth was cut and some of the more highly skilled or technologically advanced work might be performed. But much of the material was prepared for putting out to contractors. The factories also housed inspectors to receive the finished work from contractors and perhaps a crew to rework garments that did not pass inspection. It is useful to distinguish conceptually between two levels of outside shops, though in practice the distinction was often blurred. First were the contractor sweatshops. In these, the contractor congregated a small group of workers to perform specified contract work. These workshops were often located in the living quarters of the contractor, but for regulatory purposes they were generally treated as factories. During the busy season, most sweaters also further contracted work to the next level of outside shop—industrial homework. In the industrial home workshop, the household contracted for work with the sweater and performed the work within their own home. Under either arrangement, the sweater served as the middleman between the manufacturer and the workers. Professor Commons noted:

> The position of the contractor or sweater now in the business in American cities is peculiarly that of an organizer and employer of immigrants.

The man best fitted to be a contractor is the man who is well acquainted with his neighbors, who is able to speak the language of several classes of immigrants, who can easily persuade his neighbors or their wives and children to work for him, and who in this way can obtain the cheapest help.[7]

By developing a reliable network of home-based worksites, manufacturers could greatly reduce labor costs. Over time, it was estimated that homeworkers averaged one-third the wages of inside factory workers.[8] But labor cost savings were hardly the whole story. Through the use of homework, manufacturers could save money on rent and utilities and often equipment, especially in labor-intensive operations that often consumed a disproportionate share of factory space. Outsourcing the low-value-adding operations enabled enhanced efficiency in the more capital-intensive operations that remained in the factory. Availability of a network of home-based worksites also enabled factories to manage the ebb and flow of product demand, shifting more work to private homes when the factory approached capacity, pulling work back into the factory when demand slackened. Industrial homeworkers were an added blessing to the garment industry. The seasonal nature of the work, coupled with the strict piece-rate payment systems, assured productivity with little or no supervision. The garment industry had always been seasonal, and every homeworker understood the need to maximize earnings during the busy season because work would be hard to find in the slack season. Piece-rates established a clear line of sight between work inputs such as effort, intensity, and hours. Seasonality and piece-rate pay also dictated that all available hands, including the very young children, be fully engaged in the production process.

Not only did the industrial homeworkers provide the capital financing for plant and equipment, not only did they work hard without supervision, they also assumed the distribution costs associated with maintaining the network of home-based worksites. Homeworkers assumed responsibility for picking up materials at the factory or from the contractor as well as returning the finished goods. If the woman could not go to the factory herself, or send an older child, or hire a neighbor, she could arrange for delivery and pickup by the contractor and work for a reduced piece rate. Similarly, if the contractor provided any of the machinery, the family worked for a reduced rate.

Homeworkers were, in many ways, an ideal workforce. They occupied the bottom rung of the job hierarchy (and the children occupied the bottom of the bottom rung). The manufacturer often did not even know who their homeworkers were, and if they did, they could readily disclaim responsibility, displacing it to the sweaters. In the case of children, even the sweaters could disclaim responsibility—child labor was the parents' doing. Homeworkers were the worst paid, endured the worst conditions, and enjoyed the least job security of all workers in the supply chain. Ultimately, homeworker compliance was compelled by necessity. Those who were able to obtain work outside the home, in the factories, generally did so. The pay, the conditions, the lifestyle were all better. That left for homework those who needed work but could not get out. A disproportionate share of homeworkers were women with very young children, widows, women caring for sick and disabled family members, and women who were sick and disabled themselves, and, of course, their children. Women who needed work, but could not leave home, took in homework.[9]

The NCLC and Industrial Homework

Unlike the other industrial sectors highlighted in this book, the NCLC conducted relatively few large-scale or systematic investigations of industrial homework, especially during the early years. Unlike other industries, where child labor was not well documented, other organizations had studied child labor in tenement homework more thoroughly before the NCLC came on the scene. The New York Child Labor Committee had given great emphasis to the tenements in its investigative work. The National Consumers League and the trade unions were working for the abolition of homework and had conducted their own investigations. Finally, there was a much larger and much broader social movement afoot to investigate and remediate the conditions of the urban tenement slums.

Child labor was well known and understood to be a product of the poverty associated with urban tenement slums. Still, no one attempted to seriously estimate the number of children involved in industrial homework. Florence Kelley suggested the only way to estimate the number of child workers was to have two inspectors for each tenement, one by day and one by night. The New York Bureau of Labor Statistics cautioned that, in estimating the number of child tenement workers, it was "advisable to ascertain the total number of children, for even those who attend school regularly do more or less work at home."[10]

By the time the National Child Labor Committee arrived on the scene in 1904, considerable progress had already been made in eliminating labor of very young children from important sectors of the New York garment industry. The reform movement had already secured a fourteen-year minimum age for factory work and a regimen of factory inspection. The law was generally obeyed by the major garment manufacturers in their own factories. From the factories, child labor was pushed out into the contract sweatshops, but the factory laws applied to them as well, and so, by 1904, they too employed very few young children. Conditions in contract sweatshops may have remained deplorable in other respects, but they no longer presented a major child labor problem. Elimination of child labor from the contract sweatshops, in turn, pushed the problem another step deeper in the supply chain into the industrial homework settings.

Ad Hoc Investigations

During the early years of the NCLC, much of their investigative work in this industry was anecdotal, ad hoc, and opportunistic. Large-scale investigations were not conducted until the 1920s and 1930s. But there were numerous smaller-scale forays into the garment district. NCLC headquarters were located in the so-called Charities Building at Twenty-Second Street and Fourth Avenue in Manhattan. Inquiries received in the office, or information shared between the various organizations located in the building, might result in sending someone out to look into the situation.[11] The account of an unidentified investigator provides an illustration of this kind of ad hoc investigation:

> A caller at the National Child Labor Committee . . . stated that Ratanosky, a maker of caps of 55 Bond Street, conducts a very dirty factory, employs children and does not pay . . . called at 55 Bond Street. Found it to be a private house, the third floor, of which was an attic with sloping roof, is divided into four rooms. One of these rooms about 8 × 10 feet in size is occupied by Ratanosky. . . . He uses the room for his own home. The working material was piled on his bed and a small stove in the room was used for cooking purposes. There was one girl at work when I called at 8.15 A.M. . . . Her mother does work at home for [Ratanosky]. Her little sister of three helps the mother. . . . I worked from 9 to 12.45 when a half hour was allowed for lunch. R. said since he was "learning" me I would get no pay for the first day's work.[12]

Nothing came of this investigation, as nothing came of most of these small-scale investigations. Information on a single establishment had little publicity value. Further, once the investigator observed that "a printed notice from the factory inspection department hung on the wall," there was nothing that could be done legally. The "factory" was properly licensed and therefore legal.[13] Ratanosky's "factory" was, of course, not a factory at all, but rather his bedroom with cookstove where caps happened to be made. Ratanosky was a contractor. Some caps were made in Ratanosky's room, but most were made in other homes throughout the neighborhood. The factory that placed the goods with Ratanosky was required to ensure that his room was licensed. But once he had the goods, Ratanosky was free to further contract for their production with unlicensed tenements.

The Universal Brush Company

A 1912 publication on child labor in tenement homework provoked a flurry of investigative activity in cooperation with a manufacturer of hairbrushes. This investigation yielded more positive outcomes. The report included a photograph showing a family inserting bristles in to rubber pads for brushes[14] (Figure 7.2). Henry Alexander, president of the Universal Brush Company, wrote to Owen Lovejoy objecting that the situation had not been brought to his attention earlier so he could rectify it. He assured Lovejoy that:

> [I]t was never my intention of having children do this work; the work was never given out by me to children, but to women and men, who claimed that they needed the work at home for crippled members of their family, for people too feeble or old to work in factories, for people out of employment, or as an additional income needed for their daily wants.[15]

Alexander asserted that this process "is a house industry all over the world, no practical mechanical process for inserting these bristles having been invented to date," and that he was paying better rates than were paid in London, Birmingham, or Munich, the three centers of the industry in Europe. Further, Alexander pledged cooperation with the NCLC in eradicating child labor from his operation. He stated, "I feel deeply hurt and humiliated by being exhibited as an exploiter of child labor—the last thing in God's great Universe, that I could possibly be guilty of."[16]

Lovejoy took Henry Alexander up on his offer. First, Universal Brush conducted its own provisional investigation. As a result, it cut off work to twenty-six families using, or suspected of using, child labor. Next, it required families continuing to receive work to sign a pledge that no

Figure 7.2 *Filling Brushes.* New York City. January, 1912. Making hair-brushes. Hausner family, 310 E 71 St N.Y. Frank is 6 yrs old and John is 12. The mother had a sore throat and wore a great rag wrapped around it, but she took it off for the photo. They said they all (including the 6 yr old) worked until 10 P.M. when busy. Their neighbors corroborated this. She said "It's a whole lot better for the boys than doin' nothin'." The mother said the night work hurts their eyes and John said so too. He was not very enthusiastic about the beauties of the work. All together, they make about $2 a week. Father is a motorman. *(Courtesy of the Library of Congress, Prints and Photographs Division, Lewis Wickes Hine National Child Labor Committee Collection, LC-H5–2819.)*

child under sixteen would work on the brushes (Figure 7.3), establishing a fine of $10 for violations, and providing for inspections by either the company or the National Child Labor Committee.

Then Universal Brush provided the NCLC with names and addresses of all families that had received work from the company in the recent past, including the families that had been cut off. NCLC investigators visited all the addresses on the lists. Investigators found very few violations of the new company policy, and those they found were promptly rectified. Further, they were able to verify that the families the company claimed to have cut off were, indeed, no longer working on brushes. As an illustrative case, investigator Herschel Jones visited Mrs. J. Milligan at 1847 Broadway in Brooklyn and made the following notation, "Has

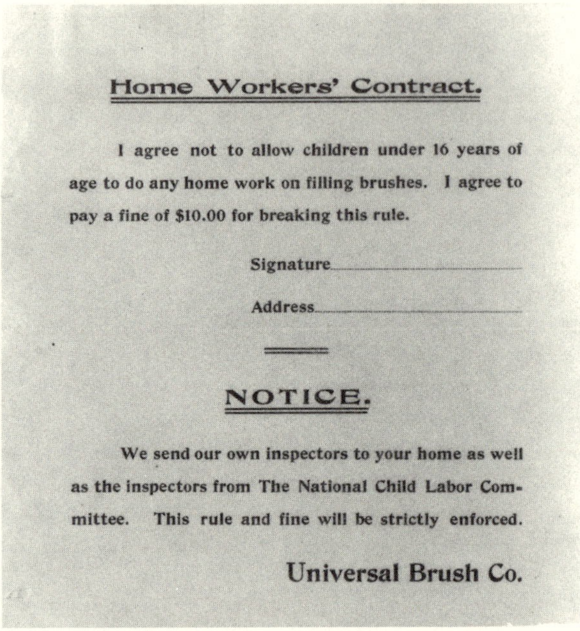

Home Workers' Contract.

I agree not to allow children under 16 years of age to do any home work on filling brushes. I agree to pay a fine of $10.00 for breaking this rule.

Signature..

Address..

NOTICE.

We send our own inspectors to your home as well as the inspectors from The National Child Labor Committee. This rule and fine will be strictly enforced.

Universal Brush Co.

Figure 7.3 *Home Workers' Contract*. NCLC Investigation Report 403, Owen R. Lovejoy, 1913, New York, tenement homework, p. 17, "Home Workers' Contract."

several children. Stopped working several months ago when they 'made this fuss about the children working.' Wants to take it up again if they will let her, but thinks there is no chance."[17]

Here was an example, then, of how the NCLC exposed child labor problems in an employer's operation, of which the otherwise responsible employer was probably genuinely unaware. The employer was then able to take a number of concrete measures—investigation, establishing a code of conduct, enforcing the code, and providing for ongoing monitoring and inspection by both internal and external agents—to effectively eradicate the child labor problem.

The New Jersey Investigations

A series of events in New York City in the early 1910s prompted a series of investigations in New Jersey in the 1920s. The 1909 shirtwaist strike by 20,000 workers, mostly young immigrant women, was followed in 1910 by the cloak makers strike when 60,000 men walked out. To settle these strikes, Louis D. Brandeis, acting as a fact finder, brokered what came to be known as the Protocol of Peace. The protocol itself did not establish substantive terms and conditions of employment such as wages and hours. Instead, it established the procedural rules through which substantive decisions would be made. One key principle was joint determination—the employer and union would jointly determine wages, hours, and terms and conditions. Another key principle was that the protocol, and substantive provisions worked out under the protocol, were to be extended to the contractors.[18] When sweatshop contractors were required to provide wages and conditions comparable to those in unionized factories, there was no longer an economic rationale for the sweatshop system. For a few years under the protocol, the sweatshops dwindled. Unions were effectively monitoring and enforcing provisions of the protocol throughout the further-contracting network. By about 1915, only 25 percent of cloakmaking was carried on as outside work; 75 percent had been moved into the factories. Eventually, however, manufacturers came to realize that the unions could only effectively enforce the protocol within their own geographic jurisdictions (which, by tradition, were determined according to streetcar lines). Contractors beyond the geographic reach of the local union were far more difficult to monitor.

The second series of events was triggered by the Triangle Shirtwaist Factory fire of March 25, 1911, in which 146 people, mostly young first- and second-generation immigrant women, perished when a fire broke out in the seventh- and eighth-floor factory into which the women had been locked. The Triangle Shirtwaist fire galvanized the nation and led to the passage of worker compensation laws in every state. But it also led to a general upgrading of New York's factory laws, including its child labor laws. A 1913 law was directed at the homework system. It prohibited production of certain goods in homework (e.g., food, dolls, doll clothing, and children's wearing apparel), banned homework in cellars and basements, required employers to tag bundles put out for homework with their own name and address, and, most significantly, banned homework by children under fourteen. While the latter provision proved impossible to enforce, it did provide "official recognition that children under fourteen should not do the work."[19]

Both the Protocol of Peace and the tightening of New York law resulted in pushing much of the further-contracting sector of the garment industry across the river into New Jersey. By the mid-1920s, 75 percent of workers in the coat and suit sector of the industry worked in contract sweatshops, reversing the ratio of a decade earlier.[20] Much of this contract work came to New Jersey. As early as 1910, Mrs. G.W.B. Cushing, head of the New Jersey Child Labor Committee, commented that the tenement licensing requirements alone in New York City were having their predictable effects. "We have found . . . very much of this sweated industry coming over because of the severe New York law."[21] So in the early 1920s, the NCLC, working with the New Jersey Child Labor Committee, conducted a series of investigations in the immigrant neighborhoods of Paterson, Passaic, Newark, and Jersey City. A. Benedict documented her account of home visits throughout the neighborhoods. An illustrative observation from each of the cities she investigated is included below.

> Crosley, 211 Martin St., Paterson . . . 6 children. Oldest 11. . . . One of the filthiest I have visited. The children, particularly the oldest, work on stockings. This is one of the worst cases. Almost all of the children are troubled with sores, and upon the admission of the Mother, Margot has not been in school since the latter part of October, because of sores in her head. . . . Two children have just returned from the hospital where they were suffering from diphtheria. Margot told me that the family was working on stockings when the children came down with the disease.[22]

> Ross, 23 McClean St., Passaic . . . 4 children. . . . Place clean. Child of about 13 worked on French knots until last June, when her father said he made her give it up as she was ruining her eyes and learning nothing. . . . She is a child who plans to go to high school, and hopes to become a teacher. Her father feels that he did well in saving her eyesight for better things.[23]

> Tobin, 41 Sheffield Street, Newark . . . 6 children. Uncertain of ages, except one of 11. Another looked about 10. . . . This place was the filthiest I had visited. It was impossible to remain longer than absolutely necessary. Refuse, soiled clothes and food littered the place. The mother's sweater was crusted with dirt. . . . The school nurse reports that these children have been sent home so many times for dirt and vermin that the mother has appeared in court about the matter. She claims she has no time to keep the children clean. She spends her time making dolls' clothes.[24]

> Pilla, 434 Second St., Jersey City . . . 5 children. Oldest 13 years. . . . School nurse reports that one of the children has recently bought glasses. This is an interesting example of the vicious circle created by child labor.

The child herself has earned the money, $6.00, at the rate of $1.00 a week with which to buy the glasses. This money was earned embroidering gowns.[25]

The NRA Investigations

In 1934, the National Child Labor Committee conducted an extensive series of investigations at the request of Robert Straus of the New York Compliance Board of the National Recovery Administration (NRA). The Code of Fair Competition for the Artificial Flower and Feather Industry was adopted on September 14, 1933. It called for a 50 percent reduction in the number of homeworkers by January 1, 1934, and complete elimination of homework by May 1, 1934. It also adopted a minimum age of sixteen, whether the work was performed in a factory or at home.

> Great dissatisfaction developed in the industry, however. One branch, ardently desired homework and felt that operations entirely within the factory were an economic impossibility. Another branch felt that the salvation of the industry required that homework be abolished. They pointed out the impossibility of paying NRA wages and maintaining NRA working conditions in competition with manufacturers who, through the system of having work done in tenements, were able to pay much lower wages and, since they did not have to provide space for workers, avoided much of the expense for rent, light and heat, which their competitors were obliged to carry.[26]

The first and most extensive investigation was conducted from February through April 1934. This was the period where homeworkers were to be reduced by 50 percent. It should be noted that child labor under sixteen was prohibited during the entire period the NRA codes were in force. Approximately 2,000 visits were made to 1,700 addresses in and around New York City using lists supplied by the code authority. In the 1,038 families actually interviewed, there were 869 children between the ages of eight and fifteen, and at least 132 were proved working. Another 29 were suspected of working. NCLC investigators considered this a substantial underestimate:

> It should be noted that it is now extremely difficult to detect cases where children are actually at work. Our investigators almost invariably report that there is an interval between the time they knock on the door and the

time they are admitted, which gives the family an opportunity to get the children away from any work they may be doing. One investigator stated that she caught a glimpse of children working in one family, but the door was slammed in her face, and ten minutes later when she was admitted, the children had been removed to the kitchen. Another investigator reported that after knocking on the door, she heard a great rustling of papers, running to and fro, etc., and when she got in, the room was bare of work. Another investigator reported that when she called at a certain apartment, the frosting was scratched off the glass in the door and she could see a small child at work. When she knocked the child ran into the other room and all traces of the work were carefully removed before she was allowed to enter.[27]

The NCLC concluded that "children are employed and will continue to be employed as long as homework is allowed, especially where very low wages are paid." They also concluded that the homework system was "utterly destructive of the standards set up by the codes."[28] Some illustrative findings include:

> The children who were found at work or admitted working, help after school sometimes until very late at night. For example, Lucy, (age 12 years) stated that she hated to work and insisted upon going to bed by 12 o'clock because she had to go to school. "The family thought her lazy." Families sometimes admit that everybody works all night if necessary to get through an order. . . . One woman told our investigator that she was glad homework had been stopped because so many children were doing it. She stated that she had seen children working from the age of 5 years up. "The mothers put them to work right after school and in the evenings." A 12-year-old school girl said "they were dopey in school, and the teachers yelled at them because they did not know their lessons." . . . Christina 8 years old finds bending wire too difficult with her hands, so she uses her teeth and James 11 years old helps. These children's thumbs were lacerated by bending wires. In this connection, it is interesting to note that we have found 8 cases of thumbs or fingers infected after such laceration by wires.[29]

A second series of interviews were conducted from May 1934 through May 1935. This was the period during which homework was to have been abolished under the NRA codes. A total of 1,376 follow-up visits were conducted, resulting in interviews with 777 families. Only twenty-four families were found doing homework in violation of the codes, and only three children under 16 were found working. A third series of interviews was conducted from June 1935 through December 1935, after the NRA had been found unconstitutional; 781 visits were made, resulting in interviews with 500 families: Fifty-nine families were found doing homework and nineteen children under 16 were found working.[30] While they had not returned to the levels existing when the codes first went into effect, both homework and child labor in homework were becoming more prevalent.

Impossibility of Regulation: Necessity of Abolition

Before the NCLC arrived on the scene, other reformers had already concluded that the entire system of industrial homework had to be scrapped. Mary Van Kleeck, who worked for both the National Consumers League and the NCLC, remarked, "The nature of this system of industry is such that its evils are its essence."[31] Robert Hunter, who as head of the New York Child Labor Committee had participated in an investigation of the tenements in 1902, concluded that child labor "probably will not be protected until the sweatshop system as a whole is abolished."[32] The NCLC inherited this conclusion as one of its operating assumptions. Assuming homework was impossible to regulate, the committee called for a prohibition on placing goods for manufacture into private homes.[33]

Correspondence between Owen Lovejoy for the NCLC and Henry Alexander of the Universal Brush Company clearly indicated the NCLC position, but also clearly indicated what they were up against in seeking a total ban on homework. In spite of the cooperative efforts between the NCLC and Universal Brush, there were a number of issues on which their leaders fundamentally and philosophically disagreed. Lovejoy asserted, "This Committee is definitely opposed to the transfer of factory occupations to the homes of the people." Unless the system of industrial homework was abolished, elimination of child labor could not be ensured:

> I venture to affirm that however definite you may be in your determination to forbid child labor in this branch of your industry, you can not be sure that it has been eliminated unless you personally follow the work into every tenement where it is done, and subject these places to frequent inspections, both by day and night.[34]

Alexander replied with a forceful and compelling articulation of the "widows and orphans" defense:

As to your remarks, that your Committee is definitely opposed to the transfer of factory occupations to the homes of people, I would state that while the principle may be a correct one, the applications of it—until some suitable work is found for people, unable to work in factories—would be most harsh and cruel.—I personally am taking quite some interest in some of the people that come here for work and I call your attention to the Buckingham family—blind people—to whom home earnings are an absolute necessity.—Or the case of Mrs. Wilson, a refined woman, near the age of seventy, with a feeble husband, unable to do outside work. ... Take the case of Mrs. Donoghue with a crippled son in her home, who I understand, assists her in this work and thereby helps her, in the only way that he can, to make a living.—What can you offer these people, when home work is taken away from them? They are much too respectable to ask for alms.[35]

There was no doubt that a ban on homework would eliminate child labor in homework. Further, limited experience with homework bans indicated such an approach could be effective. New York State banned homework on food, dolls, doll clothes, and children's apparel. Unfortunately, the ban was both sector and jurisdiction specific. It may have effectively eliminated homework in the specified sectors in New York, but it had little overall effect. Work on banned items could be shifted to New Jersey, and displaced homeworkers in New York could shift to nonbanned items.

In other cases, bans were imposed in specific sectors across a wider geographic jurisdiction. One example was in manufacture of military uniforms:

While neither the Federal Government nor any state government has undertaken to abolish tenement house work where the work is sold to private purchasers, yet where the Federal Government is itself a purchaser of clothing it has undertaken to establish this condition. Since the Spanish-American War when it seemed to be clearly demonstrated that the contagion of measles and other diseases in the army was owing directly to tenement house manufacture, the War Department has inserted in its contracts with the manufacturers of military garments that all work must be done in a regularly organized factory, and no part of the work shall be sublet to contractors.[36]

So, in 1917 during World War I, when Sidney Hillman, newly elected president of the Amalgamated Clothing Workers of America, approached

Florence Kelley with reports that a substantial amount of work on U.S. Army uniforms was being let for homework, the ban on homework was reinstituted in short order. Kelley took the reports to Secretary of War John Graham Brooks, who also happened to be president of the National Consumers League. After investigation confirmed Hillman's reports, federal contracting guidelines were tightened up, providing for improved contracts, improved safeguards to ensure that bidders were qualified (that is, they were not sweatshops), additional inspectors to enforce compliance, and a preference for letting contracts to manufacturers operating under collective bargaining agreements. At the 1918 annual meeting of the National Consumers League, Florence Kelley was able to announce that industrial homework had once again been abolished in the production of military uniforms.[37]

The only example of a broad ban on most forms of homework across the entire United States was during the short period when the NRA Codes were in effect. One complicating factor was that there was not one single code for the entire garment industry and all the needle trades. Each major sector of the industry had its own code and its own code authority. Still, most of the codes both established a sixteen-year age limit and banned homework. A few items traditionally produced in homework settings escaped the codes, but most were covered.

NCLC investigations of the codes in the artificial flower and feather industry demonstrate convincingly the effectiveness of banning homework in eliminating child labor. The NCLC conducted an extensive series of three investigations, one when the codes had just gone into effect and homework was to be phased out, a second when the ban on homework was in effect, and a third shortly after the NRA Codes had been invalidated. Table 7.1 presents and compares results from these three investigations.

The results provide support for the NCLC contention that in order to eliminate child labor in industrial homework, industrial homework itself must be banned. Investigation 1, conducted under conditions where child labor was illegal, found a large number of children working (1 child worker for every 3.65 families engaged in homework). Investigation 2, conducted under conditions where homework itself was illegal, found only three working children (one for every 259 families interviewed, and one for every eight families engaged in illegal homework). Unfortunately, Investigation 3 indicates that after the NRA Codes were lifted, not only did the prevalence of homework increase (from 3.1

Table 7.1

Summary of Three NCLC Investigations of NRA Codes in Artificial Flowers and Feathers

	Families interviewed	Families with homework (%)	Children found working	Families interviewed per child worker	Families with homework per child worker
Investigation 1 February–April 1934 (50% reduction in homework; child labor illegal)	1,038	482 (46.4)	132	7.86	3.65
Investigation 2 May 1934–May 1935 (homework and child labor illegal)	777	24 (3.1)	3	259.00	8.00
Investigation 3 June–December 1935 (NRA Codes unconstitutional)	500	59 (11.8)	19	26.32	3.11

Source: Compiled by the author from data presented in New York tenement homework, NCLC Investigation Report 421, various pages.

percent of families interviewed to 11.8 percent), but the prevalence of child labor increased as well. Once again, approximating the ratio from Investigation 1, one child under sixteen worked for every 3.11 families engaged in homework. In sum, banning child labor did not eliminate child labor from industrial homework, but banning child labor and banning homework was an effective combination. Of the two bans, the ban on homework was the most effective in eliminating child labor. Finally, however, it should be noted that even an outright ban on homework did not eliminate all homework.[38]

Ultimately, both public opinion and legal tradition made it highly unlikely that homework would be banned altogether. Neither public opinion nor law were willing to permit government intrusion into otherwise legal private conduct in private homes, even if that conduct was industrial production. In the end, it was probably just this same public sentiment that condemned the Child Labor Amendment to defeat. The broad legal contours of the debate were laid down much earlier.

The 1885 New York Supreme Court case *In re Jacobs* "cast a long shadow and prompted the drafters of future legislation to move cautiously."[39] In 1881 Samuel Gompers, then president of the Cigar-Makers Union, compiled data showing that nearly ten thousand people, including several thousand children, were working in the cigar trade in tenement home workshops and accounted for almost half of New York City's cigar production. With this data, the Cigar-Makers were successful in obtaining a law that prohibited the manufacture of cigars or preparation of tobacco in tenements.[40] Manufacturers immediately challenged the law on the basis that it unreasonably interfered with their freedom of contract and their private property rights as well as the freedoms and rights of the homeworkers themselves. Manufacturers argued that labor's main motive was to secure control of the cigar trade. The court agreed with the manufacturers.[41] The law not only unreasonably interfered with freedom of contract, but the judges even rejected the idea that homework might be harmful to either the homeworkers or the consuming public. They found it difficult to see "how the cigar-maker is to be improved in his health or his morals by forcing him from his home and its hallowed associations and beneficent influences, to ply his trade elsewhere." They asked, "What possible relation can cigar-making in any building have to the health of the general public?"[42]

Impossibility of Abolition: Necessity of Regulation

Because neither the NCLC nor anyone else was ever able to achieve a sustained ban on industrial homework, it was also never quite success- ful in eliminating child labor. In the end, therefore, regulation would have to suffice. Where homework could not be banned outright, regula- tory schemes were finally devised that kept child labor abuses at a rela- tively low level.

If industrial homework could not be banned, how could it be effec- tively regulated? The New York State Supreme Court suggested a basis for regulation when it asked what relation tenement homework had to public health. Indeed, if the *Jacobs* case had been decided a decade or so later, its outcome might have been very different, because a great deal had been learned by then about health conditions in the urban tenements.

Following publication of Charles Booth's *Life and Labour in London* and Jacob A. Riis's *How the Other Half Lives* in 1890 and 1891, respec- tively, great public interest was aroused about conditions in the urban slums of the world's major cities. In New York City, state and local governments investigated and charitable societies mobilized. The first and most obvious problem of the urban slums was the congestion. Hun- dreds of thousands of people were crowded into densely packed sec- tions of the city ringing the garment district and elsewhere. (See, for example, Figure 7.4.) Whole families, often extended families, were packed into, at most, a couple of rooms that were often poorly lit and poorly ventilated. Families often shared entrances, hallways, and toilet facilities with their neighbors. But the main problem was not the congestion, it was the sanitation. To inadequate light, ventilation, and toilet facilities, add impure water and inadequate waste disposal (coupled with the problem of improper drainage), and it was no wonder that reformer and social pho- tographer Jacob Riis concluded, "You can kill a man with a tenement as easily as you can kill a man with an ax."[43] Disease was rampant. Tubercu- losis, the great white plague, of which Robert Hunter remarked, "[T]his disease is a sort of social yardstick by which one can measure social mis- ery," was especially prevalent in the urban slums.[44] When a person fell ill with tuberculosis, or any other contagious disease, a portion of the al- ready crowded tenement was converted to a sick room. But these were the same tenements in which industrial homework was carried out.

The consuming public, even if it was indifferent to the conditions of the urban slum dwellers, was concerned for its own safety and health.

Figure 7.4 *Nursing Nutpicker.* December, 1911. Mrs. Annie De Martius, 45 Laight St., front. Nursing a dirty baby while she picks nuts. Was suffering with a sore throat. Rosie, 3 yrs. old hanging around. Genevieve, 6 yrs. old, Tessie, 6 yrs old picks too. Make $1.50 to $2 a week. Husband on railroad works sometimes. *(Courtesy of the Library of Congress, Prints and Photographs Division, Lewis Wickes Hine National Child Labor Committee Collection, LC-USZ62–90348.)*

There were plentiful accounts of homework conducted in tenements occupied by people ill and dying of contagious diseases.[45] There were occasional accounts, such as the incidents of military uniforms causing contagion among soldiers, showing that goods produced under sweatshop conditions posed a real threat to public health. The potential for the spread of contagious disease, from industrial homeworkers to the consuming public, was readily recognized and became the justification for regulation of the tenement workshops.

Early attempts at regulation of the tenements were primitive. They provided only that the tenement must be licensed to conduct industrial homework. From 1892, New York law required the licensing of tenement sweatshops producing specified classes of goods. Factories were barred from placing goods for production into unlicensed tenements. By 1910, New York City was licensing more than 10,000 tenements per year.[46] Licensing generally required only that the facility (the tenement home workshop) conform to legal specifications in affording adequate sanitary conditions (and this only at the time of the licensing inspection). If sanitary conditions deteriorated after the license was issued, or if a household member became ill with an infectious or contagious disease, the license remained valid. Even these minimal licensing requirements could be readily circumvented. First, since the license was required only for work on specified goods, production of other goods was completely unregulated. Second, the law could be circumvented through further contracting. Factories were barred from placing goods into unlicensed tenements, but the work placed into one licensed tenement was often further contracted to several unlicensed tenements.

Licensing laws did not address the question of child labor in the tenements since child labor, of itself, was not seen as presenting a public health problem. Reformers attempted, largely unsuccessfully, to portray the public health risks to child tenement workers. One particular issue that received considerable attention was eyestrain, brought about by close work in poorly lit environments.[47] But children too young to work in the factories remained free to do work for the factories in their own homes. The only laws regulating child labor in the tenements were the compulsory schooling laws. When Mary Van Kleeck visited little Angelina's home, she found a mother and four children producing artificial flowers for sixty cents a day. Angelina, age seven, and her older siblings, age nine and eleven, attended school during the day and worked on flowers after school until ten or eleven o'clock each night. The mother and the youngest child, age five, worked on flowers all day and into the night. Van Kleeck observed:

> There is no law violated by the employment of these children. They are in school when they ought to be in school. The building has been inspected by the tenement department and the factory department and found satisfactory, and there is nothing which legally can be done to prevent the work of five-, seven-, nine-, or eleven-year-old children.[48]

At this time, 1910, New York had among the most advanced child labor laws (including a minimum age of fourteen for factory work) and compulsory schooling laws in the nation. Further, it had the most stringent licensing requirements for tenement sweatshops. And yet, in thousands of tenement sweatshops, children too young for factory work, indeed children too young to be covered by compulsory schooling laws, could work unlimited hours with impunity. In spite of their limitations, however, these early licensing laws laid a foundation—got a foot in the door, so to speak—for future regulation. It was the entering wedge for government intrusion into the home. If nothing else, the laws provided a pretext for inspectors and reformers to go around knocking on doors and asking questions.

As difficult as it might have been to develop effective inspection and enforcement regimes for factories, homework was far more difficult. Ultimately, they could not be regulated in the same ways. There were simply too many home worksites that were too highly dispersed throughout urban neighborhoods to make inspection a meaningful alternative. At best, tenements could be inspected at the time of licensing, and later when licenses were to be renewed. Further, the locations of home worksites were too fluid to keep up with. Homeworkers themselves moved with some frequency from one tenement to another. Work itself could be readily moved from one neighborhood to another, or even to other cities in other states. And the ethnic composition of the home workforce changed with changing patterns of immigration. Before 1900, Jews from Eastern Europe dominated the homework trades. By 1911, only 33 percent were Jews, their place having been taken largely by Italians.[49] Finally, as concerned child labor, regulation by inspection, even if it had aimed directly at the child labor problem, would have been utterly ineffective, since children could simply lay down their work before the inspector entered the tenement.

Two forms of nongovernmental regulation were attempted, met with some success, and eventually fell by the wayside, though they also provided some impetus for more effective governmental regulation. First, there was regulation by the trade unions. Second, a few consumer labeling programs were introduced.

As noted previously, major strikes in the New York City garment industry—first the shirtwaist makers' strike in 1909 followed by the cloak makers' strike in 1910—led to the so-called Protocol of Peace that was designed to regulate conditions in the industry through an elaborate process of joint determination between the unions and employers. On the union side, the cloak makers placed Abraham Bisno in the position of chief clerk of their Joint Board—that is, he was the top union staffer dealing with the protocol.

> [Bisno's] main idea was to clean up the demoralizing conditions in the industry brought about by the contracting system. . . . The fly-by-night contractor as well as the stooge submanufacturer, attached to a single

large concern, were to be eliminated altogether as industrial termites. "Out-of-town shops" in the vicinity of New York City were to be corralled under the jurisdiction of the Protocol. [Bisno's] slogan was, "Don't let the bundles roll out of New York City."[50]

Both the union and the employer were to accept joint responsibility for prices, wages, and working conditions throughout the industry, not only in the unionized factories but also in the contract sweatshops and homework settings. The union's interest was obvious: bringing the entire industry under one umbrella was the only way to control the entire industry. For a while, under Bisno's leadership, the protocol was tremendously effective in eliminating contract sweatshops and led to a dramatic reduction in homework. In turn, it led to near elimination of child labor from key and leading sectors of the garment industry, though that was never Bisno's principal intent. That the Protocol of Peace, for a time, nearly eliminated sweatshops, homework, and child labor seems to be the consensus of history.[51] That the protocol failed to provide a lasting or final solution to any of these problems is equally obvious. In the end, the protocol could not prevent the bundles from rolling out of New York City. The union, through bilateralism, could enforce the protocol within its own jurisdiction, but was dependent on the unilateral action of employers to enforce the protocol when it was beyond the union's reach. Unilateralism predictably failed. Employers simply had too many incentives and too much at stake in the sweatshop system to give it up just yet. Likewise, the protocol could not prevent homeworkers from taking up work that was not subject to the protocol. If work on men's coats and suits and other higher-end garments was no longer available, then homeworkers could simply shift to lower-end garments or other work, such as artificial flowers, that was beyond the reach of the protocol.

The most far-reaching of the consumer labeling projects was the National Consumers League label for white goods, that is, women and children's cotton underwear. The league had struggled with the question of how the conscientious consumer, who did not want to buy goods produced under substandard conditions, could know what goods to buy and what goods to avoid. They came up with the idea of the label. The next question was how to induce manufacturers to qualify for the use of the label. To keep the project manageable, they decided to begin in one relatively small industry, white goods. The labeling project commenced in 1899 with the arrival of Florence Kelley.[52]

To qualify for the National Consumers League label, manufacturers had to meet three requirements. First, work by children under sixteen was prohibited. At the time, no other industry, except for mining in some states, had adopted the sixteen-year minimum-age standard. Second, tenement homework was prohibited. All work must be completed on the employer's own premises. Third, the factory was required to observe all state laws. By the end of the first year of the project, Kelley was able to report that fifteen factories had qualified for the label and had agreed to affix it to their products. Many more failed to qualify. After ten years, however, seventy manufacturers, that is, all of the major producers in the industry and most of the rest of the industry, were using the National Consumers League label. While there remained a few renegade manufacturers whose standards could not be guaranteed, by the end of the labeling program's fifteen-year existence, it could be fairly claimed that both child labor and tenement homework had been largely driven out of the white goods industry. Still, this was just one relatively small industry, and there were plenty of other industries that continued to provide work for children in homework settings.

Sustained progress in eliminating child labor from tenement homework was not made until the New Deal era. The role of the NRA Codes has already been mentioned. The Fair Labor Standards Act served to reduce demand for homeworkers in general, and child homeworkers in particular. Under the Fair Labor Standards Act, the sixteen-year minimum age was applied to homework. But equally important were the minimum wage, maximum hours, and provisions making homeworkers statutory employees of the contractors. These provisions dramatically reduced, but did not entirely eliminate, the incentives for manufacturers to put work out for home production. On the supply side, the Social Security Act's provisions for pensions for widows, orphans, and disabled people reduced the need for those who could not get out to work to take work into their homes. Both homework and child labor in homework were dramatically reduced. That this reduction was achieved during an economic depression speaks to the effectiveness of the regulatory regime. Still, the New Deal reforms did not and could not achieve the final abolition of child labor in homework sought by the NCLC. Under the right conditions, sufficient incentives remained for manufacturers to place work out. And among poor households, sufficient need remained to take work in. Once the work was in the home, there could be no guarantee that it would not be performed by children.

Conclusion

Under the sweating system of contracting, subcontracting, and further contracting in the garment and needle trades, labor-intensive portions of the work tend to seek the bottom. As standards for factory work are progressively elevated, the labor-intensive work runs to the less regulated sectors—to the backwaters—the dark recesses of the industry. When the work finally enters the home, it has reached the bottom where it can remain largely hidden from view behind the "hallowed associations and beneficent influences" of the home.

8. THE STREET TRADES

Figure 8.1 *Newsie.* St. Louis, Missouri. May, 1910. Francis Lance, 5 years old, 41 inches high. Sells regularly on Grand Avenue. *(Courtesy of the Library of Congress, Prints and Photographs Division, Lewis Wickes Hine National Child Labor Committee Collection, LC-H51–1393.)*

With industrialization came urbanization. And with urbanization came the street trades. And into the street trades came the children. Children provided services driving delivery wagons, working as bootblacks, messengers, and organ grinders. They sold all manner of goods such as flowers, fruit, candy bars, and, most commonly, newspapers. They seemed to be everywhere. Every busy corner of every substantial city offered a sales outlet to some enterprising child. At strategic locations where foot traffic was especially heavy, such as at train stations, a clutter of children chased after potential customers or hawked their wares from an array of booths and stands.

The NCLC recognized child labor in the street trades as a problem from the beginning. But it was a very different kind of problem from child labor in the mines, mills, and factories, and it called for different kinds of responses. First, unlike child labor in many other industries or economic sectors that was hidden away and out of sight, children worked in the streets obvious and visible to all who passed by. This might have enabled reformers to chip away at the problem simply by educating the urban consuming public. But it is a testament to the fact that consumer opinion had not yet coalesced on the question of children in the street trades that consumers who would condemn child labor in the mines, mills, and factories eagerly continued to shell out their pennies, nickels, and dimes to children plying their wares on the street. Second, unlike the mines, mills, and factories, where working children were congregated in one location, but similar to the problem of child labor in tenement workshops, the children were highly dispersed. No force of factory inspectors, however well trained and diligent, could effectively address this problem.

Third, and often the decisive factor, many of the children in the street trades had no identifiable employer. Where an employer could be identified, as in the messenger service, there was an adult, or group of adults, who could be held responsible. But where there was no employment relationship, either de jure or de facto, there was no one to be held responsible (parents might be blamed or otherwise condemned, but it was difficult to hold them effectively responsible). Many of the children in the street trades were, in effect, independent businessmen or women— little merchants—entrepreneurs. Their energy, spirit, and enthusiasm were qualities to be admired and encouraged, not condemned. Here was an army of children, all of whom were, in their own way, attempting to bootstrap themselves or their families to a better life. This was the stuff of which the American dream was made. In every city there were prominent adult citizens, true-life Horatio Alger stories, who pointed with pride to their humble beginnings in the street trades. Public opinion came around very slowly on the system of child labor in the street trades, in large part because of public admiration for many of the kids who worked in the system.

The NCLC concentrated its investigation work in two prominent sectors of the street trades—messengers and newsboys. The committee conducted an extensive series of investigations, from 1910 to 1914, in the messenger service (especially the night service), where there is a clear employer and employment relationship. These were deliberately sensational investigations that produced relatively quick and effective results in eliminating very young messengers. In contrast, the NCLC investigated the newsboy situation on at least an occasional basis almost continuously throughout its existence. The newsboy problem proved to be especially resistant to effective reform long after children had been removed from the mines, mills, and factories.

Before proceeding, it is worth mentioning one prominent child-employing sector that was not investigated by the NCLC—children in the department stores and other inside retail environments. The NCLC was well aware, as was the general public, that large numbers of young girls and boys worked as clerks, cash boys, wrappers, and delivery boys throughout the commercial retail sector. In New York City, the Consumers League and the New York Child Labor Committee had been waging an ongoing campaign in this sector. Both organizations conducted or were involved in several systematic and valuable investigations.[1] Because these organizations were investigating the department stores, the NCLC was able to focus its resources in other areas. So, while child labor in the department stores was a frequent topic of discussion at NCLC annual meetings, there were no primary investigations conducted.

The Night Messenger Service

NCLC investigators spent considerable time on the road, traveling from place to place, staying in local hotels along the way, seeing some of the sights, and transmitting reports and other correspondence via the postal, telephone, and telegraph services. The postal, telephone, and telegraph services all used boy messengers. Messengers carried correspondence between the office and its customers and delivered packages and parcels between offices, banks, factories, and stores. In large cities today, the messenger service remains a vital lubricant of commerce. Around the turn of the century, before telephone service was universally accessible, the messenger service was absolutely essential to daily commerce. Messengers typically worked for a small wage plus tips.

Over time, however, investigators came to be aware that the messenger service had a seamy side. At night—when the offices, banks, factories, and stores were closed—the messenger service lubricated the wheels of a different sort of commerce. Night traffic principally involved hotels, restaurants, and—the real shocker—whorehouses. So, in 1910, Edward F. Brown conducted the first formal investigation of the night messenger service. His report was a stunner. It is worth quoting at length his very first interview with a night messenger in Philadelphia:

> Called the Western Union Telegraph Office, stating, "I'm a stranger in town. I want a messenger who knows the town thoroughly. One who can show me where things are doing." "I understand what you want all right. He's on his way," was the reply.
>
> *Messenger*: The manager told me that you want to be shown around town. He sent me to do it because I know the town better than anyone else.
>
> *Brown*: How does it happen that night messengers are so familiar with the seamy side of life?
>
> *Messenger*: Because they see that side most. For example, a night messenger gets the whorehouse business. After nine or ten o'clock probably more than three quarters of all the business of the company until three o'clock in the morning is taking care of the disorderly house calls. They keep a force pretty busy.
>
> *Brown*: But what can the women in such places have for messengers to do that they require them at all hours of the night?
>
> *Messenger*: You might better ask what don't they have going on for messengers to do.
>
> *Brown*: How do you mean?
>
> *Messenger*: Well, there is a greater variety of work for messengers to do than any other job I know of. You get calls to buy hats for men and women in the whorehouses, they send you out with notes and telegrams, they get chop-suey, and regular meals, cigarettes, drinks, clothing, groceries. I once had a whore send me out for a box of matches, gave me a dollar, and told me to keep the change. I have been sent out for corsets, and once for

a pair of shoes. I have lots of calls for women's drawers, corset covers. I have gone for medicine and doctors, and got lots of cocaine for them when the sale was open.

Brown: They never sent you out for cocaine, did they?

Messenger: Lots of times. I used to get it a dozen times a night last year. It was easy then. They have jailed a number of men who were implicated in the traffic and it shut down for a while. I was very adventurous, and while the prosecutions were going on I continued getting dope for whores in the tenderloin. One day I went into a place to deliver a little box of "the white stuff" and a special officer stopped me, asked what I had, and where I was taking it. . . . He then said . . . , "if I ever catch any of you fellows with it, I'm going to put the police on the case." When he said that to me I lost my nerve, and ever since then I have refused to deal in dope because I don't want to be sent up. I'm scared all through. . . .

Brown: [He] was taking me through Vine, Race, Eighth, Ninth and Tenth streets, pointing out to me houses of prostitution. The streets were full of prostitutes, and many a familiar greeting was exchanged between the messenger and the women as we passed along.

Messenger: I know them all. I have been called to the houses and hotels so often that there is probably not a single whore in this district that I don't know. We get to know them pretty well. I can take you into any of these houses and introduce you to the whores by their names.

Brown: You must see some queer things in your work.

Messenger: This is the job to see things in, all right. Most of the houses along here are "dollar houses." The women sit in the reception rooms with long thin kimonos on. They wear those garments so that they won't have much trouble in getting ready to do business. They smoke, and drink all the time. Of course, the best calls are when you go right upstairs to the rooms. . . . I never knock on the door when I get a call to a woman's room. I walk right in. They don't care much. . . . Once I was sent to the room of a whore in a house, and when I came in the man was on the bed dead drunk. The woman was all naked, and she was half shot too. She sent me out six or seven times, once for chop suey, and then for drinks and cigarettes. When I was through, she took a five dollar bill from the man, and gave it to me, telling me to keep the change.

Brown: Why is it that the woman is so free with her customer's money, instead of keeping it for herself.

Messenger: Because the messengers are all "boosters," and it won't pay them to be stingy with us. We bring them a good deal of business.

Brown: What do you mean by "boosters"?

Messenger: A man like a pimp. You go out and get customers for her. Lots of strangers like you come to the office and want to be shown a good time. . . .

Brown: Don't you fear diseases in going around with these women?

Messenger: I guess I have had all the doses I want. . . . I have had three doses of "clap" one right after the other. Just as soon as I got over the first I got the second, and when I was cured of the second, I got the third. . . .

Brown: In North Callowhill Street he pointed out a French house, and told me that "you can get it in any style you want right in that house, and you can get a girl of any age too. They have girls of fourteen years with the finest forms you ever saw." . . .

Brown: Don't the police bother these women at all?

Messenger: Not as long as they pay up. They must pay the cop so much a month. If they fail, he reports them, and they are promptly raided. . . .

Brown: Before leaving me [he] took pains to write out for me his name and the address of the office in which he is employed, remarking, as he handed the slip to me—"If you want anything in the red light district just call on me." After I took the slip he asked for it again, and noting some addresses thereon, he said, "If you want to go into good whorehouses, I put some addresses on the paper. They are fine places. Just tell them I sent you up."[2]

Here was an occupation and trade that called out for condemnation by the long-haired men and short-haired women of the NCLC. Never mind the question of night work or the detrimental effects on the boys' schooling, the issue here was moral depravity. Young, sometimes prepubescent, boys were being exposed to sin, sex, drugs, disease, and danger. Moral degradation and physical dissipation of the youth were assumed to be obvious and all the NCLC needed to do was to expose the night messenger service for what it was.

From 1910 to 1914, the NCLC investigated the night messenger service in nearly every substantial city in America. The contents of these reports were so lurid that the NCLC restricted access to them. Within the NCLC, only the investigators themselves and a small handful of others were to see the original reports. Summaries would be published from which the most offensive material was redacted. Outside the NCLC, the only people to see the original reports were the messenger services—since the NCLC approached each service requesting the elimination of boys from the night service—and the occasional legislator who needed further persuasion that

Figure 8.2 *Night Messenger.* Norfolk, Virginia. June, 1911. Raymond Bykes, Western Union No. 23, Norfolk, Va. Said he was fourteen years old. Works until after one a.m. every night. He is precocious and not a little "tough." Has been here at this office for only three months, but he already knows the Red Light District thoroughly and goes there constantly. He told me he often sleeps down at the Bay Line boat docks all night. Several times I saw his mother hanging around the office, but she seemed more concerned about getting his pay envelope than anything else. *(Courtesy of the Library of Congress, Prints and Photographs Division, Lewis Wickes Hine National Child Labor Committee Collection, LC-2258.)*

things really were as bad as the committee claimed. The reports were not to be made available to scholars, writers, or the press, as other reports were. As an unfortunate consequence of the NCLC's concern for the sensibilities of others, a number of the original investigation reports could not be located for this book. Enough of the reports remain, however, to present a relatively clear and complete summary of the trade. What Edward F. Brown had observed in Philadelphia and Pittsburgh in 1910 was found to be commonplace in nearly every other large city in America (Figure 8.2).

Adolescent Boys in the Tenderloin

The night messengers working the red-light districts performed services something akin to services performed by eunuchs in a harem. They looked after the needs of the girls, procuring food, drugs, and alcohol, running errands, and performing whatever tasks were necessary so that the girls could perform their tasks. In turn, the boys were an accepted part of the harem—free to come and go almost at will. And the best boys, the ones most attentive to the needs of the girls, were the most appreciated. But the boys were hardly eunuchs. They were adolescent boys flush with the raging hormones of adolescent boys. To a boy curious about his own sexual awakening and eager to learn more, this must have seemed like the greatest job in the world.

A sixteen-year-old messenger (badge 37) for Western Union in Bridgeport, Connecticut, noting that by law the "cat houses" were supposed to close at midnight, "but many calls came from them just the same," told investigator Harry M. Bremer how routine the boy's presence in the cat houses became. "All these places are wide open to him, he informed me, and said that he sees everything that goes on. 'They do not stop for me any more. They know me. The first time I saw them at it my face got red all over.'"[3]

Many messengers interviewed described the "great fun" in getting to "see the sights." The remarks of a seventeen-year-old messenger of four years were typical:

> Lots of fun in it. Get a call to a whorehouse and go right in the parlor where the women sit around smoking cigarettes. They have long thin dresses on and you can see everything through it. When they walk across the room you see the tits bounce up and down. That's what I like to see.[4]

The opportunity to "see the sights" was not the only inducement for boys to enter the night messenger service. The pay was also better than what could be earned as a day messenger. Indeed, the pay was better than for any other job a city boy could find and often yielded higher returns than much of the work available to adult men. A seventeen-year-old messenger with the Postal-Telegraph Company of Philadelphia explained his preference for night work thusly:

> "All the night messengers know about the whore house trade. We like that business better than any other kind. More money in it. . . . There is no money in the day shift. The night is the time for tips, because then it's not all business. People are out for fun and they are sports—especially if they have a lady with them."

"How much do you ordinarily make a night in tips?"

"I'm in for one or two dollars every night, no matter how slow things are."[5]

One or two dollars on a slow night would have been a substantial daily wage even for an adult man in Philadelphia in 1910. But there were other ways the boys could boost their income. The boy went on to describe one method, overcharging: "Sometimes when we don't make it in tips, we make it in overcharges. If we get specials, all we have to do is to charge a quarter more and keep it. No one is the wiser. All the boys do it."[6] If overcharging was not enough, an especially bold messenger might report "false calls." The boy would deliver the message or service, collect the money, but, "Many times they keep the whole amount and then report 'false call,' or that the other Company's boy 'beat him to it.'"[7]

Still, tips were the best and most reliable source of money. There were essentially two methods for generating the highest tips: (1) providing enhanced services; and (2) extortion. Many boys used both methods. When it came to enhanced services, older messengers were the professionals. Louisville, at the time, had a reputation for an especially vibrant tenderloin district. In turn its messengers tended to be older and more professional. Herschel H. Jones interviewed John Meyer (Western Union badge 29), who was eighteen at the time, but had entered the service at fourteen. Meyer discussed the various houses with investigator Jones much as if he had been a hotel concierge helping him to find just the right restaurant for his wallet and taste:

"That's the best place over there (pointing to 709 W. Green St.) That's where I go myself. It's a dollar house."

"How often do you go?"

"About once a week, whenever I feel like it. There's Creoles in this house here (opposite from 709). They're pretty good. Some fellows like 'em better than any. . . . Agnes Knight's is a swell place. (And he wrote the name and address down on the blank.) That's where they have mirrors all around. It's a five dollar joint. I'll take you around there if you want to see it."[8]

It is a distinctive feature of the sex trades that many of its consumers prefer that their habits of consumption not be known. Some were prominent citizens; many had wives at home and otherwise respectable lives they wished to preserve. They most decidedly did not want their frequenting of cathouses to be revealed. In short, consumers were often vulnerable to extortion. Investigator Brown and several other investigators noted that messages were often read by the boys "who open the slightly sealed envelopes and seal them again afterwards."[9] Generally this was done out of mere curiosity, but on occasion it enabled the messenger to extort an especially generous tip as hush money.

There were the monetary tips, of course, but in-kind tips also seemed to be of considerable value to the messenger. Monetary tips—cash—were invariably provided by the customers. Even when the services were provided to the prostitute, it was the customer who paid. Numerous reports describe women "getting money out of some poor fellow's pockets." But in-kind tips were provided by the girls themselves for especially helpful messengers. An experienced messenger describes visiting the girls' rooms: "When they have a customer in the room there is nothing doing, but sometimes when they are alone you can get a chance at her for reduced prices."[10]

Similarly, Harry M. Bremer describes a conversation he had with two Lynchburg Postal-Telegraph messengers, Mal Myers, age sixteen (badge 7), and Charlie Gentry, age fourteen (badge 10):

> "Do you boys know where the 'red light' houses are?"
>
> "Sure, Go down there every night! Gee! See some great sights too!"
>
> "What do you see?"
>
> "Gee! They come out stark naked sometimes!"
>
> "Do you ever see men in there?"
>
> "Shure, when the bell rings they hide inside, and let the whores open the door."
>
> "What do you boys do down there?"
>
> "We can do anything they want. See everything they've got, and would see more if they had it. Some of them won't let you fuck them, they suck you."
>
> "Are they all young girls there?"
>
> "Shure, lots of young girls, some no older than I am."[11]

The largest houses in the most active tenderloin districts often provided additional entertainments. Some offered naked dancing girls and sexual exhibitions—the "circus" or the "show." Sixteen-year-old Dewey Harrod (Louisville Postal-Telegraph badge 7) invited investigator

Herschel H. Jones to the "circus at number 620." "What is a circus?" Jones inquired. In a most tasteful reply, Harrod observed, "Oh it's a show they put up. . . . The women do stunts with each other, and show themselves off."[12]

Dangerous Work

There were certain fairly obvious dangers associated with the night messenger service. This was rough work in the roughest part of town. Working as drug courier, pimp, conveyor of confidential messages, and such brought the messenger into constant contact with unsavory elements of society. The dangers of engaging in illicit traffic in lawless regions of the cities at night were real enough. One messenger discussed the dangers with investigator Brown, stating, "I'm used to it. Some of the fellows that are scared carry 'Billies' and some have revolvers. A little while ago one of our boys was found dead by the dock. He was robbed by some bums and then thrown overboard. When he was picked up they found him stiff."[13]

Ironically, however, the night messengers were among the safest people on the streets in the tenderloin at night. First, they were streetwise. They knew the streets better than anyone else, save maybe the pimps and the police. They learned, by necessity, to recognize signs and places of danger and avoid them. They learned how to talk their way out of trouble. Besides, the messengers were not prime targets. Drunkards could be rolled because it was so easy, but the boys were generally alert and sober. Wealthier patrons of the district were more lucrative targets and often had the added advantage of having something to hide, but the boys carried no large sums of money and were there on "legitimate" business. Finally, their role in the industry was generally appreciated by brothels, prostitutes, pimps, and customers alike. Few felt a strong need or desire to hassle the messengers.

Occupational hazards came more often in the form of venereal disease. Numerous messengers discussed both their encounters with the prostitutes and their subsequent encounters with resulting venereal diseases. A messenger described his typical experience to investigator Brown:

> "It was in one of these Italian houses that I first went with a woman. A night messenger brought me up. It was a fifty cent joint."

"Are you not afraid of getting sick by going with these women?"

"I had two doses already. That's nothing. You get over that pretty quick."

"How often do you do?"

"Once or twice a week. It depends on my cash."[14]

While experienced messengers could learn to cope with this kind of experience, novices could be quite traumatized. Investigator Brown tells a story, related to him by the night force in Western Union's Pittsburgh office, of a rookie messenger, fifteen years old, who received a rude introduction to the sex trade. He was returning from a call when he was "accosted by a veiled woman" who offered "to show him a good time." When they got to her room on the second floor of a nearby house, she essentially raped the boy (Brown notes, "There is every indication that she was a sexual pervert") and demanded a dollar. "The boy protested, but she took it from his clothes by force." A fellow messenger described the boy's return to the office, "He came running into the office with his shirt unbuttoned, one shoe in his hand, and his socks in his pocket, crying like a kid, and yelling to the biggest messenger boy we have, 'Yellow, Yellow, a whore has got me dollar.' " Yellow took the boy back to visit the woman. Their encounter, as Yellow described it to Brown, went like this:

"Did you take a dollar away from this boy?" demanded Yellow.

"Yes, but he got his money's worth didn't he," was the reply.

"That don't cut no ice, you'll have to give it up or we'll squeal," was Yellow's ultimatum.

The woman ordered him out of the house, but Yellow responded by going over to the window and calling for the police. This frightened the woman, and she promptly returned the dollar, and the incident was regarded as closed by all except the suffering messenger. . . . [F]ive days later the boy suddenly developed acute gonorrhea. It was his first experience of this kind. He was bewildered and despondent until upon the advice of a fellow messenger he sought the services of a men's diseases quack, who advertised extensively in the Pittsburgh papers.[15]

One final danger, more subtle and insidious, was that the night messenger service was often "blind alley" work. After a few years in the tenderloin, many messengers were unqualified, or were considered otherwise unsuitable, for better jobs. One former messenger remarked:

I was a messenger for about two and one-half years. At the end of that time I couldn't find a decent job that would pay a man to take. I'm twenty now but I can't find anything. I haven't any trade. . . . Most of the night messengers I knew never amounted to anything afterwards.[16]

The Managers, the Industry, and Child Labor Reform

Unlike virtually every other industry the NCLC had attacked, the postal and telegraph services came around fairly quickly to a position favoring eliminating young boys from the night messenger service. To be sure, many initially attempted to deny the problem. But when confronted by the evidence, resistance crumbled. It was obvious that the messenger service and the sex trades had developed a close, symbiotic relationship. A messenger told investigator Brown, "Most of the whore houses have call boxes. All they have to do is to turn the crank and we come up. . . . [S]ome of the whores have charge accounts and pay by the month. He makes the bills out and sends us around with them."[17] As further evidence of their "intimate complicity," Owen Lovejoy noted, "In one city the entrance to an opium den was made through the friendly offices of the [messenger service] manager."[18]

Many of the managers seemed in sympathy with the effort to keep especially young messengers out of the tenderloin. Most indicated their local operations could adjust to more mature age requirements. The sending of messages into, out of, and within the tenderloin districts was probably relatively inelastic as to price, but offices were willing to forgo profits to do the right thing. Mr. Leith, a district manager with Western Union, talking with Harry M. Bremer, "[S]poke of the order given a year or so ago to remove all call boxes from disorderly houses, and said that in one of the cities of the state the revenue of the office had at once decreased on an average of from forty to seventy-five dollars a month."[19]

Clearly the managers knew more about the activities of their messengers than they cared to admit. But it is probably also true that the messengers had a more complete understanding of the ebb and flow of the trade than the managers:

At Charleston, Mr. Phillips, manager of the local Western Union office, quizzes "Parker," one of the messengers, in my presence. Mr. Phillips had previously told me that so far as he knew the office had received only three or four calls from disorderly houses since December. . . . "Parker" informed us that before Bettie Mead's house was raided about a week previous to our conversation, the office had had an average of two calls a night from her house alone, and other calls from other houses, and that Bettie Mead's was again running wide open.[20]

A manager in West Virginia provided investigator Bremer with a statement ostensibly representing the sentiments of at least other managers in the district. The manager's statement proclaimed in no uncertain terms:

[T]he worst thing a boy can do, as far as his future development is concerned, is the carrying of messages or running errands, for the patrons of a telegraph company. . . . The worst thing that any parent can do is to allow their boys to serve as messengers, very much especially, between the hours of eight P.M. and five A.M.[21]

Bremer cautioned, "The managers mentioned in this report asked that their names and positions be kept confidential, not being willing to make any statement for publication without authorization from some higher officer of the company."[22] But the managers probably did not have to worry about the reaction of higher officers. Company officials knew they were dealing with a public relations nightmare and realized they had to respond. They could not repudiate, deny, or distance themselves from the fact that the boys were their employees—this in contrast to "little merchants" who dominated the street trades—and so the public would perceive them as responsible for the conditions of the boys' work. Lucrative as the night business may have been, it constituted only a small fraction of the total business conducted by most postal and telegraph companies. The companies were dependent for their bread and butter on maintaining a good reputation within the business community, and their role in the sex trades was damaging to that reputation.

Elimination of boys from the night messenger service turned out to be the quickest and easiest victory the NCLC ever won. Several states rapidly enacted laws prohibiting sending minors to immoral resorts, raising the minimum age for the night messenger service, and the like. But the real impetus for removal of boys from the service came from the companies that realized it was in their own interest to solve the problem. Companies removed call boxes from the whorehouses and established eighteen as the minimum age for night work. In the process, many companies also elevated their standards for boys in the day messenger service.

Moral Degradation of Girls

The moral degradation of the boys in the night messenger service may have been astonishing. The raw facts revealed by their night work may have been shocking. But perhaps the most extraordinary aspect of the NCLC's investigations into the night messenger service was the committee's complete silence on the question of young girls in the sex trades. If the work was morally degrading for the boys, what did the committee think was happening to the girls? If the committee was justified in expressing outrage that boys were exposed to sex, drugs, danger, and disease, where was their outrage on behalf of the girls? However bad the boys may have had it, clearly the girls had it far worse. But in spite of all this, the girls were more likely to be perceived and portrayed by the committee as perverts and degenerates than as victims of a morally degrading occupation and trade.

What explains the committee's silence on the question of young girls in the sex trades? It was not as if investigators were unaware of the problem. Their investigation reports are replete with references to very young girls working in the whorehouses—girls often younger than the boy messengers the committee was so concerned about. It was not even that investigators did not care about the fate of the girls. Some cared enough to act forcefully on their concern. For example, in his 1910 investigation, Edward F. Brown stumbled onto a white slavery trafficking route that brought young girls from the South through Louisville to Pittsburgh (and presumably other points north). A messenger told Brown of two young girls who had just arrived from Louisville. How did the messenger know? He had been delivering (and, of course, reading) two or three messages a day to and from the girls. Ages of the girls were not disclosed except that they were referred to as young. In their young messenger's opinion, "They were peaches to look at, too." Brown notified the authorities and, after they had confirmed the facts, arrests were made in both Pittsburgh and Louisville.[23]

There is nothing in the NCLC papers that explains why the committee deemed the work of young girls in the sex trades to be beyond their purview. But two explanations are possible. First, it may have been simple gender bias, that is, the problems of boys were considered more important than the problems of girls. After all, the committee also paid scant attention to domestic services, the sector second only to agriculture in number of child workers, and a sector where girls dominated. Nor had they focused on the department stores where, as far as child labor was concerned, it was largely a female-dominated profession. Still, gender bias seems an unlikely explanation given the influence of Hull House feminism in the committee and the committee's overall record in other industries where girls worked. A more likely explanation involved definitional demarcation of the boundaries of the concept "child labor" itself. All of the committee's work was directed to the labor of children that might otherwise have been considered legitimate work had it not done by children. Nothing about work in the sex trades was considered legitimate, and so it was treated as beyond the scope of the child labor problem. Even today it is difficult for many people to conceptualize child prostitution on the same plane as child miners, servants, pickers, or garment workers, and so it is often treated as an entirely separate problem.

Newsboys

Since the advent of the major daily newspaper, street vendors had filled the vital point-of-sale node in the distribution network. This role had long been filled by children. By the time concerns began arising about industrial child labor in other settings, child newsboys were a firmly ingrained feature of the urban landscape. Perhaps it was because their work did not appear overly "industrial" that they were not noticed. Or perhaps it was because they had always been there. Edward N. Clopper, the NCLC's best informed and most constant critic of the street trades, remarked that "Street workers have always been far more conspicuous than any other child laborers," but that society had "committed the common error of overlooking the obvious."

> At first the plight of the child in the mine and the factory, unseen except by a few, aroused the entire civilized world to vigorous protest. . . . But the street traders, that class of child laborers whose association with the great mass of people has been most intimate and constant, have been the last to meet with consideration.[24]

But there they were; they were ubiquitous; they swarmed. Lewis Hine described the scene in Washington, D.C., in 1914:

> At various times, the streets literally swarmed with youngsters, a few of them five and six years old, many of them from 7 to 12. It was impossible

for me to count, or even to estimate the number of them accurately. . . . [M]any of them [were] tiny tots moved by the spirit of adventure, the example of brothers, or too often, exploited by an older member of the fraternity.[25]

Similarly, Herschel Jones described the street scene in Detroit:

There are two hours out of the twenty-four (between two and four in the morning) when the streets of Detroit are practically free of young boys selling newspapers but there is no other hour of the day or night when they are not there in large numbers.[26]

In every city in America, children dominated the newspaper sales trade. Long after child labor was abolished from the mines, mills, and factories, children continued to work the streets. For the rural child, agriculture remained the major unregulated work opportunity. For the urban child, the streets were often the only real alternative. As other opportunities for work were foreclosed, child labor in the streets and among the newsboys continued to grow.

Organization of the Trade: Part I

Boys purchased their papers from the publisher. Papers could be obtained from the distribution counter at the publisher's office, or from a distribution wagon that dropped papers at various locations around the city, or later from satellite distribution stations. Most probably purchased directly from the publisher, but this was only the half of it. An elaborate ad hoc network of contracting and subcontracting also operated. A substantial minority of boys contracted with newsstands or worked for other boys, often older brothers or friends.

Boys purchased their papers wholesale and made their money on the markup. At the time, the markup was from one to three cents per paper (in reality, the markup was whatever the boy could extract from the customer, including tips and perhaps overcharges). To maximize earnings, boys were encouraged to "sell out"—that is, to remain on the street until all papers were sold. As independent businessmen responsible for profit, the boys also bore the risk of loss (and in so doing, also bore the publisher's cost of excess inventory). So, the compensation system created strong incentives to sell out. Boys could sell out in one of three ways. First, they could correctly gauge demand for papers and order only as many as they could sell during the rush. A strategy of conservative estimation of demand could enable the boy to sell out early, but risked missing opportunities for a big day when demand was high. Second, boys could simply remain on the street until they sold all their papers, however late that might occur. If all else failed, the boy could dump his excess down the sewer and go home, but doing so meant a financial loss since he had already paid for the papers. A third alternative was to sell the remaining papers to another boy at a discount—at cost or even somewhat below cost. The other boy, who often bought up the excess from several newsboys, would sell late after most of the boys had quit for the evening.

While newsboys could be found on the street at nearly all hours, the business was characterized by a rush period from about four-thirty to seven each evening. Most boys sold through this period and went home. Some stayed on, often buying out the boys who left early.[27] Boys who sold during the rush made the greatest volume, but those who sold later at night made better tips.[28] But when a major news story broke, all would stay out late. The papers would print "extras" and the boys would go into a frenzy of sales activity. Lewis Hine happened to be in Washington, D.C., studying the newsboys at the time of the *Titanic* disaster:

> Night after night hundreds of boys and men hung around the newspaper offices, fought their way to the distributing counters and out into the street. . . . For three consecutive nights, this week, I found them wandering about . . . hanging onto the job until one or two in the morning, simply to make a record sale, perhaps, or to unload the heavy bunch of papers in which they had unwisely invested.[29]

Newspaper sales, like all street trades, had its rough-and-tumble aspects. In the downtown street selling districts, boys vied for the best locations. A good corner was considered a prize, and boys fought, often literally, to acquire or defend prime territory. Having a good corner not only meant an adequate traffic flow, it also meant the opportunity to build up a clientele of regular customers who bought every day. Good corners were claimed as reserved and controlled territory, which others invaded at their peril. Corner boys generally made better money than freelancers who worked the spaces between controlled territory. During the rush, freelancers concentrated at areas of heavy traffic such as train stations and ferries. Later at night, the train stations and ferries became controlled territory, and the freelancers moved out to the areas vacated by the corner boys. The level of violence occasioned by the struggle over territorial control should not be overstated. After all, this was not home turf the boys were defending, it was mere economic turf, and another location could always be found. Still, many a freelancer sported a black eye as a reminder to be more careful, and occasional full-blown rumbles, as one group sought to oust another from desired territory, were not unknown.

Boys also had to be cognizant of the rules laid down by the publishers (this, even though the newspapers insisted they were not acting as employers). For example, boys found it advantageous to sell several different papers. But in many cities, especially before the advent of the newsstand, boys were actively discouraged from selling rival papers. According to Edward N. Clopper, in Cincinnati where there were two major daily papers, each paper employed "bullies" to restrict newsboy sales of the rival paper, often beating the boys up as an object lesson for all.[30]

In this kind of environment, experience—street sense—paid dividends. Earnings were generally proportionate to age, with older boys making substantially more than younger boys.[31] But all the boys remained subject to the laws of supply and demand. Any given urban landscape had only so much carrying capacity for newsboys. As opportunities for employment in other fields were increasingly foreclosed, an excess supply of newsboys developed in many cities, driving down the earnings of all.[32]

In the urban, downtown centers of early twentieth-century America, most selling was done on the streets. Outside the downtown districts, newsboys were beginning to carry regular routes from door to door. Eventually, the carrier routes would supplant street selling as the predominant mode for child involvement in the industry. Within the downtown districts, street selling would give way to newsstands, which would, in turn, be generally supplanted by vending boxes.[33] In the process, the boys would be pushed into the outlying residential and commercial routes. But through the period of the early NCLC investigations, street selling still dominated the trade.

Little Merchants

So who were these enterprising little merchants—these "diminutive business folk," as Clopper called them—who ran the street trades in America's cities? A few were girls, but the vast majority of newsboys were boys. Girls were present in other street trades—selling flowers,

Figure 8.3   *Little Fattie.* St. Louis, Missouri. Little Fattie. Less than 40 inches high, 6 years old. Been at it one year. May 9th, 1910. *(Courtesy of the Library of Congress, Prints and Photographs Division, Lewis Wickes Hine National Child Labor Committee Collection, LC-USZ62–45842.)*

candy, gum, fruits, and vegetables—and played a larger role in newspapers as sales moved from street selling to carrier routes, but they were never a large proportion of the force.[34] A few of the boys were as young as five and six (Figure 8.3), but most were between eight and fourteen. They came from whatever ethnic group lived in the particular city. Each ethnic group worked its own neighborhood and contested for key locations in downtown districts and on the boundaries between ethnic neighborhoods. These were the poor inner-city kids of America. It is no exaggeration to suggest that most urban kids worked as newsboys for at least some period of time.

There is no doubt that poverty was a significant factor, perhaps the single most dominant factor, driving boys to the street trades. Harry Bremer conducted an in-depth study—among many on the relationship between child labor and poverty—of the income and expenses of forty-eight families comprising 393 individuals. Only one-fourth of the families had as much as one dollar per person per month for all expenses exclusive of rent. Three-fourths of the families had less than a dollar per person per month, and many had less than half that amount.[35]

But poverty was by no means the whole story. Poverty may have pushed many boys into the street trades, but the street trades also boosted many boys out of poverty. Horatio Alger's stories may have been myths—for every "captain of industry" with roots in child labor there may have been hundreds of wrecked men—but for every few wrecks there was one who made it legitimately into the middle class. The street trades, and newspaper selling in particular, could be a ticket to upward mobility. It could, and often did, instill values, business sense, and responsibility and thereby fulfill its ideals for many boys, even if it failed many others. NCLC investigators had a healthy respect for the boy who was attempting to bootstrap himself to a better life, especially when he had a plan to get there. Reports were replete with positive role models. To cite just one example, Jimmy Russo was an enterprising fourteen-year-old:

> He sells afternoons and stops about 7 o'clock in order to go to night school. He intends to go to business college later on. This fall he is going to buy a delivery route for the winter. The boy from whom he is buying this route does not like the prospect of delivering on cold winter mornings.[36]

Whether it was the push of poverty or the pull of opportunity, "there would seem to be an economic pressure forcing the boy out into the street to sell papers." But the little merchants were independent businessmen in more than one sense. Certainly their relationship with the publishers was such. Publishers worked to sustain the public perception and the legal status that the boys were not their employees. This was, in part, to keep their distribution force beyond the reach of the child labor laws. But also in part because publishers sought to avoid liability for actions of the boys, whether under workers' compensation or other liability laws. Newsboys were also independent businessmen in the sense that they worked independently of the adult members of their families. This meant, among other things, that the boys controlled their own money. In most other fields of child labor, there was some assurance that the earnings of the child would be added to the meager incomes of poor families. But there was no such assurance in the street trades. "A strong argument for permitting boys to sell papers could be made from this could it be shown that all or even most of a newsboy's earnings find their way into the family purse. The argument of the poverty of the family loses all weight, however when we consider the facts shown . . . that only a few boys add any appreciable amount to the family income."[37]

Harry M. Bremer interviewed 106 New York City newsboys ages ten through thirteen on the disposition of their earnings. Nearly all the boys insisted they gave all their money to their mother or father. A few said they saved their money. Only one admitted he spent it all. Then investigator Bremer interviewed their mothers.

> Comparing the parent's statements as to earnings with the boys' statement of their earnings we find that in the majority of instances the boys earn much more than they really give home, that their parents do not know how much they earn, and that therefore the boys have this extra money to spend in ways they see fit without having to account to anyone for it.[38]

A few illustrative cases include

> [No.] 35, a boy of 12 who sells till 11 p.m. at the Hudson Terminal Building [who] told our investigator he earned 7.50 a week, of which a third came through tips. His mother said he gave her all the money he earned and that it was a dollar a week. The boy plays "crap" and no doubt loses much of the difference.

> [No.] 48, a boy 12 years old, sells at Broadway and 14th Street. He earns $6.00 a week. According to his mother he earns $3.00 of which he gives her $2.75 and spends 25 cents. This boy has been selling 5 years. He started he says in order that he might join the Newsboy's Home Club and be with his friends.

> [No.] 324, 11 years old, doesn't like to go to school, and goes only when he feels like it. He chews tobacco and is the champion hookey player in

the neighborhood. The other boys who live in the same neighborhood say there is nothing "Bonehead" doesn't do. "He is a bad one all right." He told investigators he makes $2.50 a week, that he keeps out a quarter every day, and sometimes gives his mother only a nickel. His mother says Louis does not sell papers. At least she does not know that he does. He never gives her any money.[39]

Beggars and Thieves

If more boys learned the lessons of Jimmy Russo, the enterprising four-teen-year-old, of responsibility, thrift, and the value of education, or if more boys had used more of their earnings to alleviate family poverty, the newsboy trade might have escaped the scrutiny of the reformers at the NCLC. But it was a tough business, and only a few could make it honestly and legitimately. Most who did not make it simply dropped out. Some, however, found other ways to make it in the business and turned toward dishonesty, vice, and crime. In addition to concerns over age and late selling, many within the NCLC had long held that the street trades and the newsboy profession were gateways to a life of profligacy and dissipation. There was a more general threat to morals in begging, shortchanging, truancy, delinquency, gambling, and saloon frequenting.

Many of those who professed to be legitimate street traders were, in fact, professional beggars. Harry Bremer describes "One boy [who] took his bootblack kit with no brushes or polish and made $2." Another boy, described by his cronies as a "professional beggar," "writes letters in his mother's name stating she is sick and in need of money and requesting the reader to help out. The boys say he does this frequently and makes a lot of money. They say that his mother does not know that he is doing this."[40] Bremer also describes being personally scammed by a small newsboy beggar:

> As I turned to leave a very small boy with papers under his arms begged me to give him a nickel to help him sell his papers. He could not look me straight in the eye. We talked awhile. He seemed very happy that the next day was a holiday that he would not have to go to school. Then he began to tell me of a heroic deed he had taken part in. He had killed a robber in their house. He said the robber was in the room. His father was asleep and his mother was terribly frightened. He was the only other person awake; the robber did not see him, he peered at him between his fingers and then when he got a chance, took a gun and shot the robber in the

back. The boy said he was six years old. . . . The six year old boy followed me more than a block trying to take hold of my hand and asking me all the way for a nickel. All of a sudden he left me and dodged under the swinging doors into the saloon.[41]

Beggars posing as newsboys worked only for "tips" and so they had to go where the tips were greatest. This generally meant working later at night when people were out on the streets for a good time. Probably the best location in America for newsboy begging was the theater district of New York City. The boys mingled and dodged in and out of the crowd hoping to perform some service, such as lighting cigars or opening cab doors, in order to receive tips. They were not newsboys, though each one carried papers under his arms as a foil.[42] To the consuming public, however, it was nearly impossible to distinguish the honest newsboy from the beggar or thief.

Unfortunately, just as many boys turned from honest selling to begging, many others turned from begging to theft. The first step was through the method of shortchanging:

> Drunken men fall easy prey to the boy who wants to steal his tips, as the following conversation with a twelve year-old-boy on Frankfort Street shows.
>
> "A man'll give yer a quarter, and yer'll say yer ain't got change and he'll tell yer to go get some, and yer'll go and won't come back."
>
> "And leave him standing there on the curb?"
>
> "Sure! He'll wait for yer. Last Saturday a man gave me $5, and I didn't have change—so he told me to get some. I tried one store and they didn't have it—and I went back and saw the man standing on the corner and I went around the other way!"[43]

From shortchanging some progressed to more overt crime. Professional pickpockets were not uncommon.[44] Others entered vice. Gambling was especially common among the newsboys. Reformers had long contended there was a causal link between street work and crime, or at least between child labor and juvenile delinquency. Numerous anecdotal accounts attempted to establish this link, but the proof offered was less than convincing. When the U.S. Department of Labor released its study on "Juvenile Delinquency and Its Relation to Employment," reformers considered it the "most convincing proof."[45] The study examined the Juvenile Court records of seven large cities and twelve refor-matories.[46] It showed clearly that children who worked or who had worked contributed a disproportionate share of delinquency compared to children who had never worked. And what kinds of child labor con-tributed most heavily to juvenile delinquency? There, at the very top of the list, were the newsboys.

But the newspaper industry vigorously disputed these findings, and not without some justification. Harry M. Bremer recorded these notes from a 1913 interview with Mr. Crummy, superintendent of the News-boys' Home Club in New York City:

> He laughs at the figures giving the percentages of newsboys in detention homes. He thinks that the trade is not responsible for much delinquency. Any boy who has once sold papers would call himself a newsboy. Boys who pick pockets and who stay out late at night are not bona fide news-boys and yet would call themselves such. These are the boys who go wrong and give the trade a bad name.[47]

Newsboy Regulation

The newsboy trade proved exceptionally difficult to regulate in two re-spects. First, laws aimed at regulating the street trades were difficult to obtain. By 1916, when all states had laws regulating child labor in mines or factories, in twenty-eight states there was as yet no law governing street trading by children.[48] Second, even when laws could be obtained, it was difficult to devise an effective inspection and enforcement regime.

A number of states and cities adopted the badge system. Newsboys under a certain age were required to obtain a work permit and a badge that was to be worn conspicuously while working. Typical of these badge laws was the New York law of 1903 that applied to large cities (e.g., New York City and Buffalo). Children under ten were prohibited from obtaining a work permit; children ten to fourteen were required to ob-tain work permits and wear badges and were barred from street selling after 10 P.M.

But the badge laws could not be effectively enforced. Enforcement depended on the efforts of police officers and truant officers, neither of whom were adequately equipped for the job. As far as police were con-cerned, enforcement of the street trading laws were a low priority— police were needed elsewhere. During slow times they might be willing to hassle boys without badges and keep them moving along, but very few arrests were ever made. Truant officers had their own problems. First, urban schools were often grossly overcrowded, which created its own disincentive for placing unruly boys back in school. Second, truant officers could enforce compulsory education laws during school hours, but they were unaccustomed to working evening and night hours when most of the violations in the street trades laws occurred. As a result, there were, at best, "periodic fits of enforcement" and "sporadic enforcement drives" that cleaned up the streets for a few weeks, but thereafter allowed things to drift back to normal.[49] Investigator Bremer talked with three boys (two aged thirteen and one aged nine) who told him "that the truant officer, Mr. Marks, has put the cops 'wise' to the law and now the cops chase them."[50]

There were other problems with the badge laws. Technically, the law did not prohibit boys from selling papers at any age, it only prohibited the publisher from selling to boys under ten. All of the boys selling underage were selling for older boys, as were a substantial minority of boys of legal age. So long as one boy in the group had a badge, little could be done about the others. Of course, permits and badges could always be obtained through falsification and other fraudulent means. For example, in a 1913 investigation, Harry Bremer sought to visit the homes of licensed newsboys in New York City. "Visits were made to the given address of every boy. In many cases the addresses brought us to vacant lots, or to the middle of the East River."[51] Finally, and somewhat ironically, the requirement that boys obtain a work permit opened up a new line of business for a few enterprising lads who realized that the permit itself had economic value. A school principal told investigator Bremer "that one of the boys from his school obtained his employment card before he was 14 and does not work. He rents his card to other boys for a long enough time for them to get a position in some factory."[52]

Even if authorities were willing to strictly enforce the law, the absence of a legal employer made it difficult to hold anyone responsible. Courts were understandably reluctant to mete out harsh penalties to the boys. When arrested, most child violators were let off with a warning. Since the newspapers were generally immune from prosecution, they had little incentive to reform their own systems of distribution and sales. As Jeremy Felt observed in his study of child labor reform in New York state, "An employer of child labor in a factory could be made to pay a fine, but a 'self-employed' newsboy stood before the judge alone—the publisher of the newspapers he sold could not be prosecuted."[53]

In some cities, the newspapers began adopting new distribution systems that had certain parallels to the badge system and, had it been their intent, could have been an effective complement to the child labor laws. Myron E. Adams, in a 1905 study commissioned by Hull House, reported on Chicago's system for distributing newspapers and recommended it for consideration as a method of organization that, even if it would not eliminate children from the trade, might help ensure safer and less chaotic conditions of work. Under previous arrangements, papers were distributed to whoever was there to sell them. Under the new arrangement, the Chicago papers assumed responsibility for assignment of selling territories—of corners. Circulation managers began issuing cards to boys with their name and their assigned corner on them. Cards were required to receive papers. Only boys with cards could get them, and they could get them only at their assigned location. The primary intent was to reduce the level of violence, sometimes gang violence, associated with territorial struggle, and the system appears to have helped in that respect. But this innovation also subtly transformed the economic basis for sales. "The corner, which had been merely a prize for a physical contest, now came to have a quasi-legal position that implied pecuniary value."[54] The boy with a card and the corner it conveyed had several options. He could work the corner himself and retain all the earnings. He could organize the corner by hiring assistants—younger brothers or friends—and share the proceeds. Later, if the boy wanted to move up or quit, corners could be bought and sold, acquiring, in effect, the status of a capital asset. Once corners were secure, it helped pave the way for development of fixed corner stands that would be staffed by adults.

Why were the little merchants so hard to regulate? Mainly, it was because the laws aimed at regulating the behavior of children rather than adults. In all other fields of child labor regulation attempted to control the behavior of adults, especially employers but also parents and school authorities. But in the street trades, the law sought to directly control the behavior of boys without the necessary intermediary prompts from employers, parents, and teachers. Parents and teachers could be held responsible for school attendance, and could be made to share blame when children turned to delinquency and crime, but they could not be held responsible for the presumptively legitimate business the boys conducted on the streets. More important, if employers continued to encourage the trade with impunity by selling papers to the boys, the boys had all the validation they needed that the newsboy profession was legitimate business. What did it matter that the law discouraged their participation in the trade, when so many of the adults in their lives were encouraging them into it?

But this begs the question of why the law focused, in futility, on regulating the behavior of adolescent boys. Why did the law not go after the adults—especially the employers? The short answer is that there was no employer. Above all, the newspaper industry avoided creating or acknowledging a legal employment relationship with the newsboys. Call the little merchants independent businessmen, diminutive business folk, entrepreneurs, self-employed, independent contractors, licensees, franchisees—call them anything but employees. The absence of an employment relationship meant there would be no adult employer who could be held responsible. Where there was a clear employment relationship—as in the delivery service, the messenger service, and the department stores—child labor could be effectively regulated. But where there was no employer, there was no responsible adult to regulate.

But this begs another question. How could the newspapers effectively disclaim an employment relationship with the newsboys who distributed their product? It was obvious to all that the newsboys worked de facto for the newspapers. Yet somehow the papers managed to keep their distance de jure. If the question in law was whether the newspapers effectively controlled the work of the newsboys, then an employment relationship could not be denied. Another basis had to be found. The important distinction in law was whether the child was working for wages as opposed to profits. That is, if the newspapers could maintain that the newsboys were responsible for loss as well as gain, the boys would not be subject to the same child labor laws as wage earners.

To this day, American child labor laws in most states maintain a distinction between work for wages and work for profits, echoing the concerns expressed by Edward N. Clopper in 1916:

> The laws, however, still distinguish between street occupations pursued for wages and those pursued for profits, bringing the former under the general child labor restrictions, while the latter, if covered at all, are mentioned separately and made subject to much less stringent regulations.[55]

Reformers were hopeful that the NRA Codes adopted during the depression—the same codes that played such an important role in eliminating child labor in other fields—would enable establishment of a higher standard for the newsboys and in street trading more generally. But the reformers were disappointed. At the insistence of the newspaper industry, the first code permitted children of any age to sell papers after school until 7 P.M. Chagrined at the lack of meaningful standards, reformers lobbied for more effective code provisions and, in 1934, obtained a twelve-year minimum age for carrier boys and a fourteen-year minimum for street selling. Unfortunately, the second code was adopted just shortly before the NRA was found unconstitutional.

Organization of the Trade: Part II

For an industry ostensibly organized and operated by boys acting as independent businessmen, this was a highly organized trade. Routes, corners, and territories were allocated through a more or less orderly system. Age-appropriate earnings hierarchies were well established. Those who learned the ropes could thrive; those who did not left the trade or turned to crime or vice. If it was truly the boys who organized the trade, as their entrepreneurial role would suggest, this would have been the ideal field for the study of laissez-faire capitalism. What kind of markets and institutions emerge as diminutive business folk are left to their own devices?

There is no doubt that the boys themselves, whether consciously or not, played an important role in defining industrial relationships. At the very least, adults had to deal with the children on their own terms, that is, as children. Occasionally, under especially adverse conditions, the boys themselves went so far as to create their own industrial superstructure. Herschel H. Jones described newsboy labor organizing in Detroit:

> The conditions became so bad recently that the newsboys finally took things in their own hands and, with the help of the Federation of Labor, formed the Newsboys Union. Their chief complaint was that they could not return their unsold papers, and an agreement was drawn up between the newspapers and the union under which they are now allowed to take back the papers they do not sell. They next passed a resolution to keep all boys under 16 off the streets after 9 o'clock. . . . [T]hey appointed a "freelance squad" of the older newsboys to enforce the resolution. They

demonstrated in one night that they could get rid of most of the smaller boys but it took a good many small fights to do it.[56]

But perhaps it was inevitable that adult interests would impinge upon the children and their evident self-organization of their industry. In fact, adult interests had created institutions supportive of the newsboy trade from the very beginning. Early in the industry's history, in the era of the barefoot orphan street urchin, newsboys' lodging houses had been constructed. By the time the NCLC and the reform movement had come on the scene, the lodging houses had ceased to be newsboys' lodging houses.

> The so-called newsboys' Lodging Houses no longer house newsboys. This was ascertained first from the boys at the Brooklyn Bridge. They say no decent fellow would go there. If a fellow has only a nickel he might put up there, but if he had more he would go to one of the other lodging houses along the Bowery. These boys say the Brace Memorial House contains a lot of "bums," fellows who drift in from other cities, who never sell papers, and who either hustle baggage at the ferries, or rob and steal.
>
> The superintendents of three of these houses were interviewed, and all testified that the type of newsboy for whom the houses were originally built has entirely disappeared. The homeless little street urchin, racing around in the snow, barefoot, hawking papers, or sleeping over hot gratings on cold winter nights, is no more. They say there are no homeless newsboys in New York now. A few boys may stay out all night, sleeping in doorways and the like, but they are boys who have homes but who have broken away from parental control. . . . A few of the inmates of these houses are orphaned newsboys over 15 years of age, who make their home here.[57]

Likewise, Mr. Crummy, superintendent of the Newsboys' Home Club of New York City, insisted that by 1913 the industry operated on a much higher plane. There had been a "great change in the newsboy of to-day from the boy of a few years back. The old type of bare-footed urchin has disappeared and in his place has come the intelligent, self-respecting newsboy. The Newsboys' Home Club, Mr. Crummy thinks, has been largely responsible for this change in the character of the newsboy."[58]

As the movement for child labor reform came on the scene, a variety of newsboys protective leagues and newsboys clubs were created, as early as 1902 but accelerating after 1907 when the Newsboys' Home

Club in New York City was founded. These were typically charitable organizations established for philanthropic purposes, but they were usually financed and otherwise backed by the newspaper interests. This movement went so far that, in Boston, there was established a Newsboys' Court, an officially sanctioned branch of the Juvenile Court, to hear newsboy cases, with one lawyer and two newsboys sitting in judgment.

The Newsboys' Home Club of New York City became the model, emulated in other larger cities throughout America. Its directors included such notables as William R. Hearst, Herbert F. Gunnison, Ralph Pulitzer, Ogden M. Reid, and Hector H. Havemeyer. If New York's Newsboys' Home Club caught the attention of the industry, it is no surprise that it caught the attention of the NCLC. Harry Bremer interviewed Mr. Crummy, the full-time house director and superintendent, in 1913. Edward Clopper and others referred to the club in a variety of reports and papers. Perhaps the most interesting investigation was conducted by Helen C. Dwight in 1915. Dwight was not a regular investigator for the NCLC, and there is no indication in the records that she had prior authorization from the NCLC to conduct her investigation. Nevertheless, she took it upon herself to tour the Home Club and submit her report. Dwight was, in fact, a New York socialite who had received a solicitation for the club's capital campaign and took it as an opportunity to visit. She was not impressed. From the moment the house staff, "who gave the best impersonation of a real Bowery bum I have ever seen," greeted her at the door, through her tour where she described the place as "indescribably dirty" ("The guide told me they had had the building two years, and I am certain that in those two years the place has never once been cleaned"), to her closing conference in the makeshift "office" where she was especially impressed by "A dirty St. Bernard puppy with a splotch of red paint on his nose was supposed to stay in a packing-box in the corner but really occupied himself chewing the visitors' feet, thereby adding greatly to the 'atmosphere.'"[59]

Dwight's report also includes a copy of a pamphlet published by the Newsboys' Home Club describing its activities. The club's purposes, according to the pamphlet, were these:

> It provides clean sport and entertainment and agreeable work which calls forth latent energies in the boy.
>
> It cares for the sick and needy.

It furnishes fresh-air outings during the summer months for nearly two thousand boys.

It keeps in touch with the home surroundings, habits, work and school records of its members. It helps secure steady employment for them when they graduate from school or reach working age.

Through a system of self-government, it acquaints its members with the responsibilities of citizenship.

It places a premium on good conduct and the boys soon realize that the only means of gaining distinction in the Club is to excel in this respect.[60]

It appears, for the most part, Dwight's complaints notwithstanding, that the Newsboys' Home Club actually made good on each one of its stated goals. First, it provided clean sport and entertainment. In the gymnasium they had a small, caged basketball court, a running track, and stations for boxing and other manual arts training. There was a billiard room and a full kitchen in the house. In 1915, there remained several unfinished rooms on the upper floors of the facility that were planned as libraries, lecture halls, and more manual arts training. Friday nights were reserved for basketball games. Saturday night was the show, featuring both motion picture shows and live entertainment, generally organized by the boys themselves. As to providing "agreeable work" to the boys, the club did so in two ways: first, in both the house and the camp on Staten Island, it encouraged, but did not require, the boys to do whatever work they felt motivated to perform to improve the club's facilities and programs; second, it worked to elevate the standards of the newsboy profession.

Second, the Newsboys' Home Club cared for the sick and needy. This was one of its great philanthropic appeals. The newsboys themselves said, "If any fellow is sick or needs any help all he has to do is to let some other newsie know about it. He'll tell Mr. Crummy, and it won't be long before he has what he needs."[61]

Third, it was true that the club had established a summer camp on Staten Island and that 1,710 ("nearly two thousand") had attended in 1912. These "fresh-air outings" were also enormously appealing to philanthropists, and the development of the camp was of great value to the members themselves. Beginning in 1907, on Mr. Putnam's fifteen acres, twelve boys cleared a space and erected a single tent.

Little by little the land was cleared and tent after tent added to the first. The grounds have been cleared and beautified. Floor and stationary cots built for thirty-five tents. Frame kitchens, mess rooms, store houses, and an office have been erected, chiefly by the boys themselves. Adjoining the camp grounds were three acres of uncultivated land. With Mr. Putnam's permission the boys have turned this into a productive garden, where they raise most of the vegetables used at the camp.[62]

For the price of his twenty-five cents annual dues, each member was entitled to spend a full week at the Staten Island camp each summer. The camp more specifically accommodated the work schedules of these "little businessmen."

> The boys are free to come and go at will. Being little business men, many of them are unable to leave the city for a whole week at a time. Those who cannot do so are free to come to the camp for a week-end or for one or more days, whenever convenient, and in this way make up the allotted week.[63]

Fourth, the club purported to keep "in touch with the home surroundings, habits, work and school records of its members." This it certainly did not do, if it is meant that the club systematically tracked the record of each and every one of its members. But it is also clear that the club reserved, and occasionally exercised, the right to intrude on a member's life and conduct even beyond "certain evils, such as begging, short-changing, late-selling, etc." associated with the newspaper trade. As to helping the boys secure steady employment after they left the newspaper trade, the club did, in fact, operate an employment bureau of sorts for this purpose. This helped to overcome another objection, commonly associated with many forms of child labor, that children were placed in "dead-end" jobs with little or no opportunity for career advancement.

Fifth, the club operated to a significant extent on the principle of self-governance. For example, at the summer camp, "There are no monitors, and no rules," and yet the dishes got washed, the garden was tended, and the camp was expanded, all on the initiative of the boys themselves. At the clubhouse in the city, the boys organized their own programs and entertainments, investigated cases of sickness and need, and maintained the facility itself. If they did not maintain the cleanliness of the house in accordance with Helen Dwight's housekeeping standards, it was only because their priorities lay elsewhere.

Finally, the club placed "a premium on good conduct." "Any boy who performs any special work or any creditable act of kindness to any one is entitled to have his name placed on the honor roll. Only those whose names appear on the honor roll are eligible for election to offices in the Club organizations."[64]

How could anyone object to these clubs that were unequivocally such a good influence on so many boys? There were just two problems with the newsboys home clubs. First, how could one explain why the industry was lavishing such charitable and philanthropic largesse on a group of boys with whom it, in the legal and legislative arena, disclaimed any formal employment relationship. Why were these people spending so much of their money on a problem they insisted was not their responsibility? The public relations aspect of the ploy was too transparent and too much for many reformers to stomach, thereby explaining Mrs. Dwight's predisposition to find fault. Second, and perhaps most astonishingly, while they were called newsboys clubs, they had ceased to be clubs for newsboys. Writing on the New York City club in 1917, Edward Clopper noted that, "as shown by the records of this Boys' Club, out of whose 3,000 members there are only about twenty-five who sell papers regularly." Reformers were urging the newspapers to consider "the establishment of a general boys' club, which would benefit all the boys of a community and at the same time be free from any attempt to glorify newspaper selling as an occupation for young boys."[65] In New York, the Newsboys' Home Club became the Boys' Club, and many clubs in cities around America followed suit.

Unfinished Business

Effective regulation of the newsboy trade, and by extension any street trading where there was no legal employer and where children worked for profits rather than wages, was never achieved. When the reformers turned their sights on the newsboys, the newspapers, which could generally be counted on to denounce child labor in other fields, reacted to protect their franchise in the newsboys. Using their influence in state legislatures, the papers were able to fend off intrusive regulation. Using a variety of welfare programs such as the newsboys clubs, they were able to convince enough of the alert public that the newsboys did not really have it so bad.

In spite of the absence of meaningful regulation, the number of newsboys selling in city streets declined. As early as 1916, Edward Clopper noted that, in New York City, the number of newsboys had shrunk significantly from ten or fifteen years ago as a result of the "organization of the business in the hands of adults who have established stands on the street corners where they serve the public much more economically and systematically than the boys were able to do. In fact, the stands in many public places are now controlled by corporations conducting the business on a large scale."[66] In cities throughout America, street-selling newsboys were gradually replaced by fixed newsstands staffed by adults. Concurrently, the street sellers were becoming route carriers. After World War II, street selling by boys was nearly eliminated. Furthermore, with the mass move to the suburbs, more and more of the work was going to route and carrier boys. As child labor moved out of the congested downtown districts and into the suburbs, it was more highly dispersed and, therefore, less conspicuous.

While the newsboy problem may have resolved itself without benefit of regulation, the continued absence of effective regulation has left the street trades vulnerable to a variety of abuses. A young child remains free to establish lemonade stands in front of his or her house. But he or she is also free to become a sales agent for companies peddling greeting cards, flower seeds, and the like. Schools, churches, youth athletic clubs, and other ostensibly charitable organizations are the most common users of child labor to spearhead their fund-raising programs. Probably most of this activity is innocuous; some of it is even beneficial. But because street selling remains unregulated, abuses can and do occur. In many states, state attorneys general have been investigating sham charities that bus inner-city children out to the suburbs to scam wealthier residents out of their money. Children are sometimes kept out very late or forced to work when they do not want to. A few of these organized sham charities have even transported children across state lines for these purposes. In sum, while the little merchants have moved out to residential neighborhoods, they remain with us. So, too, do the beggars and thieves.

9. AGRICULTURE AND FOOD PROCESSING

Figure 9.1 *Infant Labor*. Seaford, Delaware. May, 1910. Mother and children hulling strawberries at Johnson's Hulling Station. Cyral (in baby cart) is 2 yrs. old this May and works steadily hulling berries. At times Cyral would rest his little head on his arm and fall asleep for a few minutes and then wake up commencing all over to hull berries. This is an extreme case—by no means typical and while it was found in this investigation that children 3, 4, 5 yrs. were accustomed to start out before sunup to pick berries we have not found many cases such as this. *(Courtesy of the National Archives Still Picture Branch, Lewis W. Hine child labor collection, NWDNS-102-LH-1575.)*

Why Not Infant Labor?

Indeed, why not infant labor? What is the infant in the picture doing? Literally, he is playing with a strawberry. In imitative fashion, he is hulling it, and eventually he may actually get a good portion of it hulled, at which time he will playfully toss it in his mother's bucket. What's wrong with this picture? How is this picture different from one of a child of the same age, sitting at the edge of his mother's garden, snapping beans, and tossing them in his mother's bucket? Early in the twentieth century, no one saw a significant difference (Figure 9.1).

Parents, employers, and the children themselves saw agricultural labor as a normal, expected, and generally beneficial part of growing up. But the general public too saw nothing wrong with children working on the farms. This was wholesome work in the good outdoors under close parental supervision—who could object? Besides, if child labor on the farms was curtailed, what was next? Would children be barred from doing household chores? Even school authorities, inspectors, and occasionally reformers themselves saw child labor in agriculture in a different and more benign light than they viewed child labor in other fields. From his report of the very first investigation conducted in agriculture (conducted with Edward F. Brown), Lewis Hine cautioned, "We have met everywhere the universal feeling that there is nothing harmful in outdoor work for children, no matter how young. It will be well to keep this theory in mind, during the discussion of all points covered in this investigation."[1]

Agriculture is the economic sector most closely associated with preindustrial economy. Yet industrialization also transformed food production so that, by the early twentieth century, much of agricultural labor and most labor in food processing had been reorganized under industrial models. This was a time when commercial agriculture and mechanized farming were taking hold, but the food-processing industry, while industrializing rapidly, had not yet assumed its modern form organized around major brand names. The grower's problem was a short harvest season, varying from a few weeks to a few months and inevitably punctuated by weather-related delays. Where the crop was perishable, it had to be not only harvested but also processed in a short period of time. Recruiting a sufficient labor force to what was often a remote location to work intensively for a short period of time (thereafter agreeing to move on) was a major ongoing challenge.

Children, often beginning at extremely young ages, worked directly alongside their parents. The family wage operated in its purest form here as the entire family pooled its daily production for a single payment. This is the sector where American policy on child labor most clearly failed. Long after child labor had been eliminated from most other industries, it persisted in agriculture. Indeed, child labor remains prevalent in agriculture today.

It is impossible to present, in a single chapter, the full breadth and depth of the NCLC's investigation program in agriculture. As to breadth, the reports span the full range of years of NCLC activism. In fact, after 1921 when David F. Houston, who had been President Wilson's secretary of agriculture, succeeded Felix Adler as chair of the NCLC, almost all the organization's formal investigations were conducted in agriculture. Investigations spanned most major agricultural regions of the country and encompassed a diverse variety of crops. To provide an appropriate level of depth without sacrificing all breadth, the chapter emphasizes the annual migration of Poles, Bohemians, and Italians of Philadelphia and Baltimore. For several years, the NCLC closely studied the mass annual migration of whole families from the cities to the country. Investigations were conducted in each year from 1910 through 1915 and again in 1923. These investigations are presented in depth in this chapter. Close examination of the annual migration reveals numerous parallels to other agricultural sectors. But these investigations also provide considerable breadth—both geographically and in terms of the crops involved. From the cities, families first traveled to the berry fields of Delaware and Maryland, then to the fruit and vegetable farms in the same region, ending the growing season in the cranberry bogs of New Jersey. In the winter, many of these same families migrated to the shrimp and oyster canneries along the Gulf Coast from Florida to Louisiana. They may have maintained urban residences, but many families spent the better part of the year following the crops.

The annual migration of Poles, Bohemians, and Italians from Philadelphia and Baltimore was the focus of early NCLC investigations into agriculture and food processing. Later investigations ran the gamut. There was an extensive series of investigations of child labor in sugar beet fields from Michigan to Colorado.[2] Children working in tobacco fields were studied in Kentucky, Connecticut, and North Carolina.[3] Child cotton pickers in Texas and Oklahoma were studied.[4] And finally, child labor in the Imperial Valley of California received a great deal of attention, especially in the 1930s.[5] The crops worked by the children and their families were those requiring labor-intensive methods of cultivation or handpicking at harvest or both. For the most part, the NCLC continued to emphasize "farm laborers working out"—that is, not working on the family farm—even though they constituted a minority of child agricultural workers.

One reason for emphasizing the early investigations is internal consistency. The early investigations were conducted by some of the NCLC stalwarts—Lewis Hine, Edward Brown, Herschel Jones, Harry Bremer, Charles Chute (i.e., those most frequently mentioned in earlier chapters). Later investigations in agriculture were conducted by a new cadre of investigators who were trained in rural sociology and related disciplines and who often conducted their research in conjunction with land-grant universities and especially with the agricultural extension programs in those universities. The later investigations were more scientific in character, but they were not necessarily any more systematic than the earlier investigations. They included much more quantitative analysis, were much longer, and were generally a much drier read than the early investigations. Later investigations might be characterized as dispassionate objectivity, whereas earlier investigations were impassioned objectivity. Where material from the earlier investigations of the annual migration are sufficient to carry the story of child labor in agriculture, they are relied upon. Material from the later investigations are incorporated into the account where they extend or amplify the earlier investigations.

A number of common themes emerge when later, more scientific, investigations are compared with the annual migration of Poles, Bohemians, and Italians from Philadelphia and Baltimore. These themes include: (1) methods of labor recruitment, as exemplified by the padrone system; (2) the family wage and the child's contribution to it; (3) living conditions endured by the agricultural workers; and (4) effects of agricultural work on the children's schooling. Each of these themes is addressed in connection with the annual migration and is also summarized later in the chapter.

The Annual Migration: Interstate Commerce in Child Labor

Every year hundreds, some authorities said thousands, of Polish, Bohemian, and Italian families, mostly from Philadelphia and Baltimore, were rounded up by padrones and shipped by wagon, train, or boat, first for a summer outing in the country to the farms of Maryland, Delaware, and New Jersey, and then for a winter vacation in the Gulf Coast seafood canneries from Florida to Louisiana. One padrone remarked to Hine, "I keep 'em a-working all the year. In the winter, bring 'em down here to the Gulf. In summer, take 'em to the berry fields of Maryland and

Delaware. They don't lose many weeks' time, but I have a hard time to get 'em sometimes. Have to tell 'em all kinds of lies."[6]

Some families went out with the padrones for limited periods of time or to work specific crops and then returned to the city. Others signed on for the whole tour. Some brought the whole family along, often including extended families. In other cases, some family members, especially men and older boys, remained in the city. Some worked the summer tour only. Others worked the winter tour. Some worked both.

NCLC investigators sometimes ran across the same family at multiple points in the annual migration—the Arnao family, for example (Figure 9.2).

> In May, 1910, I made an investigation with Mr. Hine of the child workers in the berry fields and canneries of Delaware. In Cannon, Delaware we found a family of pickers from 831 Catherine Street, Philadelphia, named Arnao. The children of this family included Joe, three years, a boy of six and a girl of nine. This was on May 28th 1910. On September 28th, Mr. Hine and I found the same family picking cranberries on White's bog— four weeks after school opened.[7]

Economic necessity determined how deeply urban families became involved in rural pursuits. Where whole families went out for extended periods, it was because the family was unable to produce a comparable subsistence in the city. Where one or more family members remained in the city, it was because they had steady work at better wages than could be earned by going out. Families that went out for shortened periods were typically spot wage earners—that is, they were able to meet nominal subsistence needs in the city, but came out to the country to earn sufficient money to fund a specific project.

Several NCLC investigators described the annual migration. The early part of May saw the first wagonloads and trainloads of pickers on their way to the strawberry fields. Strawberry season started about the middle of May and lasted four to five weeks. Before the strawberry crop was over, peas came along, and the pickers spent part of the day on strawberries and part on peas. When work there was finished, the padrone shipped them off to the rich berry fields of New Jersey or the truck farms of Maryland. Gooseberries, raspberries, beans, and other crops kept the pickers out till the beginning of July. Finally, after all these crops were picked, the cranberries in the marshes of central New Jersey were beginning to ripen. Cranberry season ran through most of September.

Figure 9.2   *The Arnao Family.* Arnao family, 831 Catherine St., Rear #2. Whole family works. Jo is 3 years old. Boy is 6 years old. Girl is 9 years old. We found this family, children and all working on Hichens farm, Cannon, Del., May 28th 1910, before school closed. See photos #1582, #1586, and labels. This is the fourth week of school and the mother said they would be here for 15 or 20 days more. Whites Bog, Brown Mill, N.J. Sept. 28, 1910. Witness, E.F. Brown. *(Courtesy of the Library of Congress, Prints and Photographs Division, Lewis Wickes Hine National Child Labor Committee Collection, LC-H51–1128.)*

Around October, padrones began shipping families by train or boat to the Gulf Coast where they remained until February or March. In May, the cycle began anew.[8] Owen Lovejoy remarked that the annual migration "presents a spectacle of interstate commerce in children which this republic cannot afford longer to ignore."[9]

In Baltimore, most of the berry farms were fairly near the city, so families were carried out in farmers' wagons (Figure 9.3). In early May, "farmers will pool their wagons and carry the pickers out to their respective farms on successive days. It is a common sight I am told to see block after block of farmers' wagons passing through the streets of the Polish section of the city and out over the bridge into Anne Arundel County."[10] In the Italian section of Philadelphia, as late as September

Figure 9.3   *Farmers' Wagons.* May, 1910. A street full of Baltimore immigrants lined up and ready to start for the country to the berry farms. Wolfe Street near Canton Avenue, Baltimore, Maryland. *(Courtesy of the Library of Congress, Prints and Photographs Division, Lewis Wickes Hine National Child Labor Committee Collection, LC-USZ62–91830.)*

27, well after school had opened, "On one street nearly every house was empty for more than two blocks."[11]

In five elementary schools in Philadelphia with a predominantly Italian enrollment, from 1907 through 1910, 21 percent of students withdrew each year before the end of the school term to go with their families to pick berries. Over the same period, 9.4 percent returned late each fall after picking cranberries in New Jersey.[12]

Summer: Outing in the Country

The first investigation that intersected with the annual migration was conducted in 1910 by Edward F. Brown and Lewis Hine. They were in the berry fields of Delaware in early summer and returned to the cranberry bogs of New Jersey that fall. They did not have to look hard to find very young children at work. The berry fields were dispersed throughout the region on numerous, relatively small farms. Each farm had a few families hired to pick the fruit. Children as young as three were found picking. Alberta McNadd was in no way atypical:

> Alberta McNadd, 5 years old, said she had been working at 5 A.M. in morning and it was 4 P.M. in the afternoon when the investigators found her still at work picking berries. Mrs. McNadd, the mother of 4 children—5, 7, 8, and 11 respectively,—volunteers the information that her children worked steadily from sun-up to sun-down.[13]

When picking, families and working children were widely dispersed in small groups throughout the region. In the canning sheds, large numbers of mothers and children worked side by side in densely crowded environments. In Seaford, Delaware, at the preserving plant of H.A. Johnson and Company of Boston, Massachusetts, a station that bought up large quantities of strawberries from the surrounding countryside, child labor played out to its logical conclusion—infant labor:

> On our first visit to this place there were about 400 people sitting around hulling berries. It is estimated that there were over 200 children under 14 years of age, at least 75 of whom were apparently under 8 years of age. Children of 3 and 4 years were found at work hulling berries steadily. . . . Mothers bring nursing infants and put them to sleep while they hull berries, or lay them on a convenient box or on the ground, while they continue their work.[14]

Ultimately, however, it was the cranberry bogs of New Jersey that became the focus of the NCLC's closest scrutiny. There were several reasons for this. First, cranberries concentrated larger numbers of families (and their children) into a smaller number of work sites than any other harvest. Second, as the last stop on the summer vacation tour, the cranberry harvest occurred in the fall after the schools were in session, lending emphasis to whatever evils were associated with the harvest. Finally, the cranberry growers, feeling unfairly singled out by the NCLC, raised a challenge that only egged the NCLC on.

NCLC reports provided glimpses into what was said to be a distinctive "cranberry culture" in the cranberry regions. Cranberries grew native in a narrow belt along the Atlantic coast from Maine to New Jersey, in isolated areas along the Allegheny Mountains, and in the north-central states of Michigan, Wisconsin, and Minnesota. By 1910, New Jersey, Massachusetts, and Wisconsin were the "great centres of cranberry culture."[15] The NCLC sent investigators to both Massachusetts and Wisconsin, but the purpose of those investigations was to provide comparative data for their primary target, the New Jersey cranberry industry.

Families lived in shanties (and if the bog was large enough, in shantytowns) that were usually located on the owner's property, generally within a short walking distance or wagon ride from the bog. Hours after dark were spent around the shanties and shantytowns, but daylight hours were spent on the bog. Investigators described the bogs and the organization of work:

> Usually a large stretch of meadow is divided into squares. Bordering it on all sides is a ditch about three feet wide. There is a dike, barely sufficient to allow a loaded team to pass. This also serves as a walk for the pickers. In the morning, ordinarily about seven o'clock, the padrone blows a whistle as a signal for everyone to get into line and follow him to the spot whereon picking is to be done. When this place is reached, the families form themselves into a straight line, side by side, and picking is ordered commenced. . . . The padrone stands behind the line of pickers to see that no berries are left over. If he finds some vines not sufficiently picked, he taps the pickers behind whom the berries remain with his stick, and always with an oath, orders the picker to repick the spot.[16]

Pickers used small, hand-held scoops to gather the berries. Scoopfuls were emptied into "peck" boxes stationed immediately behind the pickers. When the peck boxes were full, they were carried to the bushelman, located on one edge of the bog. In exchange for each full peck, the family received a ticket entitling them to payment at the end of the season. In order to allow the older pickers to pick continuously, it was usually children's work to carry the full pecks, weighing anywhere from twelve to twenty pounds, to the bushelman. Conditions were arduous. Those picking spent nearly the entire day on hands and knees on the damp ground. Those carrying hauled heavy loads often over a considerable distance. Other factors contributed to the difficulty. "The large number of insects that infest the swampland settling on the open sores of the hands increase the torture of the children. Mosquitos thrive in abundance, and there are flies and a number of other insects and snakes."[17]

In 1910, Edward Brown and Lewis Hine found the New Jersey cranberry bogs swarming with children. While many of the children played a substantial amount of the time, both Brown and Hine were struck by how many children worked most of the time. They carefully documented

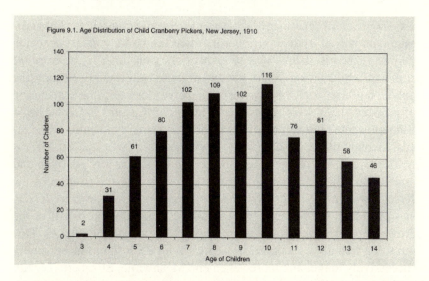

Figure 9.1. Age Distribution of Child Cranberry Pickers, New Jersey, 1910

Figure 9.4 Age Distribution of Child Cranberry Pickers, New Jersey, 1910 (*Source:* NCLC Investigation Report 205, pp. 8–9.)

living conditions of the workers and even more carefully documented working conditions. They estimated that children accounted for 40 to 50 percent of the workforce and as much as one-third of the total harvest. Investigator Brown counted 864 children from Philadelphia picking on seven bogs alone.[18] The age distribution was striking (Figure 9.4).

A few children as young as three were found picking. A majority of the child pickers were children under ten (487 of 864, or 56.4 percent). But what is really striking about the age distribution is how it tapers off at the upper end. There were fewer fourteen-year-olds than there were five-year-olds. Unfortunately, investigators did not explicitly explore the question of why the age distribution should look like this, and so the explanation is open to speculation.[19] But it does appear generally consistent with observations from other investigations that older children were fewer in number, and whatever the explanation, it strikingly demonstrates the use of very young children in the work.

The combination of Edward F. Brown's careful and systematic investigation and Hine's meticulously documented photographs enabled the NCLC to go immediately to press with a pamphlet timed to coincide with the forthcoming 1910 Thanksgiving holiday (Thanksgiving and Christmas being, by far, the biggest days for the cranberry industry). The pamphlet was widely distributed and, while carefully documented, was more sensational than was customary for the committee. The message it conveyed to the consumer was that the holiday meal for which they were giving thanks was brought to the consumer by an army of exploited child pickers. The pamphlet caused quite a stir among the public, not least with the Growers Cranberry Company, the association of growers. They were chagrined to learn that Edward F. Brown, who had represented himself as an agent for a magazine syndicate, was actually an agent of the NCLC.

The Growers Cranberry Company was located in Philadelphia and represented all the significant growers from both Cape Cod and New Jersey. Joseph J. White of White's Bog, the largest bog in New Jersey, was president. On November 29, 1910, he responded on behalf of the growers association in a letter to Owen Lovejoy of the NCLC. This reply led to a series of correspondence with each iteration becoming successively longer and more vehement. Meanwhile, Elizabeth (Lizzie) White, Joseph White's daughter and superintendent of the bog, was corresponding with Jane Addams at Hull House. Even White's faithful padrone, Gus Donato, weighed in with a letter to Lovejoy.

Mr. White objected on behalf of the industry that "Some of your statements in this leaflet are sensational and misleading, and some are absolutely untrue." His question to Lovejoy was this: "May I ask what your object is, in trying to make things appear worse than they are? And what would you do to better them, if you had the power? Would you deprive these poor people, of an outing which they and their children appear to enjoy, and an opportunity to provide food and clothing for the winter, for the sake of a few additional weeks of school for the children?"[20] Mr. White's padrone, Gus Donato, the man who brought the Italian families from Philadelphia to the bog, was indignant. He had been padrone for fifteen years, having begun by supplying two hundred pickers each year. He now supplied 900 pickers a year and many families returned year after year. If conditions were as bad as the NCLC portrayed them, then how was it that he was able to recruit 900 pickers each year? He added, "The cranberry picking is a God send for the pickers, as it means recreation and employment combined into one."[21]

Lovejoy replied, inviting the growers to show where the NCLC publication was untrue. White took Lovejoy up on his offer and laid out a statement of claims. As a result, Lovejoy was forced to make a number of concessions to the growers. First, he admitted that the rhetorical device of linkage with Thanksgiving may have been "sensational and misleading" (it may have created the impression that the entire New Jersey crop of 600,000 bushels was picked by children, when, in fact, only 200,000 were picked by children; or it may have created the impression that the entire crop was consumed on one day—the Thanksgiving holiday). Lovejoy also acknowledged that their published estimate of a ten- to twelve-hour workday should be revised downward to a nine- to 10-hour day and that, compared with other employments, hours were not exceptionally long in cranberries.[22] Still, Lovejoy argued that the NCLC pamphlet was true in its essence. As to the extent and conditions of child labor, the effects on schooling, on the padrone system, on the large "pecks," and on the housing conditions, he stood firm.

Elizabeth White, Joseph White's daughter and, for the previous seventeen years, superintendent of her father's bog, described the work of the small children to Jane Addams as play:

> As a matter of fact I have never known of children under six or seven picking any berries at all, unless it be a handful to play with. About this time, impelled by a child's imitative instinct and it may be by the coaxing of parents they fill some little cup of "kittle" several times a day and empty it into the measure of their parents, but the greater part of the time is spent in play.

White's articulate and thoughtful correspondence with Jane Addams reveals the difficulty in indicting all "exploiters" of child labor as cold and heartless. She described the evolution of the cranberry culture in New Jersey with pride:

> When I began working on the bogs all the pickers were Americans:— Americans with a remarkably well developed bump of the "I'm just as good as anybody," American spirit. Many of them were the same people who had helped my grandfather on his first bog, now more than 50 years old. One woman came every fall for 40 years; her daughter who accompanied her all through her childhood, is now clerk and stenographer in a local store. . . . Some of these Americans "put up" at the bog in "shanties" not nearly so good as the present pickers quarters, many others drove from 2 to 10 miles every day. It was the custom to bring all the children, because they were safer there with their parents than at home. A considerable number of the pickers were of that class of small farmers which has produced such a large share of the best brain and bone and sinew of the United States. The children were accustomed to help their parents at home, and continued to do so on the bogs as they were able. . . . When we

needed more pickers than the available "natives" could supply, we got a few families of Italians from Philadelphia to help us out. They worked side by side with the Americans under the same rules and conditions. Year by year the Italians have increased and the Americans have decreased, most of them not picking cranberries any more, till the pickers are chiefly Italians. . . . Of those that were children when we first began to have Italian pickers a number are married and coming back with their own babies, much better cared for too than their parents used to be.[23]

White's Bog first captured the attention of the NCLC because of the sheer magnitude of its operation.[24] Over time, the NCLC seemed to develop a grudging respect for their operation. They provided by far the best living conditions for the families—better living quarters, some attention to privacy, and the best sanitary facilities on the marshes. Their long-time padrone, Gus Donato, seemed to deal fairly with the families, at least in comparison to other padrones. Clearly, he had a faithful following of families willing to work under his regime. The Whites appeared to be very successful, and relative to others, they were also the most humane. Still, child labor was an integral part of their system. Five years after their initial investigation, Lewis Hine returned to White's Bog and counted ninety children from seven to fourteen picking steadily, adding, "The number of children from 8 to 12 years *not picking was very small*."[25]

After the 1910 investigation by Brown and Hine "met with such vehement contradiction from a prominent grower and his associates," and especially since the growers had challenged the fundamental truth of their reports, the NCLC sent crack investigator Charles L. Chute back to the region for the 1911 harvest. He visited twenty-three farms in four counties. Seventeen gangs of pickers were studied and twenty-one camps were inspected. Of 1,525 total pickers, he counted 492 (32.3 percent) under fourteen and 41 (2.7 percent) under five (not counting young children who were not picking).[26] Chute's report left no doubt that child labor was prevalent on the bogs. At Isaac Budd's Bog, the following scene was recorded:

When the padrone's whistle blew every soul left camp. Not an infant was too young or grandmother too old to join the army heading for the bog. Babies were wheeled in carriages or carried in mother's arms and "toddlers" followed after. A "baby camp" was established on the edge of the bog where about twenty babies were left to be cared for by a few older children. All the rest picked. Out of seventy pickers, 42 were under 14, 25 under 10, and 3 under 5! This is typical. . . . Children from the age of 6 and 7 up usually work regularly. . . . At Bryant's Bog, a baby of 2 was seen helping the mother a little. The owner said, "Yes they all pick some as soon as they are big enough."[27]

Chute's reports and the NCLC's use of them did little to alleviate the tension between the NCLC and the industry. All this ultimately led to formal hearings before the New Jersey Commission on Immigration. The NCLC was called upon to defend the accuracy of their earlier reports, and the industry was called upon to defend the legitimacy of their child labor practices. Ultimately, the hearings centered on the question of who compelled the children to work. Industry representatives conceded that large numbers of children worked, and worked a considerable portion of the total work time, and did so from relatively young ages. But the industry insisted that it was neither the growers nor the padrones who forced the children to work. Instead, it was the parents. Isaac Budd, of Budd's Bog, testified, "I do not think that any of them are compelled to pick under 14 years of age. If they are, they are not compelled by the owner or padrone, they are compelled by their parents." Likewise, Lizzie White asserted, "When a child does work he simply works at the request of his parents."[28] This had been a contentious issue from the very first investigation—one the NCLC was slow to address. On the basis of subsequent investigations, however, it was a point the NCLC was forced to concede. The growers and padrones did not directly force the children to work. To the extent that anyone compelled the children to work, it was the parents. In their 1915 investigation, Louise Boswell (accompanied by Lewis Hine) made careful observation of those who supervised the children:

No evidence was found that children were compelled to work by the padrones, though they obeyed him promptly and turned at once if he called their attention to some neglected spot. As seen, the padrones were civil and not unkind, though in a few instances, irritable. Occasionally considerable profanity was heard from both padrones and workers. The worst instance of harshness met, was on White's Bog where a father was seen to strike a child about eight or ten years, and pick him by the collar apparently because he had left some berries on the vine. Indications are that it is the parents who urge the children to pick, and observations among the homes and schools in Philadelphia demonstrated clearly that Italian parents, however affectionate, are frequently harsh, even brutal in their treatment of the children. Schools reported that children's ears are sometimes torn when pulled by the parents.[29]

Still, in 1915, after five years of continuous investigation and agitation, Louise Boswell and Lewis Hine found that child labor remained prevalent on the New Jersey cranberry bogs. On their return, they found that children continued to begin their socialization to picking at extremely young ages. Little had changed. Boswell reported:

> [B]etween forty and fifty bogs in New Jersey as well as a number of schools and homes of Italians in Philadelphia were visited. . . . Comparing our findings with earlier child labor reports, it is clear that but little improvement has been made. Child labor continues to be an important factor in the work on the cranberry bogs. A conservative estimate of the number of children under fourteen years of age *seen* picking on the bogs would reach above five hundred. . . . On twenty-one bogs, children of seven years or younger were found picking berries. The fact that they worked quite steadily was confirmed in many cases either by the parents or the boss.[30]

They noted that "[T]he greater part of the carrying of the berries from pickers to loading spot is still done by the children," and cited the case of the Iannaconni children:

> Millie Iannaconni, 8 years old, was carrying constantly and picking between carries. Today the distance from pickers to the bushelmen was about 350 feet, and was increasing as they picked. Millie made the trip three times in 40 minutes. Her father said she carried 51 of these boxes yesterday, and picked when not carrying. Her 7 year old brother, Dominic, picks steadily. The father said that he and his wife and these two children made $200 in a good year.[31]

Even as late as 1923, when Edith Knowles conducted the final NCLC investigation of New Jersey cranberry bogs, in eleven, she found, of 1,152 adults and children present, "a total of 303 children between 16 and 5 years of age who were working with more or less regularity."[32] But things were changing in the cranberry industry. While child labor had not yet been eliminated, as early as 1915 and clearly by 1923, child labor was on the way out. Simple, rudimentary factors affected both the labor supply and the demand for labor that mitigated against employment of children. On the supply side, Edith Knowles interviewed Philadelphia school officials and noted:

> It was the impression of both officers that fewer fathers were accompanying their families to the bogs than hitherto. Since there has been more work obtainable in Phila. they can make better money staying at home. Also, they thought more children of continuation school age had been going without their parents during the last few years. . . . When the children go off without either parent they generally say they are going with their "uncle," who is very obviously, the padrone.[33]

On the demand side, some modest improvements in bog management practices coupled with an astonishingly simple technological innovation worked to eliminate demand for child workers. "Raking" or "scooping" replaced handpicking. In contrast to handpicking, raking or scooping was heavy labor that required adult strength and endurance. As early as 1915, Louise Boswell and Lewis Hine were able to report in New Jersey that "The use of scoops as a substitute for hand picking has been tried this year on a number of bogs." Several owners indicated that "Scooping is sure to be generally adopted in a short time, for economic reasons if no other, since the cost of scooping is much less than that of the hand work."[34]

Winter: Gulf Coast Canneries

During the summer months Polish, Bohemian, and Italian families were treated to an outing in the country culminating in the cranberry bogs of New Jersey. During the winter months, many of these same families vacationed along the Gulf Coast—vacations that were financed by their labor in the oyster and shrimp canneries.

Oyster and shrimp canneries dotted the Gulf Coast from New Orleans eastward to Florida and the Atlantic Coast from Maryland to the Carolinas and Georgia. Compared with Gulf Coast canneries, many Atlantic Coast canneries employed local blacks who brought very few children to work with them. According to management, the chief advantage of hiring blacks was that it saved on the cost of transportation. The chief advantage of the whites was, "The whites work harder, longer hours, are more easily driven, and use the children much more."[35]

The Gulf Coast canneries used migrant labor from Baltimore and Philadelphia. Men and older boys generally worked the boats, leaving the women and children to the processing work. Family members who did not work the boats, were present in the processing sheds. Women took all their children, even nursing infants, along to the shed. Youngest infants and children were put in a corner out of the way on a pile of quilts or in carriages. Other children worked varying amounts, climbing the job ladder described by Lewis Hine: "At three and four years of age they play around and help a little, 'learnin' de trade.' At five and six years they work more regularly, and at seven and eight years, they put in every working day for long hours."[36] "I have witnessed many varieties of child labor horrors from Maine to Texas, but the climax, the logical conclusion of the 'laissez faire' policy regarding the exploitation of children is to be seen among the oyster-shuckers and shrimp-pickers."[37]

As in New Jersey cranberries, Lewis Hine and Edward F. Brown conducted the earliest investigations of the Gulf Coast canneries, with Hine compiling the photographic essay and Brown the journalistic documentation. During his relatively brief investigation in 1911, Hine proved fifteen children from nine to eleven years of age, twenty-five from six to eight, and thirteen three- to five-years-olds (Figure 9.5).[38] The following are representative of Brown's entries:

> Dunbar, Lopez and Dukate Company, Dunbar, Louisiana. Spoke to John Peterson, twelve years old, who lives at 705 Bond Street, Baltimore. He said he has been here four months. Works at shucking oysters. Starts usually at four o'clock in the morning, and quits when the oysters are all finished, which is sometimes four or five o'clock in the evening.

> Barataria Canning Company, Biloxi, Mississippi. Went to living quarters and met Mike and Leo Simpsky, 12 and 13, respectively. They said they both shuck. Start usually at four o'clock in the morning and work until three or four o'clock in the afternoon. Make from 15 to 20 cents per day. Live in Baltimore. Don't attend school anywhere. Adam Franklin, five years old said he shucks with the rest of his family. His sister says he gets up with the rest at four o'clock and goes to the shed. Helen Marko, seven years of age says she works also. Has started as early as three o'clock in the morning and worked as late as six o'clock at night. Makes ten or fifteen cents per day. Teresa Smith, ten years old, said she does not shuck. "I mind the baby. I would rather mind the baby because then I don't have

Figure 9.5 *Shucking Shed.* Dunbar, Louisiana. March, 1911. Four-year-old Mary, who shucks two pots of oysters a day at Dunbar. Tends the baby when not working. (See photo 2062) The boss said that next year Mary will work steady as the rest of them. The mother is the fastest shucker in the place. Earns $1.50 a day. Works part of the time with her sick baby in her arms. Father works on the dock. *(Courtesy of the Library of Congress, Prints and Photographs Division, Lewis Wickes Hine National Child Labor Committee Collection, LC-USZ6–1207.)*

to get up so early. My brother Leopold, he shucks—he's eight." Julia Smith, nine years, says she shucks steadily. Has filled as many as five pots per day, she said proudly.[39]

Several of the investigation reports suggest that the quality of the labor–management relationship was especially precarious in the Gulf Coast canneries. Paul J. Chauvet, superintendent of one of the Dunbar, Lopez and Dukate canneries in Louisiana, told investigator Brown:

This is a very poor season, and we have not had much work for the people to do. At times they get unruly because when there is no work they must eat just the same. So in such cases we advance them credit at the company store. Then when they get work they must pay back. If they knew work was so scarce they would not come down. Every year I go to

Baltimore with the boss, and we promise the people steady work, and nice houses, and good pay, and work for the children. Then when they come down they expect all these things.

Mr. Fordich, another Dunbar, Lopez and Dukate superintendent, was more direct in both his attitude and his approach to his workers:

When the Polanders come, and there is little work for them to do, they start trouble. A short time ago they went on strike, and the men even refused to bring the boats back from the reefs. I went out there and told them if they did not go to work I would blow their damned heads off, and when they saw I had a gun they got to work. When they came back to the factory they started another strike.[40]

Brown also made note of a recent case of alleged peonage where seventeen men, women, and children were reported to be held in "virtual slavery" at an isolated cannery in Mississippi. He reported that the United States attorneys for the Eastern District of Louisiana had investigated at least eight cases of alleged peonage in recent years in the canneries.[41]

The difficulty in maintaining an effective labor–management relationship prompted some to abandon the padrone system in favor of hiring blacks. Mr. Seal, a superintendent of an independent cannery in Houma, Louisiana, spoke with investigator Harry Bremer in 1914:

Once Mr. Seal brought people from Baltimore, but he found it cost too much, and the people gave him too much trouble, so he did not repeat the experiment. For transportation alone, he said it cost $5,000. "They are a load of trouble," he said. "They get down here, and then when there's no work, they want you to keep them. They go out to the Mayor and say they are starving. They are hard to manage too. You can't discharge one, or they all strike; and if they don't all strike, he goes around telling everyone that people are starving down here. You cannot send him back to Baltimore alone, because it costs too much—$75."[42]

Since the seafood canneries spanned the entire Gulf Coast, encompassing four states, there was no single employer association with which the NCLC had to contend. Rather, the influence of employers varied from section to section. In the east, John G. Ruge, proprietor of Herman Ruge and Sons of Appalachicola and Cedar Key, Florida, was the dominant influence. In the west, the firm of Dunbar, Lopez and Dukate was the largest producer, operating several canneries in both Mississippi and Louisiana. The two firms, Ruge in the east and Dunbar in the west, stood in marked contrast to one another.

Herman Ruge and Sons was run by John G. Ruge (a son, Herman, "being dead"). For a time, he was the most influential canner in Florida. According to a fellow canner, Ruge was the self-appointed protector of laissez-faire in Florida. "Whenever there was talk of taking the children out of the shucking places Ruge would raise a protest. He kept up a regular lobby at Tallahassee to fight everything he thought would hurt the business."[43]

But Ruge was a brute. His operation demonstrates the limits of employer capacity to exploit immigrant and migrant labor. He had brought his labor force, about a hundred families, mostly Poles and Bohemians, from Baltimore. Children from seven years and up worked ten-hour days, making as much as fifteen cents a day or as little as six cents a day. Living conditions were less than adequate, and, during one period when the factory was closed, the families were simply "left here stranded, . . . herded in a shack, formerly a salt ware-house, divided into partitions, and were crowded into these stalls . . . sometimes ten to twelve in one room." When several requested their promised transportation back to Baltimore "they were fired so that they would have to pay their own way back."[44] "[O]n one occasion during the second season Ruge Brothers put a force of workers to live on an old lighter in the harbor and that one night in a storm the cable parted, the lighter drifted away and all but one were drowned."[45]

Ruge was no kinder or gentler to others with whom he did business. He is alleged to have regularly cheated the oystermen out of their pay by docking them for substandard crates, even though the company processed and sold the oysters from those crates. It got so bad that members of the Oysterman's Protective Association refused to sell oysters to Ruge, and the company closed for a time for lack of boats. When they were running boats, they were accused of selling undersized oysters—the law requiring three inches from tip to hinge—resulting in "the stripping of the oyster beds." Cedar Key oysters, having been "formerly much in demand, being of fine flavor," were now being harvested, in peak season, at one-tenth the volume of previous seasons, "the industry being thus practically ruined."[46] Ultimately, Ruge was forced out of business: "Some union men burned one of his boats. He can't open his shop here any more. He is interested in some canneries in Georgia and the Carolinas."[47]

In contrast to Ruge in Florida, Dunbar, Lopez and Dukate of Mississippi and Louisiana presented the NCLC with a more traditional adversary. First of all, this was a large firm that was in the business for the long haul. They would not foul their own nest as Ruge had done. Second, they worked within established channels to ensure that the law remained favorable to their interests, and so tended to oppose restrictions on child labor. But third, they would adhere to the letter of the law—at least as it was enforced, and not necessarily in accordance with its spirit. But at least when confronted, they could be brought around.

At the time of Hine and Brown's first investigation Mississippi was the only Gulf Coast state with a law prohibiting employment of children under fourteen in the canneries. In moments of candor (that is, when they did not realize they were speaking to agents of the NCLC), management admitted the law meant little. Mr. Abley, a Dunbar, Lopez and Dukate superintendent in Pass Christian, told investigator Brown:

> It's against the law to use children, but we don't bother much with the law because if we did we would have to give up business. The Poles would not come if they were not allowed to work the children. The whole families come out at four or five in the morning and shuck oysters or pick shrimp. The children under six huddle up against the steam boxes where it is warm, while the children over six work.[48]

Similarly, Hine reports on a visit to a Dunbar, Lopez and Dukate cannery in 1916:

> In one of the Louisiana factories, I saw a sign, conspicuously posted, bearing the legend: "Children Under Fourteen Years not Permitted to Work in this Factory," and I asked the manager what it meant. "Oh," he said, "that's the law, but if the factory inspector herself should come down here, I'd tell her, 'You put 'em out,' and see what she'd do about it." In the shucking-room, the boss said: "Why it'd take a sheriff all his time to keep the kids from workin."[49]

But the official position of the company was stated by Lazoro Lopez, who asserted, "The shucking shed is not a factory, and therefore is outside the law. Besides that, we don't employ the children. They work with and for their parents."[50] This position was echoed by others in the Dunbar, Lopez and Dukate management team. For example, Mr. Abley, superintendent of the Pass Christian cannery, who had acknowledged that employment of children was against the law, nevertheless stated that "the law does not apply to the children who work here because we don't 'employ' them. They are with their parents for whom they work." He also asserted that the shucking shed is "not a factory at all" because it is open and separate from the canning line. Mr. Dunbar insisted that it was not the canners, but instead the parents, who forced the children to work: "I have seen them whip the children when they would not work. Of course, we don't want them to do that because if the child labor people knew it they would be lying about us as they are lying about the canneries up in New York."[51]

The NCLC investigations of the seafood canneries were part of a larger effort to secure better legislation, especially in Mississippi and Louisiana. The aim was to establish a fourteen-year minimum age for factory work, treat canneries as factories, and create a program of factory inspection and enforcement. Hine and Brown's investigation reports were published and widely disseminated. Predictably, industry leaders took umbrage, attacking the reports as inaccurate and sensationalist. One point they criticized was Hine's account of difficulties in shrimp picking, as opposed to oyster shucking. Hine made the claim:

> Here and elsewhere, I found considerable complaint about sore fingers caused by handling the shrimps. The fingers of many of the children are actually bleeding before the end of the day. They say it is the acid in the head of the shrimp that causes it. One manager told me that six hours was all that most pickers could stand to work. Then the fingers are so sore they have to stop. Some soak the fingers in an alum solution to harden them.[52]

The industry stressed that Hine's account of the effects of shrimp on pickers' hands was factually erroneous. It turned out, however, that Hine's only error was calling an alkali an acid. In rebuttal, the NCLC published a statement from the Bureau of Chemistry in the U.S. Department of Agriculture noting that "shrimps contain some corrosive substance. . . . It attacks the workmen's hands, causing the skin to peel, and also eats through the leather of their shoes."[53] Of course, the Department of Agriculture statement was itself inaccurate since very few of the workers were actual "workmen." Most were women and children.

In the published version of his report, investigator Brown compared activity in the Gulf Coast states to protect fish and game with activity to protect children. For example, he noted that since 1904 Mississippi had been providing large sums to the Mississippi Oyster Commission to reseed depleted oyster beds but "has not provided a single penny for factory inspection. . . . Mississippi has spent more money on paper clips for the office of the Oyster Commission than it spent on the protection of the children who toil in the state." He concluded:

> It is a high crime in Louisiana, Mississippi, Alabama, and soon will be in Florida, to gather oysters or catch shrimp out of season, because of the legally enacted principle that to do so is to endanger the preservation of this precious family. *There is no closed season for children.* These states through their acts of omission permit unscrupulous industrial poachers to hunt down the little children during all seasons, stunt their growth by exhausting toil, blunt their sensibilities by monotonous activity, and stifle their mentality by taking them from the school room and placing the unnatural burden of industry on their weak shoulders.[54]

By 1914 the law in Mississippi had changed. The age limit was now twelve for boys and fourteen for girls. More significantly, the law now covered the shucking sheds and prohibited not just the employment of children but merely permitting children to work. It also prohibited night work by children and established an eight-hour limit per day. Investigator Herschel H. Jones was sent to inspect the Dunbar, Lopez and Dukate canneries in Mississippi. He found fifty violations of age provisions and forty-five violations of hours provisions. He reported the violations to Mr. Dunbar, who assured Jones that he was willing to obey the law:

> He promised that he would immediately see that all children under age were sent out of the factory, and that none of the boys under 16 or girls under 18 years would be allowed to come before 6:00 A.M., or to work more than 8 hours per day. He said that they had had to conform to the Child Labor Law in the Louisiana Factory, and though it had been difficult to get the people themselves educated to its provisions, it had not been any detriment to them in a business way.[55]

It became apparent that the industry would obey the law if they had to, but only if they had to. The key was enforcement, and the key to enforcement was the state factory inspector. The factory inspector in Louisiana, Jean Gordon, was an ally of the NCLC (she had spoken at several of the committee's annual meetings), and she enforced the law vigorously. But David McDowell, Mississippi's factory inspector, was another matter. So, in 1916, Hine returned to Mississippi. This time he was investigating not the canneries or the industry but Inspector McDowell himself. In an interview, McDowell stated:

> I haven't had any prosecutions for violations all these two years. I get after them and they come to time. You must remember that you can *lead* these people; that you can't drive 'em. I believe in keeping on good terms with them, and then they do the things I ask them.[56]

As an illustration of what "keeping on good terms" meant, Hine located the local liveryman who drove Inspector McDowell to and from the Peerless Canning Factory that the inspector declared "had the best child labor conditions of all canneries." The liveryman stated that after each inspection, Inspector McDowell came away from the factory carrying a case of oysters.

> A boy working in one of the Biloxi canneries said that the child labor inspector comes to their factory on a certain Thursday every month. "Last year they chucked the kids under the shucking shed and into the ice box. Someone squealed on 'em and the inspector opened the ice box door and yelled, 'Gee! You got some big shrimp in here!' "[57]

Whereas technological advances resulted in the elimination of child labor from the cranberry bogs, it was regulation and enforcement that ultimately eliminated child labor in oyster and shrimp canneries. In the best traditions of gradualism, shucking sheds were brought into the ambit of factory laws where age and hours restrictions were established, and inspection and enforcement practices were gradually improved. Ironically, however, it was not child labor legislation that finally did the trick, it was pure food legislation, another object of the Progressive Era reform movement. Concern over consumer health led most coastal states to require oyster shuckers to submit to blood tests and present health certificates before they could be employed. When coupled with the age restrictions contained in the child labor legislation, the pure food laws were the final nail in the coffin that effectively eliminated children from the Gulf Coast seafood canneries.

The Padrone System

All crops that required harvesting by hand presented the grower with a labor problem—the need for a large number of hands for a short period of time. Someone who could mobilize a large number of people to migrate from some other location to the crop was needed. This need was filled by the padrone.[58] Edward F. Brown describes the development of the padrone system in New Jersey cranberries:

> The region surrounding the cranberry fields is sparsely inhabited. To meet at once the great demand for hands to gather in the fruit rural help is utterly inadequate. Formerly the cranberry growers depended on such tramps as happened in the neighborhood to pick berries. Upon the maturing of the crop there was an inrush of vagabonds who worked at their pleasure and left at will. This species of labor was wholly unreliable. Not until the Italian padrone came on the scene was a solution of this labor problem offered.[59]

In the New Jersey cranberry bogs, the padrone system had become "almost universal" as "it has proved itself the easiest way to secure the large gangs necessary." In some cases, one padrone was engaged by one grower to supply one gang. In these cases "generally he is employed by the same grower year after year." Other padrones supplied several gangs to several different growers. Some padrones specialized in supplying gangs for one crop only, such as the cranberries. Other padrones organized gangs and moved with them from crop to crop. Not surprisingly, padrones often cooperated with each other in their efforts to ensure a sufficient and coordinated labor supply.[60]

Gus Donato, long-time faithful padrone on White's Bog, the largest cranberry operation, described his work in benign terms:

> As for myself as Padrone, I only gather the pickers together, see that they are safely brought to their destination, see that they all get equal treatment, see that order is maintained, and to see that they are made comfortable during their stay there, for which I am paid a regular salary by my employer.[61]

Thus the padrone in agriculture stood in the same position as the sweater in urban environments. He was the ultimate middleman between the pickers and the growers. He was of the same ethnic background as the pickers. He knew their language, their culture, and their neighborhoods. But he also knew the growers' needs. In turn, growers typically "refuse to deal with the pickers as individuals, leaving everything relating to the harvesting to the padrone." As a middleman, the padrone was paid by both the growers and the pickers. While Gus Donato indicated he was paid a regular salary by his employer, he did not state that this was his only form of payment. In fact, regular salaries were somewhat rare. But padrones could be quite ingenious in developing multiple sources of income from their job. From the grower, the padrone might receive "a stipulated sum, ranging from fifty cents to two dollars per person" supplied.[62] The padrone might also receive a portion of the value of the crop picked. Investigator Chute described a typical arrangement: "[T]he padrone contracted for a commission on the number of bushels picked. . . . The growers contract with him for 50 cents a bushel, he takes 10 cents and the pickers get 40 cents."[63]

But the padrone also found ways to exact payment from the pickers. "By charging an excess in the actual cost of transportation; by charging for the privilege of being engaged; by requiring 'presents' at the termination of the season ranging in sums according to the amount of money earned, he largely increased his income."[64] At the beginning of the season, pickers were required to pay the padrone in order to secure employment:

> The padrone exacts a head payment from each picker, including the children if old enough to pay railroad fare, which charge is large enough to cover railroad fare, transportation of baggage and a fee for getting the job. It is very difficult to learn just what the padrone's profit is in each case. . . . The prevailing amount which is "cleaned up" by the padrone from each picker as ascertained from the growers or pickers themselves is . . . usually "about $1.00."[65]

During the picking season "the padrone is usually given the privilege of running the commissary or store." While NCLC found no evidence of exorbitant prices, it was also clear that "a good profit is made in these stores."[66] Finally, at the end of the season, pickers were expected to provide the padrone with a "present"—that is, a kickback on a portion of the family's earnings—with the amount expected as high as 10 percent of earnings.[67] Lizzie White of White's Bog commented, "The pickers have a custom of giving the padrone a 'present' at the end of each season. If the 'present' does not suit the padrone he makes sure not to engage the family the next season."[68]

Pickers had no way of knowing how or how much the padrone was paid by the grower. Likewise, "growers usually disclaim all responsibility or even knowledge of arrangements made between padrone and picker."[69] Thus the middleman was free to exploit both sides of the relationship to the extent of his cunning.

The padrone was more than just a labor recruiter. During the harvest, he also served as gang boss. As recruiter, the padrone dealt principally with the head of each family, and so had little direct relationship with the children. But as gang boss, he supervised the work of the children as well as the adults. Edward F. Brown observed:

> The children stand in great fear of the padrone. More than once I saw the padrone exercising a very strenuous supervision over the children. On Theodore Budd's bog at Turkeytown, I saw Frank, the chief padrone, grab a boy of six by the coat collar and forcibly yank him back to call the little fellow's attention to a vine with some berries left unpicked. I also saw him as he was threatening a girl of five years for not picking the vines clean. Mr. Hine and I on another occasion heard his loud cursing at a family at which time he half raised his stick as if to strike the children.[70]

With one exception in the history of American agriculture, the padrone system, or some variant of it, was used wherever and whenever hand-harvesting required large gangs of migrant workers. Even the exception serves to reinforce and illustrate the rule. It was only during the Dust Bowl years ("when Oklahoma woke up in Kansas") and thousands of "rubber tramps" migrated westward, especially to California to join the thousands of Chinese, Mexican, and Filipino families already there, that growers did not have to attend to the problem of labor recruitment. Under these extraordinary conditions, "with a gross available labor supply of more than double the peak requirements," the problem of finding enough workers was replaced by the problem of spreading the available work among the workers.[71]

When labor-intensive handwork involved not only the harvest, but also the planting and cultivation—that is, when the work gang remained on the land the entire season—various land tenancy arrangements could substitute for the padrone in securing a labor supply. Tenant farming and sharecropping were common in cotton and tobacco and were occasionally seen in sugar beets. While specific arrangements varied from crop to crop and section to section, the general arrangement was for the tenant to receive a fixed number of acres and a place to live in exchange for a share of the crop. The portion of the crop accruing to the tenant varied with the assets supplied by the tenant. Where the tenant supplied only labor, the share of the crop was relatively small. Where the tenant supplied a team, equipment, and implements, the share could be substantially larger. Acreage allotments, and thus earning potential, were also based on assets that could be supplied by the tenant. Since most tenants provided little else than hand tools and their own labor, this meant that the acreage allotment varied with family size. Under such an arrangement, it was obvious that all members of the household, including young children, would be called upon to work the fields to the extent they were able. For census purposes, children working under sharecropping arrangements on tenant farms were classed as working on the home farm.

Family Wage

Along with industrial homework, it was in agriculture where the family wage system operated most closely in conformity with preindustrial traditions of the household economy. It was often not possible to segregate the contributions of each family member from the other. But it was also not necessary to do so. All contributed to the extent they were able to the common good of the household. While labor supply, including supply of child workers, followed the preindustrial household model, there was one important difference. The household was no longer producing for its own consumption, it was selling its labor for wages in an external labor market. Preindustrial households met industrial employers.

The general rule was that whatever the family picked or shucked was pooled into common containers—pots, buckets, boxes, or baskets. Full containers were turned in to the bushelman, weighman, row boss, or padrone and were exchanged for a token or check that would be cashed in for payment at the end of the season (the tokens could also be used as currency during the season at the camp commissary).[72] The head of the household, usually a father or mother, maintained the family's account of tokens, so that the labor of the entire family was pooled into a single wage.[73]

This method of payment enabled employers to distance themselves from any responsibility for child labor conditions. In the first instance, the grower did not hire the families, the padrone did. And the padrone did not hire the children, the parents did. But it was more than mere psychological distancing. Employers used the method deliberately as an instrument to evade legal responsibility. A superintendent of one of the Louisiana Dunbar, Lopez and Dukate seafood canneries told how easy it was:

> We did use children as young as eight years picking shrimp, but the health
> department inspector came around and told us we were violating the law.
> So, after that we did not give checks to children, or employ them. They
> would come with their mothers, and pick a little, and it would all go on
> the mother's check.[74]

The family wage system had other advantages as well. It reduced transaction costs for all concerned. The grower had to deal only with the padrone. The padrone had to deal only with heads of households. In turn, each head of household assumed responsibility for management of a small crew. The family wage system placed a clear set of incentives in front of each household. These incentives favored the recruitment and selection of large families (i.e., families with more kids) and encouraged a relatively clear division of labor within the household.

On the need for large families, Gus Donato, the padrone who supplied White's Bog, told investigator Brown, "I never take a couple alone because it pays neither of us. They can make about three dollars a day together. If they had three or four children, the children would pick too, and at the end of the season they would make a good round sum."[75] Transaction costs notwithstanding, Charles L. Chute explained why padrones preferred large families:

> The relation of the padrone system to the children employed is simply
> this. The padrone prefers to engage families with many children and it is
> for his interest to make them all work as much as possible. Whether he is
> paid a commission or not it is to his interest to secure enough pickers.
> The large families furnish many pickers and are at the same time more
> docile and may be exploited more easily. It is always to his interest to get
> a large crop picked before the impending frost.[76]

This mutual preference for large families was echoed in the shrimp and oyster canneries. Harry M. Bremer spoke with the superintendent of an independent cannery: "A premium is put on large families. Mr. Seal said all the members of the family come in to help. If a man has a large family, say 8 or 10 children, he gets an easy job, but if he's got only a man and his wife he is set to wheeling oysters."[77]

The family wage system also encouraged a division of labor within the family that would maximize household earnings. In shrimp and oysters, men and older boys often worked the boats where the work was heavier but the wages were higher. Around fruit and vegetable canneries, adults and older youth might attempt to secure a position on the canning or capping line. This was considered factory work and also paid higher wages. But in some areas these positions were hard to come by, as they were reserved first for local help, and migrants were only employed when local help was insufficient. By far the greatest numerical proportion of the workforce, including all the young children who worked, were engaged in picking, hulling, or shucking. Because pay was determined by the number of measures filled, adults and older children remained at the principal task of picking, hulling, or shucking continuously. Younger children were expected to help with the principal task to the extent that they were able. But because they were slower, they were also assigned the subsidiary tasks that would enable the more productive workers to continue picking, hulling, or shucking.

One important subsidiary task that was generally assigned to children "too young to pick continuously" was carrying—that is, carrying the filled measures to wherever they were to be turned in to receive credit on the family's account. Carrying received considerable attention from NCLC investigators, especially in the New Jersey cranberry bogs (Figure 9.6). Investigators noted that a child carrying for five pickers would make fifty or more trips to the padrone each day. Each trip ranged in distance from a few feet to three or four hundred feet. In between trips, the child was encouraged to pick.[78] "One young girl on Newton's Farm, was carrying a loaded tray on her head and one in her hand, a total weight of about 50 or 60 pounds. She is only 14 years of age and working her 5th season in the fields."[79]

Growers seemed sensitive to the negative image associated with young children staggering under the weight of heavy loads. They recognized that it did not look good. But still they insisted that both they and the padrones were powerless to do anything about it. In addition to the compulsion of parents, the children themselves made carrying a game—part of their regular daily competition. Those who could carry the heaviest loads for the greatest distance in the shortest time were to be admired. In her correspondence with Jane Addams, Lizzie White observed:

> Some of this carrying is undoubtedly done at the insistence of parents, too ignorant to realize that they may thereby be doing harm to the children; but a very great deal of it is also done from the desire of the children to show how big and strong they are; the same spirit that impels them to all sorts of heavy stunts in their games. I remember one instance that

Figure 9.6   *Carrying Cranberries*. Eight-year old, Jennie Camillo, lives in West Maniyunk, Pa. (near Philadelphia). She picked cranberries this summer at Theodore Budd's Bog at Turkeytown, near Pemberton, N.J. This is the fourth week of school in Philadelphia and people will stay here two weeks more. Her look of distress was caused by her father's impatience over her stopping in her tramp to the bushelman at our photographer's request. Witness E.F. Brown, Sept. 27, 1910. *(Courtesy of the Library of Congress, Prints and Photographs Division, Lewis Wickes Hine National Child Labor Committee Collection, LC-USZ62–12870.)*

strikingly illustrates this. Domenick Tenuto has been coming to our bog ever since he was 4 or 5 years old (what a little nuisance he was too), and for two years past his feelings have been much lacerated because we have refused to put him at a man's heavy labor. His mother is the tiniest woman I have ever seen who was not deformed, and his father died before the time of my story, so there could have been no forcing from parents. When Domenick was about 12 years old he began staggering to the "bushel-man" with *four* measures of berries. It was horrible and I forbad it repeatedly, but the prohibition was always forgotten in a brief time.[80]

A second important subsidiary task usually assigned to children too young to pick continuously was baby tending. In any picking, hulling, or shucking operation of substantial scale, there were likely to be a few children, infants and toddlers, too young to be productive at all. Where they could not remain at the mother's side, they were placed in a makeshift baby camp off to the side and out of the way, but within eyesight. While parents remained close by, someone had to assume responsibility for attending to the needs of the babies. Who would perform that task? Again, it was those whose productivity and endurance in the principal task was lowest, that is, the workers whose age was closest to the infants and toddlers for whom they assumed responsibility.

> Then what do you suppose these little ones do for recreation? Of course if they can keep at work all day, they do; but if they cannot, *they tend the baby*. The pathos of the baby-tender, in such a situation, is unsurpassed. You see little ones, from four years upward, working until physical strain and monotony become unendurable, and then, for relief, go over into the corner and rock the baby or tote it around until they feel like working again. Mary, an active little child of eight, told me: "I shucks six pots a day when I don't got the baby wid me, an' two pots if I got him."[81]

An interesting phenomenon bearing on the family wage that NCLC investigators observed in New Jersey cranberries was that there was no uniform system of weights and measures from one bog to the next. On all bogs pickers filled boxes or measures that were called "pecks." Measures were as large as a little over a half bushel, weighing twenty-seven pounds full, to as small as a "peck"—a peck plus a couple quarts or so, weighing thirteen to eighteen pounds. In no case was a "peck" as small as a true peck—that is, eight quarts.[82] This phenomenon of "large pecks" was "surely a bad system" and must have created some inconvenience for farmers in obtaining picking boxes, since each farm had its own unique specifications. However, the system also prevented families from making accurate pay comparisons from one farmer to the next and encouraged farmers "to gain an advantage over his competitors and over his employees by increasing the size of his 'measure.' "[83] "Isaac Budd, a grower, speaking of his wage unit, said to me—'My "peck" boxes contain from thirteen to fourteen quarts. I exact a good measure because the pickers would cheat me every time if only I gave them a chance.'" Whether pickers would have cheated growers was rendered moot by the fact that they were not given the chance. Who was actually cheating whom was clarified by Budd's manager, Mr. Johnson, who remarked about the large pecks, "That's where we get the best of the pickers."[84]

Living Conditions

From the very first NCLC investigation conducted by Edward F. Brown and Lewis Hine in 1910, housing conditions among migrant farm workers had been a concern. Hine described conditions in 1910:

> 17 persons were found living in a one-room shack, with absolutely no care taken to insure the least privacy to the young girl berry pickers. Little or no care is exercised in regard to drainage and sanitation. In one case two families were found to be living in a made-over chicken coop. Yet it must be confessed that in some respects this chicken coop was found to be a far better living quarter than some of the shacks the farmers furnish to foreign help.[85]

In 1911, Chute confirmed Hine's report:

> In general there is one family living in each small room. . . . The rooms assigned to a family of 4, 5, or even 7 or 8 in some cases, average about 6′ × 8′ in size. . . . [S]anitary regulations or care are unknown at most camps. The growers blame the padrone, the padrone the people for the unsanitary conditions.[86]

In 1913, Harry M. Bremer further documented living conditions of the pickers. He visited eighty-nine farms in Maryland that employed nearly 4,000 pickers from Baltimore:

> Of these 89 farms, 76 gave no privacy but required many families to sleep in one large room, while only 13 furnished shanties in which not

more than 2 families occupied one room. . . . In no case did I find shanties in which provision was made to give each family a separate room. . . . As to toilet facilities, 63 of the 89 places made no provision other than the woods about the shanty . . . In most cases it was a mere appropriation of Nature's provision—the woods and bushes about the shanty.[87]

Grower attitude and attention to housing conditions of the picker families usually reflected more than simple economic interests. They usually also reflected a strong dose of ethnic prejudice. Almost invariably growers and pickers were from different ethnic backgrounds. Growers tended to be white, established and "reputable" citizens of the local community and in all ways "superior." Pickers tended to be perceived as nonwhite foreigners of inferior stock. Mr. John Forsythe, a grower, remarked, "We figure a foot per person. They are accustomed to live like pigs in Philadelphia, and we give them nothing better than they have all year round."[88] The growers seemed oblivious to the fact that the pickers felt differently. Harry M. Bremer observed:

It seemed to be the opinion of the farmers that the people were thoroughly satisfied with these living conditions, in fact that they knew nothing better. Reference would be made to the way they live in the city, that they crowded together in a few rooms and lived quite promiscuously. The contrary of this is the truth. In the city each family has its own room, and generally three or four rooms. The statements of the people when asked how they lived in the country also disprove the contention of the farmers. "Like sheep," "like pigs," "like cattle," "like animals, all in a row" are the answers I received. . . . It is a slander on their standard of decency and honor to claim that they enjoy living all together in one large room. . . . In a house to house canvass of the people of the Polish section who go out to the country I did not find one case where two families dwelt in one room, and my visits took me pretty thoroughly over the Fell's Point section of the city. What I did find was that the people resented the lack of privacy forced upon them in the country shanties.[89]

The NCLC observed slow but steady improvement in the living conditions provided on many of the farms and bogs over time. Each year investigators remarked on improvements made at select bogs, but qualified their praise by noting that conditions on many bogs remained unchanged.[90] Ultimately, the relative quality of the living conditions was left to the caprice of the grower. On some bogs and farms, growers simply paid more attention to living conditions than on others.

It is interesting to contrast the better camps with the worst camps. The best camps were consistently maintained at White's Bog, the largest cranberry operation in New Jersey. After 1910, when Brown and Hine had severely criticized the cranberry growers for the overcrowded and unsanitary conditions in their camps, Chute in 1911 observed substantial improvements at White's Bog. Several new houses had been built. They were still crowded, but less crowded than any other camp. They had built four new modern privies, each with separate compartments for the sexes. Further, White's "faithful padrone" Gus Donato had posted sanitary regulations in the camp, was requiring housecleaning every Sunday, and "had all swill and refuse about the houses periodically cleaned up and buried."[91] By 1915, Boswell and Hine reported, "Mr. White's bog still held the lead in the matter of good housing. . . . On a few bogs, notably Mr. White's, were excellent bake houses, and good shelters over the eating places."[92]

In contrast, the bogs owned by Theodore and Isaac Budd probably represented the worst in living conditions.[93] Where the Whites earned a grudging respect from NCLC investigators, the Budd operations were more likely to be treated with scorn. As late as 1923, Edith Knowles drew a pointed contrast between the Budds' ultramodern packing plant and the living conditions of the pickers:

> The cleaning shed on this bog was in marked contrast to the camp houses. The equipment was modern; the separators were painted white, a conveyor system installed and the main workroom well lighted and ventilated. The women at the machines were provided with seats the proper height and their comfort had evidently been considered. A casual visitor to the bog, or even a factory inspector, if shown only the bog proper and the cleaning house, might easily leave with a very favorable impression of what was provided for the workers. The "old maids," as a young Italian mother called the women in the packing house, come daily from nearby towns in automobiles. They were all Americans and generally the wives and daughters of nearby farmers.[94]

Effects on Schooling

The early investigations in agriculture, especially those connected to the annual migration of the Poles and Bohemians from Baltimore and the Italians from Philadelphia, established an anecdotal record of evidence on the effects of agricultural work on schooling. Later investigations approached the question much more systematically and shed additional light on the question. In some respects, the effects on schooling were obvious. Children who were picking strawberries in Delaware in May or cranberries in New Jersey in October, or shucking oysters in Louisiana in February, were obviously absent from their school in Philadelphia or Baltimore. A padrone in Dunbar, Louisiana, summed up the obvious: "These little children never go to school. They grow up and know nothing—not even to speak English. In the summer they work in the fruit fields, and in the winter they work here. They are traveling all the time, and don't get a chance to go to school."[95]

Miss Belcher, principal of the Randall School in the Italian section of Philadelphia, spoke with Lewis Hine in 1910. She made three important points.

> Hundreds of our children leave school three and four weeks before vacation to go with their families to the berry fields of Delaware and New Jersey. There is no way it seems to me to prevent this. The provision of the Compulsory Education Law is fruitless when our little charges leave the jurisdiction of the state. It seems to me, however . . . while I know the children in the fields are exploited and compelled to work at all hours, I must say it is a Godsend for the little boys and girls to be taken from the unclean and wretched tenements of the slums to breathe the good open air of the country.[96]

First she made the obvious point that hundreds of children were missing school.[97] Second, she suggested that state and local compulsory schooling laws were fruitless when interstate commerce in children was involved. In dealing with child labor in other sectors, many had expressed the view that "the best child labor law is a compulsory schooling law." It was considerably more difficult to enforce compulsory schooling laws where children crossed state or even national boundaries, passing from jurisdiction to jurisdiction—that is, when children were migratory.

Third, Belcher expressed the common sentiment that agricultural work—the outing in the country—was beneficial for the children; that, even knowing they were "exploited and compelled to work at all hours," she viewed it as a "Godsend." That school officials, of all people, who were commonly among the first to criticize other forms of child labor, felt agricultural work was a blessing to the children of the urban poor indicated how difficult the NCLC's job would be and was a portent of our national failure to solve the child labor problem in agriculture.[98]

Grower attitudes about the children's loss of schooling, like their attitudes about migrant housing, were often tinged with ethnic prejudice.
One grower remarked, "Of course they lose school, but then these Polacks
don't care."[99] Mr. Dunbar, of Dunbar, Lopez and Dukate, went even
further, asserting that education would actually be bad for the children.
"[I]t is better for these low people to be at work. They don't want school.
The children who grow up and can't read and write are always better off
than those who can because as soon as they get a smattering of education they want to strike for higher wages."[100]

Even when ethnic prejudice was not in evidence, growers were unanimous in their opinion that the children gained more than they lost in
schooling. J.J. White of White's Bog stated, "It is probably true that 690
children from the Italian quarter of Philadelphia lose 6 weeks of schooling; but in my opinion, and in the opinion of their parents, they gain
more than they lose by their outing in the Jersey pines." Mr. White's
daughter, Lizzie, appealed to Jane Addams's sense of patriotism when
she portrayed the outing to the bogs as positively the best experience
these children could have had. While children missed formal schooling,
life on the bog had its own educational value:

> I do not believe there is an occupation in which large numbers of immi-
> grants are employed which tends to more rapid making of good Ameri-
> can citizens than that of picking cranberries and similar fruits and veg-
> etables. It takes large numbers of children, dwelling in the poorer city
> districts, into the sweet air and sunshine of the country, where work and
> play are wholesomely combined. It brings families into contact and ac-
> quaintance with individual Americans, making them content to separate
> from the colony of their kind in the city without feeling utterly alone in a
> strange land. . . . Though the children miss a few weeks of schooling in
> the beginning of the year the families are enabled to return to the city
> with sufficient money to ensure the children attending school the rest of
> the term comfortably clothed and fed. The children have, besides an ac-
> cumulation of country vigor, the memory of long happy hours spent wad-
> ing the irrigating ditches catching "bu" frogs or gathering water lilies; of
> beautiful sand forts built and demolished and of all sorts of out door joys;
> they have besides the self respecting feeling that they helped to earn their
> winter clothes.[101]

While parents were by no means unanimous in their opinions about
their children's loss of schooling, they were certainly more ambivalent

about the balance of cost and benefit. One mother who had taken her family to the cranberry bogs for the very first time left no doubt about how she felt: "I hope God will paralyze me if I don't speak the truth. I never came before and I won't come again. I thought it wouldn't be bad but my children can't make enough. My boy in 3rd B. is missing a lot of school. What will I have when he grows up, only a dumbell?"[102]

The early NCLC investigations of the annual migration in agriculture established the obvious—that children missed school. What they failed to establish was that this, on net, was harmful. Strong public attitudes about the beneficial aspects of agricultural work continued to prevail. Later investigations examined more closely, and demonstrated more conclusively, the harmful effects of agricultural work on schooling.

In 1920, Gertrude Folks summarized results from seven large-scale investigations, including North Carolina and Kentucky (tobacco), Colorado and Michigan (sugar beets), Alabama and Oklahoma (cotton), and Maryland (strawberries). Results of these studies made clear some of the relationships between farm labor and schooling.[103] According to Folks, farmwork affected school attendance in three ways. First, she noted that, in every region studied, investigators found substantial numbers of children who attended no school at all. Absence from school altogether was most pronounced among children in migrant families, such that up to 15 percent of the "beet children" of school age in Michigan "had never attended school in America." Second, the school term was shorter in rural districts than urban districts, averaging 46.4 fewer days (over two months). She also noted the common practice, in many rural districts, of granting "beet vacations," "apple vacations," or "tobacco vacations" to make all hands available to harvest the dominant local crop. Third, farmwork was the leading cause of irregular school attendance.

The studies summarized by Folks compared three distinct groups of farmworker children—owner children, tenant children, and migrant children. Owner children worked on the farm owned by their parents. Tenant children worked on the farm rented or sharecropped by their parents. Finally, migrant children were those who, most typically, come out from the cities, usually with their parents, to work specific crops. Results enable some generalizations about differential effects across these groups. Most simplistically, as far as schooling was concerned, owner children fared best, migrant children fared worst, with tenant children in between. That is, the more the work took on migratory characteristics, the greater the harm. Owner children were least harmed, though they, too, fared worse in comparison with nonfarm children. Tenant children, who tended to move every few years, were next. Migrant children suffered the greatest harm, and the farther and longer the migration, the greater the harm.

If farmworker children missed more school than others, it stood to reason that they might not perform as well and that some would fall behind. Grade standing was an important dependent variable studied in NCLC investigations. While there was considerable variance from region to region, it appeared that roughly 85 percent of "regular school attenders" were performing at or above normal grade level. In contrast, among farmworker children, only 58.9 percent of owner children, 41.6 percent of tenant children, and 38 percent of migrant children were at or above grade level (excluding those who did not attend school at all).[104] The studies also demonstrated the compounding effect of farmwork on educational attainment. That is, the more years in farmwork, the further below-normal grade standing.

Child Labor in Agriculture: Failure of National Policy

Agriculture, of all economic sectors, has proven the most resistant to reform. To this day there are no restrictions on child labor when the work is performed on the parents' own farm. No restrictions apply even if the farm is worked under land-tenancy or sharecropping arrangements. For children "working out"—that is, on someone else's farm (the condition facing migrants)—restrictions remain far less stringent than in other economic sectors. When national child labor standards were codified in the Fair Labor Standards Act of 1938, agriculture was exempted altogether. It was not until 1974 that the first standards for agriculture were included. Today, agriculture has its own separate set of standards that remain well below those that apply elsewhere. As we enter the twenty-first century, the minimum age in agriculture in the United States remains twelve, there are no restrictions on hours, overtime pay need not be provided, and hazardous work can begin at sixteen. That is the current federal standard in agriculture. Only ten states have adopted a higher standard. Hundreds of thousands of children continue to work legally in American agriculture. And in spite of the lax standards, many more work illegally. Compulsory schooling laws may be better enforced today than they were in the early twentieth century (though among migrant populations that cannot be ensured). But schooling, that great bulwark against child labor, may only provide the child with a six-hour respite in the middle of a workday that runs from four or five in the morning until sundown.[105]

To say that child labor policy in agriculture has been a failure, however, is not to suggest that no gains have been made. One important gain is the near elimination of child labor in the food-processing sector of the industry. That is, children continue to pick, but not many continue to hull or shuck. As industrialization progressively permeated agriculture, its entering wedge was often the food-processing sector. Canning industrialized before processing (shucking and hulling); and shucking and hulling often industrialized before picking. A canning operation typically consisted of two main structures in which the work was performed, the processing shed and the canning shed (there was also often a storage shed). Even in early twentieth-century America, the canning sheds were clearly recognizable as factories and, in most states, came under the factory laws. Consequently, relatively few young children worked directly in the canneries. Cannery work also paid higher wages than processing work, so adults and older children sought it when available. Cannery work, however, was often hard to come by for migrants. Many canneries gave preference to local help and filled in with migrants only to the extent that the local labor supply was insufficient. Thus, some of the women and older children, but all of the young children, were channeled into processing work.

Processing work—the shucking and hulling done in the processing shed—was considered agricultural work not subject to factory laws. Because of New York's early lead in child labor laws, a state attorney general's opinion interpreting its 1903 law proved influential in most other states.[106] When the 1903 factory law was enacted, the Canned Goods Packers Association sought an interpretation as to whether their processing sheds were covered.[107] New York Attorney General Julius M. Mayer's opinion "was a green light for canneries to continue employing children." Shed work was agricultural and there were no restrictions on agricultural work. It made no difference whether the employer was an individual farmer or a corporation. In turn, New York and most other states would continue to treat shed work as agricultural until the legislature explicitly stated otherwise. But Mayer's opinion also pointed the way out. Child labor in the sheds was legal only so long as the shed was "devoid of machinery, in the open air, unconnected with a factory, and not subject to the discipline and hours governing factory employment."[108]

Even if shucking and hulling remained mostly handwork, the presence of machinery in the sheds and mechanized conveyors directly connecting the shed with the factory was increasing. The family wage, as opposed to an individual wage, may have buffered the young children from factory discipline, but in all ways, the processing sheds were coming to look and operate more like factories. As they did, more and more states began to classify them as factories and place them under factory laws. For a time, some canners attempted to evade the law,[109] but eventually the redefinition of processing sheds from agriculture to factories led to the elimination of most child labor from the food-processing sector of the industry.

While eliminating child labor from food processing stands as a major achievement, it is important to recognize the limits of that achievement. The agriculture industry never compromised on its right to hire children. The key change in the law did nothing to regulate the work of children in agriculture, it merely redefined the sheds away from agriculture and into industry. It might be said that agriculture surrendered its sheds but not its child workers.

Other gains have been made in agriculture through processes of mechanization. That is, even where work remained clearly agricultural and beyond the scope of the factory laws, technological advances continued to eliminate children from particular sectors. Sometimes the technological advances were astonishingly simple. For example, child labor was eliminated from the cranberry bogs, the very sector on which the NCLC invested such inordinate investigation resources, by the advent of "raking" and "scooping" as a substitute for handpicking methods of harvest.

At the western edge of the cranberry industry, the most recent of the cranberry sections to be developed, the Wisconsin industry was in some aspects more advanced than tradition-bound regions to the east. The NCLC studied conditions in the Wisconsin cranberry marshes in order to make comparisons with conditions in New Jersey. What investigators observed in Wisconsin was a portent of things to come in New Jersey. A major stimulus to the invigoration of the Wisconsin cranberry industry was the establishment of the University of Wisconsin Experiment Station in the center of the cranberry region. The Experiment Station advised growers and promoted advanced science and technology. Some fundamentals in bog management were emphasized: It pays to spend time weeding, and better crops are produced when the vines are encouraged to grow vertically rather than horizontally (this was done by pruning runners and sanding the marshes).[110] These simple improvements made possible a new method of harvesting the berries. "Raking" or "scooping" replaced handpicking. When bogs were weedy and matted down, raking tore up the vines, doing considerable damage and depositing considerable debris in the collection box. But with weeds removed and the vines standing upright, raking did little damage while it improved productivity by 300 to 500 percent.[111]

The rake or scoop was an astonishingly simple technological innovation. But it had decisive consequences for child labor. Handpicking was done on hand and knee. The picker used a hand-held scoop (younger children often picked literally with their hands). A half-dozen to a dozen swipes through the vines would fill the scoop, which was then emptied into the peck box behind. Pickers spent virtually the entire day on their hands and knees in the damp bogs. The rake or scoop simply put long handles on the handpicker's scoop. "The rake or scoop used is the same in size and construction as that in the New Jersey bogs" except that, in New Jersey, there is a single short handle "necessitating a cramped stooping or kneeling position to operate it." In contrast, the Wisconsin rake has two long, curved handles so the worker is in a standing position and "operates it with a wide swinging motion much as he would a scythe."[112]

Raking was heavy work, and everywhere the raking method was used, women and children were replaced by men and older boys. Women and children continued to pick where the handpicking method was used, but most owners were preparing their bogs for raking as rapidly as possible.[113] Raking had further consequences for child labor. The improved productivity of raking made it inefficient to collect berries in peck boxes. Larger bushel boxes came to be used. In the handpicked bogs, children did most of the carrying of collection boxes to the bushelman. Where peck boxes may have been difficult for young children to carry, bushel boxes were impossible. So, as raking and bushel boxes were used, carrying had to be done, again, by men and older boys. Thus, where the raking method was used, women and young children were generally absent from the bogs.

Besides eliminating much of the child labor, the transformation from handpicking to raking had other important effects on the labor supply. There was so much more money to be made in raking that men were attracted back into the bogs. This had at least two effects. First, it resulted in a free (adult) labor market. Second, what had once been a local/

rural labor market, and later had become a regional labor market, was now becoming rural/local once again. Where raking was employed, not only did men replace children, more specifically local men and older boys replaced the Polish and German women and children from the nearby cities. NCLC investigator Harry Bremer noted that a padrone system had begun to establish itself in Wisconsin cranberries. It was supplying Polish and German families from the nearby cities to the cranberry growers. He expressed relief that raking would not permit the padrone system to flourish in Wisconsin.[114] A local/rural labor force would not be so susceptible to exploitation:

> The pickers are not helpless foreigners who cannot speak the language and who do not understand our laws. Part of the exploitation in New Jersey is due to the fact that the Italian cannot speak English and do not know their rights and privileges under our laws. They must trust to the honesty of the padrone, and in their helplessness provide a rich field for his exploitation.[115]

By 1923, when Edith Knowles conducted the NCLC's final investigation in New Jersey cranberries, New Jersey had its own cranberry expert, J.C. Beckwith, provided by the New Jersey State College of Agriculture. He had been given a house on White's Bog and from there traveled throughout the region "advising owners on cranberry culture." He was encouraging the same kind of transformation that came earlier to Wisconsin. "In commenting briefly on the labor situation, Mr. Beckwith said he thought that scooping would have to replace hand picking."[116] In the end, scooping did replace handpicking, and child labor was eliminated from the bogs.

Still, today, where handpicking remains the preferred and dominant method of harvest, the children remain employed, and they remain so under conditions clearly reminiscent of early twentieth-century America. Child labor remains a problem in agriculture in twenty-first century America.

Part III

Child Labor's Legacy

10. AMERICA AND CHILD LABOR TODAY

As America entered the twentieth century, many young children were working long hours, often under arduous conditions, in mines, mills, and factories, in city streets and home-based workshops, and on farms all across the nation. As America enters the twenty-first century, children continue to work, but the mix of industries, occupations, hours, and conditions for most working children has changed so dramatically that much of this work is no longer defined as a child labor problem.

We achieved the eradication of child labor in several key sectors, but remain vulnerable in several others. Mining, manufacturing, and probably commercial retail can be regarded as successes. Child labor has been eliminated in mining and manufacturing, and commercial retail is now a prominent route for socializing youth into the labor force. Especially noteworthy is elimination of child labor from textile manufacturing. While southern cotton textiles is properly seen as a major battleground in the war against child labor, it is also true that the South came to grips with its child labor problem much more rapidly than did New England or certainly old England. By the time the industry had expanded westward to Texas, very few children were employed. Elimination of child labor from textiles—the first industry—stands as an achievement of global historic proportions.[1]

In spite of our successes, we remain vulnerable to child labor problems in certain sectors. In our street trades and in the persistent tendency toward reemergence of sweatshops, the threat of exploitative child labor remains, but our clearest policy failure is in agriculture. First, the street trades. Industrialization contributed to urbanization, which, in turn, created the street trades. Most prominent were the newsboys. As industrial child labor began to wane, child labor in the street trades boomed. The news media, which could generally be counted on to support child labor reform, reacted to protect its franchise in newsboys. The children were not employees, they were independent businessmen—little merchants. Newspapers were under close public scrutiny to ameliorate exploitative aspects of the trade, but exemptions in law for newsboys allowed the practice to continue. American children remain vulnerable to a variety of street-selling scams, sometimes under the guise of charity. Second, the sweatshops. Early on, reformers recognized that to eliminate child labor from sweatshops, it would be necessary to abolish industrial homework altogether. Especially in the garment trades, homework systems were an integral aspect of the larger sweating system. But regulating homework was tantamount to regulating private conduct in the sanctity of the home, so regulation could only go so far. We remain vulnerable to reemergence of sweatshops, especially in traditional child-employing industries like the garment trade. Further, as American business globalizes, it risks, unless it is careful, encountering sweating sectors in other nations. Finally, agriculture represents the clearest failure of American child labor policy. In contrast with most other sectors, the minimum age for employment in agriculture is twelve, and there are no restrictions on hours. While estimates are grossly imprecise, it is clear there are hundreds of thousands of children under sixteen working as hired agricultural laborers.

Most of the general public remains unaware of our nation's shortcomings in child labor policy, or of their connection to it. As in the past, at least until the NCLC and other reform organizations began their widespread agitation, most Americans today do not perceive that America has a child labor problem. As the worst forms of child labor disappeared, sector by sector, until a relatively few bad sectors remained, our attention to the social and economic problem of child labor receded. America had made its accommodation, however incomplete, and the child labor problem was redefined as a youth employment problem. America's accommodation, in turn, produced a qualitative shift in how child labor is viewed—in America's psyche, if you will. Several generations of Americans have matured into adulthood without knowing child labor, though many will properly insist that they worked very hard as children. American parents, policymakers, and pundits worry continuously over the work ethic of the next generation and believe in the importance of instilling responsibility and good work habits. But child labor is seen as something that happens to other people in some other place or time.

This chapter provides an overview of what is known about the work of children in America today. The surprising fact is that proportionately nearly as many children in America work today as at the turn of the twentieth century. The unsurprising fact is that the quantitative mix of industries, occupations, hours, and conditions has changed significantly. The chapter then wrestles with certain terms central to America's accommodation with child labor. First, how should the term "child labor" be defined? Second, what do we mean by "exploitation" in the context of child labor. What distinguishes work of children that should be condemned by epithet (either as exploitation or, more simply, as child labor) from work that should not?

Child Labor in America: Reprise

Table 2.1 in chapter 2 displayed gainful workers aged ten to fourteen as counted by the U.S. Census. It showed that labor force participation rates of these children peaked in 1890 and 1900 at 21.38 and 21.66 percent, respectively. By 1930, the labor force participation of ten-to-fourteen-year-olds had fallen to 5.56 percent. Thereafter we stopped counting gainful workers under fourteen and stopped tracking labor force activity of these youngsters. From a data perspective, this aspect of the child labor problem disappeared.

Similarly, labor force activity rates of fourteen- and fifteen-year-olds peaked at 30.9 percent in 1900 and, by 1940, had declined to 5.2 percent.[2] After 1967, the Department of Labor changed the definition of the U.S. labor force, restricting it to those aged sixteen or older, and we stopped counting fourteen- and fifteen-year-olds. The remainder of America's child labor problem was purged from the quantitative record. Anecdotal accounts of child labor abuses could be dismissed as exceptional. The absence of a quantitative record influenced economic theory and research to overlook labor force activity of children. Schooling and work were assumed to be mutually exclusive activities. For research purposes, "at school" versus "at work" could be coded as a single dichotomous (0,1) variable. More importantly, work and schooling were seen as sequential life activities—that one completed one's schooling and then entered the labor force. Operationally, schooling could be measured in years or by degrees earned, and labor force experience could be measured as age minus schooling minus six. Finally, since schooling for all but a very few extended at least to age sixteen, labor force activity under sixteen was operationally excluded from scrutiny. In an influential 1984 article, Robert Michael and Nancy Tuma observed, "[I]f one were to judge from the existing economic literature—theoretical, descriptive, or analytically empirical—one would surely infer that employment begins no earlier than age 16." They argued that "this consensus in the literature disregards substantial job experience" that "should not continue to be ignored."[3]

While children under sixteen continue to be excluded from the main labor force series published by the Department of Labor, the newest cohort of the National Longitudinal Survey, which the Department of Labor sponsors, is beginning to yield valuable information on work activities of twelve-to-sixteen-year-olds and promises to be a rich source for future research. The National Longitudinal Survey has long been recognized as the best source of quantitative data on youth employment. Based on household surveys, the NLS has tracked several cohorts of young workers into adulthood. In 1997, the NLS began studying a new cohort, age twelve to sixteen, and the survey instrument was restructured to capture early work experience. Participants were asked about their experience in "employee" jobs, where there is an ongoing relationship with an identifiable employer, and "freelance" jobs.

The portrait that emerges from the first panel of the 1997 cohort measuring work activity of twelve-to-sixteen-year-olds is, at least on the surface, astonishing. A very large proportion of twelve-to-sixteen-year olds engage in substantial amounts of work activity, and begin doing so at very young ages. Among fourteen- and fifteen-year-olds, 57.2 percent hold jobs for a least some period.[4] Even among twelve- and thirteen-year-olds, 52.5 percent have acquired paid work experience.[5] Compared to activity rates recorded at the turn of the twentieth century, it might appear that America has not come to grips with its child labor problem at all.

But a closer look at the data points to differences in the mix of industries, occupations, hours, and conditions from those observed in early twentieth-century America. Taken together, many of these changes signal qualitative changes in the nature of early work activity. First, among fourteen- and fifteen-year-olds, only 23.8 percent held employee jobs involving an ongoing relationship with an identifiable employer. The rest performed freelance jobs, the most common of which were babysitting, for girls, and yardwork, for boys.[6] Among twelve- and thirteen-year-olds, where only freelance work was counted, babysitting and yardwork together accounted for 72.1 percent work activity. Other activities among the top ten included snow shoveling, chores and odd jobs, newspaper routes, and pet care.[7] In short, these are hardly the kinds of jobs that riled society and fueled the Progressive Era reform movement of the early twentieth century. These are jobs that may be expected to foster responsibility, dependability, punctuality, and self-confidence, traits presumed to have positive effects on future endeavors whether at work or at school. Further, the data suggest that much of this work is performed within household and communal networks where children perform paid services for their parents, relatives, and their parents' friends and neighbors. A greater proportion of white children than black children hold freelance jobs and the likelihood of freelance job-holding increases as parental income increases.[8] One of today's main concerns is that blacks and other economically disadvantaged youngsters are disproportionately deprived of opportunities to gain valuable early work experience. That this is an important concern suggests just how much the qualitative nature of the phenomenon has changed.

In examining employee jobs held by fourteen- and fifteen-year-olds, there is also ample evidence that much of this work was not of the kind that the National Child Labor Committee was launched to combat. Most common industries included eating and drinking establishments, entertainment and recreation services, construction, grocery stores, newspaper publishing and printing, landscaping services, and agriculture. Most common occupations included cashiers, cooks and food preparation, wait staff, janitors and cleaners, farm workers, news vendors, sales workers, groundskeepers and gardeners, and the like. The average fourteen- or fifteen-year-old who worked was employed less than half the year. About 10 to 15 percent were employed during the school year. Both activity rates and hours tended to spike during the summer months.[9] Data on hours worked are less definitive, but it appears that relatively few, in the range of 1 to 5 percent, worked excessive hours as defined by the Fair Labor Standards Act (more than eighteen per week when school is in session; more than forty hours per week otherwise).[10] Finally, and once again, blacks and children of poorer parents are less likely to hold employee jobs at ages fourteen and fifteen, and concern over their relative deprivation reinforces the extent to which America's child labor problem has been redefined into a problem of youth employment and unemployment.[11]

Thus, when considered at a deeper level, the recent data suggest that America has, in the main, made its accommodation to child labor and has moved on to problems of youth employment and unemployment. Young children are no longer found in mines, mills, and factories. The work of very young children appears largely confined to familial and communal networks. Much of the work of older children remains in the freelance category. Most of those engaged in employee jobs work limited hours and attend school as their principal life activity. Research on the impact of employment during school yields mixed results. Working over twenty hours per week is negatively associated with academic outcomes, but whether this is because excessive work interferes with schooling, or because poorer students are more likely to turn to excessive work, is unclear.[12] But the fact that the vast majority of youth work fewer than twenty hours per week suggests minimal impact on schooling.

Remaining Trouble Spots

While America deserves credit for coming to grips with much of its child labor problem, there are indications that trouble spots remain in America's youth labor market. First, illegal child labor remains at nontrivial levels. Violations detected by the Department of Labor increased from 9,243 in 1983 to 27,528 in 1991, but there is no way of knowing what portion of all violations were detected.[13] In 1988, the U.S. General Accounting Office (GAO) estimated 166,000 fifteen-year-olds working illegally in the United States.[14] Douglas Kruse and Douglas Mahony recently constructed more conservative estimates of illegal child labor. They estimate that, in an average week, 153,600 are engaged in work that violates child labor provisions of the Fair Labor Standards Act or state law. They estimate that 300,900 work illegally at some time during the year. Of those working illegally at some time during the year, 100,900 (33.53 percent) were sixteen- and seventeen-year-olds working prematurely in hazardous occupations in industries such as manufacturing and construction where they operated motor vehicles, material moving equipment, or other dangerous power tools, equipment, and machinery. Kruse and Mahony estimate that 120,700 (40.11 percent) fourteen- and fifteen-year-olds engaged in illegal work. The most common violation was working excessive hours, but there were substantial numbers involved in hazardous work (for example, operating slicing machines in food preparation) and some placed prematurely in hazardous work in manufacturing and construction settings. The GAO estimated that 18 percent of employed fifteen-year-olds were working illegally. Kruse and Mahony offer a more conservative estimate of 10 percent, saying that 79,300 (26.35 percent) were children under fourteen who were simply employed underage in a variety of settings.[15]

Kruse and Mahony were unable to construct reliable estimates of illegal child labor in some sectors, most notably in sweatshops and industrial homework. But it is well understood that the problem has not been reduced to zero. In the late 1980s, the GAO conducted several significant studies of American sweatshops, focusing on the apparel industry. Defining sweatshops as establishments engaged in regular and multiple violations of safety and health, wage and hour, or child labor laws,[16] the GAO alerted the nation that sweatshops were, once again, on the rise in America.[17] In 1989, the GAO reported that 4,500 of New York City's 7,000 garment shops were sweatshops. Direct inspection of 339 establishments yielded 130 minors working illegally. Subsequently, the GAO has studied the garment industry in El Paso, Los Angeles, and Miami and concluded that 50 of 180 El Paso shops, 4,500 of 5,000 Los Angeles shops, and 400 of 500 Miami shops were sweatshops. Prevalence of child labor was not specified. While it is certainly possible to run a sweatshop without child labor, as many undoubtedly do, it remains a sector vulnerable to child labor so long as manufacturers are not responsible for labor conditions in their subcontract networks. Kruse and Mahony were likewise unable to estimate illegal child labor in home-based work, though they do report that the May 1997 Current Population Survey shows 16,200 homeworkers in the apparel industry and that these homeworkers had 9,300 children aged five to fourteen in their households.[18] If child labor continues to creep into subcontract workshops in the apparel industry, there is no reason to believe that child labor has been eradicated from home workshops in the same industry.

Some prominent sectors where child labor remains legal represent additional trouble spots, or potentially so. There are the newsboys, now carrying residential routes, most often in middle- and upper-middle-class neighborhoods. They are classed, by the National Longitudinal Survey, as freelancers when working at ages twelve and thirteen, but as employees when they reach fourteen. If newsboys are generally well protected from exploitation, the newsboy exception in law that permits them to work also constitutes a loophole permitting exploitative street-selling scams. Child labor in the family business and in private homes remains largely unregulated. Most children engaged in this work are under the watchful eye of parents, relatives, friends or neighbors, and are well protected from exploitation. But child abuse does occur in some proportion of homes. Better regulation of adoption and foster-care practices have largely eliminated the buying and selling of orphans and other dependent children for purposes of peonage. The greatest potential for abuse is in domestic services, an occupation and industry never investigated by the NCLC. It is known that global human trafficking networks place indeterminate, but substantial, numbers of domestic servants into situations clearly characterized as bondage. The extent to which this human trafficking involves children is not known, but it is not zero.

In a related vein, the principal occupation and industry served by the global human trafficking networks is the sex trades. Again, it is not known what proportion of those placed into bonded prostitution are children, but it is not zero. But this example serves to illustrate an important point: Most of these most abusive forms of child labor, even when not covered under child labor laws, are subject to sanctions, often criminal, on other grounds under other laws.

Then there is America's most glaring remaining child labor problem—children in agriculture. Child labor on the family's own farm remains unregulated altogether. Farm labor for hire was not regulated under the Fair Labor Standards Act until 1974. Today, children of any age may work unlimited hours, outside school hours, on small farms with their parents' written consent. Children twelve and over may work unlimited hours, outside school hours, on any farm where a parent also works. Children fourteen and over may work unlimited hours on any farm without parental consent. Finally, the minimum age for hazardous work in agriculture is sixteen, as opposed to eighteen outside agriculture.

The GAO recently estimated 300,000 youths aged fifteen to seventeen in agriculture, but they acknowledge their estimate is likely to be an undercount.[19] Youth working as hired farmworkers, as opposed to those working on the family farm, constitute the much larger proportion. Hired farmworkers are divided between migrant workers, who leave their permanent place of residence, often for extended periods, to work, and seasonal workers, who work the crops near their permanent residence. No one knows how many children under fifteen work in agriculture, but the number is in the hundreds of thousands. Most of these are children who, in any other industrial sector, would be working illegally. Human Rights Watch recently documented children as young as eight and nine working regularly in commercial agriculture. Many others work twelve- and occasionally fourteen-hour days during peak seasons (neither hours limitations nor overtime requirements prevail in agriculture).

Still others were found working in fields still wet with pesticides. Numerous others were found with injuries from cuts, heat, lack of sanitation, or simple fatigue.[20]

If child labor laws are so much less stringent in agriculture than anywhere else, and if hours and overtime laws do not apply, there are two sets of laws that should operate to curb child labor to the extent they can be effectively enforced—first, the compulsory schooling laws, and second, the minimum wage laws. Compulsory schooling laws require that children be enrolled and in regular attendance during school hours. For at least the regular school hours, no school-age children should be at work. But for seasonal farmworkers during the peak season, this often means work in the early morning before school and work into the evening after school—schooling providing a six-hour respite in the middle of a twelve-to-fourteen-hour day. For migrant children, the problem of schooling is even more vexing. Even for the child who stays in school, the continuous changes in teachers, classmates, and curricula must make learning a challenge. The child's home school district is hard-pressed to provide services—the child has migrated out of its jurisdiction—and the receiving school district has little incentive to take on the child who is just passing through. Not surprisingly, only 55 percent of farmworker children graduate from high school, at a time when high school graduation rates for the rest of America's children run in excess of 90 percent.[21] Similarly, the minimum wage law, one of the few labor laws that applies to agriculture, could serve to curb child labor. Even children are supposed to be paid the equivalent of $5.15 per hour, and so presumably only children who could produce at a rate at or exceeding $5.15 per hour would be hired. Unfortunately, employers have a number of ways to void minimum wage requirements. Human Rights Watch estimates that one-third of child workers in agriculture earned less than minimum wage. First, most agricultural work remains on piece rates—to determine hourly earnings requires a linear transformation of the data, something many educated Americans would have difficulty doing. Many do not know they are being paid less than they are entitled to. Second, many workers report that their hours are reduced for pay purposes—that is, they are paid for fewer hours than they actually worked. While this is also a violation of wage-and-hour law, it elevates the recorded value of wages paid closer to or above the legal minimum. Finally, growers can often shift liability and responsibility for labor conditions to their labor contractors—the modern-day padrones and coyotes who recruit, hire, transport, and supervise the gangs of farmworkers—by ensuring that labor contractors retain the legal status of employer.[22] While compulsory schooling and minimum wage laws undoubtedly reduce the level of child labor in agriculture, they have not proved sufficient to eliminate it.

Much of the work in seasonal and migrant agriculture remains the domain of new immigrant populations. Some proportion of these families may be expected to move up to some form of land-tenancy arrangement. And some proportion of those will eventually move up to landownership. But this is a long road, often traversing several generations, even for the families that succeed in moving up. For each family that climbs to the position and status of landowner, many others do not. Some move on to earn their livelihoods in other ways; some remain trapped in a cycle of poverty near the bottom of the agricultural labor market, in migrant and seasonal work. In the early 1900s, it was the Poles and Bohemians from Baltimore and the Italians from Philadelphia who migrated from the new immigrant neighborhoods to the truck farms of the Eastern Seaboard and the shucking sheds on the Gulf Coast. Today, the majority of seasonal and migrant farmworkers are Latino.[23] Between then and now, thousands of black families made the climb from land tenancy to landowning, but many thousands of others left agriculture for opportunities in the cities. Other new immigrant populations entered agricultural regions—Russians in sugar beets, Germans in wheat, Scandinavians in dairy. Some moved up; others moved on. Today, migrant and seasonal agricultural work is largely, but not entirely, the province of the Latino migrant and new immigrant population. Consequently, the child labor problem in agriculture is also a disproportionately Latino problem.

Some Definitional Considerations

As the preceding review of child labor in America today has shown, how we define child labor matters a great deal. If child labor is defined to include all freelance work by all youngsters and all part-time employee jobs held by fourteen- and fifteen-year-olds, it might appear that America continues to have an enormous child labor problem, indeed every bit as large as the problem of early twentieth-century America. But such a conclusion would be obviously unwarranted, at least on this basis. We want children to have opportunities for this kind of work. On the other hand, if we define child labor as illegal employment of children, then America's problem, while real, appears more limited and tractable. But this definition would ignore much of legal child labor in agriculture that remains America's largest child labor problem. Further, while a definition that turns on the legal/illegal distinction may have relevance for law enforcement, it simply will not do for historical purposes. Child labor did not come into being by having been made illegal.

Subtle differences in operational definition can yield widely varying quantitative estimates of the magnitude and scope of the child labor problem. Likewise, definitional nuances greatly determine our appreciation of the qualitative dimensions of the problem under study. If we are to effectively understand and address the problem, it would be wise to come to grips with a definition. What is child labor?

Throughout this book, child labor has been treated as a social and economic problem. This assumes that there is something at least unseemly, at worst evil, about child labor. Definitions often carry moral and judgmental connotations. In regard to child labor, it becomes nearly impossible to define the problem without impregnating the definition with implicit connotations of "bad." While most previous literature on the topic also treats child labor, either explicitly or implicitly, as a problem, this does complicate the matter of definition. A useful definition would not only clarify the construct under study, it would also serve to distinguish between that which is presumptively suspect from that which is presumptively benign.

Thus, defining child labor simply as *work performed by children* will not do. No one could seriously suggest that all work performed by children is a problem. Light household chores performed under the direction and supervision of parents within the sanctity of the home are generally viewed with approval. It is dictum among developmental psychologists that "play is the work of the child"—that play occupies an essential role in the development of the child and that, in general, children work at it. Indeed, it is possible to argue that, in some existential sense, all children work all the time. Further, consider that schooling is usually excluded from the definition of child labor. That schooling is hard work is not really in doubt. That it is coercive, in the sense that compulsory schooling laws compel participation, is plain. Yet we do not think of schooling as hard labor or even forced labor. Schooling carries positive connotations. A satisfactory definition of child labor must signal something in the nature of the work that is, at least presumptively, problematic. Likewise, defining child labor as *work for pay* is unsatis-

factory. There are too many examples from history—from the dinner toters and helpers in textiles, to the children in agriculture and food processing, to all the children who were kept off the payroll so their pay would go
to their parents—where children did not work, at least not directly, for
pay. If a teenager today mows his grandmother's lawn, or baby-sits her
nieces and nephews, whether he or she is paid for the work or not seems
irrelevant to our evaluation of its social and economic effects.

This book has implicitly, occasionally more explicitly, embraced two
distinct definitions of child labor: (1) child labor as *work detrimental to
children*, and (2) child labor as *industrial employment of children*. It is
time to explicitly examine and evaluate each of these definitions.

Work detrimental to children is the definition implicit in much of the
literature on the topic of child labor. Certainly this definition dominates
in the popular literature, but it is also prominent in much of the scholarly work. It is also the definition that underlies the efforts of such bodies as the United Nations and the International Labour Organization (ILO)
in working to eliminate global child labor today. The 1989 United Nations *Convention on the Rights of the Child*, in Article 32, condemns
"any work that is likely to be hazardous or to interfere with the child's
education, or to be harmful to the child's physical, mental, spiritual,
moral or social development." Likewise, in its 1999 Convention banning the "worst" forms of child labor, the International Labour Organization condemns, in addition to specific forms of child labor (child
slavery, military service, child prostitution, drug trafficking), "work
which, by its nature or the circumstances in which it is carried out, is
likely to harm the health, safety or morals of children."[24]

Defining child labor as *work detrimental to children* has a certain
intuitive appeal. It announces with clarity why child labor should be
viewed as a problem and points to specific effects that would distinguish good work from bad work. In condemning work detrimental to
health, education, and physical, mental and moral development, it provides some basis for making judgments about any given work situation.
Finally, work detrimental to children provides a clear justification for
intervention by policy makers.

Still, defining child labor as *work detrimental to children* creates certain problems and, while not completely rejected in this book, is ultimately unsatisfactory. First, "detriment" is a relative concept. On one
hand, it is not difficult to envision many things much more detrimental
to a child than labor. Richard Freeman, taking a hard-headed look at

child labor in the world today, observes the obvious: "In some less developed countries children may have to work for family economic survival. Better that they work and eat than starve."[25] From this point, it is but a short step to commit the logical fallacy of deriving the "ought" from the "is" and concluding that child labor is a blessing where it enables the family to avoid starvation. This is an age-old argument in defense of child labor. For example, one observer commented that the "cotton mill . . . is a real blessing, present and prospective, for it gives comfort and employment to many poor girls who might otherwise be wretched."[26] Confronting such dire alternatives, child labor might not be adjudged, on balance, as detrimental to the child. Yet there is something obviously wrong with a system that compels children to labor on pain of starvation. As Grace Abbott has observed, "[I]f you continue to use the labor of children as the treatment for the social disease of poverty, you will have both poverty and child labor to the end of time."[27]

On the other hand, it is also easy to envision circumstances that entail some moderate risk of detriment, yet which also entail real and predominant benefits for the child. For example, all work, whether performed by adults or children, carries some risk to health, safety, or physical development. How great must this risk be to condemn any particular form of work, when performed by children, as child labor? Debates over where the line is to be drawn between harmful and beneficial child labor can easily devolve to endless hairsplitting (if my teenage son mows my lawn under my supervision, few would object. But what if he is only ten? eight? What if he mows the neighbor's lawn for pay? What if he and his friends organize a neighborhood lawn service? What if my adult neighbor hires my son and his friends to provide lawn maintenance services? What if this service becomes the primary contractor with area businesses? At what point does sending young boys out to operate dangerous power equipment become a problem?)[28]

Work detrimental to children may well be the most appropriate definition of child labor from a practical, humanitarian, or welfare economics perspective. But it is also useful to have a definition grounded in the theoretical position taken here. For theoretical purposes, a definition of child labor as *industrial employment of children* is more useful. This definition is consistent with the proposition that, before industrialization, children worked, but their work was not seen as a social and economic problem. If industrialization created the child labor problem, the definition points to specific markers of the problem—that is, industrial employment. If continuing industrialization put forces into play that worked to solve the problem, then the definition of child labor as *industrial employment of children* may help to distinguish between appropriate and inappropriate work by children in a largely postindustrial society. This definition is not so broad as to be meaningless, yet is broad enough to encompass the terrain traversed here. It sheds some of the moralistic baggage that encumbers *work detrimental to children*, but it is not entirely neutral since, on theoretical grounds, *industrial employment of children* is presumptively problematic.

Three terms need attention. First, *industrial*. What signifies industrial? Is it a place, such as a factory? Is it a process? If process, should we emphasize technology (implying machines) or social processes (implying organization)? Use of the term "industrial" does connote a phenomenon of some mass and scale. It suggests, if not a large number, at least a concentration of children working together or alongside adults.

But another more fundamental defining characteristic of industrialization is production for markets. The term "industrial" implies production for markets, as opposed to production for consumption. By focusing on the product and the market for the product, the definition would include child labor in the mines, mills, and factories—that most clearly seen as industrial. But it would also include or exclude child labor in agriculture, in the home, and on the streets, depending on how the work is oriented to external markets. For example, work in commercial agriculture would be included; work in subsistence agriculture would not. Selling or distributing newspapers, greeting cards, and other products intended for distribution in organized markets would be included; selling lemonade from a makeshift neighborhood stand likely would not. Making goods in the home for distribution to external markets would be included; household chores would not.

Some may object that focusing on the market for the product construes the concept of industrialization too broadly. After all, the distinction between production for use and production for markets was important well before the industrial revolution. It is a distinction that dates to Aristotle. The term "economic" is derived from the Greek *oeconomia,* which means "householding." The essence of householding was production for the household's own consumption. Self-subsistence was the ideal.[29] Trade with external households and communities occurred, but such trade was merely incidental to the household's main goal of creating its own subsistence. As production for consumption dominates, householding proper prevails. When production for markets begins to dominate, the role of the household is threatened as the locus of production is removed from the household and household members are thrust into a competitive market for their labor. This is precisely the transformation that occurs when economies industrialize. With industrialization, the market supplanted the household as the dominant orientation of producer economics. Emphasizing industrial employment of children highlights this prominent transitional marker. Involvement of children in production and distribution for markets is the focus of concern. Production for household, kinship, or communal consumption is not.

The second term is *employment*. This implies the existence of an employment relationship—that the child works for someone or some entity—and that this employer is generally not located within the household, kinship, or communal group. Even when the work itself is performed in the home, there is an implicit third party outside the home who benefits. Economic realities considered, employment implies participation in an external labor market. Existence of an employment relationship must be judged de facto rather than de jure. Employers had strong incentives, often incentives in law itself, to avoid considering the children their employees. Where possible, employers might claim children worked for their parents, for the padrone, for the subcontractor, for themselves, or even for other children. In fact, employers almost invariably sought to avoid creating a legal employment relationship. Children in the mines often worked for their fathers. Children in the glasshouses were employed by the journeymen. In textiles it was common to keep children off the payroll and add pay to the parents' paycheck. Tenement homeworkers worked for their families first, the sweaters next, and the manufacturers and retailers only remotely. Newsboys were independent businessmen and little merchants working for themselves. Farmworker children were employed first by their parents, second by the padrones and labor contractors, third by the growers, and only remotely by manufacturers and retailers. Where the existence of a de facto employment relationship became clear, employers could be held accountable in the court of public opinion. Contrast the situations of the newsboys and the night messengers. Night messengers were obviously employees of the services—they wore the badges and uniforms of their employers—and this is where the NCLC achieved its quickest victory over child labor. But the newspapers were successful in maintaining the fiction that the boys did not work for them, and they remain largely unregulated. When de facto employment relationships came to be recognized de jure, as happened sooner in the mines, mills, and factories, moral suasion could be bolstered by compulsion. Today's child labor problem in America is concentrated in those sectors where the existence of an employment relationship has remained obscure de facto and unrecognized and unregulated de jure, but where economic realities make the relationship clear. When work is performed on a remunerative basis, regardless of who receives that remuneration, for the benefit of someone or some entity beyond the household or family/communal/kinship group, an employment relationship exists.

Defining child labor as *industrial employment of children* may be a more inclusive definition than *work detrimental to children*. More to the point, it includes some work performed by children where the potential for detriment may appear slight. The newsboys and other street sellers would be included, as would industrial homeworkers and migrant and seasonal farmworkers. But, under many circumstances, so would work in the family business and work on the family farm. Where the business or farm serves an external market, work generally meets the definition of industrial employment. Our society appears willing to tolerate limited industrial employment of children where, as with the newsboys, employers have effectively ameliorated much of the potential for harm, or in the family enterprise where parents may be presumed, in the absence of evidence to the contrary, to be less than abusive taskmasters. But their inclusion under the definition of child labor suggests that continued vigilance against abuse would be warranted.

The third term to define is *children*, a term common to both definitions of child labor. What is a child? When is a child not a child? At the risk of evasive agnosticism, it is beyond the scope of this book to resolve the riddles of childhood and maturation. As regards child labor, the concept *child* is a social construction. Children are young people who cease being children when they become adults. In between, a transitional stage called *youth* might be acknowledged. Children become adults when society determines they are no longer dependent and in need of special protection. The very conception of what a child is and when a child ceases being a child is altered by the process of industrialization. One of the important consequences of industrialization that sums up the story of child labor is that it causes a progressive prolongation of childhood as children were held out of the labor market and held in school.[30] The "useful wage-earning child" was transformed into "an economically useless but emotionally priceless child."[31] Indeed, the standards that society establishes to define childhood are based, in part, on its opposition to the phenomenon of child labor. So for present purposes, children can be defined in accordance with the standards established to limit their labor. What are the standards? In law, readers can consult a number of sources. More ethnocentric readers might prefer the standards in our Fair Labor Standards Act—generally, minimum age of sixteen, with certain exceptions and close regulation of hours from fourteen to sixteen so as not to interfere with schooling, and no dangerous work before eighteen.[32] More globally oriented readers might prefer standards commemorated in global human rights accords such as the United Nations Universal Declaration of Human Rights and the Declaration of the Rights of the Child, as more concretely codified in the various International Labour Organization conventions related to child labor—generally, a minimum age of fifteen (as soon as possible and with certain exceptions) or the maximum age of compulsory schooling, whichever is later; protection from harm to age eighteen with special attention to certain "worst forms" of child labor (e.g., slavery, prostitution, hazardous work). More adventurous readers could even choose the standards of a developing nation with a serious child labor problem and likely not be disappointed.

If standards in law, or standards in use, or standards in the heads of a few billion thoughtful global citizens define the concept of childhood as it relates to labor, then what makes one set of standards better than another? Are we resigned to a hopeless cultural relativism where every society or every citizen can choose its own preferred standards? Please entertain two working hypotheses regarding tendencies of standards: (1) they evolve; (2) they converge. First, they change over time, and, second, they tend to become more alike over time. The combination of these two tendencies creates the phenomenon optimistically referred to as "upward harmonization" and pessimistically called "the race to the bottom."

The fact that standards evolve cautions us that, whatever the standards of the moment, they should not be considered fixed for all time. At one time in America, twelve would have been considered the appropriate minimum age for factory work; it is the current standard for migratory agricultural work. The fact that standards evolve also reminds us to look beyond the law for emerging standards. To cite one example, there are few explicit age requirements for entry into professional occupations. Nonetheless, mid-twenties has emerged as the de facto minimum age for any professional occupation, late twenties for many professions. That standards converge explains why we could choose the codified standards of either the United States or a developing nation with some level of indifference. While standards may differ in myriad details, they are likely to exhibit considerable commonality, and more so over time, in their broad contours and essential aims and purposes. This in spite of vast differences in experience, past or present, with child labor. Most nations already have codified standards that are modeled, in the main, on various global conventions.

A Note on the Numbers

Policy makers, scholars, and the general public all want to know something about the numbers. Just how many child workers—absolutely, proportionately, and relatively—are we talking about? Unfortunately, good numbers (i.e., trustworthy and useful numbers) are hard to come by. For a variety of reasons, the numbers must be treated with caution, and estimates should generally be treated as conservative. Estimates of the numbers of child workers are extremely sensitive to definitional subtleties as well as who was asked (and why, when, where, and how they were asked). Fortunately, the numbers are not the main story.

Table 2.1 in chapter 2 displayed gainful workers aged ten to fourteen. It showed 1.75 million gainful child workers in 1900 as counted by the U.S. Census. But when the U.S. Census Bureau tallied wage earners under sixteen in 1899, it counted only 165,000. In fact, the number of wage earners under sixteen counted by the Census Bureau never exceeded 200,000.[33] There is, to say the least, a substantial discrepancy between these estimates derived by the same agency, and one might draw very different conclusions about the phenomenon of child labor by relying on one estimate rather than the other.

As one might suspect, there are important distinctions between gainful workers, the higher estimate, and wage earners, the lower estimate. The gainful-worker concept was used to measure occupational status rather than current employment status. Essentially, it counted people who had worked in an occupation and saw themselves as following that occupation. The measure is both broad and subjective.[34] In contrast, the wage-earner concept counted those whose names appeared on an establishment payroll on the specific day the census was taken. Thus, the wage-earner measure obviously missed many working children. First, it excluded many, even if they worked most of the year, who were temporarily out of work when the census was taken. Second, it excluded an indeterminately large portion of working children whose names did not appear on the payroll. As has been noted, employers had numerous incentives to avoiding classifying children as employees and placing them, by name, on the official payroll of the establishment. In spite of the fact that the estimate of gainful workers is tenfold larger than the estimate of wage earners, there are at least two factors that operate to bias the estimate of gainful workers downward. First, the gainful-worker measure counts children ten to fourteen, whereas the wage-earner measure counts all those under sixteen. Thus, gainful workers under ten and, most significantly, ages fourteen and fifteen are not included in the estimate. Second, in counting gainful workers, schooling and work were mutually exclusive. That is, a child could be classed as a gainful worker or gainfully in school, but not both. In contrast, wage-earning and school attendance were not mutually exclusive. If the count of gainful workers had included children who combined work with school attendance, the estimate would undoubtedly have been substantially higher.

Another key difference between the data on gainful workers and wage earners is that the former were compiled from aggregated household data, while the latter were based on aggregated establishment data. In comparative surveys, even where equivalent categories of workers are counted, household data nearly always yield higher estimates of working children than do establishment data. When employer incentives to underreport are considered, this is not surprising. Employers had a variety of opportunities to put children to work without putting them on the payroll. To opportunity add motive. First, in the presence of minimum-age or maximum-hour laws, employers would not wish to create legal liabilities (however small) by knowingly admitting to violating the law. Second, when a social movement to abolish child labor is under way, one tends not to boast about the number of children one employs. The Census Bureau observed that many employers, even those operating within the law, were disinclined to report the full number of children they employed.[35]

The problem of good data—or the lack of trustworthy data—is not only a problem for the historian. It remains a problem for both scholars and policy makers addressing the global child labor problem today. For example, in 1995, based on data from one hundred countries, the International Labour Organization estimated there were 73 million children aged from ten to fourteen at work worldwide.[36] Only a year later, however, the ILO shifted its estimates dramatically upward. Now it estimates 120 million children fully at work, and another 130 million for whom work constitutes a major life activity.[37] No one suspects there was a doubling of global child labor in a year's time. The ILO knew it had been systematically and substantially underestimating child labor. The revised estimates were based on extrapolations from somewhat experimental but more intensive investigations. As a consequence, the ILO has formally refined its estimation methods and has embarked on a program of intensive country studies that rely heavily on household surveys. As results using the new methodologies come in from more and more countries, the ILO will undoubtedly revise its estimates in the future.

Discourse on Exploitation

Sooner or later, any treatise on child labor must explicitly address and take at least a tentative stand on the issue of exploitation. No one doubts that child labor could, and sometimes did (and can, and sometimes does), involve exploitation. Workers at the occupational and industrial margins of the labor market, where most of the children work, are generally more vulnerable to exploitation than other workers. But is child labor inherently exploitative? This is, perhaps, the more fundamental and important question.

Work detrimental to children carries the implication of exploitation within the definition. Child labor is work that is detrimental, and thus exploitative. Using this definition, child labor would be considered inherently exploitative for the harm caused to the health, education, or physical, mental, or moral development of the child, even if the work is not economically exploitative. But what about *industrial employment of children*? Is that inherently exploitative?

In order to address the concept adequately, it is necessary to unpack and examine a number of closely related issues. First there is the fundamental question whether exploitation was embodied within the industrial revolution itself. To the extent that the industrial revolution resulted in exploitation of the masses—and especially the poor—children of the masses (and the poor) suffered their commensurate share of privations. But this would not necessarily be an indictment of the child labor system itself. In order to focus more clearly on the exploitation inherent in the child labor system, it is first necessary to consider the question of exploitation more generally.

Much of the literature on the question of exploitation draws on British experience with the industrial revolution. Britain was home to and progenitor of the industrial revolution. No nation had gone through it before. Whatever tendencies toward exploitation might accompany industrial revolutions, they might be expected to be, and arguably were, more extreme in industrializing Britain. From Marx to Dickens, a chorus of voices denounced the debasing of the people and the defiling of the land.

> For some seventy years, scholars and Royal Commissions alike had denounced the horrors of the Industrial Revolution, and a galaxy of poets, thinkers, and writers had branded its cruelties. It was deemed an established fact that the masses were being sweated and starved by the callous exploiters of their helplessness; that enclosures had deprived the country folk of their homes and plots, and thrown them on the labor market created by the Poor Law Reform; and that the authenticated tragedies of the small children who were sometimes worked to death in mines and factories offered ghastly proof of the destitution of the masses.[38]

Set against these established facts proving massive exploitation, however, were other established facts leading to a conclusion of steady, if uneven, progress and improvement in economic well-being. Nearly all economic indicators bearing on the well-being of the masses showed improvements associated with industrialization. From the beginning, improvements in wages, per capita gross domestic product, and household incomes were noted. Somewhat later, fertility rates began to decrease and longevity to increase. Infant mortality rates declined and other indicators of health and nutrition began to improve. When evaluated in these terms, the industrial revolution, rather than producing massive exploitation, appeared to be a boon to the masses. Whether children worked or not, they would feel some of the pains of exploitation or reap some of the benefits of economic improvement. It may not be necessary to fully reconcile the divergent judgments of history on the question of exploitation, but a few comments are in order.

Objecting to the optimistic assessment of the economists, Karl Polanyi suggests that social and cultural privation and exploitation were present in spite of improvement in measures of economic well-being. "Actually, of course, a social calamity is primarily a cultural not an economic phenomenon that can be measured by income figures or population statistics." That is, the economists were missing the point. "Nothing obscures our social vision as effectively as the economistic prejudice."[39] Where economists measured steady economic progress, Polanyi observed widespread social devastation.

A key term in this discussion is the meaning of the word "subsistence." While the term can be readily defined and operationalized, it is recognized that what is considered a subsistence level will vary from society to society. Furthermore, and more decisively, its meaning can also change over time, and did change dramatically with industrialization. In preindustrial society, when the household produced for their own consumption, the sum total of its production was its subsistence. While many households were hard pressed by poverty, it was possible to use the term "bountiful subsistence" without committing the logical fallacy of oxymoron. A household, blessed perhaps with an especially productive piece of land, could, through hard work first, but also through competent crop management, livestock management, and household management (aided and abetted by the work of children and a bit of luck), produce a bountiful subsistence. With industrialization, the meaning of the term "subsistence" changed from "whatever the household produced" to "the minimum necessary for survival." In the transition from householding to wage labor, wages and household money income could be measured more easily and accurately than before. That these measures showed improvement was not surprising; indeed, it could hardly have been otherwise since it defines the transition. But whether increasing money income signaled rising standards of living remains open to question.

Industrialization required, at the very least, that households be paid enough to keep them participating as industrial workers. Robert Hunter asserted, "There is a fundamental here. If they must work to live, they must have those necessities which will enable them to work." But under the free labor market required by industrialization, subsistence could no longer be guaranteed. From the workers' perspective, the long-term standard of subsistence was understood as that which would enable the worker to remain productive for a lifetime. "It is precisely the same standard that a man would demand for his horses or slaves." But under industrialism, employer incentive to maintain their workforce over the long term was diminished. Under industrialism, only current productivity of the workers mattered. So long as replacements could be found in a free labor market, the employer did not need to be concerned about the long-term productive capacity of any given worker. From the employers' perspective, the standard of subsistence was that which was required to keep a worker working only in the short term. As soon as any given worker became nonproductive, the employer had no interest in maintaining his or her subsistence. Hunter described industrial workers as "Wage slaves whose owners have been freed from caring for them when sick or unemployed."[40]

But what of child labor itself? The foregoing discussion suggests that the industrial revolution may have produced some exploitation of children as children—through exploitation of their parents and the corresponding degradation of the family. But what about children as workers? So far, no direct warrant has been established for the conclusion that industrial employment of children is inherently exploitative. On this question, much of the literature on exploitation of children parallels the discussion of the exploitation embodied in the industrial revolution more generally. Earlier consensus among economic historians was that "Child labor has come to be regarded as a ghastly by-product of the industrial revolution. The cruelty described in much of the historical literature has made the employment of children the industrial revolution's most despised feature."[41] If it was just cruelty to children that made child labor despicable, the definition of child labor as *work detrimental to children* would have been sufficient. But if there was something about the industrial revolution that transformed child labor into its ghastly by-product, then all *industrial employment of children* might be seen as inherently exploitative, even if some of the children escaped obvious or apparent detriment.

It does not appear, for example, that most child workers were exploited economically. Some, such as the night messengers, were very well paid. Even work in textile mills was considered among the best work, and the best paid work, available to children in textile regions. Certainly children were low productivity workers and were generally paid less than adults, even when they were performing the same work. But the question in assessing economic exploitation is not so much the absolute level of pay, but whether children were paid fairly—that is, according to their marginal productivity. While good data that would compare adult and child wages and productivity are rare, there have been a few studies. Clark Nardinelli compared wage rates and output of children and adults during the British industrial revolution and concluded there was no clear evidence that children were being exploited in their pay.[42] Likewise, Philip Holleran made similar comparisons in southern cotton textiles in the United States and reached similar conclusions—if anything, the evidence seemed to show that children were overpaid relative to adults.[43] It can also be inferred that children who produced on their parent's piece rate, as in industrial homework and most agriculture and food processing, earned wages precisely commensurate with their relative productivity. Of course there were many children who earned no money at all for their work, and many others whose paychecks went directly to their parents. Still, if economic exploitation means pay less than marginal productivity (and where pay and productivity are measured relative to adult pay and productivity), it is difficult to make the case that children were systematically exploited.

But pay commensurate with productivity is only one way to assess economic exploitation. Elementary economic theory would suggest that widespread availability of child workers should depress adult wages. While few studies have assessed this point, Donald Parsons and Claudia Goldin estimated that as much as 90 percent of the earnings of children were competed away in lower adult wages.[44] If these findings can be generalized, it means that even if children received their fair share of the wages, they contributed very little to household income. To the extent that adult wages were depressed, child labor economically exploited adults as well as children. Further, to the extent that child wages were anchored to adult wages, wages of children were likewise depressed.

As Polanyi has suggested, however, focusing solely on the economics may well miss the larger point. Even a child worker knows that social and cultural exploitation can coexist with economic betterment. Bertha Awford Black, who in 1910 moved with her family from their farm near Ashboro, North Carolina, and into the cotton mill village in Thomasville, recognized as much. At age eleven she went to work in the mill. Looking back on her life, she recounts,

> We were all anxious to go to work because, I don't know, we didn't like the farming. It was so hot and from sunup to sundown. No, that was not for me. Mill work was better. It had to be. Once we went to work in the mill after we moved here from the farm, we had more clothes and more different kinds of food than we did when we was a-farmin.' And we had a better house. They kept them mill houses up pretty good at first.

At the same time, she notes,

> Just nothing but children. You know, that ought to have been stopped a long time before it was. We didn't get no education. We weren't old enough to go to work. That thar child labor law was wonderful when it came in. We, every one, should have been in school.[45]

There is a more fundamental objection to the industrial employment of children. Labor markets are institutions based on contract. And free labor markets require that contracts be freely entered. Children, by definition, are not capable of freely and rationally contracting for their own labor. Thus, as regards child workers, freedom of contract is a myth and there can be no free market for child labor. This was recognized long ago by John Stuart Mill, who argued that child labor should not be permitted, "for if permitted it may always be compelled. Freedom of contract, in the case of children, is but another word for freedom of coercion."[46] Or, as Samuel Taylor Coleridge said it, even earlier and more colorfully, "If the labor were indeed free, the contract would approach, on the one side, too near suicide, on the other to manslaughter."[47]

A free market assumes individuals transacting in their own rational self-interests. Even if it could be assumed that children were equipped with sufficient rationality to avoid bad bargains, the fact is, with rare exceptions, children did not transact for their own labor. It must always be borne in mind that child labor is not merely something that children do, it is something that is done to children. There was nearly always a third party standing between the child and the employer and acting on behalf of the child in contracting for the child's labor. Often there were multiple layers of third parties. Padrones in agriculture, sweaters in urban tenement homework, labor recruiters and agents in glass, textiles, and other industries, all preferred larger families with more children who could be put to work. Whether other third parties were present or absent, it was usually the parent, or someone standing in the place of the parent, that contracted for the child's labor. Thus, Marx's famous quote condemning the factory system:

> Machinery, by throwing every member of the family on the labor market, spreads the value of the man's labour-power over his whole family. In order that the family of four may live, four people must now, not only labour, but expend surplus-labour for the capitalist. Previously, the workman sold his own labour power, which he disposed of nominally as a free agent. Now he sells wife and child. He has become a slave dealer.[48]

So the market for child labor was inherently unfree. It could be redeemed, then, only through an assurance that parents would act in the best interests of their children. But no such assurance could be given. Certainly there were many examples of abusive or greedy parents, but the argument here is not premised on the capacity and inclination of some parents to abuse their children. Nor is the argument aimed at those parents who were "tricked"—either by outright deception or simply through the parents' own inability to consider fully the alternatives— into placing their children in a bad situation. Assume rational parents who truly care about their children. When it comes to a question of industrial employment for their children, parents cannot be trusted to act in the best interests of any given child. Assume that decisions about employment of the children (weighed against the alternatives) are conditioned by considerations of household subsistence. The child's interests in subsistence are included with the household mix, but any given child is just one of several household members. Furthermore, the parents' own subsistence is at stake in the decision. Thus, parents may act in what is seen as the household's best interests even if it is not the child's best interests. Parents, along with others in the household, stand to gain by the employment of any given child. When the parents' own subsistence is involved, parental decisions are "tainted" by the parents' own rational household interest. There is no one involved in these contract negotiations to represent the best interests of the child. The child is incompetent to do so, and the parents have broader issues— the household—to consider.

Thus, when household subsistence is an issue in the decision to send a child to work, there can be no assurance that the best interests of the child have been considered. What about, on the other hand, situations where subsistence is not an issue? When parents do not stand to gain materially from the labor of their children, it can generally be assumed that parents act in the best interests of their children. Under these circumstances, children are not likely to be placed in situations detrimental to health, education, or physical, mental, or moral development. Objections against child labor lose much of their moral and ethical force when the harm to children has been eliminated. There may still be occasional greedy or abusive parents, but these would be the exceptional cases. Furthermore, when subsistence is no longer a salient concern, both the institution of child labor and the child labor problem are altered dramatically. We already know—theoretically, empirically, and historically—that the child labor problem is associated with poverty and that the problem is solved when subsistence is no longer precarious. Most of the work of children today is of the freelance variety and has returned to the preindustrial model where services are provided within household, kinship, and communal networks and the services provided contribute to household consumption. Work such as babysitting, mowing lawns, raking leaves, shoveling snow, and cleaning house for their parents, relatives, and neighbors is neither inherently exploitative nor likely to be detrimental. Even in many of the areas where industrial employment of children continues—delivering newspapers, work in the family business or on the family farm—the work is performed under conditions that ameliorate much of the potential for harm (farmworkers are the glaring exception).

The problem with permitting remaining forms of industrial employment of children to continue, even though most families are well-off enough to protect their children from harm, is that some families are not so well-off. Subsistence remains precarious for substantial proportions of American families. Permitting well-off children, who are not likely to be harmed, to work in industrial employment, means permitting poor children, who are much more vulnerable to harm, to do so as well. Ken Swinnerton and Carol Ann Rogers, defining exploitative child labor as work detrimental to children, demonstrate theoretically that nonexploitative child labor cannot exist without some level of exploitation, and conversely, that exploitative child labor cannot exist unless nonexploitative child labor also exists.[49] What Swinnerton and Rogers have demonstrated theoretically, we have observed in American history. Where children were permitted to work in industrial employment, some proportion, often a very large proportion, was harmed.

11. GLOBAL CHILD LABOR
Past as Prologue

Global child labor is a problem of immense social and economic proportions. In the world today, the International Labour Organization estimates there are 250 million working children under the age of fifteen in the developing nations alone. Of these, 120 million are considered to be fully at work. According to the ILO, 61 percent of child workers are found in Asia, 32 percent in Africa, and 7 percent in Latin America. While Asia has the largest number of child workers, Africa has the highest labor force participation rate at around 40 percent of children between five and fourteen years old.[1]

Table 11.1 presents a broad overview of child labor in recent world history. More than a little caution must be urged in viewing these numbers, as the ILO's current estimate of global child labor implies more than a threefold increase in the estimates presented here.[2] The source of the data in Table 11.1 is the ILO's *Economically Active Population*. It counts only children from ten to fourteen and relies, for the most part, on official estimates from the member countries. From the table, it appears that, in absolute numbers, global child labor peaked around 1980. But the percentage of children in the total labor force and labor force participation rates of children peaked much earlier, sometime before 1950. Both of these indicators are now on a steady downward path. Rough parallels can be observed in both magnitudes and directional trends between global labor force participation rates and presence of children in the workforce with those observed in U.S. history. To the extent that the data are comparable, which they really are not, global child labor today stands at roughly the level where U.S. child labor stood in 1920, when the United States was on the verge of eliminating child labor from key sectors, especially the mines, mills, and factories. Further, there are a number of striking parallels between the kinds of work performed by children in the world today and the kinds of work performed in the United States then. A majority of the world's working children are in agriculture. It is not known what portion of them are in preindustrial subsistence

Table 11.1

**Economically Active Population, Aged Ten to Fourteen, in the World:
1950–1990** (in thousands)

Year	Workers 10–14	Population 10–14	Total workers	Children as % of workforce	Activity rates of children (%)
1950	71,022	257,838	1,206,527	5.89	27.55
1960	76,968	310,607	1,377,254	5.59	24.78
1970	90,104	404,423	1,656,125	5.44	22.28
1980	99,530	499,846	2,054,245	4.85	19.91
1990	75,630	518,289	2,505,793	3.02	14.59

*Source: International Labour Organization, Economically Active Population, 1950–
2010* (Geneva: ILO, 1997), vol. 5, table 4.

farming and what portion are in commercial agriculture. Next most
prominent sectors are domestic services and the street trades. The National Child Labor Committee never investigated domestic services, and
little is otherwise known about the American record at the turn of the
twentieth century. It is understood that domestic service was not an uncommon occupation, especially for girls. We certainly had a rich body
of experience in the street trades. In addition to agriculture and the street
trades, global child labor problems exist in each of the sectors investigated by the NCLC and examined in this book. Child labor is common
in small-scale mining and quarrying operations. Children work in
glassmaking and ceramics. Not so many work in textile factories today,
but many work in hand-woven textiles and especially the garment and
needle trades in subcontractor and home workshops.

Global child labor is correctly perceived as a problem of economically underdeveloped nations. But if all advanced nations had to pass
through a stage of pervasive child labor on the path to advancement,
then the economic history of advanced nations may serve as guide to
eradication of child labor in the developing nations.

Toward a Theory of Child Labor

Over the last decade or so, there has been a growing awareness in the
United States of the problem of global child labor. Media stories, especially when they have involved celebrities or celebrity corporations, have
heightened public attention to the problem. Accompanying this growing

awareness has been a modest burgeoning of scholarly writing and research on the topic. Important steps have been taken to integrate various perspectives into a more unified and general "theory of child labor." This section assesses the contribution that insights from U.S. history can make to a theory of child labor.

The thesis advanced here, that industrialization is the cause of both the child labor problem and, later, its eradication, is not entirely novel. During early phases of industrialization, forces came into play that virtually ensured that children would be put to work. In later stages of industrialization, factors conspired to curb child labor.

While child labor has long been a topic of interest to many disciplines, much of the best recent integrative theoretical work on child labor has been in economics. Considerable progress had been made in articulating a formal theory of child labor that appears to have great potential for integrating the work of many disciplines.[3] Professor Kaushik Basu of Cornell University, formerly with the World Bank, has developed an elegant formal economic theory of child labor based on a multiple equilibrium model.[4] In a very poor society, where adult wages are very low, children must work. In a well-off society, where adult wages are high, no children work. But in between, there may be a societal equilibrium with massive child labor, and another equilibrium with relatively higher adult wages and no child labor. It is only in this middle stage that bans on child labor are warranted. In the earlier stage, a ban will make the poor, including the children, worse off. In the later stage, a ban is no longer needed, even if it remains in place as a vestigial "benign" intervention. By suggesting a "tipping point" in a society's development at which child labor can be eliminated, the theory has enormous policy implications. On the positive side, it is a fundamentally optimistic theory. It points the way to the elimination of child labor through "general economic development, equitably distributed."[5] On the other hand, the theory urges caution—if we push too hard too soon (or in the wrong way) to eliminate child labor, we can make things worse for everyone, including the children. Furthermore, the theory suggests that a poor society may fall into a "child labor trap"—stuck in the bad equilibrium—where one generation of child workers becomes the next generation's impoverished adult workers who must, in turn, send their children into the workforce.[6]

Taking certain liberties with Basu's theory, it is generally consistent with the premise advanced here regarding industrialization. Accepting the multiple equilibrium premise, a key question involves locating the tipping point where child labor can, at least theoretically, be eliminated. Locating the tipping point concurrent with industrialization has a number of important implications for both the rise and eradication of the child labor problem. First, in preindustrial society where adult wages were low, at least as they would be measured today, we would expect work of children to be a mass phenomenon, but we might not condemn it as a social and economic problem. Children from as early an age as possible, within the confines of a kinship-based household, contributed to production for the group's own consumption. As society began to industrialize, it entered the multiple equilibrium stage of the model where child labor came to be perceived as a problem but also where a solution was possible. Finally, with the continuing advance of industrialization, our society moved beyond child labor in most sectors. Second, placing the tipping point in industrialization invites us to revisit the intriguing and age-old question whether child labor—assumed to be evil—is a necessary evil. If the tipping point was correctly located at the very beginnings of industrialization, then the answer, at least in theory, would be no, child labor is not necessary. A society could choose to industrialize using child labor and hope to grow out of it later. Or a society could industrialize without child labor from the beginning. The latter would be a large claim. Empirical evidence offers very few examples of industrialized societies that have not gone through a stage of pervasive industrial child labor. Nevertheless, the theoretical proposition advanced here is that with industrialization, social and economic forces are unleashed that could do without child labor if necessary, but which are likely to result in child labor unless anticipated.

Kaushik Basu credits rising real money income and elevated standards of living as the forces eliminating child labor, phenomena which should occur shortly after industrialization begins. Thus, poverty is the main explanatory variable. Poor families send their children to work; well-off families do not. That child labor is associated with poverty is well accepted. How poverty relates to child labor is less well understood. Child labor in the United States was clearly a problem of poor Americans. The well-to-do never had a child labor problem, the notable exception being the controversy over child actors, which led to the so-called Jackie Coogan Laws.[7] Indeed, it is a sure sign that a society has gotten beyond most of its child labor problems when it hoards all the best work opportunities for middle- and upper-middle-class children, leaving the poor out of work. It is certainly true that, in the long run, child labor diminished as incomes rose. But the relationship between child labor and poverty was more complex than that. In America, we saw examples of rising incomes causing a reduction in child labor. As incomes rose in cities like Philadelphia and Baltimore, participation in the annual migration to the berry fields of the Eastern Shore and the seafood canneries on the Gulf Coast diminished.[8] But the process was slow. First, fathers skipped the migration and remained in the city. Then young adults began staying at home. Finally, when incomes had risen sufficiently, the women and children stayed at home. But there are also counterintuitive examples showing that child labor diminished as incomes declined. The most rapid reduction in child labor in southern cotton textiles occurred during the industry depression of the 1920s when work-sharing programs were instituted. Likewise, child labor in tenement homework probably reached its lowest ebb during the Great Depression when the NRA Codes were in effect (at least in those sectors regulated by the codes).

Rising incomes may provide an economic foundation for withdrawal of children from the market, but it was also necessary to attack the cultural underpinnings of child labor. For example, when journeymen glassblowers no longer found the industry suitable for their own sons ("I'd rather send my boys straight to hell"), it was the beginning of the end of child labor. While the industry continued to use boys for some time, it was never able to establish a reliable labor supply and eventually turned to substitutes. The rising incomes of skilled workers, secured through their craft unions, may have afforded them the luxury of withholding their boys. But it was the truncation of the craft career ladder, when "dog boy" became dead-end work, that child labor in the glasshouses was doomed. While poverty undoubtedly motivates child labor, the role of custom, habit, and tradition probably played as decisive a role. If the potential tipping point on child labor is coincident with industrialization, it implies that we could have done without child labor. In economic terms, employers should be indifferent as to better paid and more productive adults versus lower-paid and inefficient children. But since children had always worked, custom, habit, and tradition brought them to work in industry. Child labor remained prevalent, long after its justification in economic necessity, until old habits were broken.

Supply of Child Workers

Child workers are supplied to the labor market by the household. Supply can generally be understood within the framework of household economy, for which there is a rich theoretical and empirical literature in both economics and sociology. Earlier theories of household economy treat the household as a unit seeking to maximize a single utility function.[9] Decisions regarding allocation of time—whether and how much to devote to labor or leisure, labor or schooling, production or consumption, production for the household or production for markets, production for markets within the household or in the external market—are made so as to maximize the common good of the household. The head of the household, generally the father but, if absent, then the mother, is assumed to be the decision maker. Under these models, the time of children will be allocated to labor, and more importantly, to the labor market, when returns to household utility are perceived as greater than returns to alternative uses of the time of children.

More recent theories of household economy treat it as a collection of individuals who each possesses his own unique utility function.[10] The family strategy, then, is to maximize a weighted sum of these utility functions. The weight accorded to any given family member's utility function is determined by his or her bargaining power within the family. Thus, these theories incorporate various bargaining and game-theory models into the household decision-making process.[11] The major contribution of the newer theories is the suggestion that, as children become workers and contribute larger shares to household income, their status in the bargaining hierarchy of the family, and thus their influence on household decisions, is enhanced. This theoretical nuance may alter decision-making processes at the margins in special circumstances, but would generally yield the same behavioral predictions as the simpler unitary theories. First, at the point of the initial decision whether the child should work, children are presumed to have near zero bargaining power. Thus, the decision is made by powerful parents without consideration of the child's own utility function because it has no weight. Once the decision to work is made, the child may gain some bargaining power within the family, but this would, ceteris paribus, encourage continued work so as to enhance influence further. Next, under many circumstances—such as pure family wage situations—contributions of individual family members may be inseparable and indistinguishable and so, by necessity, are treated as unitary.[12] The earlier model of the unitary family may be a better fit to the historical period under consideration.[13]

An important theoretical issue in household decision making is the question of parental altruism. In economic terms, parental altruism implies that parents are willing to forgo some portion of the family's current utility to enhance the child's future utility. Thus, a child may be held out of work, even though it means a current loss of income, in favor of school that may increase future earnings. Most recent economic theories of child labor assume some degree of parental altruism. Generally, under these models, parental poverty drives the decision to supply children to the market. When child labor is seen as essential to economic survival, children will work. But when family income rises above some threshold level of subsistence, children are withdrawn from the labor market. Within the framework of household economy, poverty is widely acclaimed as the first cause of child labor. Everywhere and always, child labor is associated with poverty.[14]

But the assumption of parental altruism is grounded in an overly simplistic view of the role of poverty in child labor, as discussed above, and it is not clear that the assumption of parental altruism is warranted, at least not as it has been articulated. While there is ample evidence that many caring but desperate parents, both historically and today, sincerely regretted sending their children into the labor market, there is also ample evidence of low parental altruism. Parents in mining camps and mill villages sent their children to work in accordance with habituated age-based rites of passage and viewed their right to the child's earnings as an entitlement. Altruism was irrelevant to the parents who took their children to the berry fields or the seafood canneries. Once the children were there, what else was there for them to do but work? Donald Parsons and Claudia Goldin constructed models of parental choice with and without altruism and concluded that the data for 1890 in the United States, when child labor was near its peak, were consistent only in the model without parental altruism. They concluded:

> The empirical results suggest that parents did not have strong [economic] altruistic concerns for their children. The presence of industries with a high demand for child labor sharply reduced the future wealth position of the offspring. Child labor had the obvious, almost definitional, negative effect on schooling attainment. At the same time, the family provided little ... to compensate children for their lost schooling and future earnings. The increased family income was apparently absorbed in higher current

family consumption. Indeed much of the apparent gain to family income from child earnings was illusory; the greater child earnings were almost wholly offset by lower earnings for the adult male.[15]

There is additional evidence that suggests we should be cautious about adopting the assumption of high parental altruism. Working-class Americans viewed their children as income-producing assets—as poor man's capital. Where children are viewed as income-producing assets, it tends to skew fertility decisions upward.[16] Industrialization is commonly associated with a dramatic decline in fertility rates as parents traded quantity of offspring for quality of offspring. When long-run trends are examined more closely, however, fertility rates remained high through protoindustrialization and well into early industrialization before they finally began to fall. The notion that early industrialization caused fertility rates to drop "belongs to the historian's dustbin; if anything family size increased slightly"[17] as parents sought to exploit the income-producing potential of large families.

The foregoing discussion of parental altruism again suggests the importance of custom, habit, and tradition in determining supply of child workers. Even if parents are generally economically rational, at the same time, they are largely guided by custom, habit, and tradition. In any historical transition, customs, habits, and traditions that were shaped in the period prior to the transition in turn shape behavior of the participants into and during that transition. So, too, preindustrial traditions of child labor were carried forward into industrialization. Since children worked in preindustrial times, they would work into industrial times and would continue working until preindustrial customs, habits, and traditions were broken. Economic rationality might generally and ultimately prevail, but not until overcoming these inertial forces. Custom, habit, and tradition delay the altering of economic behavior as families may persist in sending their children into the labor market long beyond the point demanded by economic necessity for no other reason than that they have always done so.

> Consequently the existing practice among craftsmen of working from sunup to sundown, even when this involved fourteen or sixteen hours a day, was carried over into the factory without recognizing the fact that the intermingling of leisure and work which had relieved the fatigue of the craftsman was impossible for the operative. Women and children were employed without thought to the difference in the effect upon them between factory employment and sharing in family craftsmanship.[18]

Consider that mass child labor is not simply a family phenomenon or a societal phenomenon, it is also, at an intermediate level, a community phenomenon. At one extreme, if none of my associates and neighbors send their children to work, despite crushing poverty, I am not likely to send my children to work—I might behave altruistically without being strong on altruism. At the other extreme, if all my associates and neighbors send their children to work, in spite of being fairly well off, I probably will too, even if I am generally altruistic.

On the Role of Schooling

Parental decisions regarding allocation of their children's time, however altruistic the parents may be, are conditioned by the range of available alternatives. Schooling has come to be viewed as the generally preferred alternative to work for children.[19] In allocation of a child's time, schooling is the antithesis of work. A child cannot at the same time be both at work and at school, though part-work–part-school arrangements are not uncommon. Effective schooling presumptively eliminates the detrimental effects of child labor and substitutes acquisition of human capital and earning potentials. It is, as the saying goes, a "win-win situation" for both society and the children.[20] It is impossible to overstate the importance of schooling in eliminating child labor and, indeed, in redefining the concept of childhood for the industrial age. As Hugh Cunningham has noted:

> There is also little doubt that the introduction of compulsory schooling, normally in the late nineteenth century, did more than any other factor in these five centuries to transform the experience of and the meanings attached to childhood by removing children, in principle if not immediately in fact, from the labour market, now reserved for those who were no longer "children."[21]

During early industrialization, however, schooling was not necessarily seen as a gain by either the parents or the employers, who lost the current returns on the labor of the children. Their resistance had to be overcome. Eventually, parental values habituated to a view of children as income-producing assets had to become reoriented toward schooling. Only when working-class parents began accepting the view of the economically worthless but emotionally priceless child could they clearly perceive the long-run gains (including but not limited to earnings potential) in schooling for their children. Likewise, employers eventually came to value schooling. Enlightened employers and their representatives came to see a greater long-run return to sending the children to school while they were young and employing them later, after they had acquired some of the elementary human capital so useful in advanced industrial employment. But during early industrialization, both parental and employer short-term interests always argued for continuation of the child labor system.

While it is easy to identify schooling as the solution to the child labor problem, it was not an easy solution to implement. To be an effective alternative to child labor, schooling must first be available. Making schooling universally available requires a massive and ongoing public investment, one that all advanced nations eventually made. In America, widespread availability of schooling came sooner to urban areas, where people were concentrated, than to rural areas, where the population was more widely dispersed. In this regard, the mill schools in the southern cotton mill villages made available the only opportunity for any schooling at all for many southern children.

Second in importance to availability is cost. When parents choose schooling over work for their children, they necessarily incur an opportunity cost in lost earnings of the children. To the extent that additional costs are incurred—say for tuition, books and supplies, uniforms, transportation—schooling is a less attractive alternative. Where families are truly dependent on their children's earnings, compulsory schooling may exacerbate poverty. A popular policy-option today suggests providing subsidies to families to keep their children in school. We experimented with a number of "scholarship" programs in our own history. Relief agencies in major cities established scholarship programs designed to enable school attendance without harming the family economically. Some were income-replacement programs calculated on probable lost earnings. Others were means-tested based on household need. Still others provided subsidies for books, supplies, or clothing. We found that these scholarship programs were vital for some families. But we also found that most eligible families never even applied, and of those who did, most needed only a small amount of help for only a short while. The entire cost was borne, in that era, by private charity. The major cost of universal compulsory schooling is provision of the school system itself. Ameliorative incentive programs, even added to compliance and enforcement costs, should add only modestly to the total.

Making universal schooling available at low cost was necessary, but not sufficient, to transfer the children from work to school. Schooling had to be made compulsory. Customs and habits of parents and employers had to be changed through societal compulsion. But simply establishing age-based enrollment and attendance requirements was also insufficient.[22] Additional enforcement mechanisms were required. Parents, employers, and county ordinaries could not be counted on to attest truthfully to the ages of children. The ultimate solution to the problem of trustworthy age-certification was the creation of systems for keeping accurate birth records. Factory inspectors and other law enforcement officials proved inadequate in enforcing compulsory school attendance. This responsibility was to be shifted to the schools themselves as embodied in the truant officer. Migratory families presented, and continue to present, especially difficult problems in enforcement of compulsory schooling laws. These problems are undoubtedly exacerbated by our American tradition of local control over school systems. As migratory children regularly passed from one jurisdiction to the next, no local school system was willing to accept responsibility, or bear the costs, of educating them.

Industrialization confronts society with a quality–quantity trade-off similar to that confronting parents. An educated citizenry eventually proves to be an economic, political, social, and cultural asset. Industrialization creates not only a mass labor market to satisfy a mass consumer market, it also creates a market for schooling of the masses. As with child labor, there appears to be a societal tipping point on school enrollment. When none of my neighbors and associates consider schooling their children, neither do I. When my neighbors and associates start considering school, I might also. Indeed, there is reason to suggest that a number of societal tipping points may converge. Tipping points on child labor, school enrollment, fertility rates, child health, and underdevelopment are all likely to be causally interconnected. Certainly the earlier a society can provide schooling for the masses, the better. Universal compulsory schooling is an enormous investment that is not accomplished overnight. Societies that wait until they discover their child labor problem to address the issue of schooling are likely to prolong child labor, as we undoubtedly did in America.

Demand for Child Workers

If a theory of supply of child workers is fairly well developed, employer demand for child workers is less well understood. We know much less about demand for child workers than we do about supply. Simply positing employer greed as the principal motivation is tempting but theoretically inadequate. Most recent economic theory assumes employers are generally indifferent as to whether they hire adults or children. To be sure, child labor is cheap labor, but it is also low-productivity labor. It is assumed that children and adults are paid in accordance with their marginal productivity, and so, in terms of cost of production, the choice between children and adults is a wash. That employers are generally indifferent, at least on economic grounds, to the choice between children and adults is the most reasonable starting point for theory, and there is at least some historical evidence supporting the assumption, but it is far from the whole story.[23] We cannot explain employer demand for child workers by assuming it away.

Coupling elementary economics with elementary knowledge of children, a number of propositions can be asserted. We know child labor, relative to adult labor, is low-productivity labor. We also know there are limits on the kind of work children can perform. Children can perform work that does not require too much strength, knowledge, or skill and where pressure on employers for high productivity is subdued. Conditions favorable to low-productivity labor would include piece-rate and family-wage payment systems, few restrictions on hours, wages, or conditions, and smaller investments in capital. Piece-rate systems make labor costs more fixed than variable and subdue productivity pressures. Pure family wage systems made productivity of the children utterly irrelevant to employers. On the other hand, any restriction on hours of work, minimum hourly wages, or health and safety requirements would increase employer incentives to get more work from each hour of labor. In the United States, hours restrictions played the more important role in reducing child labor, health and safety played a role that seemed significant but difficult to pin down, and minimum wages were less important (they came later). In the world today, restrictions in any or all of these areas may be expected to have an effect. Finally, increased capital per worker heightens employer concern for productivity. So, we would expect children to be found in labor-intensive than in capital-intensive settings—handwork would be the ideal. Furthermore, where the employer can shift capital costs—for example, by subcontracting or homework—interests in productivity are further subdued. Taken together, these factors suggest we would expect to find child labor exactly where we have found it—in the least advanced, least protected economic backwaters.

But this still does not adequately explain demand for child labor and, more particularly, persistence of that demand. If, on economic terms, children and adults are effective substitutes, employers would be expected to make that substitution at the first sign that child workers were becoming a social or political cost. It is probably fair to say that new industrial employers "merely took what they found"—that is, they found the preindustrial household economy and took it, at least for a time, to be an effective solution to their labor problem. In doing so, they carried child labor forward into the new industrial regime.[24] But we also know that many employers vigorously resisted child labor reform efforts and continued to employ children long after it was fashionable to do so.

There are many reasons that employers might view children as "ideal workers"—why they might, within constraints outlined above, actively prefer child labor. First, even where children and adults are effective substitutes and wages are proportionately adjusted to productivity, as it is assumed they are, employment of large numbers of children can bring economic advantage by depressing adult wages. In theory, where large numbers of children compete with adults for the available work, adult wages must be driven down (or adult unemployment increased, or both). This is an oft-voiced, but rarely tested, proposition. However, in one clear test, Parsons and Goldin found that, in 1890 America, fully 90 percent of child earnings were competed away through lower adult wages.[25]

Second, employers can reduce transaction costs by hiring whole families. Up-front costs are reduced as the employer transacts for the whole gang at the time of initial hire. Second, turnover costs are reduced as family wage arrangements make it more difficult to move. These savings in transaction costs could be especially important where labor mobility and turnover were otherwise high.

Third, many have suggested that children are more compliant and obedient than adult workers—they are more willing to do as they are told and less likely to cause certain kinds of trouble like organizing unions. It was certainly true that children were less aware of their rights and how to assert them, and that very young children could be intimidated easily. But it was not really true that children were more compliant and obedient. They were often loud and boisterous, careless and inattentive, and they played like children. Task-oriented management in a mine, mill, or factory kindergarten was severely challenging. It might be more appropriate to suggest that the presence of large numbers of children in the workplace made adults more compliant and obedient than they would otherwise have been. While there is little direct evidence of a causal connection, child labor declined most rapidly in southern cotton textiles concurrent with the growing labor unrest of the 1920s.

Finally, there is the "nimble fingers" argument that children can perform some work better than adults—that, by virtue of small, supple bodies, there are things children can do that adults cannot. While the nimble fingers argument has been debunked in recent writings,[26] it has been a persistent argument throughout history and cannot be dismissed out of hand. Certainly there were advantages to being a child in performing much of the work that children performed. Working for long stretches sitting down and hunched over bent double may have been difficult for breaker boys or mold boys, but it would have been excruciating for most adult men. Dog boys worked at a rapid pace in tight quarters, again giving the advantage to young (slender) boys. The small, nimble doffer boys had an edge in climbing up on the spinning frames, and there was no doubt that supple fingers helped the girls learn spinning. But in each and every case, there were human or mechanical substitutes available that would have performed the work equally effectively or better.[27]

On the Role of Mechanization

Early mechanization not only created the factory system, it created demand for children. In her examination of child labor during the British industrial revolution, Carolyn Tuttle advances a theory of "biased technological change" suggesting that technologies developed for the early factories favored employment of children.[28] She cites three classes of technological change that operated to increase demand for children: (1) labor-intensive technology, (2) labor-substituting technology, and (3) labor-specific technology. There were examples of each in American history. Sometimes uneven technological advance, especially when coupled with division and specialization of labor, left gaps in the work process between the difficult or skilled jobs. These labor-intensive jobs created a need for a large number of assistants and helpers, roles that could often be filled by children. Doffers and sweepers in textile mills and the dog boys in the glasshouses are prime examples. Other technology allowed employers to substitute unskilled for skilled labor in certain machine-tending production processes and, again, created a demand for children. When ring-spinning replaced mule-spinning in cotton textiles, men were displaced and were replaced by girls and young women.

Finally, some technology was labor specific in that the machines specifically required children, rather than adults, to operate them. For example, before the advent of electricity, when textile mills ran on a complex system of belting connected to a central power source, and when much machinery was still made from wood, spinning rooms were located on the top floor of multistory textile mills. In order to reduce vibration, the spinning frames were built close to the floor. For an adult to operate them required back-breaking "stoop" labor. Children, being of shorter stature, could often operate the machinery more easily.[29]

Whatever the effects of early mechanization, it is clear that advancing mechanization created forces opposed to employment of children. Hand operations and labor-intensive tasks were mechanized, and steadily increasing investments in capital per worker steadily increased both skill requirements of the work and employer concern over worker productivity. Employers eventually realized that it no longer paid to run a kindergarten in a coal breaker, a glasshouse, or a textile mill. In coal mining, mechanical slate pickers replaced boys in the breakers, and machine-powered or electric haulage systems eliminated the need for most of the boys underground. In glasshouses, introduction of pressed-glass technologies reorganized the production processes and automated conveyor systems (along with blacks and immigrants) replaced the dog boys. In textiles, it was not so much the introduction of new machinery that replaced the children, but rather new management strategies to achieve greater efficiencies in use of the existing machinery. In industrial homework, the street trades, and agriculture, the record is mixed. The garment and needle trades remain relatively labor intensive, and where handwork can be put out to subcontractor sweatshops and home workshops, children can still be found working. In newspapers, children in downtown districts have been replaced by vending boxes, but children continue to carry papers on residential routes. In agriculture, wherever hand-harvesting methods were mechanized, child labor was eliminated, but where hand-harvesting remains the method of choice children continue to work.

If, on the supply side, poverty can create a child labor trap, technology can create a child labor trap on the demand side. In discussing technology, it is always important to distinguish between available technology and technology in use. There was often a lag between the time when a technological advance became available and when it was put to use in industry (and eliminated child labor). For example, mechanical slate pickers were available well before boys were removed from the coal breakers. So long as boys were cheap and readily available, employers had little incentive to invest in advanced technology. They could continue to profitably use a low-productivity production process. When the continued child labor agitation made it more difficult to hire boys, one by one mines began installing mechanical pickers and, one by one, eliminating boys from the breakers. Once the capital investment was made, however, the production process had to be reorganized to spread the increased capital cost over more units of production. Thus, the presence of child workers delayed technological advance and, by the same token, removal of child workers spurred technological advance and productivity improvements.

It should be noted that even modest technological advances could have large implications for child labor. For example, the simple expedient of putting long handles on the hand-held scoops of cranberry pickers displaced the children by requiring adult strength while, at the same time, making cranberry picking a more lucrative proposition for adults. In attacking global child labor, it may often be possible to use simple technologies as low-cost tools for simultaneously eliminating child workers and boosting productivity (and pay) for adult workers. For example, the simple expedient of providing wheelbarrows in quarries around Bogotá, Colombia, displaced the children who had previously carried rock piece by piece.[30]

On Law and Reform

A prominent theme in economic history is that law matters little in the regulation of child labor. State child labor laws are given little credit for the reduction of child labor in early twentieth-century America.[31] Likewise, compulsory schooling laws are given little credit for either increasing school enrollment or decreasing child labor.[32] Finally, there is abundant evidence that, in spite of our laws, widespread and persistent violations occur.[33]

A superficial review of the reform movement's efforts in the realm of U.S. federal regulation would seem to support the view that law matters little. After all, according to census data, child labor peaked in the United States in 1900, before a national child labor movement coalesced. Our first serious attempt at federal legislation, the Beveridge bill of 1906, went nowhere. It was nearly a decade before another bill was seriously considered. Our first federal child labor law, banning interstate commerce in goods produced by children, was enacted in 1916, but was found unconstitutional. A second attempt—the Child Labor Tax Act of 1918—was also found unconstitutional. In the mid-1920s, Congress recommended a constitutional amendment to the states, but it, too, failed. The Fair Labor Standards Act (FLSA) of 1938 was our first enduring federal child labor legislation. But by the time it was enacted, child labor had largely and long been relegated to the past. On the surface, it appears entirely plausible that federal regulation played little role in abolition of child labor. At best, it may have formally ratified the abolition, but it does not appear to have brought it about.

This skepticism over the role of law carries over to the present debate over global child labor. Legal bans are inherently suspect as not too thinly veiled protectionism designed to remove the common competitive advantage of developing nations—cheap labor.[34] Under conditions of crushing poverty, legal bans can leave everyone—from the children to the parents to the employers—worse off.[35] The cautionary tale is told how thousands of young girls were summarily dismissed from the Bangladeshi garment industry in 1992 when the Harkin bill banning imports made with child labor was merely introduced in Congress. Many were forced into far worse situations, including prostitution.[36] To be sure, economic theory recognizes that, in the long run, banning child labor and promoting schooling is welfare enhancing.[37] Legal bans can be effective only to the extent that they hasten the arrival of the long run while cushioning the potentially devastating effects of the short run. Probably the most optimistic view of legal bans in recent theory is that they can help "jolt" an economy out of its reliance on child labor. But once achieved, economics would enforce the ban, and a legal ban would no longer be needed, even if it remains in place as a vestigial "benign" intervention.[38]

But this view could lead to the quite erroneous conclusion that legal-reform efforts matter little. This would be an utterly dangerous conclusion for today's and tomorrow's child workers around the world. It would also be utterly wrong with respect to American history. When federal efforts are examined more deeply than their surface failures, and when federal efforts are examined alongside state efforts, and when the long-run accomplishments of the reform movement itself are examined, a different picture emerges. Coercive powers of the state were critical—necessary even if not sufficient—for the abolition of child labor. As adjunct measures in the larger struggle against child labor, laws did indeed ratify milestone achievements, but they were also instrumental in bringing about real reform.

Did the enactment of the Fair Labor Standards Act in 1938 have a measurable effect on the reduction or elimination of child labor in America? Absolutely not. Child labor had been almost entirely eliminated from mining and manufacturing, and was generally well regulated in retail trades, several years earlier. No one seriously claims, let alone has been able to document, any substantial reduction in child labor in these sectors directly attributable to enactment of the FLSA. This would seem to support, if only superficially, the school of thought that laws do not matter much.

But did the movement toward federal regulation have a palpable effect on the reduction of child labor in America? Of course it did. If enactment of the FLSA had no measurable effect on numbers of working children, the movement for which the FLSA was a crowning achievement had a large and decisive effect. It is tempting to note only the reform movement's lack of achievements at the federal level and conclude it was feeble, belated, and ultimately, unnecessary. It is also tempting to conclude that, because the reform movement lost most of the major battles, that it also lost the war. But this overlooks too much. There were other important federal milestones. The formation of a Children's Bureau in 1912 and the commissioning of a massive study by the Labor Bureau (authorized in 1906 and completed from 1910 to 1913) were important first steps. The Children's Bureau would assume responsibility for investigating child labor in the traditional sectors (mining and manufacturing), which freed the NCLC to emphasize other sectors (agriculture, the street trades, and industrial homework). After the 1916 law was found unconstitutional, its provisions were imposed by executive order, as a wartime measure, on federal contractors. The 1918 law remained in force for three full years, at a critical economic juncture, before it was struck down. And finally, many consider the child labor provisions of the NRA Codes to have been the final nail in child labor's coffin. Each of these events, not to mention the great national debate over the Child Labor Amendment, contributed to driving child labor out of industrialized America.

Constitutional considerations dictated that the major battles of the child labor movement would be waged at the state level. This required a sustained, multicentered, multifaceted humanitarian reform movement to carry the banner. Progressive states, usually but not always the more industrialized, led; others eventually followed. Specific provisions in law tended toward convergence on a common standard, but specific provisions were often less important than effective compliance and enforcement provisions. As Daniel Nelson has noted, "[T]he exact provisions were often less important than the extent of the enforcement effort. . . . In the last analysis it was the inspectors rather than the legislators who determined the impact of progressive legislation."[39] Furthermore, as the child labor reform movement intersected with other movements, the complexity of law magnified. It was not just minimum ages, hours restrictions, and compulsory schooling that mattered; a wide variety of reforms, from abolition of slavery to adoption of widows' pensions, were also important.

Our American history of child labor reform may be especially informative about the political and geographic contours of the reform movement in the world today. We established ourselves as a republic of sovereign states. Constitutionally protected states' rights effectively barred a federal role regulating the workplace until 1937. Before then, all labor law, whether regulating factory conditions, workers' compensation, or child labor, was state law. At the same time, however, the sovereign states had become increasingly integrated into a strong national economy. In this respect, the United States—then—represents in microcosm the world—now—in which sovereign nations struggle to come to grips with their own child labor problems in the larger context of an increasingly integrated global economy.

Rather than a gradual articulation and refinement of a uniform national policy, America's child labor reform movement and its manifestation in enacted legislation proceeded on a patchwork and piecemeal basis throughout the sovereign states. Unofficially, the federal standard set the standard for the states to follow. The Beveridge bill articulated the first national standard for the states to emulate. Before the Keating-Owen Act was passed, only nine states measured up to its standards. Between 1916 and 1933, most states came into substantial conformity with the federal standard, but only four states exceeded the basic age standard before it was raised by the NRA Codes of 1933. Then the NRA standard rapidly became the norm. Nowhere is this illustrated more clearly than when North Carolina adopted the sixteen-year standard after the NRA was invalidated by the Supreme Court.[40] The unofficial and unenforceable federal standard established the point of convergence.

But each sovereign state made its own separate, but not entirely independent, accommodation to that standard. A few states led, many followed the federal standard closely, and a few lagged.

Similarly, a relatively clear set of official, but still unenforceable, global standards exist. They have been worked out gradually by the representative governments. Basic principles are articulated in the United Nations Declaration of Universal Human Rights (1948), the International Covenant on Economic, Social and Cultural Rights (1966), and the Convention on the Rights of the Child (1989). More specific standards are spelled out in the International Labour Organization's minimum-age convention (Convention 138 [1973]) and the more recent convention on worst forms of child labor (Convention 182 [1999]). Carrying the added cachet of being associated with human rights, these are the standards that developing nations are striving to achieve. At the same time, each sovereign nation must make its own separate, but not entirely independent, accommodation to the global standard within the context of its own unique child labor problems.

Concluding Remarks on the Global Child Labor Problem

We may never completely eradicate global poverty. It is unlikely that we will ever eliminate all abuse and exploitation of children. But it is entirely possible that we will achieve effective abolition of global industrial child labor, and it may happen within the lifetimes of children who are working today. We know how to do it. And we know that we will all be better off for it once it is done, even if transitional costs can sometimes be wrenching. There are a number of optimistic signs that a global movement of sufficient critical mass to abolish global child labor is now under way. Before the 1990s there were a few dedicated policy analysts and scholars soldiering away on the problem of global child labor.[41] Since the 1990s there has been a modest burgeoning of scholarly work and policy analysis. This has been accompanied by a substantial mobilization of resources by the International Labour Organization and other agencies of the United Nations, by national and local governments in several areas, and by a variety of trade associations and human rights, worker rights, and social welfare organizations. Finally, there are indications that the numbers of child workers may be turning downward in many parts of the world.

Consumers from wealthy nations have, so far, proven to be an unreliable but potentially very powerful ally in the struggle against global child labor. On the positive side, most consumers have little stomach for exploiting third-world children. When they become aware that their consumer goods were made by poor children, many react with moral indignation, some alter their spending habits, and a few enlist as activists in various labor and environmental rights campaigns. On the negative side, consumers have little capacity to learn much about the conditions under which there goods are produced; collectively, consumers tend to have short memories; and, in the main, their spending decisions are driven more by price than quality. Still, even relatively low levels of consumer awareness and activism can have a substantial impact on the margins of vulnerable firms.

Multinational corporations from wealthy nations have become more sensitive to the potential problem of child labor within their sourcing networks. Whether motivated by humanitarian or economic interests, many multinationals are coming to recognize that they had better accept responsibility for clean sourcing because they are likely to be held responsible for problems that are exposed. When textile interests from Lowell, Massachusetts, moved south to take advantage of cheap labor, they were willing to accept, and allow their local agents to defend, the child labor system. This is becoming more difficult for multinational corporations. In turn, local partners, contractors, and subcontractors that desire to maintain their contracts with multinationals are beginning to recognize a competitive advantage in maintaining conditions that will not be a source of embarrassment to their wealthy benefactors. Historically, few instruments, aside from trade unions and occasionally insurance interests, existed for establishing and enforcing the principle of joint liability for labor conditions throughout the commodity chain (from retailer to manufacturer to contractor to subcontractor). Today, additional instruments exist—from corporate and trade association codes of conduct, to social accounting and certification standards, to global trade agreements and human rights accords—that have the capacity to reinforce principles of joint liability for labor conditions.

While global standards and a global movement are important, and while wealthy consumers and multinational corporations can play a critical role, most of the heavy lifting in the struggle to abolish child labor must necessarily take place on the ground, in one country or region and then the next, in one industrial or occupational sector and then the next. There are some important additional steps that advanced nations can take. In America we could start, for example, by finally resolving some of our own residual child labor problems in agriculture, the street trades, and sweatshop homework. Even if it is only a symbolic gesture, we could ratify the United Nations Convention on the Rights of the Child and the International Labour Organization's minimum-age convention. That we have ratified neither diminishes our global credibility when we claim to be champions of human rights. Finally, we could take the lead in advocating incorporation of labor standards into global trading accords. This includes, most importantly, the World Trade Organization, but also institutions such as the World Bank and the International Monetary Fund. There is little doubt that, if the advanced economies spoke with one voice on the question of labor standards, those standards would be adopted. If all we insisted on were the consensus global human rights in employment, it would require the abolition of industrial child labor. Beyond this, we can offer our moral, financial, institutional, and legal support to those in the developing world who are working to eliminate their own domestic child labor problems.

Each developing nation must ultimately make its own unique accommodation to its own unique child labor problem: As nations and regions move from less advanced to more advanced, whether that movement is characterized as industrialization, development, growth, democratization, or whatever, the strictures of a rigorous laissez-faire capitalism must be relegated to the ashbin of history, and children must be deliberately, consciously, and forcibly removed from the industrial labor market (and placed in school). Coming to grips with child labor, if not a ticket to advancement, at least appears to be a cultural requisite of advanced nations and regions. In their efforts to abolish child labor, developing nations should be mindful of the history of the developed nations that have already been through the process. In addition to attacking work detrimental to children, for example, it might be useful to attack all industrial employment of children, as that phrase was defined in the previous chapter. Distinguishing preindustrial and postindustrial patterns of work with industrial employment of children, and attacking the latter, may help developing nations seeking to abolish child labor accomplish the task sooner and more completely. Children have always worked and will always continue to do work, but industrial child labor can be eradicated.

If past is prologue, once a sustainable global movement to abolish child labor is under way, child labor is no longer sustainable. Most employers will eventually surrender their child workers, even if some employers must be coerced into letting them go. As light shines on child labor, it predictably retreats to the economic backwaters of society. But even if much child labor is hidden from public view, we know where to look to find it. The movement will pursue abolition of child labor to the point of a societal accommodation. The movement may not achieve all of its aims. But it will achieve some. Child labor will be abolished in a few nations at a time. If past is prologue, there are likely to be holes in society's accommodation—holes that pockets of working children can slip through. But if we learn from the past, we know where these holes are likely remain—in agriculture, in the street trades, in homework.

American history with child labor does not answer all the questions developing nations must confront in order to eliminate child labor. For example, in many parts of the world, child labor is reinforced by systems of slavery, debt bondage, indenture, and other forms of forced labor. In the United States we effectively abolished slavery well before we turned our attention to industrial child labor. Likewise, our experience with the effects of war, famine, epidemic, and other catastrophic events on child labor was limited. We know that whatever impoverishes the working classes, or enfeebles the adults, or results in a proliferation of widows and orphans, exacerbates whatever child labor problems are already present. Furthermore, that which enfeebles and impoverishes one generation exacerbates the child labor problems of the next generation. Finally, American experience in the abolition of child labor tells us little about how child labor might be effectively abolished in nondemocratic, totalitarian nations. Judging from American experience, our pluralistic and democratic traditions and institutions seem critical to the reform movement's success. The movement relied on freedom of speech, freedom of association, freedom of the press, and the freedom to elect (or defeat) to achieve its aims. Whether similar success can be achieved in the absence of pluralism and democracy cannot be deduced from American experience. But clearly, lessons learned from American experience with child labor can be valuable to many developing nations seeking to overcome their child labor problems.

A final word regarding costs. In the short run, the costs of abolishing child labor can be substantial, even prohibitive. Thus, for policy purposes, it may be necessary to proceed on a step-by-step basis absorbing costs as they can be afforded. Gradualism and incremental gains may be dictated by necessity. But in the long run, there are no costs, only gains.

The major costs in eliminating child labor are in establishing and maintaining the schools and school systems. The cost of universal compulsory schooling is enormous. But schooling is not simply a cost, it is principally an investment. An educated citizenry is a valuable economic asset and a priceless cultural asset. Other costs associated with abolishing child labor, including the direct costs of forgone income and production, as well as the gamut of indirect costs for everything from regulation, inspection, and enforcement, and compliance, to establishing systems of birth records and widows' and orphans' pensions, are, in the long run, more than compensated for by the increase in productivity (and the consequent increase in adult pay) that comes from getting the children out of the workplace so the adults can get the work done. In the long run, as Karl Polanyi observed, "An industrial society can afford to be free."[42]

NOTES

Chapter 1

1. Walter I. Trattner, *Crusade for the Children*, p. 21. See also Robert Hunter, *Poverty*, p. 225, "Children have always worked; but their labor was not an evil, but rather it was a good thing, in the earlier days." John Spargo, *The Bitter Cry of the Children*, p. 127, "Children have always worked, but it is only since the reign of the machine that their work has been synonymous with slavery." Hugh Cunningham notes "children had always worked" in "The Employment and Unemployment of Children in England c.1680–1851." Likewise, see Carolyn Tuttle, *Hard at Work in Factories and Mines*, various pages. See also Viviana A. Zelizer, *Pricing the Priceless Child*, p. 59.

2. Judith Mara Gutman, *Lewis W. Hine and the American Social Conscience*; Walter Rosenblum, Naomi Rosenblum, and Alan Trachtenberg, *America and Lewis Hine*; John R. Kemp, *Lewis Hine: Photographs of Child Labor in the South.*

Chapter 2

1. Richard Thurnwald, *Economics in Primitive Communities*, p. 212.

2. Allen Tullos, *Habits of Industry*, pp. 57–58.

3. Robert Hunter, *Poverty*, pp. 201–202.

4. As an interesting aside, the father in the photo was not some randomly selected Vermont yeoman farmer. He was John Spargo, author of *The Bitter Cry of the Children*, published in 1906. The book was an impassioned condemnation of child poverty in America, loaded with fact after fact—probably the most complete work on the subject published up to its time. Spargo and the National Child Labor Committee would seem to have been natural allies in the fight against child labor. But, Spargo was a Socialist, and the NCLC was a mainstream progressive organization that deliberately distanced itself from radical taint. So, while Spargo graciously acknowledged assistance from the NCLC in his book, Hine's visit to Spargo's Vermont farm is one of the very few recorded contacts with Spargo initiated by the NCLC.

5. Likewise, Richard T. Ely et al. note, "It is interesting to observe that, owing to the progressive western movement of the population of the country, the stages in the history of man's productive efforts appeared in regular order from west to east," Ely et al., *Outlines of Economics*, p. 62.

6. Ibid., p. 75.

7. Ibid., p. 66.

8. Indentured servitude is in violation of the United Nations Declaration of Universal Human Rights, the Treaty on the Rights of the Child, and numerous hu-

man rights conventions of the International Labour Organization, most notably bans on slavery, forced labor, and, to the extent that children were involved, the various child labor conventions.

9. Abbott E. Smith, *Colonists in Bondage*. See also, Richard S. Dunn, "Servants and Slaves: The Recruitment and Employment of Labor"; Sharon V. Salinger, *To Serve Well and Faithfully*. Salinger estimates that in mid–eighteenth century Philadelphia, half the labor force was "unfree."

10. Foster Rhea Dulles and Melvyn Dubofsky, *Labor In America*, pp. 3–4.

11. Ely et al., *Outlines of Economics*, p. 66.

12. Salinger, *To Serve Well and Faithfully*, p. 9.

13. Ibid.

14. Dulles and Dubofsky, *Labor in America*, p. 9.

15. Ely et al., *Outlines of Economics*, pp. 66–67.

16. Tullos, *Habits of Industry*, p. 82.

17. "The tenement workers in the so-called 'sweated trades' to-day are, so far as the method of their employment is concerned, the direct descendants of the women who were employed in weaving, or in making cards for the 'manufactory' of the eighteenth century. Although the women of the earlier period did their work at home, their materials were often furnished and they were employed by a manufacturer to whom they returned the product when finished and by whom they were paid for what they had done." Edith Abbott, *Women in Industry*, p. 42.

18. Karl Polanyi asserts more broadly, "Mercantilism, with all its tendency towards commercialization, never attacked the safeguards which protected these two basic elements of production—labor and land—from becoming the objects of commerce." Polanyi, *The Great Transformation*, p. 70.

19. Hugh Cunningham, *Children and Childhood in Western Society*, pp. 88–89.

20. Dulles and Dubofsky, *Labor in America*, pp. 14–15. See also Abbott, *Women in Industry*, pp. 334–36, and U.S. Bureau of Labor, *The Beginnings of Child Labor Legislation in Certain States*, pp. 21–23.

21. Abbott, *Women in Industry*.

22. See John Sugden, *Tecumseh*. Tecumseh and his confederated warriors stopped the American invasion of Canada effectively at Detroit. By the War of 1812, regularized patterns of trade had developed through the western edge of the Great Lakes. Note that the boundary between the United States and Canada runs along a straight line westward, the 49th parallel, from 1812 forward.

23. Ely et al., *Outlines of Economics*, p. 82.

24. Ibid. The distinction between the earlier "manufactories" and Slater's "factory" is grounded in technology, the former based in traditional hand methods, the latter based in state-of-the-art machinery.

25. Thomas Dublin, *Women at Work*; Jonathan Prude, *The Coming of Industrial Order*.

26. E.O. Smith and R.L. Nyman, "Effects of Technological Change on Occupational Structure," pp. 63–69.

27. Abbott, *Women in Industry*, p. 121. Furthermore, to tie the two ends of the age spectrum together, it appears that the few young children were often daughters of the boardinghouse chaperones. For example, Lucy Larcom, publisher of the famed *Lowell Offering*, began work at age eleven. Her widowed mother ran one of the corporate tenement boardinghouses.

28. Discussed in Dulles and Dubofsky, *Labor in America*, pp. 70–71.

29. See Howard M. Gitelman, "The Waltham System and the Coming of the Irish." See also discussion in David M. Gordon, Richard Edwards, and Michael Reich, *Segmented Work, Divided Workers*, pp. 67–77.

30. Gitelman, "The Waltham System," p. 244.

31. Barbara M. Tucker, *Samuel Slater and the Origins of the American Textile Industry*.

32. Caroline Ware, *The Early New England Cotton Manufacture*, p. 199.

33. Abbott, *Women in Industry*, pp. 43–44.

34. Ely et al., *Outlines of Economics*, p. 62.

35. Tullos, *Habits of Industry*, pp. 60–61.

36. Ibid., p. 139.

37. Elizabeth H. Davidson, *Child Labor Legislation in the Southern Textile States*, p. 5.

38. Ibid.

39. See, for example, Esther Boserup, *Women's Role in Economic Development*; Guy Standing, *Labour Force Participation and Development*; and William Rau and Robert Wazienski, "Industrialization, Female Labor Force Participation, and the Modern Division of Labor by Sex," pp. 504–21.

40. Dulles and Dubofsky, *Labor in America*, pp. 75, 93. In 1864, a contract-labor law was enacted that permitted the advance of passage money to immigrants as a lien on wages. Dulles and Dubofsky cite (p. 92) the American Emigrant Company, capitalized at $1 million and backed by Chief Justice Samuel Chase, Secretary of the Navy Gideon Welles, Senator Charles Sumner, and Henry Ward Beecher as an example of a company established to import European labor.

41. C. Vann Woodward, *Origins of the New South, 1877–1913*; Jacquelyn Dowd Hall et al., *Like a Family: The Making of a Southern Cotton Mill World*.

42. Ronald D. Eller, *Miners, Millhands, and Mountaineers*, pp. 124–27.

43. Kenneth Sokoloff, "Industrialization and the Growth of the Manufacturing Sector in the Northeast"; Claudia Goldin and Kenneth Sokoloff, "Women, Children, and Industrialization in the Early Republic," pp. 741–74; Goldin and Sokoloff, "The Relative Productivity Hypothesis of Industrialization," pp. 461–87; Kenneth Sokoloff, "Was the Transition from the Artisanal Shop to the Nonmechanised Factory Associated with Gains in Efficiency?" pp. 351–82.

44. This situation was due to characteristics of Yankee farmsteads and in contrast with the South or Midwest, where relative productivity of women and children more closely approximated that of men. Stated alternatively, the high relative price of adult male labor created incentives for employers to organize their processes so as to utilize alternative sources of labor provided by women and children. See also Stanley Lebergott, *Manpower in Economic Growth*, pp. 125–29.

45. Goldin and Sokoloff, "Women, Children, and Industrialization in the Early Republic." Donald O. Parsons and Claudia Goldin, "Parental Altruism and Self-Interest," pp. 637–59.

46. Alexander Hamilton, "Report on Manufactures."

47. The term "family wage" has been given two distinct meanings in history. The first meaning—the entire family works for a single wage—is the one used here. The second meaning—one family member earns a sufficient wage to provide for the

entire family—came about later and can be seen as society's reaction to the earlier family wage systems. See Michelle Barrett and Mary McIntosh, "The 'Family Wage' Debate."

48. Hall et al., *Like a Family*.

49. Cathy L. McHugh, *Mill Family*, p. 20; Gay L. Gullickson, "Technology, Gender, and Rural Culture," pp. 33–37; Hall et. al., *Like a Family*, p. 62; Davidson, *Child Labor Legislation in Southern Textile States*, p. 15. Note that under the Pelzer Contract, as the law progressively raised the minimum age for employment, the school/work ridge could easily be adjusted to comply.

50. Charles Loring Brace *The Dangerous Classes of New York*, p. 225. For a recent account of the orphan trains, see Janet Liebl, *Ties that Bind*. Liebl estimates that the number of orphans who rode the orphan trains was about the same as the number of slaves brought to the United States.

51. Brace, *The Dangerous Classes of New York*, p. 247.

52. "A few of the boys are bound to trades, but the most insisted upon being farmers, and learning to drive horses. They are to receive a good common-school education, and one hundred dollars when twenty-one." Ibid., p. 253.

53. Dulles and Dubofsky, *Labor in America*, p. 15.

54. Gary R. Freeze, "Poor Girls Who Might Otherwise Be Wretched"; Hall et al., *Like a Family*, p. 33.

55. Lewis W. Hine, NCLC Investigation Report 302, p. 2, emphasis in original.

56. Robert Hunter, *Poverty*, pp. 3–4.

57. Ibid., p. 200.

58. Ibid., p. 202.

Chapter 3

1. Long ago, the economist Richard Ely observed that "certain classes, particularly women and child wage workers, have found it nearly impossible to organize for collective bargaining. In their case the state has entered upon a program of positive protection, acting so far as children are concerned *in loco parentis*. Adult men, with their trade unions, have been left very largely to take care of themselves." Richard T. Ely et al., *Outlines of Economics*, p. 471.

2. This argument parallels that advanced by Hugh Cunningham regarding Great Britain, in "The Employment and Unemployment of Children in England." It is undoubtedly true, however, that unemployment of children and youth never reached the proportions in America that it had in Britain. In this sense, the American reform program can be seen as preventive in nature.

3. See Edith Abbott, *Women in Industry*, especially Appendix A, pp. 327–38. See also U.S. Bureau of Labor, *The Beginnings of Child Labor Legislation in Certain States*, pp. 9–26.

4. Quotes from colonial Massachusetts laws, cited in Abbott, *Women in Industry*, Appendix A, p. 328.

5. "The economic advantages of a free labor market could not make up for the social destruction wrought by it. Regulation of a new type had to be introduced under which labor was again protected, only this time from the working of the market mechanism itself." Karl Polanyi, *The Great Transformation*, p. 77.

6. "Accordingly, the countermove consisted in checking the action of the mar-

ket in respect to the factors of production, labor, and land. This was the main function of interventionism." Ibid., p. 131.

7. Quoted in Robert Hunter, *Poverty*, p. 259.

8. Ibid., pp. 205–206.

9. Beatrice Webb, arguing the familiar refrain that child labor was injurious to both the child and to society, began the use of the word "parasitic" to refer to the child-employing industries. Webb, "The Economics of Factory Legislation." It might also be noted that counterreformers sometimes referred to the reformers themselves as parasites.

10. Hunter, *Poverty*, p. 253.

11. Ibid., p. 248.

12. Edgar Gardner Murphy, *Problems of the Present South*, p. 325.

13. Quoted in Foster Rhea Dulles and Melvyn Dubofsky, *Labor in America*, p. 47.

14. Ibid., pp. 125–26, 150.

15. The best history of the National Child Labor Committee is provided by Walter I. Trattner, *Crusade for the Children*.

16. Ibid., pp. 11–12.

17. Lewis W. Hine, "Baltimore to Biloxi and Back," p. 12.

18. Lewis W. Hine, *Child Labor in Gulf Coast Canneries*, NCLC Publication 158, p. 121.

19. "The manufacturers were not altogether unjustified in calling the committee a northern organization. While the membership of the committee included a few southerners, the predominant influence was northern. In 1910 there were only two southern members on the board." Elizabeth H. Davidson, *Child Labor Legislation in the Southern Textile States*, p. 253.

20. Mrs. John Van Vorst and Marie Van Vorst, *The Woman Who Toils*; and Mrs. John Van Vorst, *Saturday Evening Post* (January 16, February 23, and July 20, 1905, and June 21, 1906).

21. John Spargo, *The Bitter Cry of the Children*,

22. Edwin Markham, "Children at the Loom."

23. Broadus Mitchell, *The Rise of Cotton Mills in the South*.

24. C. Vann Woodward, *The Origins of the New South*; James A. Hodges, *New Deal Labor Policy and the Southern Cotton Textile Industry*.

25. U.S. House Committee on Labor, *A Bill to Prevent Interstate Commerce in the Products of Child Labor*, pp. 93–96.

26. Allen Tullos, *Habits of Industry*, p. 160.

27. George Taylor Winston, *A Builder of the New South*, p. 142.

28. Ibid., pp. 276–77.

29. Ibid. In a similar vein, Tompkins also felt that providing adult workers too much in the way of either leisure or·wages would be ruinous to the average worker. See Tullos, *Habits of Industry*, p. 159.

30. Stephen B. Wood, *Constitutional Politics in the Progressive Era*, pp. 42–46.

31. The other great potential advantage, location in the middle of the cotton fields, Clark claimed, had already been mooted by discriminatory freight rates, again at the behest of northern interests.

32. His position, like that of many other laissez-faire propagandists, however, was internally inconsistent. He sought only freedom from intervention in the internal affairs of private business, but had no hesitation about advocating in favor of

protective tariffs for the South's "infant industries." In this way, his position was no different from that of the laissez-faire protectionists of Britain who were criticized by Polanyi: "The free trade origins of the cotton industry are a myth. Freedom from regulation in the sphere of production was all the industry wanted; freedom in the sphere of exchange was still deemed a danger." Polanyi, *The Great Transformation*, p. 160. The National Child Labor Committee was able to make effective rhetorical use of Clark's advocacy for protection of "infant industries" as opposed to his stance against abolition of "infants in industry."

33. While a state role in regulating child labor might have been irritating, it was a matter for pragmatic accommodation; but a federal role in child labor, or any condition of internal production, was anathema. Clark was fond of reminding his readers that several southern states, most notably the Carolinas, would not have ratified the U.S. Constitution without the inclusion of the Tenth Amendment, which reserved to the states all rights not specifically enumerated.

34. U.S. Bureau of Labor, *The Cotton Textile Industry.*

35. See Daniel J.B. Mitchell, "A Furor Over Working Children and the Bureau of Labor," pp. 34–36.

36. Thomas Robinson Dawley Jr., *The Child That Toileth Not.* The title parodied the 1903 book highly critical of the mills and mill villages, Van Vorst and Van Vorst, *The Woman Who Toils.*

37. Here, also, was an easy explanation and remedy for the "mill pallor" of the children, which had been attributed by reformers to premature overwork.

38. Ron Chernow, *Titan: The Life of John D. Rockefeller, Sr.*, pp. 487–91.

39. Florence Kelley, *Some Ethical Gains Through Legislation*, p. 103.

40. "While every legislature followed a separate course, there was a tendency for the less progressive states to follow the lead of the more progressive and in time to narrow the gap between them. This was due to the gradual diffusion of ideas and the growth of regional and national reform groups." Daniel Nelson, *Managers and Workers*, p. 123.

41. Davidson, *Child Labor Legislation in Southern Textile States*, preface.

42. Forest Ensign, *Compulsory School Attendance and Child Labor*; William F. Ogburn, *Progress and Uniformity in Child-Labor Legislation*; August W. Steinhilber and Carl J. Sokolowski, *State Laws on Compulsory Attendance.*

43. See Davidson, *Child Labor Legislation in Southern Textile States.* Since 1887 Alabama had the first restrictive child labor legislation. Georgia had a sixty-six-hour (per week) law since 1889, and South Carolina passed an eleven-hour (per day) law in 1892. Also in the 1880s, several bills were introduced in North Carolina, though none were adopted. All these were at the instigation of the Knights.

44. But note, while North Carolina lagged in child labor legislation, a Bureau of Labor Statistics established in 1887 in the Department of Agriculture, Immigration, and Statistics gave North Carolina more data on the problem than other southern states had.

45. Davidson, *Child Labor Legislation in Southern Textile States*, pp. 100–101.

46. As Richard Ely commented, "But yesterday a slave, it is inevitable that the negro should be forced to traverse in the forward path the intermediate steps of serfdom, peonage, and tenancy before becoming farm operative and owner." Ely et al., *Outline of Economics.*

47. Alexander J. McKelway, *The Child Labor Problem—A Study in Degeneracy*, NCLC Publication 022.

48. Florence Kelley, *Obstacles to the Enforcement of Child Labor Legislation*, NCLC Publication 046.

49. Davidson, *Child Labor Legislation in Southern Textile States*, mentions a North Carolina Supreme Court case from around 1902 where Chief Justice Walter Clark (who was David Clark's father) held that the contributory negligence defense was not available in the case of a fourteen-year-old boy even though North Carolina had no minimum age law at the time.

50. Nelson, *Managers and Workers*, pp. 12–13.

51. This is the same Dwight Manufacturing Company that figured in the repeal of Alabama's earlier child labor law. Alabama was the first southern state with a child labor law. Its statute dated from 1877. In 1894 the statute was repealed, ostensibly at the behest of the company, which began building its first large mill in Alabama City the following year. See Davidson, *Child Labor Legislation in Southern Textile States*.

52. U.S. Bureau of Labor, *Report on Condition of Woman and Child Wage Earners in the United States*. (Washington, DC: Government Printing Office [U.S. Senate Doc #645], 1910–1913.

53. Trattner, *Crusade for the Children*, p. 89, discusses Roosevelt's refusal to support the Beveridge bill and the commissioning of the report. Trattner, pp. 119–120, discusses Julia Lathrop's appointment as head of the Children's Bureau.

54. A. Mitchell Palmer, a young reform-minded Democrat from Pennsylvania, was the first sponsor of a serious child labor bill since the Beveridge bill. His path through progressivism, though perhaps more extreme, was not entirely unusual. From this auspicious beginning as first sponsor of the first serious child labor bill, he later became Wilson's attorney general and chief architect of the Palmer Raids, an effort to round up and incarcerate foreign-born subversives toward the latter part of World War I. The raids were concentrated especially on those of a leftist, laborist persuasion (to be sure, the bombing of Palmer's personal residence by anarchists may have provided the decisive motivation). Countless progressives traversed a similar path, first embracing the progressive ideals of Wilson's New Freedom, later questioning, and eventually outright rejecting the populist impulse it implied.

55. U.S. House Committee on Labor, *A Bill to Prevent Interstate Commerce in the Products of Child Labor*, pp. 93–96.

56. Davidson, *Child Labor Legislation in Southern Textile States*, p. 257.

57. Wood, *Constitutional Politics in the Progressive Era*, p. 78.

58. Wood cautions that Captain Ellison Smyth should be distinguished from another prominent South Carolinian with virtually the same name, Ellison Durant "Cotton Ed" Smith. Cotton Ed also played an important role in the child labor issue as a U.S. senator and special protector of the state's cotton interests. Ibid., p. 44.

59. Ibid., pp. 47–80, 206–209.

60. Ibid., pp. 51–55.

61. *Southern Textile Bulletin* (August 10, 1916): 10.

62. *Southern Textile Bulletin* (August 23, 1917): 10.

63. The idea that a poor man like Dagenhart, who claimed that the compensation earned by his sons was essential to his subsistence, would hire such a distinguished

group of nationally known corporate attorneys was laughable on its face. Payment of attorney fees would have required the labor of the two boys in perpetuity.

64. Lowell Mellett, "Reuben Dagenhart in 1923."

65. Quoting Justice Louis Brandeis, see Alexander M. Bickel, *The Unpublished Opinions of Mr. Justice Brandeis*, pp. 1–20.

66. Wood, *Constitutional Politics in the Progressive Era*, pp. 130–31.

67. Elizabeth Sands Johnson, "Child Labor Legislation."

68. In another interesting irony, the Revenue Bill of 1919, to which the Pomerene Amendment was attached, the Simmons-Kitchen Act, bore the name of House Majority Leader Claude Kitchen of North Carolina. Claude Kitchen was the son of former governor W. W. Kitchen, who was hired by David Clark and the Executive Committee to defeat the Keating-Owen Act in Congress.

69. Wood, *Constitutional Politics in the Progressive Era*, p. 238.

70. *Southern Textile Bulletin* (March 4 and 25, 1920): 22.

71. See discussion in Wood, *Constitutional Politics in the Progressive Era*, pp. 240–51. Quote at p. 244.

72. Quoted in Bickel, *The Unpublished Opinions of Mr. Justice Brandeis*, p. 17.

73. Wood, *Constitutional Politics in the Progressive Era*, p. 269.

74. These are my estimates, compiled from various sources, including NCLC files, various issues of the *Southern Textile Bulletin,* and Wood, *Constitutional Politics in the Progressive Era*, pp. 262–63.

75. The textile industry was well into a postwar depression by May 1922, a depression from which it never fully recovered until after the Great Depression of the 1930s.

76. Samuel Gompers, *American Labor and the War*, p. 337. See also Steve Charnovitz, "The Influence of International Labour Standards on the World Trading Regime."

77. A similar pro and con outline is provided in Julia E. Johnsen, *Child Labor.*

78. Pamphlet by James A. Emory, general counsel, National Association of Manufacturers, New York, 1924. See also remarks of New York senator Wadsworth on May 29, 1924, cited in Johnsen, *Child Labor*, pp. 90–91.

79. Pamphlet by James A. Emory, cited in Johnsen, *Child Labor*, pp. 89–90.

80. Cited in Johnsen, *Child Labor*, p. 107.

81. Gilbert E. Hyatt, "The Farmers' States Rights League and Ratification of the Child Labor Amendment," p. 4.

82. *Southern Textile Bulletin* 27, no. 3 (February 5, 1925): 20.

83. They got what they wished for. Unfortunately, it turned out to be an extremely volatile bargain. The minimum wage resulted in a modest increase in hourly labor costs, thereby creating pressure for enhanced productivity—the stretch-out. At the same time, the new minimum wage resulted in reduced weekly income for many workers. Once reduced hours were factored in, even with an increase in the hourly rate, income fell. The dramatic intensification of work effort, for less pay, was one of the leading causes of the General Textile Strike of 1934, the largest strike in American labor history to its time.

84. Hodges, *New Deal Labor Policy and the Southern Cotton Textile Industry*, p. 32.

85. Liston Pope, *Millhands and Preachers*, p. 198.

86. Davidson, *Child Labor Legislation in Southern Textile States*, p. 271.

87. Letter dated January 27, 1934. From the papers of the National Child Labor Committee, Library of Congress.

88. Herbert Hoover, *The Challenge to Liberty*, p. 83.

89. Code provisions dealing with rights to organize and bargain collectively had been restored and strengthened earlier in the Wagner Act, or National Labor Relations Act, of 1935.

90. *United States v. Darby Lumber Co.*, 312 U.S. 100 (1941).

Chapter 4

1. Owen R. Lovejoy, *In the Shadow of the Coal Breaker*, NCLC Publication 061, emphasis in original.

2. Owen R. Lovejoy, *Child Labor in the Coal Mines*, NCLC Publication 027.

3. Lewis W. Hine, NCLC Investigation Report 408, p. 5.

4. Ibid., pp. 5–6.

5. Lovejoy, *Shadow of the Coal Breaker*, p. 14.

6. Ibid., p. 6.

7. Anthracite Coal Strike Commission, *Report to the President on the Anthracite Coal Strike*, p. 40.

8. "No colliery has been visited in which children have not been found employed at ages prohibited by the law of the state. Lovejoy, *Child Labor in the Coal Mines*. Independently, Peter Roberts estimated nearly 18,000 breaker boys, a majority of whom were under fourteen. See Peter Roberts, *Anthracite Coal Communities*, p. 174.

9. Quoted on p. 36, Owen R. Lovejoy, *Extent of Child Labor*, NCLC Publication 045.

10. Foster Rhea Dulles and Melvyn Dubofsky, *Labor In America*, pp. 177–85.

11. Lovejoy, *Extent of Child Labor*, p. 35.

12. Ibid.

13. On Sunday, Hine had been visiting with the boys around their homes. "On Sunday, January 8th, I found a number of very young boys around their homes and got their photos, names, and addresses. These were mostly Breaker-boys, working in the Ewen Breaker of the Pennsylvania Co., at Port Griffeth, South Pittston. Several of them admitted twelve years of age, others insisted they were fourteen, but I was sure they all overstated their ages, as they were very suspicious of my motives. Two of those who said 12 years old, also said they had been working, one for six months, and one for a year at the Breaker. One who said 14 years old, said he had been working at Breaker for 3 years." Lewis W. Hine, NCLC Investigation Report 408, p. 2.

14. Edward Brown, NCLC Investigation Report 409, p. 6.

15. Florence Taylor, NCLC Investigation Report 410, p. 4.

16. Owen R. Lovejoy, *Child Labor in the Soft Coal Mines*, NCLC Publication 044. See also the only formal investigation report filed by Lovejoy, NCLC Investigation Report 422.

17. Edward N. Clopper, *Child Labor in West Virginia*, NCLC Publication 086.

18. Lovejoy, *Child Labor in the Coal Mines*.

19. Lovejoy, *Child Labor in the Soft Coal Mines*.

20. In anthracite, roughly only 20 percent of the mining families lived in company housing. See Roberts, *Anthracite Coal Communities*, p. 122.

21. Lovejoy, *Child Labor in the Soft Coal Mines*.

22. Ibid.

23. See Hugh Cunningham, *Children and Childhood in Western Society*; Carolyn Tuttle, *Hard at Work in Factories and Mines*.

24. Owen R. Lovejoy, "The Coal Mines of Pennsylvania," pp. 133–38.

25. Hine, NCLC Investigation Report 408, p. 4.

26. Ibid., pp. 4–5.

27. U.S. Children's Bureau, *Children in an Anthracite Coal-Mining District*, p. 9.

28. Lovejoy, *Shadow of the Coal Breaker*.

29. Clopper, *Child Labor in West Virginia*, NCLC Publication 086, p. 11.

30. Hine, NCLC Investigation Report 408, p. 3.

31. Ibid., p. 4.

32. Ibid., p. 6.

33. Brown, NCLC Investigation Report 409, p. 7.

34. Quoted in Roberts, *Anthracite Coal Communities*, pp. 349–50.

35. Hine, NCLC Investigation Report 408, p. 3.

36. Lovejoy, "The Coal Mines of Pennsylvania," pp. 136–37.

37. Brown, NCLC Investigation Report 409, p. 4.

38. Lovejoy, *Shadow of the Coal Breaker*, p. 5.

39. Lovejoy, *Child Labor in the Soft Coal Mines*.

40. Roberts, *Anthracite Coal Communities*, pp. 164–74.

41. Anthracite Coal Strike Commission. *Report to the President on the Anthracite Coal Strike*.

42. Lovejoy, *Shadow of the Coal Breaker*, quote on p. 12. "De gob" was the pile of debris, mostly dirt and slate, that lined the sides of the tunnels.

43. Lovejoy, *Child Labor in the Coal Mines*.

44. Ibid.

45. Ibid.

46. Ibid.

47. Lovejoy, *Shadow of the Coal Breaker*, p. 8.

48. Hine, NCLC Investigation Report 408, pp. 6–7.

49. Lovejoy, *Child Labor in the Coal Mines*, p. 36.

50. Lovejoy, "The Coal Mines of Pennsylvania," p. 134.

51. Lovejoy, *Child Labor in the Coal Mines*.

52. Brown, NCLC Investigation Report 409, p. 2.

53. Ibid.

54. Ibid., p. 10.

55. Hine, NCLC Investigation Report 408, p. 7.

56. Quoted in Brown, NCLC Investigation Report 409, p. 10.

57. Quoted in Hine, NCLC Investigation Report 408, p. 7.

58. Ibid., pp. 9–10.

59. Brown, NCLC Investigation Report 409, p. 11.

60. Hine, NCLC Investigation Report 408, p. 8.

61. Brown, NCLC Investigation Report 409, p. 13.

62. Taylor, NCLC Investigation Report 410, p. 4.

63. Ibid., p. 3.

64. Ibid., p. 5.

65. Ibid., p. 3.

66. Lovejoy, *Child Labor in the Soft Coal Mines*, pp. 28–30.

67. Ibid., p. 30.

68. Owen R. Lovejoy, NCLC Investigation Report 422, p. 1.

69. Ibid., p. 1.

70. Lovejoy, "The Coal Mines of Pennsylvania," p. 137.

71. Taylor, NCLC Investigation Report 410, pp. 3–5.

72. Ibid., pp. 3, 6.

73. Harry M. Bremer, NCLC Investigation Report 423, p. 2.

74. Ibid., p. 2.

75. U.S. Children's Bureau, *Children in an Anthracite Coal-Mining District* and *Children in a Bituminous Coal-Mining District.*

76. Charles E. Gibbons, *Child Labor in the Tiff Mines*, NCLC Publication 373.

77. Ibid., p. 8.

78. The NCLC report includes tables indicating that children in the tiff constitute a large portion of those not enrolled in school. Further, of those enrolled, tiff and related obligations caused a large proportion of absences.

Chapter 5

1. Upton Sinclair, *The Jungle*; Florence Kelley, *Some Ethical Gains Through Legislation.*

2. Owen R. Lovejoy, *Child Labor in the Glass Industry*, NCLC Publication 028.

3. Charles L. Chute, NCLC Investigation Report 314, p. 4.

4. In contrast to the bottle or blown-glass industry centered in East St. Louis, the NCLC conducted no investigations in the flat glass industry that centered around Toledo, Ohio. As Charles L. Chute noted in his investigation report, "Plants manufacturing window glass and other kinds of building glass . . . form a separate industry employing very few children." Ibid., p. 5.

5. Josephine Goldmark, *Impatient Crusader*, p. 41.

6. Harriet Van der Vaart, NCLC Investigation Report 310, pp. 23–28.

7. Harriet Van der Vaart, *Child Labor in the Glass Works of Illinois*, NCLC Publication 050.

8. Ibid., p. 6.

9. Van der Vaart, NCLC Investigation Report 310, p. 10.

10. Edgar T. Davies, "The Difficulties of a Factory Inspector," *Proceedings of the 3rd Annual Meeting of the National Child Labor Committee*, pp. 125–31.

11. Davies, "The Difficulties of a Factory Inspector."

12. For more on the Illinois Glass Company prosecutions and the tensions confronted by factory inspectors, see Daniel Nelson, *Managers and Workers*, pp. 132–39.

13. Van der Vaart, *Child Labor in the Glass Works of Illinois.*

14. Herschel H. Jones, NCLC Investigation Report 321, p. 8.

15. Chute, NCLC Investigation Report 314, p. 14.

16. U.S. Bureau of Labor, *Glass*, p. 83. See also Nelson, *Managers and Workers*, p. 20.

17. Chute, NCLC Investigation Report 314, p. 15.

18. Jones, NCLC Investigation Report 321, p. 20.

19. Anna Herdina's notes include these: "Man (blower) said boys struck regularly every Spring, but did not gain any raise by it, simply got 'Spring fever.'" "Boys went on strike for more pay this Fall but came back without getting a raise." Herdina, NCLC Investigation Report 311, pp. 5, 7.

20. Chute, NCLC Investigation Report 314, p. 13.

21. Ibid., p. 13.

22. Jones, NCLC Investigation Report 321, p. 9.

23. Lovejoy, *Child Labor in the Glass Industry.*

24. Interestingly, one factory that did not operate at night was the glass-blowers' cooperative at Marion, Indiana. "Manager Schofield stated that the men objected to night work 'unless necessary' and that they got along, filled orders and made a profit without night work." Chute, NCLC Investigation Report 314, p. 31.

25. Jones, NCLC Investigation Report 321, p. 15.

26. Chute, NCLC Investigation Report 314, p. 36.

27. Quoted in ibid., p. 37.

28. Ibid., pp. 37–38.

29. Jones, NCLC Investigation Report 321, p. 33.

30. Harriet B. Jones, MD, from Wheeling, quoted in Chute, NCLC Investigation Report 314, pp. 39–40.

31. Dr. J.E. Patterson, Washington, Pa., a physician of many years experience in a large glass manufacturing town, quoted in Jones, NCLC Investigation Report 321, p. 40.

32. A.D. Endsley, superintendent of public schools, Tarentum, Pa., quoted in ibid., p. 44.

33. Dr. J.F. Edwards, Bureau of Infectious Diseases, Department of Public Health, Pittsburgh, quoted in ibid., p. 41.

34. Ibid., p. 10.

35. Harry Braverman, *Labor and Monopoly Capital.*

36. Frank Tannenbaum, *A Philosophy of Labor*; Karl Polanyi, *The Great Transformation.*

37. See, for example, Clark Nardinelli, *Child Labor and the Industrial Revolution*; Rondo Cameron, *A Concise Economic History of the World.*

38. Chute, NCLC Investigation Report 314, pp. 16, 18.

39. Herdina, NCLC Investigation Report 311, pp. 28–29.

40. Chute, NCLC Investigation Report 314, pp. 16–18.

41. Jones, NCLC Investigation Report 321, p. 21.

42. Chute, NCLC Investigation Report 314, pp. 18, 21.

43. Jones, NCLC Investigation Report 321, p. 21.

44. Ibid., p. 24.

45. Herdina, NCLC Investigation Report 311, pp. 22–23.

46. Lewis W. Hine, NCLC Investigation Report 308, p. 3.

47. Lovejoy, *Child Labor in the Glass Industry.*

48. In the East St. Louis region, an official of the Illinois Glass Company acknowledged, "The difficulty in getting boys he admits is not due to the law chiefly. It is due to the limited number of boys here, the coming in of a number of other plants lately which takes away the older boys by offer of higher wages and to the dissatisfaction of the older boys because not given a chance to learn a trade. The

Union last year allowed no apprentices, this year very few (1 to 20 journeymen); said he had had a number of boys leave directly on this account." Herdina, NCLC Investigation Report 311, p. 25.

49. For more on employer response to the boy shortage problem, see Nelson, *Managers and Workers*, p. 89.

50. Herdina, NCLC Investigation Report 311, pp. 11, 21–22.

51. "Men (blowers) get $8.00 to $10.00 a day, while all boys young and old get only $1.00 except cracking-off, who get $1.25. Evident from talking with a number of men and boys that the real reason for shortage of boys here is because 'they don't pay enough.'" Ibid., p. 7.

52. Van der Vaart, NCLC Investigation Report 310, p. 21.

53. Herdina, NCLC Investigation Report 311, p. 28. Other illustrative reports include these: "No trouble getting the foreign men. Mr. P. said he didn't import them but some were here on the railroad and they passed the work along, 'probably sent word over to the old country that they had a good job for some relative and they came in.' Greeks good steady workers. Takes them some years to learn the language; some manufacturers won't bother with them on that account." Ibid., p. 31. "In these plants, as in other places, I have found a number of Greeks, Italians, and negroes. A bookkeeper in the Whitney Glass Co., as Glassboro, told me that on account of the law and the inspector the glass people were employing these people instead of boys, and my observations would bear him out." Hine, NCLC Investigation Report 308, p. 1.

54. Herdina, NCLC Investigation Report 311, p. 19.

55. Van der Vaart, NCLC Investigation Report 310, pp. 32–33.

56. Herdina, NCLC Investigation Report 311, p. 19.

57. Van der Vaart, NCLC Investigation Report 310, pp. 11–13. Similarly, Anna Herdina observed that "Fruit jars made by semi-automatic machines never had great need for younger boys." Herdina, NCLC Investigation Report 311, p. 30.

58. Herdina, NCLC Investigation Report 311, p. 1.

59. Jones, NCLC Investigation Report 321, p. 29.

60. Quoted in Lewis W. Hine, NCLC Investigation Report 304, pp. 1–2.

61. Herdina, NCLC Investigation Report 311, p. 24.

62. Jones, NCLC Investigation Report 321, p. 29.

63. "To facilitate the investigation the writer enrolled as a graduate student in Ohio State University and carried letters of introduction from its faculty." Chute, NCLC Investigation Report 314, p. 5.

64. He might also have acknowledged that, given its standing in the industry, the eleven Illinois plants visited represent an undersampling of Illinois glass factories.

65. "Assuming the same proportion of children employed in the 154 establishments not investigated, there were employed at the time of the investigation approximately 5,240 children under 16 in all plants in operation." Chute, NCLC Investigation Report 314, p. 20.

66. Chute's report does not permit a test of whether the difference was statistically significant.

67. Chute, NCLC Investigation Report 314, p. 44.

68. Ibid., p. 45.

69. Nonunion plants generally ran longer shifts. "The longest hours in any furnace room were found in the Federal Glass Company, Columbus, Ohio, where the shifts worked 10 hours day or night." Ibid., pp. 26–27.

70. Ibid., pp. 28–29.

71. Ibid., pp. 21–22.

72. Ibid., p. 52.

73. "You know the Law in Indiana allow boys to work at night, and only requires an affidavit from the Father, or Mother, to prove the child's age. The Glass Factories have their own Notaries; so the transaction is only between the employer and the parent." Van der Vaart, NCLC Investigation Report 310, p. 19.

74. Chute, NCLC Investigation Report 314, p. 52.

75. Ibid., pp. 57–58.

76. Herdina, NCLC Investigation Report 311, pp. 17–18.

77. Ibid., p. 24.

78. Ibid., p. 1.

79. According to Harriet Van der Vaart, the previous owners had encountered financial difficulties and the glassblowers had loaned them money. Shortly thereafter, the factory burned down, and the blowers got the site and what remained of the factory for their debt. They were able to raise funds to rebuild the plant and reopened as a producer cooperative. Van der Vaart, NCLC Investigation Report 310, p. 15.

80. "Mr. P.W. Schofield, the manager, said they avoided the small boy as much as possible. He needed too much watching and they did not consider him a profitable employee. I only saw three whom one would question as being under sixteen. They employed one hundred and fifty altogether." Ibid., p. 16.

81. Ibid., p. 32.

82. Ibid., pp. 22, 26–28.

83. Jones, NCLC Investigation Report 321, p. 35.

84. Van der Vaart, NCLC Investigation Report 310, pp. 26–28.

85. Ibid., pp. 16–17.

86. Ibid., p. 20.

Chapter 6

1. This is not to suggest that the NCLC did not investigate northern mills. Numerous investigations were conducted, but they were generally of a different character from those conducted in the South. Southern investigations were conducted for purposes of exposing and documenting conditions of child labor and were usually conducted on a larger scale than northern investigations. Northern investigations were most often conducted to obtain salient comparisons with conditions in southern mills or for the purpose of assessing the effects of various legislative proposals.

2. U.S. Bureau of Labor, *Cotton Textile Industry*, pp. 20–28.

3. Alexander J. McKelway, *Child Labor in the Southern Cotton Mills*, NCLC Publication 021.

4. See, for example, the address of Lewis W. Parker, one of the leading mill owners in South Carolina, to the NCLC annual meeting in Atlanta in 1908, in which he attempted to debunk Alexander McKelway's estimates. "Thus do the 62,000 estimated by Dr. McKelway dwindle to 9,000, or an exaggeration of seven to one," in Lewis W. Parker, "Compulsory Education, the Solution to the Child Labor Problem," *Proceedings of the Fourth Annual Meeting of the National Child Labor Committee.*

5. I present Harriman's theory here because it probably represents the enlightened northern stereotype about the South. Except for some of the condescending factual inaccuracies, the basic contours of the theory were embraced by the millmen themselves and their allies. See Parker, "Compulsory Education, the Solution to the Child Labor Problem"; see also Thomas R. Dawley, *The Child That Toileth Not.*

6. Mrs. J. Borden Harriman, "The Cotton Mill a Factor in the Development of the South," *Proceedings of the Sixth Annual Meeting of the National Child Labor Committee.*

7. Alexander J. McKelway, "The Mill or the Farm," *Proceedings of the Sixth Annual Meeting of the National Child Labor Committee.* This was a theme McKelway emphasized. For example: "It may be fairly said, therefore, that the South has acquired this system of child labor from New England just as New England learned it from Old England," McKelway, *Child Labor in Southern Industry,* NCLC Publication 012.

8. "Southern labor was so hard pressed at the time that the mill conditions were usually better than those on the farms. In spite of long hours and low wages, the growing industry brought relief." E.O. Smith and R.L. Nyman, "Effects of Technological Change on Occupational Structure," pp. 63–69.

9. Statement of a boardinghouse keeper, Lewis W. Hine, NCLC Investigation Report 302, p. 2.

10. Marie Hunter, NCLC Investigation Report 303, pp. 6–7.

11. Grover Hardin interview, quoted in Allen Tullos, *Habits of Industry,* pp. 267–68, 274.

12. Lewis W. Hine, NCLC Investigation Report 307, p. 1.

13. Elizabeth H. Davidson, *Child Labor Legislation in the Southern Textile States,* p. 110, citing North Carolina Bureau of Labor Statistics *Tenth Annual Report,* 1896, pp. 61–62.

14. Lewis W. Hine, NCLC Investigation Report 323, p. 2.

15. Herschel H. Jones, NCLC Investigation Report 411, pp. 9–10.

16. Harvey P. Vaughn, NCLC Investigation Report 320, p. 13.

17. George Z. Owen, NCLC Investigation Report 330, pp. 14–17.

18. See, for example, Vaughn, NCLC Investigation Report 320, pp. 26–27. One principal observed, "He thought the mill people encouraged dinner toting because in that way they trained the children to work. I learned from him and from other sources that children who carried dinner often took the place of the people whose dinners they carried."

19. Alfred E. Seddon, NCLC Investigation Report 301, p. 21.

20. Hine, NCLC Investigation Report 302, p. 1.

21. See, for example, Alexander M. Fleischer, NCLC Investigation Report 317, p. 6: "Prof. Lee, Principal of the School and in charge of the four upper grades (5th to 8th) has enrolled in his classes 24 children and in present attendance about 21. Practically all of these children are the sons and daughters of the foremen, managers, and superintendent of the mill, practically no mill hands being represented."

22. Captain Ellyson A. Smyth of the Pelzer Mills was quoted in Alexander J. McKelway, *Child Labor in the Carolinas,* NCLC Publication 092. While very few children were found working regularly as weavers, many occasionally tended their parent's looms helping for short periods under close parental supervision.

23. Quoted in Victoria Byerly, *Hard Times Cotton Mill Girls,* p. 65.

24. Lewis W. Hine, NCLC Investigation Report 315, p. 4.

25. Samuel B. Platt, superintendent at the Sibley Manufacturing Company in Augusta, to Lewis Hine. Reported in Vaughn, NCLC Investigation Report 320, p. 7.

26. Quoted in Byerly, *Hard Times Cotton Mill Girls*, p. 65.

27. McKelway cited two examples. First, "A witness described to us an instrument for whipping children at a factory in Rhode Island, consisting of a leather strap eighteen inches long, with tacks driven through the striking end." Second, from an 1870 report of the Bureau of Labor, an "overlooker" with seven years' experience explained, "Six years ago I ran night work from 6.45 P.M. to 6 A.M., with 45 minutes for meals, eating in the room. Children were drowsy and sleepy, having known them to fall asleep standing up at their work. I have had to sprinkle water to awaken them after having spoken to them until hoarse. This was done gently, with no intention of hurting them." Cited in Alexander J. McKelway, *The Cotton Mill: The Herod Among Industries*, NCLC Publication 162.

28. Paul Cline interview, quoted in Tullos, *Habits of Industry*, p. 9.

29. Seddon, NCLC Investigation Reports 301 and 305.

30. Quoted in McKelway, *Child Labor in the Carolinas*, NCLC Publication 092, p. 6.

31. Ibid., p. 11.

32. Hine, NCLC Investigation Report 315, p. 1.

33. Ibid., p. 3.

34. Ibid., p. 6.

35. Alfred E. Seddon, "The Education of the Mill Children in the South." *Proceedings of the Fourth Annual Meeting of the National Child Labor Committee*; also cited in McKelway, *Child Labor in the Carolinas*, NCLC Publication 092.

36. Vaughn, NCLC Investigation Report 320, pp. 24–25.

37. Alexander J. McKelway, *Child Labor in Georgia*, NCLC Publication 194, p. 26.

38. Davidson, *Child Labor Legislation*, p. 216.

39. Hine, NCLC Investigation Report 307, pp. 1–2.

40. Fleischer, NCLC Investigation Report 317, p. 2.

41. Herschel H. Jones, NCLC Investigation Report 412, p. 33.

42. Seddon, NCLC Investigation Report 305, p. 1.

43. Ibid., p. 2.

44. Even though he never got to visit the mill, Seddon did have an extended interview with the mill's top brass, and he obtained some valuable information. Superintendent Towers reported 339 hands, 70 under sixteen and 20 between twelve and fourteen. Seddon mentioned seeing a number of very small children, some of whom were surely under twelve. "Mr. John Porter, the General Manager, said that these were children of widows or invalid fathers, or else 'little kids' whose mothers had taken them into the factory as the best way to keep them out of mischief." Ibid., pp. 2–3.

45. Edgar Gardner Murphy, *Problems of the Present South*; Davidson, *Child Labor Legislation*.

46. Explanation and quotes found in Hine's 1913 report of his investigation in Massachusetts, NCLC Investigation Report 319, pp. 3–4.

47. Lewis W. Hine, NCLC Investigation Report 325, pp. 3–4.

48. Lewis W. Hine, NCLC Investigation Report 318, pp. 1–3. Hine continues, "I cannot understand how it is that directors, superintendents and other interested

parties with ordinary eyes in their heads can see these tiny, immature children coming and going four times a day, and then say they do not have violations of the law. One little chap of eight years (according to the School Record) gravely passes for twelve years, because his parents say he is twelve. One glimpse of his tiny figure and immature face refutes that assertion, but as it is in the case of a dozen others right here, it is easier to wink at the thing because the children are needed" (p. 4).

49. Ibid., p. 5.

50. Seddon, NCLC Investigation Report 301, p. 9. Investigator Seddon continues, "The system of employing children of tender years serves as a premium to wife desertion. There is an unusually large number of deserted wives with children working in all the factories. The wife deserter as well as the lazy loafing father often escapes the punishment due to him, because of the ease by which those dependent upon him can be kept from starvation by flying for the refuge of the mills" (pp. 26–27).

51. Ibid., p. 17.

52. Ibid., p. 11, and Jones, NCLC Investigation Report 411, p. 1.

53. Seddon, NCLC Investigation Report 301, p. 11. Similarly, Seddon met the overseer of the spinning room of the Meridian Cotton Mill. "Mr. Neil Grayson overseer of the spinning room pointed out 6 boys and 8 girls who did not come into the mill until after they were 12 yrs of age, who are doing better work than children who had been longer in the mill and who came in at an earlier age."

54. Hine "found, in the spinning room, with 50 hands, ten under 14, six of these doffers and helpers I judged to be under 12,—one of these said seven years and one said nine." Hine, NCLC Invstigation Report 302, pp. 9, 11.

55. Jones, NCLC Investigation Report 411, pp. 2–3.

56. Fleischer, NCLC Investigation Report 317, p. 2, and Jones, NCLC Investigation Report 412, p. 33.

57. Fleischer, NCLC Investigation Report 317, pp. 3, 5.

58. Jones, NCLC Investigation Report 412, pp. 32–33.

59. Jones, NCLC Investigation Report 411, p. 15.

60. Seddon, NCLC Investigation Report 301, p. 25. Seddon tested the literacy of twenty-four of the Laurel Mill's workers under fourteen and found twenty to be illiterate.

61. Jones, NCLC Investigation Report 411, pp. 26–30.

62. Lewis W. Hine, NCLC Investigation Report 327.

63. Quoted in Parker, "Compulsory Education, the Solution to the Child Labor Problem," *Proceedings of the Fourth Annual Meeting of the National Child Labor Committee*, p. 46.

64. John Porter Hollis, *Child Labor Legislation in the Carolinas*, NCLC Publication 159.

65. The county was also home to the famous Loray Mill strike of 1929, about which much has been written. See Irving Bernstein, *The Lean Years: A History of the American Worker, 1920–1955*; William F. Dunne, *Gastonia, Citadel of the Class Struggle in the New South*; Liston Pope, *Millhands and Preachers: A Study of Gastonia*; John A. Salmond, *Gastonia, 1929: The Story of the Loray Mill Strike*; Tom Tippett, *When Southern Labor Stirs*. For compelling accounts of these same events in novels, see Grace Lumpkin, *To Make My Bread*, and Mary Heaton Vorse, *Strike*.

66. Pope, *Millhands and Preachers*, p. 195.

67. Wiley H. Swift, *The Child That Toileth Not: A Reply to Mr. Dawley*, NCLC Publication 186.

68. Yates Snowden, *History of South Carolina*, pp. 407–22.

69. Seddon, NCLC Investigation Report 301.

70. See Davidson, *Child Labor Legislation*, pp. 275–78.

71. Under the prevailing political system of "one-party white man's rule," a false bargain was struck "based on a false consensus between Mr. Rich White Man and Mr. Poor White Man over the division of available 'public work' (wage labor), excluded black workers from operating the machinery of the new cotton mills and tobacco factories." Lillian Smith, *Killers of the Dream*, pp. 154–69. See also John Gaventa, *Power and Powerlessness*, pp. 29–30.

72. See, for example, Hunter, NCLC Investigation Report 303, p. 3: "Man taking me through said negro children couldn't be worked because the hum of the machinery put them to sleep."

73. See Vaughn, NCLC Investigation Report 320, p. 2, and Lewis W. Hine, NCLC Investigation Report 419, p. 20, respectively. The NCLC also received reports of two mills in Fayetteville, North Carolina, that employed blacks for inside work.

74. Hine, NCLC Investigation Report 307, p. 3.

75. Ibid., p. 4.

76. See Alexander J. McKelway, *The Child Labor Problem—A Study in Degeneracy*, NCLC Publication 022. For the views of enlightened mill men, see the 1907 statement of the South Carolina Cotton Manufacturers Association: "There are already more negro children than whites enrolled in the public schools of our State—the percentage of attendance of the negro children is larger. How much longer will the senseless fear of forcing the negroes into school deter us from requiring an acceptance by the children of illiterate whites of the opportunities of learning which our public school system offers?" Quoted in Parker, "Compulsory Education, the Solution to the Child Labor Problem," *Proceedings of the Fourth Annual Meeting of the National Child Labor Committee*, p. 45.

77. Jean Gordon, *Why the Children Are in the Factory*, NCLC Publication 076.

78. Seddon, NCLC Investigation Report 301, p. 3.

79. Pope, *Millhands and Preachers*, p. 197.

80. Seddon, NCLC Investigation Report 305, p. 9.

81. Herschel H. Jones, NCLC Investigation Report 335, p. 3.

82. McKelway, *Child Labor in Southern Industry*, NCLC Publication 012.

83. Consider, for example, "The southern textile states were much slower to act." Nelson, *Managers and Workers*, p. 126.

Chapter 7

1. Quoted in Mary Van Kleeck, *Child Labor in Home Industries*, NCLC Publication 134. Similarly see A. Benedict's investigation in Jersey City: "Anna [age 13] tells me that she works steadily after school and until 11:30 or so at night. I asked her when she played. She replied 'Never.'" A. Benedict, NCLC Investigation Report 432, p. 5.

2. "The roots of the sweatshop can be found in the home." Leon Stein, *Out of the Sweatshop*, p. 3.

3. "There was no standardization of prices or wages or shop conditions. It was an industrial jungle." Benjamin Stolberg, *Tailor's Progress*, p. 10.

4. This is not to suggest that homework was not prevalent in other industries. It was common, for example, in many early processing phases of agriculture (nut picking, tobacco stripping, bean snapping, etc.).

5. George A. Hall, *What the Government Says About Child Labor in Tenements*, NCLC Publication 151.

6. NCLC, *Who Made What You Buy?* NCLC Publication 252.

7. John R. Commons, *Report of the U.S. Industrial Commission*. Also cited in Stein, *Out of the Sweatshop*, p. 45. NCLC investigators "[r]eport an intense dislike, distrust and fear of these contractors on the part of the workers. . . . One of our workers was told by an elevator man in a building that women would come with great boxes of work and depart weeping at the small amount of wages they received. Nearly all the workers state that the contractor receives from the manufacturer twice as much as they are paid. 'He makes 50 percent.' " Another homeworker "stated that she thought the contractors were very lucky—'all one needed was enough cash to make a deposit on the work taken out, then put an ad in the paper for home workers, make $6.00 a day without any labor, or give it out to the neighbors and make 50 percent profit.' " NCLC Investigation Report 421, p. 7.

8. Jeremy P. Felt, *Hostages of Fortune*, p. 141.

9. Homework was considered by many to be "a godsend to the poor widow." Hall, *What the Government Says About Child Labor in Tenements*, NCLC Publication 151.

10. Florence Kelley, *Some Ethical Gains Through Legislation*. See also Felt, *Hostages of Fortune*, pp. 6–7.

11. The Charities Building was home to a number of prominent organizations including the NCLC, the New York Child Labor Committee, the National Consumers League, the Charitable Organization Society, and the Southern Education Board. The building also housed important publications, including *Outlook* and *Charities* (which would later become *Survey Graphic*). In addition, the building housed several local (New York City) charitable and social service organizations. Josephine Goldmark, *Impatient Crusader: Florence Kelley's Life Story*, pp. 68–69.

12. NCLC Investigation Report 328, p. 1.

13. Ibid., p. 2.

14. NCLC, *Child Workers in the Tenements*, NCLC Publication 181, p. 42.

15. Owen R. Lovejoy, NCLC Investigation Report 403, p. 1.

16. Ibid., pp. 1, 12.

17. Ibid., p. 8.

18. In the meetings leading to the protocol, two groups of employers were represented: the manufacturers and the jobbers, or contractors. The manufacturers clearly exerted the greater influence, and it appears that the jobbers only reluctantly accepted the principles of the protocol. Stein, *Out of the Sweatshop*, pp. 102–125.

19. Felt, *Hostages of Fortune*, pp. 146–50.

20. Alan Howard, "Labor, History, and Sweatshops," pp. 151–73.

21. Van Kleeck, *Child Labor in Home Industries*, NCLC Publication 134.

22. A. Benedict, NCLC Investigation Report 430, p. 2.

23. A. Benedict, NCLC Investigation Report 424, p. 1.

24. Ibid., pp. 9–10.

25. Benedict, NCLC Investigation Report 432, p. 4.

26. NCLC Investigation Report 421, p. 21.

27. Ibid., pp. 3–4.

28. Ibid., pp. 1–2.

29. Ibid., p. 4.

30. Ibid., pp. 22–23.

31. Van Kleeck, *Child Labor in Home Industries*, NCLC Publication 134.

32. Robert Hunter, *Poverty*, p. 238.

33. Scholars, too, have come to this same conclusion. "The historical evidence on tenement homework indicated the futility of regulatory measures and demonstrated that complete prohibition was the only answer." Felt, *Hostages of Fortune*, p. 153.

34. Lovejoy, NCLC Investigation Report 403, p. 4.

35. Ibid., p. 11.

36. Commons, *Report of the U.S. Industrial Commission*, p. xxxi.

37. Goldmark, *Impatient Crusader*, pp. 128–31.

38. Similarly, a study in men's clothing in four states found that, of 2,301 homeworkers employed by forty-eight firms before the NRA, 2,153 remained employed during the NRA. U.S. Children's Bureau, *Prohibition of Industrial Homework in Selected Industries*, p. 12.

39. *In re Jacobs*, 98 N.Y. 98 (1885); cited and discussed in Felt, *Hostages of Fortune*, p. 145.

40. Samuel Gompers, *Seventy Years of Life and Labour*, vol. 1, p. 189.

41. Attorney Roscoe Conkling, retained by Adolph Strasser for the union, failed to appear in court for oral arguments. Felt, *Hostages of Fortune*, pp. 10–13.

42. Cited in Felt, *Hostages of Fortune*, pp. 12–13.

43. Jacob A. Riis, *How the Other Half Lives*; Charles Booth, *Labour and Life of the People in London*.

44. Hunter, *Poverty*, p. 344. In the years around 1900, approximately 150,000 people died of tuberculosis each year in America. One-third of them were between the ages of fifteen and thirty-five.

45. The NCLC and others attempted to emphasize unsanitary conditions when they found them in their investigations. For example, "Demora, 357 Railroad Avenue, Jersey City . . . 7 children. The oldest claims to be 15 but looks younger. . . . These rooms were horribly dirty. . . . The school nurse states that the children are sent home daily because of dirt and vermin. The settlement worker states that previously this family lived in the same tenement with a family that had tuberculosis while living in this tenement. The worker assures me that the Demoras were working, and that there were children in both families. . . . Even a child of 7 was embroidering about 8:30 in the morning when I called." Benedict, NCLC Investigation Report 432, p. 6.

46. In 1908 9,805 were licensed; 11,162 in 1909; and 13,195 in 1911. Van Kleeck, *Child Labor in Home Industries*, NCLC Publication 134; George Hall, *Unrestricted Forms of Child Labor in New York State*, NCLC Publication 168.

47. For example, "Paresi, 94 Brunswick St., Jersey City . . . 4 children. Ages 12 and 8 and two younger. . . . The school nurse states that Antoinette has complained a great deal of headache, and has recently been fitted with glasses by the oculist. . . . Her little brother Pete can embroider very well but has not been doing this recently.

His sister told me Pete said 'Antoinette I can't work, my eyes hurt.'" Benedict, NCLC Investigation Report 432, p. 5.

48. Van Kleeck, *Child Labor in Home Industries*, NCLC Publication 134.

49. Felt, *Hostages of Fortune*, p. 141.

50. Stolberg, *Tailor's Progress*, pp. 79–80.

51. Felt, *Hostages of Fortune*; Goldmark, *Impatient Crusader*; Howard, "Labor, History, and Sweatshops"; Stein, *Out of the Sweatshop*; Stolberg, *Tailor's Progress*.

52. Goldmark, *Impatient Crusader*, pp. 56, 61–64.

Chapter 8

1. For accounts of child labor in the department stores, see Jeremy P. Felt, *Hostages of Fortune*; or Florence Kelley, *Some Ethical Gains Through Legislation*.

2. Edward F. Brown, NCLC Investigation Report 426, pp. 1–8.

3. Harry M. Bremer, NCLC Investigation Report 416, p. 1.

4. Brown, NCLC Investigation Report 426, pp. 10–11.

5. Ibid., p. 11.

6. Quoted in ibid., p. 11.

7. Harry M. Bremer, NCLC Investigation Report 433, p. 5.

8. Quoted in Herschel H. Jones, NCLC Investigation Report 427, pp. 2–3.

9. Brown, NCLC Investigation Report 426, p. 16.

10. Ibid., pp. 10–11.

11. Quoted in Harry M. Bremer, NCLC Investigation Report 420, p. 3.

12. Quoted in Jones, NCLC Investigation Report 427, p. 4. A more lurid account of the "show" in a Pittsburgh brothel where the women "will exhibit the most depraved forms of sexual perversion" is provided in the first report of Edward F. Brown: "A messenger boy has described to me such a 'show,' as it is called, in one of the largest 'Dollar Houses' in Pittsburgh. . . . The show opened with a suggestive dance by several naked girls, after which they successively performed the act of cunnilingus upon each other. A girl reclined in such a manner as to expose her genital organs to the audience, then placed a lighted cigarette within the orifice, and, by working her stomach up and down succeeded in smoking the cigarette in that fashion. Another girl had sexual intercourse with a dog. Another balanced herself on her back and shoulders after the manner of an acrobat and caught tossed coins in her vagina. . . . (T)he exhibition continued about half an hour." Brown, NCLC Investigation Report no. 426, p. 24.

13. Ibid., p. 13.

14. Ibid.

15. Ibid., pp. 22–23.

16. Quoted in Owen R. Lovejoy, *Child Labor and the Night Messenger Service*, NCLC Publication 141, p. 9.

17. Quoted in Brown, NCLC Investigation Report 426, p. 11.

18. Lovejoy, *Child Labor and the Night Messenger Service*, NCLC Publication 141, p. 11.

19. Bremer, NCLC Investigation Report 433, p. 3.

20. Ibid., p. 2.

21. Ibid., pp. 4–5.

22. Ibid.

23. Brown, NCLC Investigation Report 426, pp. 17–18.

24. Edward N. Clopper, *The Child Merchants of the Streets*, NCLC Publication 203. Clopper was longtime NCLC secretary for the northern states. He held a Ph.D. from the University of Cincinnati, and the street trades was his major area of expertise. His book, *Child Labor in the City Streets*, was his Ph.D. thesis and was based, in part, on work he performed for the NCLC.

25. Hine is quoted in Alexander J. McKelway, *Child Labor at the National Capital*, NCLC Publication 213, p. 10.

26. Herschel H. Jones, *Unregulated Street Trading in a Typical City*, NCLC Publication 264, p. 3.

27. For example, "John Linfante, 13 years old, sells till 11 p.m. and earns 60 cents a week between 8 p.m. and 11 p.m. With three or four other boys he sells during the rush, then goes to the movies, and comes out in time to buy out boys who sell cheap in order to get home early. 'This is where we make our money,' he said." Harry M. Bremer, NCLC Investigation Report 407, p. 10.

28. "When asked about the per centage of their earnings that came through tips two-thirds of the boys between 10 and 13 inclusive said they got very little, two or three cents a day. The other third, 32 boys, averaged about a dollar a week. On holidays and special occasions the boys receive large sums as tips, but generally a customer pays only what the paper is worth. The boys who sell to the late crowd, either to the business man detained at his office, or to the pleasure seeker, receive the tips. . . . The largest tips were made by the boys who sell latest." Ibid., pp. 13–14.

29. Hine is quoted in McKelway, *Child Labor at the National Capital*, NCLC Publication 264, pp. 10–11.

30. Edward N. Clopper, "Children on the Streets of Cincinnati," *Proceedings of the Fourth Annual Meeting of the NCLC*.

31. "The boys of 10 and 11 years old earned about a dollar less per week than the boys of 12 and 13 years. . . . This bears out the statement of many of the older newsboys to the effect that the 'kids' don't make much, and is in accord with the findings of other investigations." Bremer, NCLC Investigation Report 407, pp. 8–10.

32. A 21-year-old who had been selling papers for several years at the ferry in Jersey City complained that the work was harder than in earlier years. "He said that there were too many boys now so that none of them can make very much." Harry M. Bremer, NCLC Investigation Report 418, p. 10.

33. Newsstands were clearly an intermediate stage between street selling by newsboys and the vending boxes. Street selling and vending boxes could not have coexisted for fairly obvious reasons—for the price of one paper the boy could both replenish his supply and eliminate his competition.

34. Hine's 1916 report on Vermont street trades includes this note from Bennington: "Mr. F.E. Howe, Editor of the Banner said that about 30 children from 8 to 16 yrs old deliver & sell papers here, for a couple of hours after school. Only a few girls, but he would like to have more as he thinks they are more honest than the boys generally." Lewis W. Hine, NCLC Investigation Report 434, p. 3.

35. Bremer, NCLC Investigation Report 407, p. 21.

36. Bremer, NCLC Investigation Report 418, p. 11.

37. Bremer, NCLC Investigation Report 407, pp. 21–22.

38. Ibid., p. 14.

39. Ibid., pp. 15, 17–18.

40. Bremer, NCLC Investigation Report 418, pp. 15–16, 32.

41. Ibid., p. 5.

42. "Boys who do this are not newsboys even though they have papers under their arms. Knowing they should not be on the street, and that would arouse suspicion if they dodged in and out of the crowd around the theatre entrance they provide themselves with papers as a license to be there. . . . [I]n front of the Republic Theatre on West 42nd Street, I saw three boys between the ages of 11 and 13. One had two papers, another had one, and the third had none. I bought the paper from the boy who had only one and in answer to my question he said he would now go home. . . . A half hour later, at 11:15 p.m. I returned to this spot and mixed with the crowd leaving the theatre. As I had anticipated the three boys were on the job dodging in and out of the crowd looking for opportunities to do something that would procure tips. The boy from whom I had bought the last paper, and who had said he would go home, had procured another 'last' paper." Bremer, NCLC Investigation Report 407, pp. 27–28.

43. Ibid., p. 13.

44. "The chief probation officer testifies that several of the newsboys are professional 'dips'—they can pick a man's pocket in broad daylight without his knowing it." Jones, *Unregulated Street Trading in a Typical City*, NCLC Publication 264, p. 3.

45. Edward N. Clopper, *Street Work and Juvenile Delinquency*, NCLC Publication 221.

46. U.S. Bureau of Labor. 1910–1913. *Report on the Condition of Woman and Child Wage Earners in the United States*, vol. 8.

47. Harry M. Bremer, NCLC Investigation Report 402, p. 1.

48. Edward N. Clopper, *Street Trades Regulation*, NCLC Publication 272.

49. Felt, *Hostages of Fortune*, pp. 158–64.

50. Bremer, NCLC Investigation Report 418, p. 3.

51. Bremer, NCLC Investigation Report 407, p. 21.

52. Bremer, NCLC Investigation Report 418, p. 19.

53. Felt, *Hostages of Fortune*, p. 160.

54. Myron E. Adams, "Children in the American Street Trades," *Proceedings of the First Annual Meeting of the National Child Labor Committee*, p. 27.

55. Clopper, *Street Trades Regulation*, NCLC Publication 272, pp. 2–3.

56. Jones, *Unregulated Street Trading in a Typical City*, NCLC Publication 264, p. 5.

57. Bremer, NCLC Investigation Report 407, pp. 25–27.

58. Bremer, NCLC Investigation Report 402, p. 2.

59. Helen C. Dwight, NCLC Investigation Report 429, pp. 2–4.

60. Quoted from pamphlet included with Dwight, NCLC Investigation Report 429.

61. Ibid.

62. Ibid.

63. Ibid.

64. Ibid.

65. Clopper, *Street Trades Regulation*, NCLC Publication 272, pp. 6–7.

66. Ibid., p. 2.

Chapter 9

1. Lewis W. Hine, NCLC Investigation Report 216, p. 2.

2. For examples, see Edward N. Clopper and Lewis W. Hine, *Child Labor in the Sugar-Beet Fields of Colorado*, NCLC Publication 259; Walter W. Armentrout,

Sara A. Brown, and Charles E. Gibbons, *Child Labor in the Sugar Beet Fields of Michigan*, NCLC Publication 310; Sara A. Brown and Robie O. Sargent, *Children Working in the Sugar Beet Fields of the North Platte Valley of Nebraska*, NCLC Publication 318.

3. For example, see Edward N. Clopper, *Farmwork and Schools in Kentucky*, NCLC Publication 274.

4. For example, see Edward N. Clopper, *Causes of Absence from Rural Schools in Oklahoma*, NCLC Publication 281; Charles E. Gibbons, *Child Labor Among Cotton Growers of Texas*, NCLC Publication 324; Kate Clugston, *Cotton or School*, NCLC Publication 387.

5. For example, see Emma Duke, *California the Golden*, NCLC Publication 304; George B. Mangold and Lillian B. Hill, *Migratory Child Workers*, NCLC Publication 354; James E. Sidel, *Pick for Your Supper*, NCLC Publication 378.

6. Lewis W. Hine, "Baltimore to Biloxi and Back," in *The Child's Burden in Oyster and Shrimp Canneries*, NCLC Publication 193, p. 12.

7. Edward F. Brown, NCLC Investigation Report 205, p. 8.

8. See ibid., p. 3, and Harry M. Bremer, NCLC Investigation Report 207, p. 3.

9. Quoted in Lewis W. Hine and Edward F. Brown, *The Child's Burden in Oyster and Shrimp Canneries*, NCLC Publication 193, p. 31.

10. Bremer, NCLC Investigation Report 207, p. 4.

11. Edith Knowles, NCLC Investigation Report 219, p. 16.

12. Compiled from Brown, NCLC Investigation Report 205, pp. 5–7.

13. Hine, NCLC Investigation Report 216, p. 4.

14. Ibid., pp. 5–6.

15. Brown, NCLC Investigation Report 205, p. 17.

16. Ibid., pp. 9–10.

17. Ibid., p. 11.

18. Children were counted as "picking" if they were picking (or carrying) at the time Edward F. Brown observed them. This, in contrast to the measure taken in later investigations—"picking steady"—which meant they were observed picking (or carrying) for an extended period of time. Ages were those reported by the workers themselves, not Brown's estimates.

19. Plausible yet speculative explanations would include: older children remaining home in the cities; older children working in processing as opposed to the harvest; families with younger children being drawn into picking; or, more artifactually, maybe investigator Brown was more likely to inquire about the ages of the younger looking children.

20. Owen R. Lovejoy, NCLC Investigation Report 213, pp. 2, 12. Note that Report 213 is not a true investigation report. Lovejoy undertook no fieldwork. This folder collects correspondence between him and industry representatives.

21. Ibid., pp. 19–20.

22. Cranberries could not be picked until the dew was off, so while 7 A.M. may have been the desired starting time, picking often did not commence until 9 or 10 in the morning.

23. Lovejoy, NCLC Investigation Report 213, pp. 23, 25–26.

24. Investigator Brown noted, "Special mention should be made of White's, because of the large scale on which they do business. Gus Donato, the chief padrone on White's Bog estimates that there are nine hundred and ninety seven pickers actu-

ally working on the marsh. Miss Lizzie White estimates that there are nine hundred, four hundred of whom are children. These nine hundred people are housed in seventeen shacks, an average of fifty two people to a house. Seven pickers' shanties constitute the 'Province of Rome,' and seven more the 'Province of Florence.' There is another colony called Naples. . . . On this bog three hundred and forty seven children from Philadelphia, between three and fourteen years were found picking four weeks after school had reopened." Brown, NCLC Investigation Report 205, pp. 25–26.

25. Louise Boswell and Lewis W. Hine, NCLC Investigation Report 218, p. 71. Hine commented, "Miss Elizabeth White was on the bog all the time I was there, (although she did not notice me fortunately), and I cannot see how she can avoid the realization of the fact that, even on their high-grade bogs and after five years of agitation on our part, children are picking much too young, for a long day in the hot sun, and some are being overworked at all times carrying the berries for long distances and under conditions that are difficult for children."

26. Compiled from Charles L. Chute, NCLC Investigation Report 204, pp. 1, 7.

27. Ibid., p. 6.

28. Testimony included in Harry M. Bremer, NCLC Investigation Report 211, p. 22.

29. Boswell and Hine, NCLC Investigation Report 218, pp. 5–6.

30. "One child of 33 months was on its knees by father, who proudly showed her off. She was picking a few berries into her apron. Father said she could 'do a little.'" Ibid., pp. 2–3, 35.

31. Ibid., pp. 4, 35.

32. Knowles, NCLC Investigation Report 219, p. 28.

33. Ibid., p. 5.

34. Boswell and Hine, NCLC Investigation Report 218, p. 6.

35. Hine, "Baltimore to Biloxi and Back," in *The Child's Burden in Oyster and Shrimp Canneries*, NCLC Publication 193, p. 13.

36. Ibid., p. 10.

37. Lewis W. Hine, *Child Labor in Gulf Coast Canneries*, NCLC Publication 158.

38. "The mother of three-year-old Alma told me proudly, 'Yes, I'm learnin' her de trade.'" Ibid.

39. Edward F. Brown, NCLC Investigation Report no 206, pp. 3, 9.

40. Ibid., pp. 4, 5.

41. Edward F. Brown, "The Toiling Children of the Gulf Coast Canneries," in *The Child's Burden in Oyster and Shrimp Canneries*, NCLC Publication 193, p. 25.

42. Harry M. Bremer, NCLC Investigation Report 212, pp. 2–3.

43. Brown, NCLC Investigation Report 206, p. 14.

44. NCLC Investigation Report 203. Report 203 is not a true investigation report, but rather several notarized affidavits submitted by E.G. Newmann, inspector and secretary of the Oysterman's Protective Association, and John W. Bishop, a wholesaler with the Union Fish Company.

45. Ibid.

46. Ibid.

47. Quoted in Brown, NCLC Investigation Report 206, p. 15.

48. Quoted in ibid., p. 8.

49. Lewis W. Hine, *Child Labor in Gulf Coast Canneries*, NCLC Publication 158.

50. Quoted in Brown, NCLC Investigation Report 206, p. 11.

51. Quoted in ibid., p. 13.

52. Quoted in Alexander J. McKelway, *Child Labor in Mississippi*, NCLC Publication 169, p. 18.

53. Ibid.

54. Brown, "The Toiling Children of the Gulf Coast Canneries," pp. 24–25, 28.

55. Herschel H. Jones, NCLC Investigation Report 214, pp. 5–6.

56. Lewis W. Hine, NCLC Investigation Report 415, p. 1.

57. Ibid., p. 3.

58. The term "padrone" generally refers to labor recruiters, agents, contractors, or bosses of eastern or southern European origin. But the role played by the labor contractor, regardless of ethnic origin and regardless of the specific title given the contractor, is essentially that of the padrone. The labor contractor is usually of the same ethnic background as the workers he recruits.

59. Brown, NCLC Investigation Report 205, pp. 1–2.

60. Chute, NCLC Investigation Report 204, p. 3.

61. Quoted in Lovejoy, NCLC Investigation Report 213, p. 20.

62. Brown, NCLC Investigation Report 205, pp. 2–3.

63. Chute, NCLC Investigation Report 204, p. 4.

64. Brown, NCLC Investigation Report 205, p. 2.

65. Chute, NCLC Investigation Report 204, pp. 3–4.

66. Ibid., p. 5.

67. This is my own estimate of the upper limit on kickbacks. It is based on a combination of investigator Brown's report that the "present ranges in amounts from one to twenty dollars" (Brown, NCLC Investigation Report 205, p. 15) coupled with estimates of total earnings reported in various publications.

68. Quoted in Brown, NCLC Investigation Report 205, p. 16.

69. Chute, NCLC Investigation Report 204, p. 4.

70. Brown, NCLC Investigation Report 205, p. 12.

71. Sidel, *Pick for Your Supper*, NCLC Publication 378.

72. "At the end of the season the pickers turn over to the padrone the checks they received as evidence of the number of pecks picked. These the padrone delivers to the grower who cashes them delivering the cash to the padrone. The padrone then pays his following." Brown, NCLC Investigation Report 205, p. 15.

73. "The method of paying for work is such that the child does not participate in the returns. The paste-board checks received as evidence of the work go to the head of the family who cashes them in." Hine, NCLC Investigation Report 216, p. 4.

74. Quoted in Brown, NCLC Investigation Report 206, p. 5.

75. Brown, NCLC Investigation Report 205, p. 3.

76. Chute, NCLC Investigation Report 204, pp. 5–6.

77. Bremer, NCLC Investigation Report 212, p. 2.

78. Brown, NCLC Investigation Report 205, p. 16.

79. Hine, NCLC Investigation Report 216, p. 4.

80. Quoted in Lovejoy, NCLC Investigation Report 213, p. 24.

81. Hine, *Child Labor in Gulf Coast Canneries*, NCLC Publication 158.

82. Unfortunately, investigation reports in other agricultural and food-processing sectors make no mention of this phenomenon, so we can draw no conclusions about how widespread this practice might have been at the time in places beyond cranberry bogs.

83. Chute, NCLC Investigation Report 204, pp. 7–9.

84. Investigator Brown estimated the impact of large pecks on picker earnings. The total 1910 yield in New Jersey was 600,000 bushels, but pickers were paid only for about 450,000. At the going rate of about 50 cents per bushel, pickers were cheated out of roughly $75,000 for the season. Brown, NCLC Investigation Report 205, pp. 12–14.

85. Hine, NCLC Investigation Report 216, p. 5.

86. Chute, NCLC Investigation Report 204, pp. 10–11.

87. Bremer, NCLC Investigation Report 207, pp. 12–13.

88. Quoted in Brown, NCLC Investigation Report 205, p. 25.

89. Bremer, NCLC Investigation Report 207, pp. 5–12.

90. In 1911, Chute observed, "The housing conditions, though improved since last year by more care on the part of growers and by less crowding consequent to a smaller number of pickers, are in the main unspeakably bad still." Chute, NCLC Investigation Report 204, p. 10. In 1913, Bremer reported less crowding (in part due to the small number of pickers due to a poor crop) so that, in many cases, each family had two rooms. Bremer, NCLC Investigation Report 211, p. 3. In 1915, Boswell and Hine observed, "There have undoubtedly been some improvements in the conditions about the shacks. A few additions to buildings were found. Quite frequently, one family was found having two rooms instead of one. . . . On many other bogs however, the forlorn shacks and crude cooking arrangements remained unchanged." Boswell and Hine, NCLC Investigation Report 218, p. 9.

91. Chute, NCLC Investigation Report 204, pp. 11–12. Likewise, in 1913, Bremer remarked, "An honest attempt at improving conditions had been made at White's Bog, and this seems to have been continued in the erection of more privies at the Rome colony. These are of the sanitary concrete type, and provide a privy for each shanty at this camp." Bremer, NCLC Investigation Report 211, p. 3.

92. Boswell and Hine, NCLC Investigation Report 218, pp. 9–10.

93. It is worth noting that J.J. White of White's Bog (the best) was the president of the Growers Cranberry Association, but Theodore Budd of Budd's Bog (the worst) was first vice president.

94. Knowles, NCLC Investigation Report 219, pp. 21–22.

95. Quoted in Brown, NCLC Investigation Report 206, pp. 4–5.

96. Hine, NCLC Investigation Report 216, p. 5.

97. Similarly, Miss Arnold, principal of the Hawthorne School noted, "The exodus of school children to the berry fields of New Jersey before the regular close of the school term, and their return long after the resumption of school activity has long been a source of demoralization to our system." Quoted in Brown, NCLC Investigation Report 205, p. 4. Consider also this from Boswell's 1915 report: "Seven of the leading schools in the Italian district reported approximately 1600 children late in entering this fall, a majority of whom were held by work in the canneries and fields of New Jersey. . . . 70 percent of these children had also left school for the early berry work from one to seven weeks before school closed in the spring." Boswell and Hine, NCLC Investigation Report 218, p. 15.

98. These attitudes on the part of school officials could also produce some quirky outcomes. Hine observed, "A peculiar state of affairs was found in Cannon, Del., where the local high school principal was found to be the time keeper in the cannery." Hine, NCLC Investigation Report 216, p. 6.

99. Harry M. Bremer, NCLC Investigation Report 209, p. 16.

100. Quoted in Brown, NCLC Investigation Report 206, p. 13.

101. Quoted in Lovejoy, NCLC Investigation Report 213, pp. 5, 26.

102. Knowles, NCLC Investigation Report 219, p. 24.

103. Gertrude Folks, *Farm Labor vs. School Attendance*, NCLC Publication 300. Aggregated across these studies, investigators visited 670 rural schools and collected attendance and related data for 37,837 children. Additional well-designed studies were conducted after 1920, but, in the main, they merely reinforce, rather than extend, the results summarized by Gertrude Folks in 1920.

104. Ibid. Folks insists these are conservative estimates because the "three-year basis" was used to measure "normal" grade standing. Under this method a child of eight was normal if in the first, second or third grade, a child of nine if in the second, third, or fourth grade, and so on.

105. The most current account of child labor in U.S. agriculture is provided by Lee Tucker, *Fingers to the Bone*. Another good account is provided by Ronald G. Taylor, *Sweatshops in the Sun*.

106. Edward F. Brown, *Child Labor in New York Canning Factories*, NCLC Publication 188.

107. Actually, the packers association sought to ensure that their processing sheds were not covered. They had opposed the 1903 law on the assumption they would be covered. But, "after some thought the canneries decided that perhaps sheds were not covered under Factory Law." So, they sought an opinion from an attorney general who was perceived to be sympathetic to their interests. Jeremy P. Felt, *Hostages of Fortune*, pp. 171–72.

108. Quoted in ibid., p. 171.

109. When the New York law was amended in 1913 to explicitly incorporate the processing sheds, some canners effectively evaded the law by erecting tents (the shed law had not specifically mentioned tents). Ibid., p. 178.

110. Of equal value was the weather station that provided early frost warnings. Frost was deadly to the crop, but an early warning allowed growers to flood the bogs to avoid damage.

111. "The growers were unanimous in their verdict that raking is three to five times cheaper than picking, and a majority said they were going to do away with pickers as soon as they could get their marshes into condition for raking." Bremer, NCLC Investigation Report 209, p. 6.

112. Ibid., pp. 5–6.

113. "The pickers are chiefly women and children. Rarely does one see a man among the pickers, tho' among the Indians it is much more common. . . . Raking is done altogether by men." Ibid., pp. 4–5.

114. Ibid., pp. 7–8.

115. Bremer, NCLC Investigation Report 211, pp. 5–6.

116. Knowles, NCLC Investigation Report 219, p. 14.

Chapter 10

1. If one is careful in distinguishing industry sectors, it is probably a valid claim, in the main, that child labor has been largely abolished from textile manufacturing worldwide. In making this claim, textile manufacturing must be distinguished from garment manufacturing and from handwork (textiles produced in manufactories as

opposed to factories—for example, hand-knotted carpets) where child labor often continues to flourish.

2. See Stanley Lebergott, "Labor Force and Employment Trends," p. 103.

3. Robert T. Michael and Nancy Brandon Tuma, "Youth Employment: Does Life Begin at 16?" pp. 464, 465.

4. Donna S. Rothstein, "Youth Employment in the United States."

5. Lynn Huang, Michael Pergamit, and Jamie Shkolnik, "Youth Initiation into the Labor Market."

6. Rothstein, "Youth Employment in the United States."

7. Huang et al., "Youth Initiation into the Labor Market."

8. Rosella M. Gardecki, "Racial Differences in Youth Employment."

9. Rothstein, "Youth Employment in the United States."

10. Douglas L. Kruse and Douglas Mahony, "Illegal Child Labor in the United States: Prevalence and Characteristics."

11. See, for example, Richard B. Freeman and David A. Wise, *The Youth Labor Market Problem.*

12. Christopher J. Ruhn, "Is High School Employment Consumption or Investment?"; Sharon Wofford Mihalic and Delbert Elliott, "Short- and Long-Term Consequences of Adolescent Work"; Mark Schoenhals et al., "The Educational and Personal Consequences of Adolescent Employment"; Kusum Singh, "Part-Time Employment in High School and Its Effects on Academic Achievement"; Gerald S. Oettinger, "Does High School Employment Affect High School Academic Performance?"

13. U.S. General Accounting Office, *Child Labor: Information on Federal Enforcement Efforts.*

14. U.S. General Accounting Office, *Child Labor: Characteristics of Working Children.*

15. Kruse and Mahony, "Illegal Child Labor in the United States."

16. This definition contrasts somewhat, but overlaps considerably, with the historically anchored definition of a sweatshop as any establishment in the backward chain of a subcontracting network. Both definitions imply establishments in the backwaters of the industry.

17. U.S. General Accounting Office, *Sweatshops in the U.S.: Opinions on Their Extent and Possible Enforcement Options*; U.S. General Accounting Office, *Sweatshops in New York City: A Local Example of a Nationwide Problem*; U.S. General Accounting Office, *Child Labor Violations and Sweatshops in the U.S.*; U.S. General Accounting Office, *Garment Industry Efforts to Address the Prevalence and Conditions of Sweatshops.*

18. Kruse and Mahony, "Illegal Child Labor in the United States," pp. 26–27.

19. U.S. General Accounting Office, *Child Labor in Agriculture: Characteristics and Legality of Work.*

20. Lee Tucker, *Fingers to the Bone.*

21. Ibid., p. 2.

22. Ibid., pp. 42–46.

23. Ibid., p. 3. Eighty-five percent of migrant and seasonal farmworkers are racial minorities. Blacks continue to constitute a significant portion of them, but the vast majority are Latino.

24. United Nations, *Convention on the Rights of the Child*, http://www.unicef.org/crc/fulltext.htm; International Labour Organization, *Worst Forms of Child Labour Convention*, http://ilo.org/public/english/standards/ipec/publ/ipec 9915.htm.

25. Richard B. Freeman, "A Hard-Headed Look at Labor Standards," p. 31.

26. Quoted in Gary R. Freeze, "Poor Girls Who Might Otherwise Be Wretched," p. 27.

27. U.S. House of Representatives, Sixty-Eighth Congress, First Session, "Proposed Child Labor Amendments to the Constitution of the United States," p. 268.

28. For a humorous account that illustrates the same point, see the story of Tommy the Batboy in Robert B. Reich, *Locked in the Cabinet*, pp. 113–16.

29. Discussed in Karl Polanyi, *The Great Transformation*, pp. 53–54. He credits Aristotle by noting, "His famous distinction of householding proper and money-making, in the introductory chapter of his *Politics*, was probably the most prophetic pointer ever made in the realm of social sciences; it is certainly still the best analysis of the subject we possess. Aristotle insists on production for use as against production for gain as the essence of householding proper."

30. "If attendance compulsorily at school marked a person as a child, then childhood has been progressively prolonged as the school leaving age has risen." Hugh Cunningham, *Children and Childhood in Western Society*, p. 174.

31. Viviana A. Zelizer, *Pricing the Priceless Child*, p. 57.

32. See 29 United States Code, Section 212 (1994) and 29 Code of Federal Regulations, Section 570 (1997).

33. U.S. Bureau of the Census, *The Statistical History of the United States*.

34. Many who were retired or disabled and had not worked for some time reported their former line of work and were counted as gainful workers. Likewise, many who were currently employed were not counted because they did not consider work their primary activity.

35. U.S. Bureau of the Census, *Census of Manufactures*, part 1, p. 75. Cited in Daniel Nelson, *Managers and Workers*, p. 137.

36. Kebebew Ashagrie, *Methodological Child Labour Surveys and Statistics*.

37. International Labour Organization, *Targeting the Intolerable*.

38. Polanyi, *The Great Transformation*, p. 156.

39. "By the accepted yardsticks of economic welfare—real wages and population figures—the Inferno of early capitalism, they maintained, never existed; the working classes, far from being exploited, were economically the gainers and to argue the need for social protection against a system that benefited all was obviously impossible." Ibid., pp. 157, 159. Polanyi referred to economic liberalism and laissez-faire as a "crusading passion" and a "militant creed," p. 137. Faith in the system produced "a mystical readiness to accept the social consequences of economic improvement, whatever they might be," p. 33.

40. Robert Hunter, *Poverty*, pp. 6–7, 144.

41. "[T]he well being of several generations of children was sacrificed to make Great Britain wealthy." Clark Nardinelli, *Child Labor and the Industrial Revolution*, pp. 2–3.

42. Ibid.

43. Philip M. Holleran, "Child Labor and Exploitation in Turn-of-the-Century Cotton Mills."

44. Donald O. Parsons and Claudia Goldin, "Parental Altruism and Self-Interest."

45. Bertha Awford Black, quoted in Victoria Byerly, *Hard Times Cotton Mill Girls*, pp. 64–65.

46. John Stuart Mill, *Principles of Political Economy*, p. 958.

47. Cited in Hugh Cunningham, *Children of the Poor*, pp. 63–64, and *Children and Childhood in Western Society*, p. 140.

48. Karl Marx, *Capital*, vol. 1, p. 373.

49. Kenneth A. Swinnerton and Carol Ann Rogers, "A Theory of Exploitative Child Labor."

Chapter 11

1. International Labour Organization, *Targeting the Intolerable.*

2. Kebebew Ashagrie, *Methodological Child Labour Surveys and Statistics.*

3. The centers for this theory development have been, interestingly enough, institutions such as the World Bank, the International Monetary Fund, the U.S. Department of Labor, the International Labour Organization, and scholars associated with those institutions.

4. See especially, Kaushik Basu and Pham Hoang Van, "The Economics of Child Labor," and Kaushik Basu, "Child Labor: Causes, Consequence, and Cure." For other recent important theoretical contributions, see Sylvain E. Dessy, "A Defense of Compulsory Measures Against Child Labor"; Jean-Marie Baland and James A. Robinson, "Is Child Labor Inefficient?"; and Kenneth A. Swinnerton and Carol Ann Rogers, "The Economics of Child Labor: Comment."

5. Christiaan Grooteart and Ravi Kanbur, "Child Labour: An Economic Perspective."

6. Other recent theoretical treatments of child labor that identify likely child labor or underdevelopment traps, though their policy implications differ somewhat in emphasis, include Baland and Robinson, "Is Child Labor Inefficient?" and Dessy, "A Defense of Compulsory Measures Against Child Labor."

7. Everett W. Lord, *Children of the Stage*, NCLC Publication 137A. See also Viviana A. Zelizer, *Pricing the Priceless Child*, pp 85–96.

8. See, in contrast, Martin Brown, Jens Christiansen, and Peter Philips, "The Decline of Child Labor in the U.S. Fruit and Vegetable Canning Industry." Brown, Christiansen, and Philips measured wages in the canning sheds and found no significant effect on child labor. But the more salient comparison would be wages in the city. Rising wages in the canneries would only pull more families, and thus more children, out of the cities.

9. T.W. Schultz, "Investment in Human Capital"; Gary Becker, *A Treatise on the Family*; Becker, "A Theory of the Allocation of Time"; Becker, *Human Capital: A Theoretical and Empirical Analysis.*

10. François Bourguignon and Pierre-André Chiappori, "Collective Models of Household Behavior: An Introduction"; Martin Browning and Pierre-André Chiappori, "Efficient Intra-Household Allocations: A General Characterization and Empirical Tests."

11. Pierre-André Chiappori, "Introducing Household Production in Collective Models of Labor Supply"; Ariel Rubenstein, "Perfect Equilibrium in a Bargaining Model."

12. At the other extreme, where children secure their own employment, work completely independently of their parents, and control their own earnings, newer theories of household economy may offer more insights. But, I suggest, these insights are likely to tell us more about consumption decisions than production decisions.

13. Cunningham notes, in regard to the period of industrialization in Britain, "The phrase 'family strategy' conveys a sense of a family rationally, if perhaps half-heartedly, considering a range of options open to it: of a family in control of its own destiny and making a choice. . . . Few families undergoing the process of industrialization would have greeted this with anything other than a hollow laugh. In truth there comes a point where the 'parameters,' 'constraints' and 'delimiting factors' become meaningless." Hugh Cunningham, *Children and Childhood in Western Society*, pp. 87–88.

14. The notion that children have always worked is not only incorrect today, but even historically it was an overbroad generalization. Some children have never worked. Children of the well-to-do are generally not subject to the kind of child labor that people find objectionable. Even when child labor was at its peak in the United States, large proportions of children escaped its grip and did so principally as a function of wealth.

15. Donald O. Parsons and Claudia Goldin, "Parental Altruism and Self-Interest," p. 656.

16. Partha Dasgupta, "The Population Problem: Theory and Evidence."

17. Cunningham, *Children and Childhood in Western Society*, p. 88.

18. E.O. Smith and R.L. Nyman "Effects of Technological Change on Occupational Structure." Continuing, "Factory walls now guarded the formerly open border between work and leisure which the craftsman had been able to cross at will. . . . He could no longer control his own speed of work but had to keep pace with a power loom which was utterly indifferent to his comfort or fatigue."

19. The traditional conception of a labor–leisure trade-off is not readily applicable to child labor. Leaving the children to their leisure while both parents were off at work was never a socially satisfactory option. The more appropriate conception is the labor–schooling trade-off. But this underscores the need to define schooling as more than an investment in human capital. Schooling should be defined broadly enough that it encompasses some notion of the child care that parents need in order to be free to work.

20. On schooling and child labor, see especially George Psacharopoulis, "Child Labor Versus Educational Attainment"; Patrick Horan and Peggy G. Hargis, "Children's Work and Schooling in the Late Nineteenth-Century Family Economy"; Pamela Barnhouse Walters and Philip J. O'Connell, "The Family Economy, Work, and Educational Participation in the United States, 1890–1940."

21. Cunningham, *Children and Childhood in Western Society*, p. 17.

22. See, for example, William M. Landes and Lewis C. Solomon, "Compulsory Schooling Legislation"; Robert A. Margo and T. Aldrich Finegan, "Compulsory Schooling Legislation and School Attendance."

23. Clark Nardinelli, *Child Labor and the Industrial Revolution*; Philip M. Holleran, "Child Labor and Exploitation in Turn-of-the-Century Cotton Mills."

24. On British history, B.L. Hutchins and A. Harrison observe, "The evils and horrors of the industrial revolution are often vaguely ascribed to the 'transition stage' brought about by the development of machinery and the consequent 'upheaval.' But the more we look into the matter, the more convinced we become that the factory system and machinery merely took what they found, and that the lines on which the industrial revolution actually worked itself out cannot be explained by the progress of material civilization alone; rather, the disregard of child-life, the greed of child-

labour, and the maladministration of the poor law had, during the eighteenth century, and probably much farther back still, been preparing the human material that was to be so mercilessly exploited." B.L. Hutchins and A. Harrison, *A History of Factory Legislation*, p. 13.

25. Parsons and Goldin, "Parental Altruism and Self-Interest."

26. Deborah Levison, Richard Anker, Shahid Ashraf, and Sandhya Barge, *Is Child Labour Really Necessary in India's Carpet Industry?*; Elinor Spielberg, "The Myth of Nimble Fingers."

27. For example, it is obviously true that small, thin young boys were better suited to be chimney sweeps than adult men (who would not fit). This remains true even if it is also true that chimneys are more efficiently cleaned with brushes.

28. Carolyn Tuttle, *Hard at Work in Factories and Mines*.

29. It is debatable whether designers of textile machinery built machines with the deliberate aim of employing children, but it is clear that designers were aware of the implications for employing children.

30. M.C. Salazar, "Child Labour in Colombia."

31. Martin Brown, Jens Christiansen and Peter Philips, "The Decline of Child Labor in the U.S. Fruit and Vegetable Canning Industry"; Carolyn M. Moehling, "State Child Labor Laws and the Decline of Child Labor."

32. Landes and Solomon, "Compulsory Schooling Legislation"; Joshua Angrist and Alan Krueger. "Does Compulsory School Attendance Affect Schooling and Attendance?"; Margo and Finegan, "Compulsory Schooling Legislation and School Attendance."

33. Douglas L. Kruse and Douglas Mahony, "Illegal Child Labor in the United States: Prevalence and Characteristics."

34. T.N. Srinivasan, "International Labour Standards Once Again!"; Basu, "Child Labor: Causes, Consequence, and Cure."

35. Richard B. Freeman, "A Hard-Headed Look at Labor Standards"; Basu and Van, "The Economics of Child Labor."

36. UNICEF, *The State of the World's Children*.

37. Baland and Robinson. "Is Child Labor Inefficient?"

38. Basu, and Van, "The Economics of Child Labor."

39. Daniel Nelson, *Managers and Workers*, pp. 125, 132.

40. Elizabeth Sands Johnson, "Child Labor Legislation"; Elizabeth H. Davidson, *Child Labor Legislation in the Southern Textile States*, p. 257; Stephen B. Wood, *Constitutional Politics in the Progressive Era*, pp. 56–57.

41. See Elias Mendelievich, *Children at Work*; Gerry Rodgers and Guy Standing, *Child Work, Poverty, and Underdevelopment*.

42. Karl Polanyi, *The Great Transformation*, p. 256.

NOTE ON SOURCES

A variety of primary and secondary source materials were consulted in the research that resulted in this book. At the heart of the primary materials are the investigation reports of the National Child Labor Committee. The NCLC investigation reports comprise some four hundred documents. These include investigator field notes, reports from investigators to the NCLC, and reports and publications from the NCLC to various publics. The "raw" investigation reports (investigator field notes and reports to headquarters) are contained in ninety-one folders in three containers in the National Child Labor Committee papers housed in the Manuscript Division of the Library of Congress. These are supplemented, where necessary, by various publications and other source material found in the National Child Labor Committee Collection distributed between the Manuscript Division and the Prints and Photographs Division of the Library of Congress.

The "raw" investigation reports themselves range from a single page to several hundred. The typical report consists of the notes and report of a single investigator studying child labor conditions in a single industry in a single state or region. In some cases, a report covers multiple states, regions, or industries, or includes separate reports from multiple investigators. In a few cases, the "investigation report" is not truly a separate investigation, but rather a piece of significant documentation or correspondence pertaining to some other investigation.

The NCLC investigation reports possess a number of strengths. The first strength is the incredibly rich detail in many of the reports. A number of the field investigators, especially those who produced the largest proportion of the reports, were extremely systematic, methodical, rigorous, and meticulous in their approach to their studies. While some reports were only cursory in nature, many reports contain lengthy summaries, with verbatim quotes, of interviews with children, parents, employers, inspectors, and others. Most contain detailed notes of first-hand observations. Some contain itemized lists of children; ages; and pay, production, health, or education records that permit, at least in some instances, some simple quantitative analyses.

An equally important strength of the reports is that they encompass a wide variety of industries in an array of states over a substantial time interval. Field investigators were assigned to any industry where substantial numbers of children worked. As reports accumulate, it is possible to compare practices across industries, to compare within an industry across states or over time, or to plot a trend within a given industry within a given state. The cumulative body of these reports have never, not even by the NCLC, been integrated into a single body of work for analysis.

The NCLC placed a high premium on factual accuracy and avoidance of radicalism or sensationalism, even if they were not entirely objective. Investigators frequently laced their reports with editorial comment, but they were expected, first and foremost, to be factually accurate. Through the 1920s, the NCLC developed a cadre of experienced and expert investigators. Some specialized in a single industry, such as Harriet Van der Vaart and Anna Herdina in glass or A. Benedict in tenement homework. Others took on multiple industries. Key investigators during the early years of the NCLC included Harry M. Bremer, Edward F. Brown, Charles L. Chute, Edward N. Clopper, Lewis W. Hine, Herschel H. Jones, and Alfred E. Seddon. Altogether, these seven investigators accounted for sixty-five of the ninety-one investigation reports. Of these investigators only Edward N. Clopper, who published his Ph.D. dissertation *Child Labor in the City Streets,* which was based in part on his work for the NCLC, and Lewis W. Hine, the great social photographer, achieved any significant measure of fame for their work. Of these, Hine exemplified the tenacity and the meticulous, systematic, and thorough approach taken by other investigators. While his reports, complete with accompanying photographs, could have tremendous public impact, his approach was really no different from that of the other investigators. He would resort to subterfuge when necessary to enter a plant or procure an interview (posing as a magazine representative, a postcard salesman, or an insurance salesman). He learned to measure height from the buttonholes on his coat. And he always took detailed notes, sometimes doing so on a piece of paper concealed inside his pocket. Each one of his photos has its own caption card on which Hine recorded, again in detail, the origin of each photo.

While the NCLC investigation reports constitute a strong data set,

they have their limitations as well. First, the reports are of uneven quality. Generally, the more experienced investigators submitted the most
systematic and thorough reports, but occasionally they were sketchy
and cursory. The quality of the reports from less experienced investigators runs the gamut from excellent to barely useful. I have attempted to
rely, most heavily, on reports from the most experienced investigators.

A more substantial limitation of the investigation reports is that they
encompass only a portion of American history with child labor. The
reports encompass the period from 1904 to1937, but the greatest concentration of reports were produced between 1908 and 1915. Thus, the
reports document child labor during the period of its waning in the United
States, but not during the period of its emergence. One consequence of
this can be seen in the reports on cotton textiles. The cotton textile industry originated in New England employing large numbers of children. But by the time the NCLC was founded and initiated its program
of investigations, most New England states had more or less effectively
regulated child labor in cotton textiles, and a thriving and as yet unregulated industry had developed in the South. So child labor in southern
cotton textiles is featured prominently in the NCLC investigation reports and the role of child labor in New England textiles is largely ignored. At the same time, however, the last investigation in southern cotton
textiles was conducted in 1915. That is, the NCLC left the field before
child labor had been fully eradicated.

Another limitation of the NCLC investigation reports is that certain
biases must be recognized. Even though the committee placed a high
premium on factual accuracy and objectivity, the NCLC was at the center of a reform movement, and the investigation program was a purposive instrument of that reform. In reading the reports, it is obvious that
they were aimed at reform. Bias was introduced in two principal ways.
The first, and most obvious, source of bias was the investigators themselves. While disciplined toward factual accuracy and objectivity, the
investigators were also ardent advocates of child labor reform. So, many
investigation reports, and especially investigator field notes, were
sprinkled with editorial commentary. Generally, however, these notes
do not detract from our capacity to glean the facts. A second source of
bias was in sampling. The industries and regions selected for investigation were chosen in large measure because they supported the
committee's current objectives. So, while there were no investigation
reports prior to 1910 in agriculture and food processing, industrial home-

work, or the street trades, the NCLC launched numerous investigations in each of those industries in subsequent years. The reason was straightforward. By that time, significant progress regulating child labor in mining and manufacturing was evident. But agriculture and food processing, industrial homework, and the street trades were generally exempt from regulation. Thus, investigations were often launched to establish a factual basis for proposed regulation.

A final limitation is that the collection of investigation reports is incomplete. For example, very few of the many investigations in agriculture conducted after 1916 are included in the collection. This is not a major problem since it appears that most of these investigations were published in NCLC publications. Apparently, investigators retained their own field notes and went straight to publication. At any rate, for purposes of this book, these later investigations in agriculture are given less attention. More problematic, some of the earlier investigation reports are missing from the collection. For example, due to their salacious content, many of the reports of the night messenger service were handled differently from other investigation reports and are not included in the NCLC collection. Fortunately, at least a few of these reports were filed, and there is no choice but to rely on them, supplemented by information from NCLC publications, as representative of the rest. A few other investigation reports are missing from the collection. For example, there is no report of Hine's first visit to the Carolinas in 1908. In this case, Hine's photo caption cards can provide the chronology and much of the detail. Further, it is highly probable that all of the most important investigations are covered in various NCLC publications. Still, the fact that some investigation reports are missing raises the question whether others are missing, for which we have no other source of information. While this collection does not contain all the NCLC investigation reports ever produced, it does contain the most complete body of work from the most active period of the NCLC.

I have attempted to allow the "raw" NCLC investigation reports to carry the story of child labor in America as much as possible, turning to other NCLC publications and secondary sources only to the extent that they supplemented and complemented the original reports. A list of the ninety-one investigation reports housed in the National Child Labor Committee papers in the Manuscript Division of the Library of Congress, as they have been cited in the text, follows. The numbering system and pagination system are of my own construction. The first digit in the report number indicates the container in which the report was located. The final two digits indicate the folder. Thus, Report 203 represents the third folder found in container number two. As to pagination, I could not consistently rely on the pagination of investigators. Many folders included transmittal letters and other correspondence that were not paginated. Furthermore, many folders contained multiple reports with each report paginated separately. Page numbers reported in this book were determined by counting the number of pages into the folder, from first to last, regardless of how they may have been numbered by the investigators themselves.

NCLC Investigation Report Roster

Benedict, A. NCLC Investigation Report 430, New Jersey tenement homework, 1922.
————. NCLC Investigation Report 432, New Jersey tenement homework, 1922.
————. NCLC Investigation Report 424, New Jersey tenement homework, 1923.
————. NCLC Investigation Report 431, New Jersey tenement homework, 1923.
Boswell, Louise, and Lewis W. Hine. NCLC Investigation Report 218, New Jersey agriculture, 1915.
Bremer, Harry M. NCLC Investigation Report 201, Michigan agriculture, 1911.
————. NCLC Investigation Report 418, New Jersey street trades, 1912.
————. NCLC Investigation Report 207, Maryland agriculture, 1913.
————. NCLC Investigation Report 209, Wisconsin agriculture, 1913.
————. NCLC Investigation Report 211, New Jersey agriculture, 1913.
————. NCLC Investigation Report 402, New York street trades, 1913.
————. NCLC Investigation Report 407, New York street trades, 1913.
————. NCLC Investigation Report 420, Virginia street trades, 1913.
————. NCLC Investigation Report 423, New Jersey mining, 1913.
————. NCLC Investigation Report 212, Louisiana canneries, 1914.
————. NCLC Investigation Report 416, Connecticut street trades, 1914.
————. NCLC Investigation Report 428, Connecticut street trades, 1914.
————. NCLC Investigation Report 433, West Virginia street trades, 1914.
————. NCLC Investigation Report 210, Maryland agriculture, 1915.
Brown, Edward F. NCLC Investigation Report 205, New Jersey agriculture, 1910.
————. NCLC Investigation Report 426, Pennsylvania street trades, 1910.
————. NCLC Investigation Report 409, Pennsylvania mining, 1912.
————. NCLC Investigation Report 206, Gulf Coast canneries, 1913.
————. NCLC Investigation Report 329, Maryland light manufacturing, 1913.
Chute, Charles L. NCLC Investigation Report 405, Ohio glass, 1910.
————. NCLC Investigation Report 204, New Jersey agriculture, 1911.
————. NCLC Investigation Report 314, Midwest glass, 1911.
Dwight, Helen C. NCLC Investigation Report 429, New York street trades, 1915.
Fleischer, Alexander. NCLC Investigation Report 317, Mississippi textiles, 1912.
Fleischer, Isabella. NCLC Investigation Report 208, California agriculture, 1913.

Gibbons, Charles E. NCLC Investigation Report 333, Indiana glass, 1923.
Herdina, Anna. NCLC Investigation Report 311, Illinois glass, 1910.
———. NCLC Investigation Report 312, Indiana glass, 1910.
Hine, Lewis, W. NCLC Investigation Report 304, West Virginia, glass, 1908.
———. NCLC Investigation Report 306, New England textiles, 1909.
———. NCLC Investigation Report 308, New Jersey glass, 1909.
———. NCLC Investigation Report 315, Georgia textiles, 1909.
———. NCLC Investigation Report 202, New York agriculture, 1910.
———. NCLC Investigation Report 216, Delaware agriculture, 1910.
———. NCLC Investigation Report 307, Alabama textiles, 1910.
———. NCLC Investigation Report 309, Illinois glass, 1910.
———. NCLC Investigation Report 302, Mississippi textiles, 1911.
———. NCLC Investigation Report 313, Florida light manufacturing, 1911.
———. NCLC Investigation Report 408, Pennsylvania mining, 1911.
———. NCLC Investigation Report 419, Virginia, multiple industries, 1911.
———. NCLC Investigation Report 316, South Carolina textiles, 1912.
———. NCLC Investigation Report 318, Alabama textiles, 1913.
———. NCLC Investigation Report 319, Massachusetts textiles, 1913.
———. NCLC Investigation Report 323, Mississippi textiles, 1913.
———. NCLC Investigation Report 325, Georgia textiles, 1913.
———. NCLC Investigation Report 327, Texas textiles, 1913.
———. NCLC Investigation Report 404, Texas, multiple industries, 1913.
———. NCLC Investigation Report 215, Colorado agriculture, 1915.
———. NCLC Investigation Report 217, California agriculture, 1915.
———. NCLC Investigation Report 406, New York tenement homework, 1915.
———. NCLC Investigation Report 222, Midwest agriculture, 1916.
———. NCLC Investigation Report 401, Illinois agriculture, 1916.
———. NCLC Investigation Report 415, Mississippi, multiple industries, 1916.
———. NCLC Investigation Report 434, Vermont street trades, 1916.
———. NCLC Investigation Report 220, Michigan agriculture, 1917.
———. NCLC Investigation Report 332, New Jersey glass, 1917.
Hunter, Marie. NCLC Investigation Report 303, Virginia textiles, 1908.
Jones, Herschel H. NCLC Investigation Report 321, Pennsylvania glass, 1912.
———. NCLC Investigation Report 322, Illinois glass, 1912.
———. NCLC Investigation Report 326, New York textiles, 1913.
———. NCLC Investigation Report 427, Kentucky street trades, 1913.
———. NCLC Investigation Report 214, Gulf Coast canneries, 1914.
———. NCLC Investigation Report 335, Georgia textiles, circa 1914.
———. NCLC Investigation Report 411, Mississippi textiles, 1914.
———. NCLC Investigation Report 412, Mississippi textiles, 1914.
———. NCLC Investigation Report 413, Mississippi textiles, 1914.
———. NCLC Investigation Report 414, Georgia textiles, 1914.
Knowles, Edith. NCLC Investigation Report 219, New Jersey agriculture, 1923.
Lovejoy, Owen R. NCLC Investigation Report 422, Maryland mining, 1906.
———. NCLC Investigation Report 403, New York tenement homework, 1913.
———. NCLC Investigation Report 213, New Jersey agriculture, 1914.
NCLC Investigation Report 203, no author attribution, Gulf Coast canneries, 1911.

NCLC Investigation Report 324, no author attribution, New York light manufacturing, 1913.

NCLC Investigation Report 328, no author attribution, New York tenement homework, 1913.

NCLC Investigation Report 417, no author attribution, West Virginia, multiple industries, 1914.

NCLC Investigation Report 425, no author attribution, Pennsylvania tenement homework, 1923.

NCLC Investigation Report 421, No author attribution, New York tenement homework, 1934.

NCLC Investigation Report 331, no author attribution, New Jersey light manufacturing, year not specified.

Owen, George Z. NCLC Investigation Report 330, Georgia textiles, 1915.

Seddon, Alfred E. NCLC Investigation Report 301, Mississippi textiles, 1907.

———. NCLC Investigation Report 305, Georgia textiles, 1908.

———. NCLC Investigation Report 334, South Carolina textiles, 1908.

Stokes, Barbara. NCLC Investigation Report 221, Maryland agriculture, 1937.

Taylor, Florence. NCLC Investigation Report 410, Pennsylvania mining, 1916.

Van der Vaart, Harriet. NCLC Investigation Report 310, Illinois glass, 1904.

Vaughn, Harvey P. NCLC Investigation Report 320, Georgia textiles, 1913.

The NCLC did not collect investigation reports in order to store them in file folders. Investigations were collected in order to be published. Public awareness was central to the NCLC's mission, so the committee had an extensive publication program. While publications were not limited to reporting on investigations, many of the most important investigations were published, either as stand-alone publications, or in publications that summarized multiple investigations in a related industry, occupation, or region. NCLC publications are a valuable supplement and complement to the raw investigation reports.

Several investigators authored NCLC publications pertaining to their investigative work. Edward N. Clopper was especially prolific. But publications were more likely to be authored by Owen R. Lovejoy, Alexander J. McKelway, or others among the committee's luminaries.

A collection of 420 NCLC publications has been preserved on microfilm by the Library of Congress as part of the larger NCLC collection. Many of these provide valuable information about investigations, and these are the NCLC publications cited throughout this book. The Library of Congress placed the publications on microfilm in chronological order. I used their numbering system throughout the book.

Many of the stand-alone NCLC publications were also published in other outlets. During the early years of the committee, significant reports and papers from the NCLC's annual meetings were published in the *Annals of the American Academy of Political and Social Sciences*. The NCLC also published its own periodical journal, the *Child Labor Bulletin* (later renamed *American Child*), and many investigations were summarized here as well. So, there is considerable redundancy in these sources. Throughout the text of the book, I have identified NCLC publications by their publication number without attempting to indicate whether it was also published elsewhere. In the list of publications cited that follows, I have attempted to indicate the complete publication record for each of the publications.

NCLC Publications Cited

Adams, Myron E. "Children in the American Street Trades." *Proceedings of the First Annual Meeting of the NCLC*, 1905. Also appears in the *Annals of the American Academy of Political and Social Science* 25, no. 3 (May 1905): 23–44.

Armentrout, Walter W., Sara A. Brown, and Charles E. Gibbons. *Child Labor in the Sugar Beet Fields of Michigan*. NCLC Publication 310. New York, 1923.

Brown, Edward F. *Child Labor in New York Canning Factories*. NCLC Publication 188. New York, 1913. Reprinted in *Child Labor Bulletin* 1, no. 4 (February 1913).

———. "The Toiling Children of the Gulf Coast Canneries." In *The Child's Burden in Oyster and Shrimp Canneries*. NCLC Publication 193. New York, 1913.

Brown, Sara A., and Robie O. Sargent. *Children Working in the Sugar Beet Fields of the North Platte Valley of Nebraska*. NCLC Publication 318. New York, 1924.

Clopper, Edward N. *Child Labor in West Virginia*. NCLC Publication 086. New York, 1908.

———. "Children on the Streets of Cincinnati." *Proceedings of the Fourth Annual Meeting of the NCLC*, 1908, pp. 113–23. Also appears in the *Annals of the American Academy of Political and Social Science* (July 1908).

———. *The Child Merchants of the Streets*. NCLC Publication 203. New York, 1913.

———. *Street Work and Juvenile Delinquency*. NCLC Publication 221. New York, 1914.

———. *Street Trades Regulation*. NCLC Publication 272. New York, 1917. Reprinted from *Child Labor Bulletin*, 5, no. 2 (August 1916).

———. *Farmwork and Schools in Kentucky*. NCLC Publication 274. New York, 1917. Reprinted from the *Child Labor Bulletin* 5, no. 4 (February 1917).

———. *Causes of Absence from Rural Schools in Oklahoma*. NCLC Publication 281. New York, 1917. Reprinted from the *Child Labor Bulletin* 6, no. 2 (August 1917).

Clopper, Edward N., and Lewis W. Hine. *Child Labor in the Sugar-Beet Fields of Colorado*. NCLC Publication 259. New York, 1916. Reprinted from the *Child Labor Bulletin* 4, no. 4 (February 1916).

Clugston, Kate. *Cotton or School*. NCLC Publication 387. New York, 1943.

Davies, Edgar T. "The Difficulties of a Factory Inspector." *Proceedings of the Third*

Annual Meeting of the National Child Labor Committee, 1907, pp. 125–31. Reprinted in the *Annals of the American Academy of Political and Social Science* 29, no. 1 (January 1907).

Duke, Emma. *California the Golden.* NCLC Publication 304. New York, 1920. Reprinted from *The American Child* 2, no. 3 (November 1920).

Folks, Gertrude. *Farm Labor vs. School Attendance.* NCLC Publication 300. New York, 1920.

Gibbons, Charles E. *Child Labor Among Cotton Growers of Texas.* NCLC Publication 324. New York, 1925.

———. *Child Labor in the Tiff Mines.* NCLC Publication 373. New York, 1938.

Gordon, Jean. *Why the Children Are in the Factory.* NCLC Publication 076. New York, 1908.

Hall, George A. *What the Government Says About Child Labor in Tenements.* NCLC Publication 151. New York, 1911.

———. *Unrestricted Forms of Child Labor in New York State.* NCLC Publication 168. New York, 1911.

Harriman, Mrs. J. Borden. "The Cotton Mill a Factor in the Development of the South." *Proceedings of the Sixth Annual Meeting of the National Child Labor Committee*, 1910. Reprinted in the *Annals of the American Academy of Political and Social Science* (1910): 47–51.

Hine, Lewis W. *Child Labor in Gulf Coast Canneries.* NCLC Publication 158. New York, 1911. Also appears in *Proceedings of the Seventh Annual Meeting of the National Child Labor Committee*, 1911. Reprinted in the *Annals of the American Academy of Political and Social Science* (July supplement, 1911):118–22.

———. "Baltimore to Biloxi and Back." In *The Child's Burden in Oyster and Shrimp Canneries.* NCLC Publication 193. New York, 1913.

Hine, Lewis W., and Edward F. Brown. *The Child's Burden in Oyster and Shrimp Canneries.* NCLC Publication 193. New York, 1913.

Jones, Herschel H. *Unregulated Street Trading in a Typical City.* NCLC Publication 264. New York, 1916.

Kelley, Florence. *Obstacles to the Enforcement of Child Labor Legislation.* NCLC Publication 046. New York, 1907. Also appears in *Proceedings of the Third Annual Meeting of the National Child Labor Committee*, 1907. Reprinted in the *Annals of the American Academy of Political and Social Science* (January 1907): 50–56.

Lord, Everett W. *Children of the Stage.* NCLC Publication 137A. New York, 1910.

Lovejoy, Owen R. *Child Labor in the Coal Mines.* NCLC Publication 027. New York, 1906. Also appears in *Proceedings of the Second Annual Meeting of the National Child Labor Committee*, 1906. Reprinted in the *Annals of the American Academy of Political and Social Science* (March 1906): 35–41.

———. *Child Labor in the Glass Industry.* NCLC Publication 028. New York, 1906. Also appears in *Proceedings of the Second Annual Meeting of the National Child Labor Committee*, 1906, pp. 42–53. Reprinted in the *Annals of the American Academy of Political and Social Science* 27, no. 2 (March 1906).

———. *In the Shadow of the Coal Breaker.* NCLC Publication 061. New York, 1906. Reprinted in *Woman's Home Companion* (September 1906).

———. *Child Labor in the Soft Coal Mines.* NCLC Publication 044. New York, 1907. Also appears in *Proceedings of the Third Annual Meeting of the National*

Child Labor Committee, 1907. Reprinted in the *Annals of the American Academy of Political and Social Science* (January 1907): 26–34.

———. *The Extent of Child Labor in the Anthracite Coal Industry*. NCLC Publication 045. New York, 1907. Also appears in *Proceedings of the Third Annual Meeting of the National Child Labor Committee*, 1907. Reprinted in the *Annals of the American Academy of Political and Social Science* (January 1907): 35–49.

———. *Child Labor and the Night Messenger Service*. NCLC Publication 141. New York, 1910.

———. "The Coal Mines of Pennsylvania." *Annals of the American Academy of Political and Social Science* (July 1911): 133–38.

Mangold, George B., and Lillian B. Hill. *Migratory Child Workers*. NCLC Publication 354. New York, 1929. Also appears in *Proceedings of the Twenty-fifth Annual Meeting of the National Child Labor Committee*, 1929.

McKelway, Alexander J. *Child Labor in Southern Industry*. NCLC Publication 012. New York, 1905. Also appears in *Proceedings of the First Annual Meeting of the National Child Labor Committee*, 1905. Reprinted in the *Annals of the American Academy of Political and Social Science* 26, no. 2 (March 1905): 16–22.

———. *Child Labor in the Southern Cotton Mills*. NCLC Publication 021. New York, 1906.

———. *The Child Labor Problem—A Study in Degeneracy*. NCLC Publication 022. New York, 1906. Also appears in *Proceedings of the Second Annual Meeting of the National Child Labor Committee*, 1906. Reprinted in the *Annals of the American Academy of Political and Social Science* (March 1906): 54–68.

———. *Child Labor in the Carolinas*. NCLC Publication 092. New York, 1909.

———. "The Mill or the Farm." *Proceedings of the Sixth Annual Meeting of the National Child Labor Committee*, 1910. Reprinted in the *Annals of the American Academy of Political and Social Science* (1910): 52–57.

———. *The Cotton Mill: The Herod Among Industries*. NCLC Publication 162. New York, 1911. Also appears in *Proceedings of the Seventh Annual Meeting of the National Child Labor Committee*, 1911. Reprinted in the *Annals of the American Academy of Political and Social Science* (July supplement, 1911): 39–52.

———. *Child Labor in Mississippi*. NCLC Publication 169. New York, 1911.

———. *Child Labor in Georgia*. NCLC Publication 194. New York, 1913.

———. *Child Labor at the National Capital*. NCLC Publication 213. New York, 1914.

National Child Labor Committee. *Child Workers in the Tenements* (reprint of Appendix 7, preliminary report, New York State Factory Investigating Commission). NCLC Publication 181. New York, 1912.

———. *Who Made What You Buy?* NCLC Publication 252. New York, 1916.

———. *Poems of Child Labor.* NCLC Publication 316. New York, 1924.

Parker, Lewis W. "Compulsory Education, the Solution to the Child Labor Problem." *Proceedings of the Fourth Annual Meeting of the National Child Labor Committee*, 1908. Reprinted in the *Annals of the American Academy of Political and Social Science* (July supplement, 1908): 40–56.

Seddon, Alfred E. "The Education of the Mill Children in the South." *Proceedings of the Fourth Annual Meeting of the National Child Labor Committee*, 1908. Reprinted in the *Annals of the American Academy of Political and Social Science* (July supplement, 1908): 72–79.

Sidel, James E. *Pick for Your Supper: A Study of Child Labor Among Migrants on the Pacific Coast*. NCLC Publication 378. New York, 1939.

Swift, Wiley H. *The Child That Toileth Not: A Reply to Mr. Dawley*. NCLC Publication 186. New York, 1913.

Van der Vaart, Harriet M. *Child Labor in the Glass Works of Illinois*. NCLC Publication 050. New York, 1907. Also appears in *Proceedings of the Third Annual Meeting of the National Child Labor Committee*, 1907, pp. 77–83. Reprinted in the *Annals of the American Academy of Political and Social Science* 29, no. 1 (January 1907).

Van Kleeck, Mary. Child Labor in Home Industries. NCLC Publication 134. New York, 1910. Also appears in *Proceedings of the Sixth Annual Meeting of the National Child Labor Committee*, 1910. Reprinted in the *Annals of the American Academy of Political and Social Science* (July supplement, 1910): 145–49.

BIBLIOGRAPHY

Abbott, Edith. *Women in Industry: A Study in American Economic History*. New York: D. Appleton, 1910.

Abbott, Grace. *Legal Status in the Family, Apprenticeship and Child Labor*, vol. 1 of *The Child and the State*. New York: Greenwood, 1938.

————. *The Dependent and the Delinquent Child*, vol. 2 of *The Child and the State*. New York: Greenwood, 1938.

Angrist, Joshua, and Alan Krueger. "Does Compulsory School Attendance Affect Schooling and Attendance?" *Quarterly Journal of Economics* 106 (1991): 979–1014.

Anthracite Coal Strike Commission. *Report to the President on the Anthracite Coal Strike of May-October, 1902*. Washington, DC: Government Printing Office, 1903.

Ashagrie, Kebebew. *Methodological Child Labour Surveys and Statistics: ILO's Work in Brief*. Geneva: ILO Bureau of Statistics and International Programme on the Elimination of Child Labour, 1996.

Baland, Jean-Marie, and James A. Robinson. "Is Child Labor Inefficient?" *Journal of Political Economy* 108, no. 4 (2000): 663–79.

Barrett, Michelle, and Mary McIntosh, "The 'Family Wage' Debate: Some Problems for Socialists and Feminists." *Capital and Class* 11 (1980): 51–72.

Basu, Kaushik. "Child Labor: Causes, Consequence, and Cure, with Remarks on International Labor Standards." *Journal of Economic Literature* 37 (1999): 1083–1119.

Basu, Kaushik, and Pham Hoang Van. "The Economics of Child Labor." *American Economic Review* 88 (1998): 412–27.

Becker, Gary. *A Treatise on the Family*. Cambridge, MA: Harvard University Press, 1981.

————. "A Theory of the Allocation of Time." *Economic Journal* 75, no. 299 (1965): 493–517.

————. *Human Capital: A Theoretical and Empirical Analysis, with Special Reference to Education*. New York: Columbia University Press, 1964.

Bernstein, Irving. *The Lean Years: A History of the American Worker, 1920–1955*. Boston: Houghton-Mifflin, 1960.

Bickel, Alexander M. *The Unpublished Opinions of Mr. Justice Brandeis*. Cambridge, MA: Harvard University Press, 1957.

Booth, Charles. *Labour and Life of the People in London*. London: Williams and Norgate, 1889.

Boserup, Ester. *Women's Role in Economic Development*. London: Allen and Unwin, 1970.

Bourguignon, François, and Pierre-André Chiappori. "Collective Models of Household Behavior: An Introduction." *European Economic Review* 36, no. 3 (1992): 355–365.

Brace, Charles Loring. *The Dangerous Classes of New York and Twenty Years' Work Among Them*. New York: Wynkoop and Hallenbeck, 1872. Reprinted in Abbott, *The Dependent and the Delinquent Child*.

Braverman, Harry. *Labor and Monopoly Capital: The Degradation of Work in the Twentieth Century*. New York: Monthly Review Press, 1974.

Brown, Martin, Jens Christiansen, and Peter Philips. "The Decline of Child Labor in the U.S. Fruit and Vegetable Canning Industry: Law or Economics?" *Business History Review* 66 (Winter 1992): 723–70.

Browning, Martin, and Pierre-André Chiappori. "Efficient Intra-Household Allocations: A General Characterization and Empirical Tests." *Econometrica* 66, no. 6 (November 1998): 1241–78.

Byerly, Victoria. *Hard Times Cotton Mill Girls: Personal Histories of Womanhood and Poverty in the South*. Ithaca, NY: ILR Press, 1986.

Cameron, Rondo. *A Concise Economic History of the World: From Paleolithic Times to the Present*. Oxford: Oxford University Press, 1989.

Charnovitz, Steve. "The Influence of International Labour Standards on the World Trading Regime." *International Labour Review* 126, no. 5 (1987): 565–84.

Chernow, Ron. *Titan: The Life of John D. Rockefeller, Sr.* New York: Random House, 1998.

Chiappori, Pierre-André. "Introducing Household Production in Collective Models of Labor Supply." *Journal of Political Economy* 105, no.1 (1997): 191–211.

Clopper, Edward N. *Child Labor in the City Streets*. New York: Macmillan, 1912.

Commons, John R. "Report of the U.S. Industrial Commission," vol. 15, 1901.

Cunningham, Hugh. "The Employment and Unemployment of Children in England c.1680–1851." *Past and Present* 126 (1990): 115–50.

———. *Children of the Poor: Representations of Childhood Since the Seventeenth Century*. Oxford: Blackwell, 1991.

———. *Children and Childhood in Western Society Since 1500*. London: Longman, 1995.

Dasgupta, Partha. "The Population Problem: Theory and Evidence." *Journal of Economic Literature* 33 (December 1995): 1879–1902.

Davidson, Elizabeth H. *Child Labor Legislation in the Southern Textile States*. Chapel Hill: University of North Carolina Press, 1939.

Dawley, Thomas Robinson, Jr. *The Child That Toileth Not: The Story of a Government Investigation Hitherto Suppressed*. New York: Gracia, 1912.

Dessy, Sylvain E. "A Defense of Compulsive Measures Against Child Labor." *Journal of Development Economics* (2000): 261–75.

Dublin, Thomas. *Women at Work: The Transformation of Work and Community in Lowell, Massachusetts, 1826–1850*. New York: Columbia University Press, 1979.

Dulles, Foster Rhea, and Melvyn Dubofsky. *Labor in America: A History*, 4th ed. Illinois: Harlan Davidson, 1984 [originally published 1949].

Dunn, Richard S. "Servants and Slaves: The Recruitment and Employment of Labor." In *Colonial British America: Essays in the New History of the Early Modern Era*, ed. Jack P. Greene and J.R. Pole. Baltimore: Johns Hopkins University Press, 1984, 157–94.

Dunne, William F. *Gastonia, Citadel of the Class Struggle in the New South*. New York: Workers Library Publishers, 1929.

Eller, Ronald D. *Miners, Millhands, and Mountaineers: Industrialization of the Appalachian South, 1880–1930*. Knoxville: University of Tennessee Press, 1982.

Ely, Richard T., Thomas S. Adams, Max O. Lorenz, and Allyn A. Young. *Outlines of Economics*, 3d ed. New York: Macmillan, 1919.

Ensign, Forest. *Compulsory School Attendance and Child Labor.* Iowa City: Athens Press, 1921.

Felt, Jeremy P. *Hostages of Fortune: Child Labor Reform in New York State.* Syracuse University Press, 1965.

Freeman, Richard B. "A Hard-Headed Look at Labor Standards." In *International Labor Standards and Global Economic Integration: Proceedings of a Symposium*, ed. Gregory K. Schoepfle and Kenneth A. Swinnerton. Washington, DC: U.S. Department of Labor, 1994.

Freeman, Richard B., and David A. Wise. *The Youth Labor Market Problem: Its Nature, Causes, and Consequences.* Chicago: University of Chicago Press, 1982.

Freeze, Gary R. "Poor Girls Who Might Otherwise Be Wretched: The Origins of Paternalism in North Carolina's Mills, 1836–1880." In *Hanging by a Thread: Social Change in Southern Textiles*, ed. Jeffrey Leiter, Michael D. Schulman, and Rhonda Zingraff. Ithaca, NY: ILR Press, 1991.

Gardecki, Rosella M. "Racial Differences in Youth Employment." *Monthly Labor Review* 124, no. 8 (August 2001): 51–67.

Gaventa, John. *Power and Powerlessness: Quiescence and Rebellion in an Appalachian Valley.* Urbana: University of Illinois Press, 1980.

Gitelman, Howard M. "The Waltham System and the Coming of the Irish." *Labor History* 8 (Fall 1967): 227–53.

Goldin, Claudia, and Kenneth Sokoloff. "Women, Children, and Industrialization in the Early Republic: Evidence from the Manufacturing Censuses." *Journal of Economic History* 42, no. 4 (1982): 741–74.

———. "The Relative Productivity Hypothesis of Industrialization: The American Case, 1820–1850." *The Quarterly Journal of Economics* (August 1984): 461–87.

Goldmark, Josephine. *Impatient Crusader: Florence Kelley's Life Story.* Urbana: University of Illinois Press, 1953.

Gompers, Samuel. *American Labor and the War.* New York: G.H. Doran, 1919.

———. *Seventy Years of Life and Labour.* 2 vols. London: Hurst and Blackett, 1925.

Gordon, David. M., Richard Edwards, and Michael Reich. *Segmented Work, Divided Workers: The Historical Transformation of Labor in the United States.* New York: Cambridge University Press, 1982.

Grooteart, Christiaan, and Ravi Kanbur. "Child Labour: An Economic Perspective." *International Labour Review* 134, no. 2 (1995): 187–203.

Gullickson, Gay L. "Technology, Gender, and Rural Culture: Normandy and the Piedmont." In *Hanging by a Thread: Social Change in Southern Textiles*, ed. Jeffrey Leiter, Michael D. Schulman, and Rhonda Zingraff. Ithaca, NY: ILR Press, 1991.

Gutman, Herbert. "Work, Culture, and Society in Industrializing America, 1815–1919." *American Historical Review* 78 (June 1973): 531–88.

Gutman, Judith Mara. *Lewis W. Hine and the American Social Conscience.* New York: Walker, 1967.

Hall, Jacquelyn Dowd, James Leloudis, Robert Korstad, Mary Murphy, LuAnn Jones, and Christopher Daly. *Like a Family: The Making of a Southern Cotton Mill World.* New York: Norton, 1987.

Hamilton, Alexander. 1791. "Report on Manufactures." In *Papers on Public Credit, Commerce and Finance*, ed. Samuel McKee. New York: Liberal Arts Press, 1957.

Hodges, James A. *New Deal Labor Policy and the Southern Cotton Textile Industry, 1933–1941*. Knoxville: University of Tennessee Press, 1986.

Holleran, Philip M. "Child Labor and Exploitation in Turn-of-the-Century Cotton Mills." *Explorations in Economic History* 30 (1993): 485–500.

Hoover, Herbert. *The Challenge to Liberty.* New York: Scribner's, 1934.

Horan, Patrick M., and Peggy G. Hargis. "Children's Work and Schooling in the Late Nineteenth-Century Family Economy." *American Sociological Review* 56 (October 1991): 583–96.

Howard, Alan, "Labor, History, and Sweatshops in the New Global Economy." In *No Sweat: Fashion, Free Trade, and the Rights of Garment Workers*, ed. Andrew Ross. New York: Verso, 1997, pp. 151–72.

Huang, Lynn, Michael Pergamit, and Jamie Shkolnik. "Youth Initiation into the Labor Market." *Monthly Labor Review* 124, no. 8 (August 2001): 18–24.

Hunter, Robert. *Poverty.* New York: Macmillan, 1904.

Hutchins, B.L., and A. Harrison. *A History of Factory Legislation*. London: P.S. King and Son, 1903.

Hyatt, Gilbert E. "The Farmers' States Rights League and Ratification of the Child Labor Amendment." *Labor* (January 1925). Reprinted in Abbott, *Legal Status in the Family*, and in *Southern Textile Bulletin* 27, no. 3 (February 5, 1925).

International Labour Organization. *Targeting the Intolerable*. Geneva: ILO, 1996.

Johnsen, Julia E. *Child Labor.* The Reference Shelf 3, no. 9. New York: H.W. Wilson, 1926.

Johnson, Elizabeth Sands. "Child Labor Legislation." In John R. Commons, *Labor Legislation*, vol. 4 in *History of Labor in the United States, 1896–1932*, ed. Elizabeth Brandeis. New York: Macmillan, 1935, pp. 403–57.

Kelley, Florence. *Some Ethical Gains Through Legislation*. New York: Macmillan, 1905.

Kemp, John R. *Lewis Hine: Photographs of Child Labor in the South*. Jackson: University of Mississippi Press, 1986.

Kruse, Douglas L., and Douglas Mahony. "Illegal Child Labor in the United States: Prevalence and Characteristics." *Industrial and Labor Relations Review* 54, no. 1 (2000): 17–40.

Landes, William M., and Lewis C. Solomon. "Compulsory Schooling Legislation: An Economic Analysis of Law and Social Change in the Nineteenth Century." *Journal of Economic History* 22 (1972): 54–91.

Lebergott, Stanley. *Manpower in Economic Growth: The American Record Since 1800*. New York: McGraw-Hill, 1964.

———. "Labor Force and Employment Trends." In *Indicators of Social Change*, ed. E.B. Sheldon and W.E. Moore. New York: Russell Sage Foundation, 1968.

Levison, Deborah, Richard Anker, Shahid Ashraf, and Sandhya Barge. *Is Child Labour Really Necessary in India's Carpet Industry?* Labour Market Papers no. 15. Geneva: ILO, 1996.

Liebl, Janet. *Ties That Bind: The Orphan Train Story in Minnesota*. Marshall, MN: Southwest State University Press, 1994.

Lovejoy, Owen R. "The Coal Mines of Pennsylvania." *Annals of the American Academy of Political and Social Science* (July 1911): 133–38.

Lumpkin, Grace. 1932. *To Make My Bread*. New York: Macaulay, 1932. Republished by University of Illinois Press, 1995.

Margo, Robert A., and T. Aldrich Finegan. "Compulsory Schooling Legislation and School Attendance in Turn-of-the-Century America: A 'Natural Experiment' Approach." *Economic Letters* 53 (1996): 103–10.

Markham, Edwin. "Children at the Loom." *Cosmopolitan* (September 1906).

Marx, Karl. 1867. *Capital: A Critique of Political Economy*, vol. 1. New York: International Publishers, 1967.

McHugh, Cathy L. *Mill Family: The Labor System in the Southern Cotton Textile Industry, 1880–1915*. New York: Oxford University Press, 1988.

Mellett, Lowell. 1923. "Reuben Dagenhart in 1923: How Sharper Than a Serpent's Tooth It Is to Have a Thankless Child." *Nation* (November 17). Reprinted in Abbott, *The Child and the State*, vol. 1, *Legal Status in the Family, Apprenticeship, and Child Labor*. Chicago: University of Chicago Press, pp. 515–17.

Mendelievich, Elias. *Children at Work*, Geneva: International Labor Office, 1979.

Michael, Robert T., and Nancy Brandon Tuma. "Youth Employment: Does Life Begin at 16?" *Journal of Labor Economics* 2, no. 4 (1984): 464–76.

Mihalic, Sharon Wofford, and Delbert Elliott. "Short- and Long-Term Consequences of Adolescent Work." *Youth and Society* 28, no. 4 (June 1997): 464–98.

Mill, John Stuart. 1848. *Principles of Political Economy, with Some of Their Applications to Social Philosophy*. London: Longmans, Green, 1909.

Mitchell, Broadus. *The Rise of Cotton Mills in the South*. Baltimore: Johns Hopkins University Press, 1921.

Mitchell, Daniel J.B. "A Furor Over Working Children and the Bureau of Labor." *Monthly Labor Review* (October 1975): 34–36.

Moehling, Carolyn M. "State Child Labor Laws and the Decline of Child Labor." *Explorations in Economic History* 36 (1999): 72–106.

Murphy, Edgar Gardner. *Problems of the Present South: A Discussion of Certain of the Educational, Industrial, and Political Issues in the Southern States*. New York: Macmillan, 1904.

Nardinelli, Clark. *Child Labor and the Industrial Revolution*. Bloomington: University of Indiana Press, 1990.

Nelson, Daniel. *Managers and Workers: Origins of the New Factory System in the United States—1880–1920*. Madison: University of Wisconsin Press, 1975.

Ogburn, William F. *Progress and Uniformity in Child-Labor Legislation: A Study in Statistical Measurement*. New York: Columbia University Press, 1912.

Oettinger, Gerald S. "Does High School Employment Affect High School Academic Performance?" *Industrial and Labor Relations Review* 53, no. 1 (October 1999): 136–51.

Parsons, Donald O., and Claudia Goldin. "Parental Altruism and Self-Interest: Child Labor Among Late Nineteenth-Century American Families." *Economic Inquiry* 27 (October 1989): 637–59.

Piore, Michael J. "International Labor Standards and Business Strategies." In *International Labor Standards and Global Economic Integration: Proceedings of a Symposium*, ed. Gregory K. Schopfle and Kenneth A. Swinnerton. Washington, DC: U.S. Department of Labor, 1994, pp. 21–25.

Polanyi, Karl. *The Great Transformation: The Political and Economic Origins of Our Time*. Boston: Beacon, 1944.

Pope, Liston. *Millhands and Preachers: A Study of Gastonia*. New Haven: Yale University Press, 1942.

Prude, Jonathan. *The Coming of Industrial Order: Town and Factory Life in Rural Massachusetts, 1810–1860*. New York: Cambridge University Press, 1983.

Psacharopoulis, George. "Child Labor Versus Educational Attainment: Some Evidence from Latin America." *Journal of Population Economics* 10, no. 4 (1997): 377–86.

Rau, William, and Robert Wazienski. "Industrialization, Female Labor Force Participation, and the Modern Division of Labor by Sex." *Industrial Relations* 38, no. 4 (October 1999): 504–21.

Reich, Robert B. *Locked in the Cabinet*. New York: Alfred A. Knopf, 1997.

Riis, Jacob A. *How the Other Half Lives: Studies Among the Tenements of New York*. New York: Scribner's, 1890.

Rodgers, Gerry, and Guy Standing, *Child Work, Poverty, and Underdevelopment*. Geneva: International Labor Office, 1981.

Rogers, Carol Ann, and Kenneth A. Swinnerton. 2000. "Inequality, Productivity and Child Labor: Theory and Evidence." Working Paper.

Roberts, Peter. *Anthracite Coal Communities: A Study of the Demography, the Social, Educational and Moral Life of the Anthracite Regions*. New York: Macmillan, 1904.

Rosenblum, Walter, Naomi Rosenblum, and Alan Trachtenberg. *America and Lewis Hine*. New York: Aperture, 1977.

Rothstein, Donna S. "Youth Employment in the United States." *Monthly Labor Review* 124, no. 8 (August 2001): 6–17.

Rubenstein, Ariel. "Perfect Equilibrium in a Bargaining Model." *Econometrica* 50 (1982): 97–109.

Ruhn, Christopher J. "Is High School Employment Consumption or Investment?" *Journal of Labor Economics* (October 1997): 735–76.

Salazar, M.C. "Child Labour in Colombia: Bogota's Quarries and Brickyards." In *Combating Child Labour*, ed. Assefa Bequele and Jo Boyden. Geneva: International Labour Organization, 1988.

Salinger, Sharon V. *To Serve Well and Faithfully: Labor and Indentured Servants in Pennsylvania, 1682–1800*. New York: Cambridge University Press, 1987.

Salmond, John A. *Gastonia, 1929: The Story of the Loray Mill Strike*. Chapel Hill: University of North Carolina Press, 1995.

Schoenhals, Mark, Marta Tienda, and Barbara Schneider. "The Educational and Personal Consequences of Adolescent Employment." *Social Forces* 77, no. 2 (December 1998): 723–62.

Schultz, T.W. "Investment in Human Capital." *American Economic Review* 51, no. 1 (1961): 1–17.

Sinclair, Upton. *The Jungle*. New York: Doubleday, Page, 1906.

Singh, Kusum. "Part-Time Employment in High School and Its Effects on Academic Achievement." *Journal of Educational Research* 91, no. 3 (January/February 1998): 131–39.

Smith, Abbott E. *Colonists in Bondage: White Servitude and Convict Labor in America, 1607–1776*. Chapel Hill: University of North Carolina Press, 1947.

Smith, E.O., and R.L. Nyman (1939). "Effects of Technological Change on Occupational Structure: A Case Study." Reprinted in Sigmund Nosow and William H. Form, *Man, Work, and Society*. New York: Basic Books, 1962.

Smith, Lillian. *Killers of the Dream*. New York: Norton, 1949.

Snowden, Yates. *History of South Carolina*. Chicago: Lewis Publishing, 1920.

Sokoloff, Kenneth. "Industrialization and the Growth of the Manufacturing Sector in the Northeast: 1820–1850." Ph.D. diss., Harvard University, 1982.

———. "Was the Transition from the Artisanal Shop to the Nonmechanised Factory Associated with Gains in Efficiency?" *Explorations in Economic History* 21 (1984): 351–82.

Spargo, John. *The Bitter Cry of the Children.* New York: Macmillan, 1906.

Spielberg, Elinor. "The Myth of Nimble Fingers." In *No Sweat: Fashion, Free Trade, and the Rights of Garment Workers,* ed. Andrew Ross. New York: Verso, 1997, pp. 113–22.

Srinivasan, T.N. "International Labour Standards Once Again!" In *International Labor Standards and Global Economic Integration: Proceedings of a Symposium,* ed. Gregory K. Schoepfle and Kenneth A. Swinnerton. Washington, DC: U.S. Department of Labor, 1994, pp. 34–40.

Standing, Guy. *Labour Force Participation and Development.* Geneva: International Labor Organization, 1981.

Stein, Leon. *Out of the Sweatshop: The Struggle for Industrial Democracy.* New York: Quadrangle Books, 1977.

Steinhilber, August W., and Carl J. Sokolowski. *State Laws on Compulsory Attendance.* Washington, DC: U.S. Department of Health, Education and Welfare, 1966.

Stolberg, Benjamin. *Tailor's Progress: The Story of a Famous Union and the Men Who Made It.* New York: Doubleday, Doran, 1944.

Sugden, John. *Tecumseh: A Life.* New York: Holt, 1997.

Swinnerton, Kenneth A., and Carol Ann Rogers. "The Economics of Child Labor: Comment." *American Economic Review* 89, no. 5 (1999): 1383–88.

———. 2001. "A Theory of Exploitative Child Labor." Working Paper.

Tannenbaum, Frank. *A Philosophy of Labor.* New York: Knopf, 1951.

Taylor, Ronald G. *Sweatshops in the Sun.* Boston: Beacon, 1973.

Thurnwald, Richard. *Economics in Primitive Communities.* London: H. Milford, 1900.

Tippett, Tom. *When Southern Labor Stirs.* New York: Jonathan Cape and Harrison Smith, 1931.

Trattner, Walter I. *Crusade for the Children: A History of the National Child Labor Committee and Child Labor Reform in America.* Chicago: Quadrangle, 1970.

Tucker, Barbara M. *Samuel Slater and the Origins of the American Textile Industry, 1790–1860.* Ithaca, NY: Cornell University Press, 1984.

Tucker, Lee. *Fingers to the Bone: United States Failure to Protect Child Farmworkers.* New York: Human Rights Watch, 2000.

Tullos, Allen. *Habits of Industry: White Culture and the Transformation of the Carolina Piedmont.* Chapel Hill: University of North Carolina Press, 1989.

Tuttle, Carolyn. *Hard at Work in Factories and Mines: The Economics of Child Labor During the British Industrial Revolution.* Oxford: Westview, 1999.

UNICEF. *The State of the World's Children: Focus on Child Labour.* London: Oxford University Press, 1997.

U.S. Bureau of the Census. *Census of Manufactures.* Washington, DC: Government Printing Office, 1905.

———. *Historical Statistics of the United States, Colonial Times to 1970.* Washington, DC: U.S. Census Bureau, 1997.

————. *The Statistical History of the United States from Colonial Times to the Present.* Washington, DC: Government Printing Office, 1965.

U.S. Bureau of Labor. 1910–1913. *Cotton Textile Industry*, vol. 1 of *Report on Condition of Women and Child Wage Earners in the United States.* Washington, DC: Government Printing Office (U.S. Senate Doc. 645).

————. 1910–1913.*Glass*, vol. 3 of *Report on Condition of Women and Child Wage Earners in the United States.* Washington, DC: Government Printing Office (U.S. Senate Doc. 645).

————. 1910–1913. *The Beginnings of Child Labor Legislation in Certain States: A Comparative Study*, vol. 6 of *Report on Condition of Women and Child Wage Earners in the United States.* Washington, DC: Government Printing Office (U.S. Senate Doc. 645).

————. 1910–1913. *Juvenile Delinquency and Its Relation to Employment*, vol. 8 of *Report on the Condition of Woman and Child Wage Earners in the United States.* Washington, DC: Government Printing Office (U.S. Senate Doc. 645).

U.S. Children's Bureau. *Children in an Anthracite Coal-Mining District.* (Publication 106). Washington, DC: Government Printing Office, 1922.

————. *Children in a Bituminous Coal-Mining District* (Publication 117). Washington, DC: Government Printing Office, 1923.

————. *Prohibition of Industrial Homework in Selected Industries Under the National Recovery Administration* (Mary Skinner, Publication 244). Washington, DC: Government Printing Office, 1938.

U.S. General Accounting Office, *Sweatshops in the U.S.: Opinions on Their Extent and Possible Enforcement Options.* GAO/HRD-88–130BR. Washington, DC, 1988.

————. *Sweatshops in New York City: A Local Example of a Nationwide Problem.* GAO/HRD-89–101BR. Washington, DC, 1989.

————. *Child Labor Violations and Sweatshops in the U.S.* T/HRD-90–18. Washington, DC, 1990.

————. *Child Labor: Characteristics of Working Children.* GAO/HRD-91–83BR. Washington, DC, 1991.

————. *Child Labor: Information on Federal Enforcement Efforts.* GAO/HRD-92–127FS. Washington, DC, 1992.

————. *Garment Industry Efforts to Address the Prevalence and Conditions of Sweatshops.* GAO/HEHS-95–29. Washington, DC, 1994.

————. *Child Labor in Agriculture: Characteristics and Legality of Work.* GAO/HEHS-98–112R. Washington, DC, 1998.

U.S. House Committee on Labor, 63d Cong., 2d Sess. Hearings on H.R. 12292, *A Bill to Prevent Interstate Commerce in the Products of Child Labor.* May 22, 1914.

U.S. House of Representatives, 68th Cong., 1st Sess., Serial 16. *Proposed Child Labor Amendments to the Constitution of the United States.* Washington, DC: Government Printing Office, 1924.

Vorse, Mary Heaton. *Strike.* New York: R. Livernight, 1930. Republished by University of Illinois Press, 1991.

Van Vorst, Mrs. John. *Saturday Evening Post* (January 16, February 23, and July 20, 1905, and June 21, 1906).

Van Vorst, Mrs. John, and Marie Van Vorst. *The Woman Who Toils: Being the Experience of Two Ladies as Factory Girls.* New York: Doubleday, 1903.

Walters, Pamela Barnhouse, and Philip J. O'Connell. "The Family Economy, Work, and Educational Participation in the United States, 1890–1940." *American Journal of Sociology* 93, no. 5 (1988): 1116–52.

Ware, Caroline. *The Early New England Cotton Manufacture: A Study in Industrial Beginnings.* Boston: Houghton-Mifflin, 1931.

Webb, Beatrice "The Economics of Factory Legislation." In *The Case for the Factory Acts*, ed. Beatrice Webb. London: G. Richards, 1901.

Winston, George Taylor. *A Builder of the New South: Being the Story of the Life Work of Daniel Augustus Tompkins.* New York: Doubleday, 1920.

Wood, Stephen B. *Constitutional Politics in the Progressive Era: Child Labor and the Law.* Chicago: University of Chicago Press, 1968.

Woodward, C. Vann. *Origins of the New South, 1877–1913.* Baton Rouge: Louisiana State University Press, 1951.

Zelizer, Viviana A. *Pricing the Priceless Child: The Changing Social Value of Children.* New York: Basic Books, 1985.

INDEX

Hugh D. Hindman is Associate Professor of Labor and Human Resources at Appalachian State University. He received his undergraduate degree from the College of Wooster in 1972 and his Ph.D. in labor and human resources from Ohio State University in 1989. Before the age of sixteen he sold greeting cards door to door, mowed lawns and shoveled snow, carried newspapers, caddied, and bagged groceries, but as a boy he never had the opportunity to work in a mine, mill, or factory.